# Lecture Notes in Computer Science 4785

*Commenced Publication in 1973*
Founding and Former Series Editors:
Gerhard Goos, Juris Hartmanis, and Jan van Leeuwen

Alexander Clemm
Lisandro Zambenedetti Granville
Rolf Stadler (Eds.)

# Managing Virtualization of Networks and Services

18th IFIP/IEEE International Workshop
on Distributed Systems: Operations and Management, DSOM 2007
San José, CA, USA, October 29-31, 2007
Proceedings

 Springer

Volume Editors

Alexander Clemm
Cisco Systems
170 West Tasman Drive (SJC23/2)
San Jose, CA 95134-1706, USA
E-mail: alex@cisco.com

Lisandro Zambenedetti Granville
Federal University of Rio Grande do Sul (UFRGS)
Instituto de Informática Av. Bento Gonçalves
9500 - Bloco IV - Agronomia 91501-970 - Porto Alegre, RS Brazil
E-mail: granville@inf.ufrgs.br

Rolf Stadler
School of Electrical Engineering
KTH Royal Institute of Technology
KTH/EE/S3, Osquldas väg 10
SE-100 44 Stockholm, Sweden
E-mail: stadler@ee.kth.se

Library of Congress Control Number: 2007936689

CR Subject Classification (1998): C.2.4, C.2, D.1.3, D.4.4, K.6, K.4.4

LNCS Sublibrary: SL 5 – Computer Communication Networks
and Telecommunications

ISSN     0302-9743
ISBN-10   3-540-75693-0 Springer Berlin Heidelberg New York
ISBN-13   978-3-540-75693-4 Springer Berlin Heidelberg New York

Springer is a part of Springer Science+Business Media

springer.com

© IFIP International Federation for Information Processing 2007
Printed in Germany

Typesetting: Camera-ready by author, data conversion by Scientific Publishing Services, Chennai, India
Printed on acid-free paper     SPIN: 12175086     06/3180     5 4 3 2 1 0

# Preface

This volume of the Lecture Notes in Computer Science series contains all papers accepted for presentation at the *18th IFIP/IEEE International Workshop on Distributed Systems: Operations and Management (DSOM 2007)*, which was held in the heart of Silicon Valley, San Jose, California, USA, on October 29–31, 2007.

DSOM 2007 was the 18th event in a series of annual workshops. It followed in the footsteps of previous successful meetings, the most recent of which were held in Dublin, Ireland (DSOM 2006), Barcelona, Spain (DSOM 2005), Davis, California, USA (DSOM 2004), Heidelberg, Germany (DSOM 2003), and Montreal, Canada (DSOM 2002). The goal of the DSOM workshops is to bring together researchers from industry and academia working in the areas of networks, systems, and service management, to discuss recent advances and foster future growth. In contrast to the larger management conferences, such as IM (Integrated Network Management) and NOMS (Network Operations and Management Symposium), DSOM workshops have a single-track program in order to stimulate more intense interaction among participants.

The theme of DSOM 2007 was *"Managing Virtualization of Networks and Services"*. Virtualization, in which the properties of a service are decoupled from its physical realization over networking and IT infrastructure, is capturing the imagination of industry and the research community alike. Questions need to be addressed such as: what is different about virtualization in 2007 compared with virtualization in the mainframe era, which advances in network control and self-management may advance virtualization technologies, which new problems will we incur when managing virtualized networks and services, and in which ways may management itself benefit from virtualization. At the same time, DSOM 2007 continued its tradition of giving a platform to papers that address general topics related to the management of distributed systems. As a result, DSOM 2007 included sessions on decentralized and peer-to-peer management, fault detection and diagnosis, performance tuning and dimensioning, problem detection and mitigation, operations and tools, service accounting and auditing, and Web services and management as well as a session with short papers.

Like the previous two DSOM workshops, DSOM 2007 was co-located with several related events as part of the Third International Week on Management of Networks and Services (MANWEEK 2007). The other events were the 10th IFIP/IEEE International Conference on Management of Multimedia and Mobile Networks and Services (MMNS 2007), the 7th IEEE International Workshop on IP Operations and Management (IPOM 2007), the 2nd IEEE International Workshop on Modeling Autonomic Communications Environments (MACE 2007), and the 1st IEEE/IFIP International Workshop on End-to-End Virtualization and Grid Management (EVGM 2007). Co-locating those events provided the opportunity for an exchange of ideas between research communities that work on related topics, allowing participants to forge links and exploit synergies.

DSOM 2007 attracted a total of 54 paper submissions by authors from 21 different countries. Each paper received at least three, and in most cases four, reviews by experts in the field. The authors were invited to write a rebuttal to the reviews. The final paper selection was based on the reviews, the authors' feedback, and (in some cases) online discussions among Technical Program Committee members. A total of 20 submissions were finally accepted into the program as full papers, 5 as short papers.

DSOM 2007 owes its success in large part to a dedicated community of researchers from academia and industry, which has formed over many years. First and foremost, we want to thank the authors of the submitted papers – without them, there would be no program. We also want to thank the members of the Technical Program Committee and the additional reviewers for their constructive and detailed reviews. A big "thank you" goes to Tom Pfeifer, our publications chair, who played a big part in creating these proceedings. Finally, we want to thank our patrons, Cisco Systems and France Telecom, whose financial support was essential to making DSOM 2007 a great event.

October 2007                                              Alexander Clemm
                                              Lisandro Zambenedetti Granville
                                                              Rolf Stadler

# DSOM 2007 Organization

**Program Committee Co-chairs**

Alexander Clemm                                          Cisco, USA
Lisandro Zambenedetti Granville    Federal University of Rio Grande do Sul, Brazil
Rolf Stadler                        Royal Institute of Technology (KTH), Sweden

**Publication Chair**

Tom Pfeifer                         Waterford Institute of Technology, Ireland

**Publicity Chair**

Sumit Naiksatam                                         Cisco, USA

**Treasurers**

Raouf Boutaba                          University of Waterloo, Canada
Brendan Jennings               Waterford Institute of Technology, Ireland

**Website and Registration Co-chairs**

Edgar Magana                                        UPC/Cisco, USA
Sven van der Meer              Waterford Institute of Technology, Ireland

**Submission Chair**

Lisandro Zambenedetti Granville    Federal University of Rio Grande do Sul, Brazil

**Manweek 2007 General Co-chairs**

Alexander Clemm                                         Cisco, USA
Silvia Figueira                         Santa Clara University, USA
Masum Z. Hasan                                          Cisco, USA

**Manweek 2007 Advisors**

Raouf Boutaba                          University of Waterloo, Canada
Brendan Jennings               Waterford Institute of Technology, Ireland
Sven van der Meer              Waterford Institute of Technology, Ireland

## DSOM 2007 Technical Program Committee

| Burkhard Stiller | University of Zurich and ETH Zurich, Switzerland |
| John Strassner | Motorola Labs, USA |
| Sven van der Meer | Waterford Institute of Technology, Ireland |
| John Vicente | Intel Corporation, USA |
| Vincent Wade | Trinity College Dublin, Ireland |
| Felix Wu | University of California at Davis, USA |
| Geoffrey Xie | Naval Postgraduate School, USA |
| Makoto Yoshida | The University of Tokyo, Japan |
| Xiaoyun Zhu | HP Laboratories, USA |

## DSOM 2007 Additional Paper Reviewers

| Florence Agboma | University of Essex, UK |
| Khalid AlBadawi | DePaul University, USA |
| Mina Amin | University of Surrey, UK |
| Kamal Bhattacharya | IBM Research, USA |
| Steffen Bleul | University of Kassel, Germany |
| Pieter-Tjerk de Boer | University of Twente, The Netherlands |
| Aimilios Chourmouziadis | University of Surrey, UK |
| Alan Davy | Waterford Institute of Technology, Ireland |
| Steven Davy | Waterford Institute of Technology, Ireland |
| Walter M. Fuertes | Universidad Autónoma de Madrid, Spain |
| Tom Gardos | Intel Corporation, USA |
| Stylianos Georgoulas | University of Surrey, UK |
| José Alberto Hernández | Universidad Autónoma de Madrid, Spain |
| Mohammad Ullah Khan | University of Kassel, Germany |
| Ling Lin | University of Essex, UK |
| Xue Liu | HP Laboratories, USA |
| Henrik Lundqvist | NEC Europe Ltd., Germany |
| Maitreya Natu | University of Delaware, USA |
| Pradeep Padala | University of Michigan, USA |
| Roland Reichle | University of Kassel, Germany |
| Anna Sperotto | University of Twente, The Netherlands |
| Martin Stiemerling | NEC Europe Ltd., Germany |
| Yongning Tang | DePaul University, USA |
| Michael Wagner | University of Kassel, Germany |
| Zhikui Wang | HP Laboratories, USA |
| Yi Zhu | University of Essex, UK |

# Table of Contents

## Session 5: Operations and Tools

## Session 6: Short Papers

# Session 7: Service Accounting and Auditing

# Session 8: Web Services and Management

# Botnets for Scalable Management

Jérôme François, Radu State, and Olivier Festor

MADYNES - INRIA Lorraine, CNRS, Nancy-Université, France
{jerome.francois,radu.state,olivier.festor}@loria.fr

**Abstract.** With an increasing number of devices that must be managed, the scalability of network and service management is a real challenge. A similar challenge seems to be solved by botnets which are the major security threats in today's Internet where a botmaster can control several thousands of computers around the world. This is done although many hindernesses like firewalls, intrusion detection systems and other deployed security appliances to protect current networks. From a technical point of view, such an efficiency can be a benefit for network and service management. This paper describes a new management middleware based on botnets, evaluates its performances and shows its potential impact based on a parametric analytical model.

## 1  Introduction

Network and service management is an important component to assure the well functioning of a network. It is divided into five domains: fault management, configuration, accounting tasks, performance and security monitoring. However network management planes face several problems to be scalable. Authors of malware (bots, worms) already faced these challenges and some of their achievements are very surprising. There are cases, where one botmaster can control up to 400 000 bots [1]. It is thus natural to investigate if it is possible to use a botnet to perform management operations on a large scale infrastructure. This approach is somehow a time travel, since long time ago, among the first IRC (Internet Relay Chat) [2] bots, Eggdrop [3] was created not for hackers but for helping administrator of IRC networks. The main contribution of this paper is to propose a management plane based on a botnet model, evaluate its performance and show its feasibility. Our paper is structured as follows. In section 2, we introduce the malware communication system and its possible adaption for managing networks. In section 3, the mathematical model and the associated metrics are explained in details. The next section 4 highlights our first experimental results. Related works are presented in section 5. Finally, we conclude the paper and outline future works.

## 2  Malware-Based Management Architecture

### 2.1  Classical Management Architecture and Challenges

Network management solutions show their limits today due to several reasons. First of all, there are more and more hosts to be managed and the management

A. Clemm, L.Z. Granville, and R. Stadler (Eds.): DSOM 2007, LNCS 4785, pp. 1–12, 2007.

domains have no well delimited boundaries. The management domain is split on several sites and a lot of tasks are usually delegated to other companies which need to access to the network. Moreover, a management operation could be performed on different locations in different countries and has to pass through a lot of active equipments like firewalls or network address translators (not only under the responsibility of the company). For a comprehensive overview, please refer to [4]. The main challenges that we address are related to scalability.

## 2.2   Internet Worm and Malware Communication Paradigms

A worm primary goal is to infect multiple machines without being detected or countered. To reach this goal, the worm can exploit security holes and there are various ways to improve the infection rate. In [5], some existing mechanisms are listed. Malware contain generally malicious payload. The most dangerous malware are stealthy and are able to retrieve private information (password, credit card number...) or to get the control of a system in order to use it as a proxy for future malicious activities (spamming, distributed denial of service attacks, beginning a worm infection, password cracking...).

This kind of malware is based on a control mechanism as in figure 1. Once the bot software is installed on a computer, the bot connects itself to the botnet. This technique is able to bypass most of firewalls and network address translators related problems, since outgoing connections are used. If a firewall blocks outgoing traffic too, it should allow some traffic like web traffic. Thus the IRC server can use different ports to bypass this kind of firewalls.

## 2.3   Malware Based Management Framework

We consider that malware communication scheme can be a reliable middleware solution for network and service management [4]. Firstly, the exchange of commands is simple and multiple operations are possible. Moreover, the decentralized communication topology of these networks allows to manage many bots. In [1] some statistics about botnets show that controlling 400 000 bots is possible contrary to the current management framework. In [6], the authors model and evaluate distributed management approaches and the main result is that a botnet management architecture is scalable.

IRC is one communication channel used to control a botnet as in the figure 1. A user wanting to chat connects to a server and chooses a chat channel. Many users can be connected simultaneously to the same channel due to the architecture of an IRC network. In fact, several servers are interconnected and share the different channels conceptually equivalent to a multicast group. Thus all the participants are not connected to the same server and this decentralized architecture avoids server overloading. The quantity of messages is well adapted because they are often sent to the channel. The servers form a spanning tree. In a botnet, the master is connected to one server and sends the orders on a channel, the bots are connected to any servers in the network and get the orders through the chat channel. The responses can be sent to the master in the same way also.

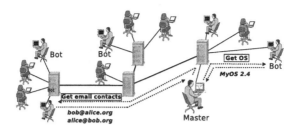

**Fig. 1.** An IRC botnet

These previous facts are the motivation to build a management system based on an IRC botnet where an administrator requests management operations through an IRC network. However an administrator need a proof of the real efficiency and benefits of this system before deploying it. In this study, our goal is to model IRC botnet and evaluate this approach from a network management point of view by asking several questions like:

- what is the probability to reach 80% of the hosts ?
- how many servers I need to deploy ?
- how should the servers be connected ?
- how much time is needed to reach 75% of hosts ?
- what is the server load ?

Since this new management framework is based on botnet, deploying some IRC servers is needed which is not necessary with a typical centralized management solution. In all cases, the devices to be managed have to execute a specific software: an agent for a typical solution or a modfied IRC client in our case.

## 3   An IRC Botnet Mathematical Model

Although IRC based botnets proved their efficiency in practice, little is known related to their analytical performance. The tree of servers is the main component of an IRC architecture. Thus our model is based on interconnected nodes (the servers) within a tree. We assume two kinds of failure. The first is due to the overloading of a server. The second introduces the risk to be attacked. In this case, a node or a server can be discovered by an attacker and we consider that once one node is discovered, all the system is unreliable because the attacker is able to use this server to compromise and command all the servers and bots.

The bots connected on the servers are not yet considered. The branching factor parameter $m$ is the maximum number of adjacent links for every nodes in the network. The number of adjacent links has to be between 1 and m and the probability function is equiprobable.

The overloading factor $\alpha(m)$ models the fact that the more a server can have connections with others, the more possible the server can be crashed due to needed operations to maintain the connectivity and synchronize the messages with the other servers. As mentionned, the worst case of the maximal possible branching factor is used which can be different from the real branching factor. Thus $\alpha(m)$ decreases when $m$ increases and the probability for a node to have k neighbors is $p_k = \alpha(m) \times \frac{1}{m} = \frac{\alpha(m)}{m}$ when $1 \leq k \leq m$ i.e. $k$ is a possible node degree except the node failure case. Obviously the degree can not be greater than the branching factor so $p_k = 0$ when $k > m$. The sum of probabilities has to be equal to one and so $p_0 = 1 - \sum_{i=1}^{m} p_i = 1 - \alpha(m)$.

The generating function of the probability function is defined as:

$$G_0(x) = \sum_{k=0}^{\infty} p_k x^k = \sum_{k=0}^{m} p_k x^k = p_0 + \sum_{k=1}^{m} p_k x^k = p_0 + \frac{\alpha(m)}{m} \times \sum_{k=1}^{m} x^k$$

This is a simple tool to compute the mean value by differentiating it;

$$\mathbb{E}(k) = G_0'(1)$$

We compute the generating function for the probability function to have $k$ neighbors at the $j$th hop in a similar way as in [7] and we obtain a recursive formula;

$$G^j(x) = \begin{cases} G_0(x) & \text{when } j = 1 \\ G^{j-1}(G_1(x)) & \text{when } j \geq 2 \end{cases} \tag{1}$$

where $G_1(x) = \dfrac{G_0'(x)}{G_0'(1)}$ which is the distribution function of outgoing connections from a k degree reached node.

The average number of nodes at the $j$th hop is $z_j = (G^j)'(1)$. As the same manner as in [7], we have:

$$z_1 = (G^1)'(1) = G_0'(1) \qquad z_2 = (G^1(G_1))'(1) = \frac{G_0''(1)}{G_0'(1)} \times G_0'(1) = G_0''(1)$$

$$z_j = \left[\frac{z_2}{z_1}\right]^{j-1} z_1$$

Because $p_0$ is constant, we have:

$$G_0'(x) = \frac{\alpha(m)}{m} \sum_{k=1}^{m} k x^{k-1} \qquad G_0''(x) = \frac{\alpha(m)}{m} \sum_{k=1}^{m} k(k-1) x^{k-2}$$

Moreover the formula to compute the number of neighbors is recursive and thus the number of neighbors at the hop $j+1$ depends on the number of neighbors at hop $j$.

## 3.1   Reachability

One important entity is reachability. Assuming $N$ nodes (servers), the reachability is the average number of reached nodes at a maximal distance $k$ divided by the total number of nodes in the tree $\frac{\sum_{j=1}^{k} z_j}{N}$. From a network manage-ment point of view, we are able to know the potential impact of requesting a management operation and thus evaluate the possible needed additional oper-ations for non reached hosts if necessary. We introduce the probability to have a node failure: the bigger the tree is, the more detectable it becomes and thus the probability of being attacked increases. Thus we consider that detecting the IRC network depends only on the single node/server detection probability $\beta$. So the IRC network remains undetected if all servers are not detected, that is the probability $(1 - \beta)^N$. The reachability is expressed as:

$$reachability(k) = \frac{(1 - \beta)^N \times min(\sum_{j=1}^{k} z_j, N)}{N} \qquad (2)$$

Our model is focused on the IRC server only. Considering randomly and uni-formly connected B bots, the average number of reached bots in k hops is:

$$bots(k) = reachability(k) \times B$$

The reachability metric for bots is the proportion of reached bots:

$$reachability\_bots(k) = \frac{bots(k)}{B} = reachability(k)$$

Due to the random uniform connection of bots, the different reachability metrics are the same for the bots and the servers.

## 3.2   Average Reachability

Another useful metric is the average reachability over all possible distance in the tree. The minimal distance is one and the maximal distance is $N$ in the case the tree is a chain. This metric gives a global overview of performance corresponding to a given $N$.

$$avg\_reachability(k) = \frac{\sum_{k=1}^{N} reachability(k)}{N} \qquad (3)$$

## 3.3   The Load of the System

In order to compare the botnet based management plane with typical solutions, we consider $load_s$; the overload of a server to maintain its connections with other servers and $load_c$; the overload to deal with a computer or a bot connected to the server. Thus any server needs to have sufficient resources, the load for managing $C$ computers with a typical management solution is; $load\_server_{typical} = C \times load_c$ and the worst case in our framework (when the server has the maximal branching factor $m$) is; $load\_server_{botnet} = C_{server} \times load_c + m \times load_s$ where $C_{server}$ is the average number of bots per server. This formula takes in account the resources to deal with each connected bots and each of the $m$ connected servers.

### 3.4   Time Evaluation

Be the time $t_h$, the network transmission time to send a management instruction to a final host and $t_s$ the time to forward a message between two IRC servers. In a standard management plane, the manager sends each request after sending the previous request and so the total time is; $time_{typical} = C \times t_h$

Since a server can be forced to forward message to other servers firstly, the total time is composed of the time to reach the last server (at k hops) and the time for this server to send the message to all the connected bots; $time_{botnet} = k \times t_s + C_{server} \times t_h$

This metric allows to evaluate when a request should be sent but an administrator could compute the total time of a management operations list and choose to execute urgent operations if he has not enough time.

## 4   Experimental Results

### 4.1   Experimental Settings

The function $\alpha(m)$ has to decrease when $m$ increases. It has values between 0 and 1 for $2 \le m \le \infty$ to exclude the specific case of $m = 1$ which is limited to two nodes only. Two functions can be used for $\alpha(m)$:

- $\alpha(m) = \alpha_1(m) = 1/m$
- $\alpha(m) = \alpha_2(m) = e^{(m-i)}$

The second function decreases more slowly than the first and the parameter i is chosen to have not too low values for the little $m$ values. For example if we want to test $m$ from three to five we will fix $i = 3$.

A node can be discovered with a probability $\beta = 0.01$ . Other values can be used based on domain specific knowledge.

### 4.2   The Average Reachability

The first experiment is about the average reachability for different values of the branching factor $m$ and number of nodes $N$. On the figure 2(a) with $\alpha(m) = \alpha_1(m)$, a curve represents a value of $m$ between one and ten. The curves are plotted against the total number of nodes. At the beginning, more nodes can be reached and that is the reason why the curves increase. However, from a certain value of $N$ close to 10 the curves decrease due to the parameter $\beta$: the tree is easily detectable and the reachability is affected. Thus choosing a graph with more than 10 nodes has limited performances in term of reachability. Since the branching factor concerns the children and the parent link, the values of the curve for $m = 2$ are very low (chain tree) as we can see on the figure 2(a), this is also one of the reason to exclude this trivial case.

The results with $\alpha(m) = \alpha_2(m)$ are on the figure 2(b). The difference is at the beginning because the curves with little branching factors are less affected when using $\alpha_2(m)$ i.e $\alpha_2(m) > \alpha_1(m)$. Therefore the maximal branching factor

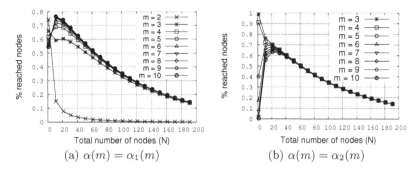

(a) $\alpha(m) = \alpha_1(m)$          (b) $\alpha(m) = \alpha_2(m)$

**Fig. 2.** The average reachability with different branching factors

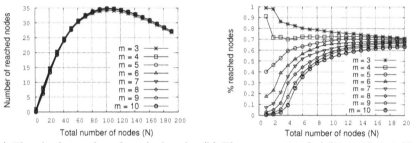

(a) The absolute value of reached nodes (b) The average reachability with $1 \leq N \leq 20$

**Fig. 3.** Reached nodes with $\alpha(m) = \alpha_2(m)$

$m$ has only an impact on the average reachability for small value of $N$ (less than 20). When there are more than twenty nodes, the curves depend more on $\beta$.

The absolute number of reached nodes is plotted on the figure 3(a). All the curves are similar and there is a maximum number of reached nodes of about 35 nodes for 100 nodes in the graph. This means that there is no need to have more than 100 nodes in the tree because the more nodes there are, the fewer they could be reached. Thus, a management architecture can be based on the absolute value of reached nodes or on the reachability depending on the constraints and the choices of the target environment and the business requirements. For example, with only 100 bots on a server, we can manage 3500 computers. Thanks to formula in subsection 3.3, the total load of the managing station is;

$$load\_server_{typical} = 3500 \times load_c$$

Considering 100 hosts per server in our framework, the total load of a server is;

$$load\_server_{botnet} = 100 \times load_c + m \times load_s$$

Our goal is to diminish the load of a server which implies to have:

$$load_s < \frac{3400}{m} load_c$$

We assume that $load_s > load_c$. Indeed a server has to maintain channels, to synchronize the messages and to maintain the connections and the topology. However even though a server is connected to many others as 10 for example, $load_s$ can be equal to $340 \times load_c$ without loss of performance. This can be improved by decreasing the branching factor.

Except for $m = 2$, the curves are different with low values for $N$. With $\alpha_1(m)$, the higher the branching factor is, the higher the reachability is. This is in contradiction with the second case with $\alpha_2(m)$ presented on the figure 3(b). The reachability is the results of two antagonist "forces": the branching factor and $\alpha(m)$ i.e. the probability to have a node failure.

### 4.3   The Number of Hops

The impact of the number of hops is studied with different values of $N$, respectively 20, 50, 100 and 200 on respectively the figure 4(a), 4(b), 4(c) and 4(d). All figures highlight a maximum value. This value depends only on $\beta$ as can be observed in formula (2). For example for $N = 20$, the maximum of nodes that can be reached is limited by $(1 - \beta)^{20} = (1 - 0.01)^{20} = 0.81$ which is the probability to not be discovered. Using this method, we can know the maximum number of nodes/servers by fixing the maximal reachability.

The number of needed hops is very important because it is equivalent to the time needed to perform management operations. In this test only the function $\alpha_2(m)$ is used. On the figure 4(a), N is equal to 20 and the probability to be

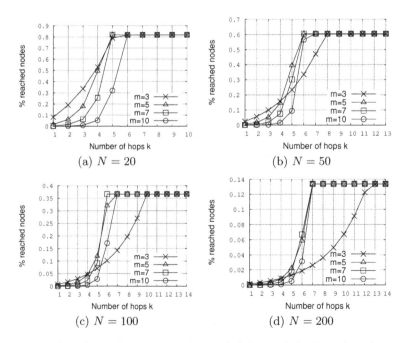

**Fig. 4.** The relationship between the reachability and the branching factor

discovered is not important, which contrasts with the probability to have a node failure. Therefore a small branching factor is needed to have the best performances. We assume that the more there are nodes, the more effective a high branching factor is. This is highlighted by other curves in figure 4. For instance a branching factor of three has worse performances when N increases. However, as we can observe, an high branching factor like ten is never better than seven. To be brief, depending on how many bots have to be managed and so how many servers can be used, a different value for the branching factor has to be selected. A good compromise for high and low values of $N$ is $m = 5$. Moreover the maximum value is reached within 5, 6 or 7 hops in main cases. So for a botnet based management plane, the request will not pass through many servers which saves a lot of resources.

On the figure 4(b) with $m = 5$, $0.6 \times 50 = 30$ servers are reached in 6 hops. If there are 100 bots per server, it corresponds 3000 hosts. The total needed time to send a management request is given in 3.4 and is $6 \times t_s + 100 \times t_h$ which has to be lower or equal to $3000 \times t_h$ i.e $t_s < 483 \times t_h$ to obtain equivalent performance. To conclude, even though intermediate nodes are added, the delay is greatly reduced. In the previous section, we saw that a typical management solution implies more server overloading which can increase the delay.

## 4.4   The Impact of the Number of Nodes

There are two factors which affect the reachability: the probability to be discovered $\beta$ and the probability to have a node failure $\alpha(m)$. The figure 5 shows the reachability for a fixed number of hops k and with $\alpha(m) = \alpha_2(m)$. There is always a first stage where the curves decrease slowly. This first stage corresponds to reach all nodes limited by the probability to be discovered. After this moment, the curves decrease drastically when a specific $N$ value is reached. In fact this value depends on the branching factor which limits the value of reached nodes (antagonist effects of $m$ and $\alpha(m)$). Once again the branching factor $m = 5$ is the best compromise for different number of hops because on the figure 5(a), it's

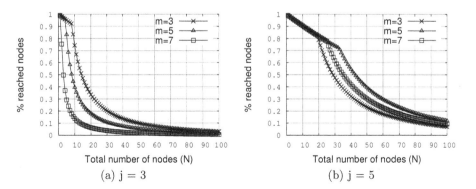

**Fig. 5.** The reachability according the number of nodes in the graph and the number of hops j

the best curve and on the figure 5(b) it is the second best curve. We tested also $j = 7$ and saw that the branching factor $m = 5$ was the best case again.

## 5   Related Works

Botnets are a powerful tool for attackers needing to manage large armies of compromised machines. Since a botnet can be build by a worm infecting several machine, the authors in [8] give full details about worms: definition, traffic patterns, history, ideas about future worms, detection and defense. Many papers about worm propagation were published and [9] describes the propagation of the CodeRed worm where the classical Kermack-McKendrick model is extended. The authors in [10] aim to determine the characteristics of some well known botnet families and show that all of them are based on IRC. In [11], the different ways to construct a botnet are discussed and the authors highlight that using IRC networks limits the latency and preserves the anonimity of the controller. With respect to these works we are the first to build an analytical model and evaluate experimentally the performances. A classical network and service management framework is a simple direct exchange of commands between the manager and the agents to manage. Several solutions were proposed to deal with a large scale management like the management by delegation [12]. Another solution is to deploy cascaded managers managers [13]. The mid-level managers can translate a management request into subrequests for each device they manage or get the results and analyze them. A similar approach is based on active network [14] [15] [16] where the network equipments execute and forward a light management program but the main disadvantage is that dedicated network equipments are needed. Our approach needs only to deploy some servers. In [17] a decentralized management is proposed where a query is send to a starting node which is responsible to distribute subqueries and get the results thanks to the echo pattern. Thanks to another subquery, each node is able to create an aggregate result which is sent to the upstream node in the echo pattern. The starting node can finally provide the final result by using another subquery. In [18], the authors propose a solution for the specific case of the distribution of Windows update patches unlike our work which can be used for various applications. First of all, they observe that efficient clustering of patches is possible and so the generation of delta files (the final file which depends on a specific configuration) should be delegated to the servers in order to reduce the traffic. A dedicated solution to ad-hoc networks in [19] determines groups of machines which have a high connectivity within a group and elect a manager inside it. In [20], a worm is designed to patrol on different hosts to get information before coming back to the manager. The authors propose to use a worm which moves on the different hosts by looking for a way to reach them. However the experiments are very limited and the worm acts only as a monitor. Finally, some real examples of salutary worms exist like Code-Green [21] which counters the Code-Red. However these worms are not controlled and not limited to certain hosts. As mentionned, a lot of these approaches need to have active components like active mid-level managers which are in charge of analyzing and translating the queries. Our system is composed of passive servers which forward only the requests. Furtermore bypassing most of active equipments is an advantage of a botnet based management plan since only outgoing connections are used.

## 6   Conclusion and Future Works

The current malware seems to have a highly efficient communication channel. The effectiveness and the scalability of botnets is a proof that a large scale management is possible by adapting the botnet model. In this paper, we described a model for IRC based communication in a network management environment. A mathematical model of an IRC network and different performance metrics are proposed. The reachability metric is the percentage of reached hosts and can be calculated according the time delays. Secondly, as requests are transmitted through huge networks like the Internet, the system exposed to different problems: network failures or delay, denial of service attacks against the mid-level managers. We introduce these elements to evaluate the ability of our approach to continue to work when facing these issues. Now, we are able to determine the number of reached hosts for a certain network configuration and optimize it to have specific results. Due to the possibility to be attacked, the number of IRC servers has to be large enough but not too large in order to have a high reachability. Since our model is only analytical, the next step is to test an implementation. A case study is introduced in [4] where we defined a malware based large scale management plane to create and manage a honeynet to detect criminal predators in a P2P environment. Future work will consist in modeling epidemic propagation and experimenting our solution on a large grid network.

**Acknowledgment.** This paper was supported in part by the EC ISTE-MANICS Network of Excellence (#26854).

## References

1. McLaughlin, L.: Bot software spreads, causes new worries. IEEE Distributed Systems Online 5(6) (2004)
2. Oikarinen, J., Reed, D.: rfc 1459: Internet relay chat protocol (1993)
3. Canavan, J.: The evolution of malicious irc bots. In: VB 2005. Proceedings of the Virus Bulletin Conference, Dublin, Ireland (October 2005)
4. State, R., Festor, O.: Malware: a future framework for device, network and service management. Journal in Computer Virology 3(1), 51–60 (2007)
5. How to Own the Internet in Your Spare Time, USENIX Association (2002)
6. Chen, T.M., Liu, S.S.: A model and evaluation of distributed network management approaches. Selected Areas in Communications, IEEE Journal on 20(4), 850–857 (2002)
7. Ramachandran, K., Sikdar, B.: Modeling malware propagation in gnutella type peer-to-peer networks. In: International Parallel and Distributed Processing Symposium, 2006 (2006)

8. Nazario, J.: Defense and Detection Strategies against Internet Worms. Artech House, Inc., Norwood, MA, USA (2003)

9. Zou, C., Gong, W., Towsley, D.: Code red worm propagation modeling and analysis (2002)

10. Barford, P., Yegneswaran, V.: 1. In: An inside look at Botnets, Springer, Heidelberg (2006)

11. Cooke, E., Jahanian, F., Mcpherson, D.: The zombie roundup: Understanding, detecting, and disrupting botnets, pp. 39–44 (June 2005)

12. Goldszmidt, G., Yemini, Y.: Distributed management by delegation. In: 15th International Conference on Distributed Computing Systems, IEEE Computer Society Press, Los Alamitos (1995)

13. SNMP, Research: The mid-level manager (accessed on 07/30/07) http://www.snmp.com/products/mlm.html

14. Schwartz, B., Jackson, A.W., Strayer, W.T., Zhou, W., Rockwell, R.D., Partbridge, C.: Smart packets: applying active networks to network management. ACM Transactions on Computer Systems 18(1), 67–88 (2000)

15. Brunner, M., Stadler, R.: The impact of active networking technology on service management in a telecom environment. In: IFIP/IEEE International Symposium on Integrated Network Management, Boston (1999)

16. Brunner, M., Stadler, R.: Management in telecom environments that are based on active networks. Journal of High Speed Networks (2001)

17. Lim, K.S., Stadler, R.: Real-time views of network traffic using decentralized management. In: Integrated Network Management, 2005. 9th IFIP/IEEE International Symposium on, IEEE Computer Society Press, Los Alamitos (2005)

18. Gkantsidis, C., Karagiannis, T., VojnoviC, M.: Planet scale software updates. SIG-COMM Comput. Commun. Rev. 36(4), 423–434 (2006)

19. Badonnel, R., State, R., Festor, O.: Probabilistic management of ad-hoc networks. In: NOMS 2006. 10th IEEE/IFIP Network Operations and Management Symposium, IEEE Computer Society Press, Los Alamitos (2006)

20. Ohno, H., Shimizu, A.: Improved network management using nmw (network management worm) system. In: Proceedings of INET 1995, Honolulu, Hawai'i (June 27-30, 1995)

21. Szor, P.: The Art of Computer Virus Research and Defense. Addison-Wesley Professional, Reading (2005)

# Self-organizing Monitoring Agents for Hierarchical Event Correlation

Bin Zhang and Ehab Al-Shaer

School of Computer Science, Telecommunications and Information Systems
DePaul University, USA
{bzhang,ehab}@cs.depaul.edu

**Abstract.** Hierarchical event correlation is very important for distributed monitoring network and distributed system operations. In many large-scale distritbuted monitoring environments such as monitions senor networks for data aggregation, battlefield compact operations, and security events, an efficient hierarchical monitoring agent architecture must be constructed to facilitate event reporting and correlation utilizing the spacial relation between events and agents with minimum delay and cost in the network. However, due to the significant agent communication and management overhead in organzine agents in distributed monitoring, many of the existing approaching become inefficient or hard to deploy. In this paper, we propose a topology-aware hierarchical agent architecture construction technique that minimizes the monitoring cost while considering the underlying network topology and agent capabilities. The agent architecture construction is performed in a purely decentralized fashion based on the agents' local knowledge with minimal communication and no central node support.

## 1 Introduction

A Distributed network monitoring (DNM) system has become an indispensable component for current enterprise network. The high speed and large scale properties of enterprise network have imposed new requirements on DNM system. The DNM system should not only detect and transfer the network events efficiently, but also limit event propagation to save computing and network resources. A DNM system is composed of a set of distributed monitoring agents which cooperate together to fulfill the monitoring tasks. These agents form an architecture which determines the event delivery and aggregation path in the network. So DNM architecture is crucial to the system performance. Many DNM systems have been proposed in the past [15,3,6]. These works focus mainly on the network events detection and correlation models, dynamic monitoring job update and programmable action interface. However, the mechanism of constructing and maintaining the monitoring agent architecture was insufficiently addressed. In many DNM systems, the agent architectures are static and sometimes manually constructed and maintained. In other DNM systems, the agent architectures are constructed based on the logical relations between agents, which may not reflect the underlying network topology or agents' capabilities. These limitations

A. Clemm, L.Z. Granville, and R. Stadler (Eds.): DSOM 2007, LNCS 4785, pp. 13–24, 2007.
© IFIP International Federation for Information Processing 2007

impose long construction time, low efficiency and unbalance monitoring task distribution in DNM systems.

In this paper, we introduce distributed self-organized topology-aware agents for constructing a hierarchical distributed monitoring architecture. We describe a number of algorithms and management protocols that enable agents to co-operate together to build a hierarchical architecture in a decentralized fashion. Agents work collaboratively but based on their local knowledge to select the most suitable set of leaders in each level in the hierarchy such that the monitoring information delivery cost is minimized. No central node or global knowledge is assumed in this work and the number of messages exchanged between agents is minimized by using scope-controlled multicast. Our proposed work takes into consideration of spacial event correlation which is important for many distributed applications such as security alarm correlation and sensor network data aggregation. In addition, topology-aware hierarchical correlation does not only restrict event propagation but it also allows sensors to save energy in transmitting events during the correlation/aggrtegation operation.

This paper is organized as follows. In section 2, we describe and formalize the problem that we address in this work. Section 3 describes our heuristic algorithm to develop hierarchical monitoring architecture using decentralized self-organizing agents. In section 4, we evaluate this approach and show the simulation results. Section 5 compares our work with related works. In section 6, we give the conclusion and identify the future work.

## 2   System Model and Problem Definition

A large number of monitoring agents might be distributed in a large-scale enterprise network. To address the scalability problem of having a large amount of agents in the distributed monitoring system, hierarchical monitoring structure is used. Agents are organized into different layers such that each layer contains a set of agents that are selected as leaders to which other agents report their events. Each leader filters and aggregates the incoming event and reports to higher level agent. In order to improve the system performance and reduce events propagation, the agent architecture should not only consider the underlying network topology and agent processing capability, but also the event traffic rate generated by each agent. Thus, in each layer, we want to find the optimal subset of agents as leaders and assign each non-leader agent to the most suitable leader. The assignment of an agent to a leader is associated with a communication cost, that is equal to the traffic rate of that agent multiplied by the distance (e.g., number of hops) from that agent to its leader. Our objective in each layer is to find the optimal subset of leaders and the assignment that can minimize the total communication cost while respecting the leaders' processing capability. Thus, the hierarchical agent architecture construction can be viewed as a set of recursive solutions to the Leader Selection and Assignment Problem (LSAP) described above.

Suppose we have a set of $n$ monitoring agents in one layer. Let $d_{ij}$ denote the distance between agent $i$ and agent $j$. Let $c_i$ denote the processing capability of agent $i$, which is decided based on the CPU speed and memory. Let $b_i$ represent the event rate of agent $i$, which is defined by $b_i = \theta \mu_i + \sigma_i$. Here, $\mu_i$ and $\sigma_i$ denote the mean and standard deviation of event rate of node $i$ respectively. The LSAP at each layer can be formalized as an integer linear program:

$$minimize \quad \sum_{i=1}^{n} \sum_{j=1}^{n} d_{ij} x_{ij} b_i \tag{1}$$

subject to:

$$\sum_{i=1}^{n} b_i x_{ij} < c_j \tag{2}$$

$$\sum_{j=1}^{n} x_{ij} = 1 \tag{3}$$

$$x_{ij} \le y_j \tag{4}$$

$$\sum_{j=1}^{n} y_i \le \lceil \frac{\sum_{i=1}^{n} b_i}{\sum_{i=1}^{n} c_i/n} \rceil \tag{5}$$

$$x_{ij} \in \{0, 1\} \tag{6}$$

$$y_j \in \{0, 1\} \tag{7}$$

The binary variable $x_{ij}$ represents whether agent $i$ treats agent $j$ as its leader. The binary variable $y_j$ represents whether agent $j$ is selected as a leader. The objective function (Eq.1) is to minimize the communication cost between agents and their leaders. The constraint in Eq.2 guarantees that each leader will not receive events more than a fraction of its capacity. The constraint Eq.3 restricts that each agent can report to one leader only. The relation between variable $x_{ij}$ and $y_j$ is defined by Eq. 4, which means if agent $i$ report to agent $j$, then agent $j$ must be a leader. The constraint Eq.5 is to specify that the total number of leaders in each layer can not be greater than the maximum number of agents required to accommodate all the event traffic coming from the this layer when using the average agent capacity ($\sum_{i=1}^{N} c_i/n$). We use this constraint to limit the depth of the monitoring hierarchy and thereby reduce the monitoring delay.

## 3   Optimal Self-organizing Monitoring Agents

Traditionally, to find a solution for this kind of optimization problem, we need one central agent that has the global knowledge of the network. When the network topology changes due to the nodes or network devices failure, the reconstruction has to be performed by the central node. This can easily causes a bottleneck in the monitoring system and creates a single point failure. In addition, to measure the distance between each agent pair and aggregate this information to the central node, a large number of probe messages ($O(N^2)$) should be exchanged. To overcome these shortcomings of using a centralized approach, we propose a decentralized agent architecture construction technique. The hierarchical structure is built in a bottom-up fashion such that all agents join the first layer and then the optimal subset of leaders are collaboratively discovered and selected based on agents' local knowledge. The rest agents are assigned to these leaders. Then, the leaders from lower layer form the higher layer (ex. leaders of layer 1 form layer 2) and the leader selection and agent assignment process will be repeated at each layer till the agents at certain layer detect that there are no enough agents left and it is not necessary to further build the hierarchy, then these agents will directly report to the manager.

Based on the definition in section 2, we can see that the agents' architecture construction in each layer is an instance of the LSAP problem. So in this paper, We will focus the discussion on our distributed solution to LSAP. The LSAP can be proved to be NP-hard by a mapping from capacitated P-median problem (CPMP) [13]. Many approximation algorithm have been proposed for CPMP [14], but these approaches require a central node with global knowledge. So they are not suitable to large-scale monitoring architecture.

In the following section, we introduce our distributed solution for LASP and show how this algorithm can be repeatedly used to construct the hierarchical agent architecture. Our solution targets the monitoring architecture in large-scale enterprise network, where multicast and broadcast are normally available. Also, it is commonly known that in enterprise network, the hop counts relatively indicates the network delay between two nodes [5]. Our solution is totally distributed and efficient in terms of processing complexity and message exchange.

### 3.1   Distributed Leader Selection and Assignment Algorithm

Because the data from different monitoring nodes are often correlated and the correlation is usually stronger between data from nodes close to each other, we should select agents which have a small average distance to their members with high processing capacity as leaders. Thus, all data from nodes which share the same leader can be filtered, aggregated and correlated locally by the leader. Two tasks need to be accomplished in order to solve LSAP problem: (1) selecting the optimal subset of leaders, and (2) assigning each agent to the most suitable leader. Our algorithm combines these two tasks together into one step. The operation of our algorithm is divided into rounds and the length of round is represented by $T$. Before the agent architecture construction, each agent $i$ computes its initial potential to become a leader (represented by $P_i$) based on its processing capability $c_i$. The $P_i$ can be computed as $P_i = \eta \frac{c_i}{c_{max}}$. $c_{max}$ is a constant which represents the maximal processing capability and $\eta < 1$ is used to control the initial value of $P_i$.

We assume agents can synchronously start the hierarchy construction about the same time based on a specific broadcast or control message sent by the system manager. At the beginning of each round, each agent sends out multicast search messages with limited scope as discussed below to inform other agents about its existence and status. The scope is used to control the distance the search message can travel in the network. We limit the scope to control the message propagation. The scope is implemented by setting the time-to-live (TTL) field in IP header of the search message equal to the scope value. The scope is increased by 1 at each searching round. In the search message, each agent embeds its unique ID, event traffic rate $b_i$, and current scope. When one agent receives a search message from another agent, it computes the distance (i.e., number of hops) from the source by subtracting the TTL value in the IP header of received search message from the scope value in that search message. At the end of each round, each agent first updates its member list based on the search messages received so far. Because of the processing capacity limitation, each agent chooses its members based on the ascending order of distance, and at the same time the total traffic rate of its members should respect its capacity. Assume set $M_i$ represents agent $i$'s potential members, $d_{ji}$ represents the distance between node $i$ and $j$. The communication cost of agent $i$ can be computed as follows: $cost_i = \sum_{j \in M_i} d_{ji} b_j$. Based on updated member list and communication cost, $P_i$ value can be updated as follows:

$$(P_i)_{new} = (P_i)_{old}(1 + \alpha_1 \frac{s_i}{s_{max}} + \alpha_2(1 - \frac{cost_i/s_i}{\lambda})) \tag{8}$$

Here the parameter $s_i$ represents the selected member list size of agent $i$, $s_i = |M_i|$. $S_{max}$ is a constant which represents the maximal number of members any node can possibly have. And $\lambda$ is a constant and used to normalize the average communication cost. In above equation, $\alpha_1$ and $\alpha_2$ are used to control how many percent each term contributes to $P_i$ increase, $\alpha_1 + \alpha_2 = 1$. From equation 8, we can see that $P_i$ value will increase inevitably at the end of each searching round. But how fast the $P_i$ value increase is different for each agent. As member list size $s_i$ increases (first term in Eq. 8), its contribution to $P_i$ increase, and as the average communication cost $cost_i/s_i$ increases (second term in eq. 8), its contribution of it to $P_i$ decreases. The more the members, the smaller the average communication cost, the faster the $P_i$ value increases. Since the increase of $P_i$ reflects both agent's processing capability and its distance to other agents, $P_i$ is used as primary factor to decide whether an agent should become a leader. The agents with high $P_i$ value has more possibility to become a leader.

## 3.2   Node Status

In this approach, each node has five status which can change based on its $P_i$ value and its local knowledge.

- Unstructured: It means the agent doesn't belong to any leader's member list.
- Structured: It means the agent is included in some leader's member list.
- Leader candidate: The agent can be a leader candidate if the $P_i$ value is larger than certain threshold $P_T$ and less than 1.
- Leader: An agent becomes a leader if its $P_i$ value reach 1.
- Isolated leader: An agent becomes an isolated leader when after $R_T$ rounds it still can not become a leader or a member, or its $P_i = 1$ but it has no members.

In our algorithm, the initial status of all agents is unstructured. As the agent's $P_i$ value increases at each search round, the agent status changes accordingly.

When an agent changes its status to a leader candidate or a leader, it sends out a multicast announcement to the selected members to make them stop searching. The leader candidate announcement is sent out periodically till this node becomes a leader. Leader node sends out beacon message (leader announcement) to its members periodically. The current members of a leader candidate or a leader are embedded in these announcements. If an unstructured agent receives a leader candidate announcement that includes its ID in the member list, it stops searching. If unstructured agent receives leader announcement that includes its ID, it change its status to structured and start membership determination.

The agent's status can also be changed reversely from a leader candidate to unstructured when it receives a leader candidate announcement from other agent which is more suitable to become a leader. Then how two leader candidates can compete with each other to determine which one is more suitable to become a leader? According to the definition of $P_i$, the node with higher $P_i$ value is more suitable to become a leader. However, this is only true if they are closely related to make them competitors. The relation $L_{ij}$ used to measure the competition relation between two candidate agents $i$ and $j$ can be computed as follow:

$$L_{ij} = \beta_1 \frac{|M_i \cap M_j|}{|M_i \cup M_j|} + \beta_2 (1 - \frac{d_{ij}}{d_{max}}) \tag{9}$$

$M_i$ and $M_j$ is the member list in agent $i$ and $j$ respectively, and $d_{ij}$ is the distance (number of hops) between the agents $i$ and $j$. Here $d_{max}$ is a constant which stands for the largest distance in the network. $\beta_1$ and $\beta_2$ are used to control how many percent each term contributes to $L_{ij}$ , $\beta_1 + \beta_2 = 1$. Intuitively, we can see that the more members these two leader candidates share, the smaller the network distance between them, the higher the competition relation value. Only when the relation $L_{ij}$ between two agents $i$ and $j$ is larger than certain threshold $L_T$, these two agents become competitors. In this case, the agent with larger $P_i$ prevails and keep its status as leader candidate. The other competitor changes its status to unstructured. The complete algorithm for leader selection can be found in [2]. This approach favors those agents which have small distances to their members and sufficient processing power to become leaders. To control the convergence speed, we set the threshold $R_T$ as the maximal number of searching round for each node in the construction of one layer. After $R_T$ round, if an agent still can not become a leader or a member, it will stop sending search message and declare itself as an isolated leader as will be discussed in section 3.3.

## 3.3   Agent Membership Determination

For unstructured node, member determination phase is the phase where the agent decides which leader to join in. When receives and included in a leader announcement, an unstructured agent waits for a short time $T_d$ to see if other agents become leaders and include itself as member during that period. If it appears in multiple leaders' member list, the agent always chooses the closest leader by sending a multicast membership confirmation message with TTL equal to the distance to the farthest leader. This message causes other leaders or leader candidates to remove this agent from their member lists. If a leader doesn't receive anything from its member, it assumes that agent agrees to be its member. For leader candidate, the member determination phase is the phase where the leader candidate decides whether it should become a leader. A leader candidate can reach $P_i = 1$ without any member, this means either no other leader agent is willing to accept this agent or all its potential members already join other leaders. In this case, this leader sends join request to all of its known leaders to see if any leader will accept its traffic at this phase. If it still can not get accepted, it promotes itself as an isolate leader. The algorithm for agent member determination can be found in [2].

### 3.4   Resilience of The Agent Hierarchical Architecture

**Resilience to Message Loss.** The message exchange between agents in our distributed approach is through multicast. Multicast is not a reliable protocol, packets can be lost during the operation of our algorithm. But due to the periodically sending of search message, leader candidate and leader announcement, this approach can tolerate message loss and still construct the complete agent architecture. The search message loss of an unstructured agent can be compensated by the next round message. The unstructured agent will keep sending till it is covered by a leader candidate or reach maximal round $R_T$. The loss of leader candidate announcement only causes the unstructured agents sending more searching messages. The loss of leader announcement can cause unstructured agents join suboptimal leader. In extreme case where all leader announcements to an agent get lost, that agent can still send join request during the member determination phase or become an isolate leader which can join higher level or directly report to the manager. So, the packet loss can influence the result architecture, make some agents join suboptimal leaders. But our algorithm guarantees that each agent will find a leader or become a leader, no agent will be isolated from the resulting architecture, this will complete the architecture.

**Resilience to Nodes Failure and Topology Change.** When network topology changes or agents fail to perform its monitoring tasks, the hierarchical architecture should be reconstructed to reflect these changes. In our proposed algorithm, the distributed leader selection and assignment component contributes significantly to the resiliency of the monitoring infrastructure as the topology changes can be accommodated locally in the affected areas without globally impacting the rest of the architecture. Each leader monitors the topology change in the area it controls and keeps the statistical record of its members' average communication cost. If an abnormal average communication cost lasts for more than a certain period, the leader can assume topology change happens in the network. Then the leader sends out a reconstruction notification message to its members to trigger the selection of new leader. The reconstruction only happens within the scope of old leader and its members such that other areas are not effected. As for agent failure, the normal agent failure will not influence the monitoring architecture. The architecture only need be changed when a leader node fails. Since each leader node periodically sends out beacon message to its members, when the member agents lose contact from their leader for certain time, they set its status back to unstructured and restart the leader selection. The new selected leader promotes itself to higher level to receive leader beacon messages at that level, so it can select the best leader to join at that level.

### 3.5 Dynamic Parameters Selection

The proposed distributed algorithm is significantly impacted by two important thresholds: leader candidate threshold $P_T$ and competition relation threshold $L_T$. In order to make this approach suitable for different networks and agent distributions, these parameters should be dynamically chosen to reflect the target system properties. Since the construction of agent hierarchy structure is totally distributed without any central node assistance, and there is no agent has global knowledge, we propose the following technique for parameters selection. At the beginning of architecture construction, each agent randomly send out a multicast search message ($TTL = 255$) with probability $p$, which is a small value to limit only a small fraction of agent sending out messages. Upon receives these messages, each agent can calculates the distance to other agents and sends these information to the agent with smallest ID. So the agent with smallest ID has a sample of global knowledge. It then calculate the mean and standard deviation of agent capability, distance, and event rate for the sample agents set. Based on these information, it estimate how many search rounds needed for an agent with average capability and average distance to make its $P_i$ value reach 1. Because the agents need some time to resolve the competition between leader candidates, so the $P_T$ value is set as $P_i$ value of the estimated agent at third last round. And the $L_T$ value is set as the estimated $L_{ij}$ value between two leader candidates share half of their members with average distance. The details of how these thresholds are calculated are shown in [2]. After calculation, the agent with smallest ID will multicast these thresholds to all other agents.

## 4   Evaluation

In this section, we evaluate the performance of our distributed agents hierarchical architecture construction algorithm using networks with various topologies and sizes. Our simulation focuses on studying the accuracy, scalability and efficiency of our heuristic distributed approach to the LSAP problem and compare the results with the optimal centralized approximation algorithm [12].

Because the target of this approach is enterprise network, so we assume that the network links for each agent have enough capacity to accommodate the event traffics to and from that agent. Agents have different processing capabilities and event traffic rates. The distances between agents are network distances. We assume no path restriction in our model, which implies that each agent can send a message to any other agent. Based on these assumptions, we construct many network topologies for our evaluation study by distributing agents randomly into a two-dimensional graph. The geometry distance between agents symbolize the

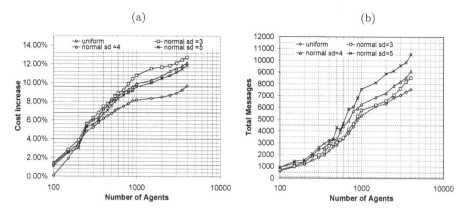

**Fig. 1.** Performance evaluation (a) Total cost increase ratio (b) Total messages change as agents number changes

network distance. The coordinates of agents are generated with uniform and normal distribution. We use the following performance metrics in our study: (1) total transferring cost which is the summation of the communication cost for each agent,(2) total messages which is the summation of the messages used between agents during the construction,(3) finishing round which represents how long it will take for each agent to finalize its status.

### 4.1 Accuracy

Recall that the objective of our distributed agents structure construction algorithm in each layer is to find the best subset of agents as leaders and assign member agents to these leaders to achieve minimal total communication cost. We apply our algorithm to several network topologies with agents number varies from 80 to 4000 and compare the total transferring cost ($Cost_{dist}$) with the result of the centralized local search approximation algorithm ($Cost_{cent}$). We use the increase ratio (IR) represent the difference between these two results which is calculated as follows: $IR = (Cost_{dist} - cost_{cent})/Cost_{cent}$. The IR value for different network topologies is shown is in Fig. 1.a. From this graph, we can see that IR value increases slowly as agents number increases dramatically. Our approach uses the hop counts as the distance between agents/nodes, which is obtained by rounding up the geometric distance divided by the predefined distance of one hop. This may lose precision when compared with the centralized approach that uses network distance without rounding. From this figure we can see that, for network generated based on normal distribution, higher standard deviation network gets lower IR value in our approach. This means our approach can achieve better results when agents are widely distributed.

### 4.2 Scalability

Scalability is another very important criteria to evaluate our distributed agents structure construction algorithm. We want to prevent the search messages from

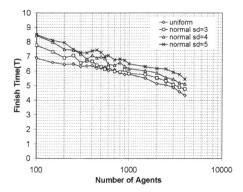

**Fig. 2.** Average finish time changes as agents number changes

flooding the network. Our objective is to use the minimal number of messages to finish the construction. We evaluate the scalability of our work by applying it on different network topologies and calculate the total messages used for the construction. The result is shown in Fig. 1.b. From this graph we can observe that the total number of messages increases almost linearly as the number of agents increases, make our approach suitable to large-scale networks.

### 4.3   Efficiency

How fast the agent architecture can be built is crucial to the performance of the distributed monitoring system. Slow construction implies slow detection and reaction to network events. In each level of the agent hierarchy, each agent finishes the construction of the current level (finalize its status) when it becomes a leader or a member of another leader. So different agents might finish the construction at different search round. We evaluate the efficiency of our approach by studying the average finishing time of agents in different network topologies. We set the threshold $R_T = 20$ to terminate the construction for some agents with small processing power and far from rest agents. Fig. 2 shows the average finishing round of agents at different network topologies. We can see that the finish time keep in certain range regardless the network topology changes. Also, as the number of agents increases, each agent receives more search messages during each round. So the $P_i$ value will also increase faster. This is why we can see that as the number of agents increases, the average finishing time decreases.

## 5   Related Work

To our best knowledge, there is no prior work which addresses the problem of how to construct the agent architecture in a complete distributed and autonomous fashion in large-scale enterprise network based on network topology and nodes capacity. Our related work study will focus on those works address the agents structure of large-scale monitoring and management system. HiFi [1] is a hierarchical events monitoring systems for large-scale network. In HiFi, the monitoring agent architecture has to be manually configured, which limits its fast deployment in large-scale network. Grid resource and application monitoring tools have been proposed in [4] and [10]. Although these system adopt hierarchical architecture, none of these architectures consider the underlying network topology, nodes traffic and capability.

A topology-aware overlay construction technique was proposed in [11]. In this approach, every overlay node will independently pings a set of predefined landmarks. Each node will sort the set of landmarks Based on the Round_Trip Time (RTT) to them. Thus, each node will have a landmark order vector, which reflects the topology position of that node. All nodes with same landmark order will independently join the same group. This approach can cluster large amount of agents in distributed fashion, but the accuracy of the result depends on the selection of landmarks. It can only sparsely cluster the nodes, and it may create nodes unevenly distribution problem. LEACH [9] proposes a distributed cluster algorithm for sensor networks. Nodes in LEACH make autonomous decisions to become cluster head based on energy consumption without any centralized control. But LEACH doesn't guarantee good head selection and distribution, its objective is to evenly distribute the energy load among all the nodes. On the contrary, in our approach, agents compete with each other to become leaders.

## 6   Conclusion and Future Works

In this paper, we have addressed the problem of automatic construction of topology-aware hierarchical agent architecture for large-scale event monitoring and correlation systems. Our distributed approach overcomes the shortcomings of centralized approaches and provides a scalable mechanism that can accommodate topology changes. The agent architecture is built in a bottom-up fashion and no central manager is required to organized the agents. We show how to build an optimal architecture based on the network topology and agents' capabilities. The possibility of one agent to become a leader in the hierarchy is determined by its processing power and proximity to other agents. In our approach, the agents compete with each other to become leaders but our algorithm favors the agents with high processing power and more close agents. The simulation results show that this approach can construct the agent architecture efficiently with reasonable communication cost for a large distributed monitoring system.

Our future work will focus on two tasks. First, we will improve dynamic parameters selection algorithm, analyze the influence of different threshold calculation methods and sample size to the accuracy of our approach. Also, we will study the impact of the proposed recovery and reconstruction technique on the optimality of the agent architecture.

# References

1. Al-Shaer, E., Abdel-Wahab, H., Maly, K.: HiFi: A New Monitoring Architecture for Distributed System Management. In: ICDCS 1999. Proceedings of International Conference on Distributed Computing Systems, Austin, TX, pp. 171–178 (May 1999)
2. Zhang, B., Al-Shaer, E.: Self-Organizing Monitoring Agents for Hierarchical Monitoring Architecture. Technical Report, multimedia research lab, Depaul University (2007)
3. Carzaniga, A., Rosenblum, D.S., Wolf, A.L.: Design and evaluation of a wide-area event notification service. ACM Transactions on Computer Systems (TOCS) 19(3) (August 2001)
4. Baker, M., Smith, G.: GridRM: An Extensible Resource Monitoring System. In: CLUSTER 2003. Proceedings of the 5th IEEE Cluster Computing Conference, Hong Kong (December 2003)
5. Fei, A., Pei, G., Liu, R., Zhang, L.: Measurements on Delay and Hop-Count of the Internet. In: Proc. IEEE GLOBECOM 1998 Internet Mini-Conf., IEEE Computer Society Press, Los Alamitos (1998)
6. Gruber, R.E.: Balachander Krishnamurthy and Euthimios Panagos: High-level constructs in the READY event notification system. In: Proceedings of the 8th ACM SIGOPS European workshop on Support for composing distributed applications, Sintra, Portugal (1998)
7. Carzaniga, A., Rosenblum, D.S., Wolf, A.L.: Design and evaluation of a wide-area event notification service. ACM Transactions on Computer Systems (TOCS) 19(3) (August 2001)
8. Gruber, R.E., Krishnamurthy, B., Panagos, E.: High-level constructs in the READY event notification system. In: Proceedings of the 8th ACM SIGOPS European workshop on Support for composing distributed applications, Sintra, Portugal (1998)
9. Heinzelman, W.R., Chandrakasan, A., Balakrishnan, H.: An Application-Specific Protocol Architecture for Wireless Microsensor Networks. IEEE Transactions on Wireless Communications 1(4), 660C670 (2002)
10. Truong, H.-L., Fahringer, T.: SCALEA-G: a Unified Monitoring and Performance Analysis System for the Grid. Technical report, Institute for Software Science, University of Vienna (October 2003)
11. Ratnasamy, S., Handley, M., Karp, R., Shenker, S.: Topologically-aware Overlay Construction and Server Selection. In: INFOCOM (2002)
12. Korupolu, M.R., Plaxton, C.G., Rajaraman, R.: Analysis of a Local Search Heuristic for Facility Location Problems. In: Proceedings of the 9th Annual ACM-SIAM Symposium on Discrete Algorithms, pp. 1–10. ACM Press, New York (1998)
13. Osman, I.H., Christofides, N.: Capacitated clustering problems by hybrid simulated annealing and tabu search. Transactions in Operational Research 1, 317–336 (1994)
14. Jain, K., Vazirani, V.: Primal-dual approximation algorithms for metric facility location and k-median problems. In: Proceeding of the 40th Annual IEEE Symposium on Foundation of Computer Science, pp. 1–10. IEEE Computer Society Press, Los Alamitos (1999)
15. Yemini, S.A., Kliger, S., Mozes, E., Yemini, Y., Ohsie, D.: High Speed and Robust Event Correlation. IEEE Communication Magazine, 433–450 (May 1996)

# Market-Based Hierarchical Resource Management Using Machine Learning

Ramy Farha and Alberto Leon-Garcia

University of Toronto, Toronto, Ontario, Canada
ramy.farha@utoronto.ca, alberto.leongarcia@utoronto.ca

**Abstract.** Service providers are constantly seeking ways to reduce the costs incurred in managing the services they deliver. With the increased distribution and virtualization of resources in the next generation network infrastructure, novel resource management approaches are sought for effective service delivery. In this paper, we propose a market-based hierarchical resource management mechanism using Machine Learning, which consists of a negotiation phase where customers are allocated the resources needed by their activated service instances, and a learning phase where service providers adjust the prices of their resources in order to steer the network infrastructure towards the desired goal of increasing their revenues, while delivering the mix of services requested by their customers. We present the operation of such a market where distributed and virtualized resources are traded as commodities between autonomic resource brokers performing the negotiation and learning on behalf of service providers. We perform extensive simulations to study the performance of the proposed hierarchical resource management mechanism.

## 1 Introduction

Service providers (SPs) are reacting to competitive pressures by transitioning from being providers of individual services (voice, data, video) to providers of service bundles. SPs must deal the challenge of reducing the costs of managing these services and the network infrastructure over which these services are deployed and offered. The requirements for a powerful service management system motivate the need to automate management by evolving to self-managing infrastructures, in order to ensure automated service delivery to customers.

The Autonomic Computing [1] concept presented by IBM to reduce software complexity and cost of service delivery in the IT domain is attractive in the sense that a similar concept could be mapped in the telecommunications domain to perform autonomic service management. In a previous work [2], we had introduced the Autonomic Service Architecture (ASA), which aims to give SPs the needed solutions to dynamically marshal their service delivery infrastructure and to support the required service mix at a given point in time using a hierarchy of Autonomic Resource Brokers (ARBs) which perform resource management.

The network infrastructure for telecommunications service delivery could be viewed as a set of competing SPs, similar to players in a game-theoretic problem [3]. Given the difficulty to represent this game using classical game theory,

A. Clemm, L.Z. Granville, and R. Stadler (Eds.): DSOM 2007, LNCS 4785, pp. 25–37, 2007.

we explore an alternative approach using Machine Learning [4], where Reinforcement Learning [5] agents built into the ARBs of ASA incrementally improve their strategies according to trial-and-error interactions with the external world. As a result, SPs adjust the prices of their resources to achieve better performance for the autonomic resource management approach performed by ASA.

In this paper, we present a market-based hierarchical resource management approach, using Machine Learning to autonomically steer the network infrastructure towards the desired goals for both SPs and their customers. The remainder of this paper is structured as follows. In section 2, we review some related work. In section 3, we summarize the design of ASA, prior to explaining the hierarchical resource management approach in section 4. In section 5, we integrate Machine Learning into ASA to improve the strategy of SPs. In section 6, we illustrate some simulation results to show the performance of the proposed scheme. Finally, in section 7, we conclude the paper and suggest some future work.

## 2   Related Work

Game Theory is aimed at understanding situations in which several decision makers (also called players) interact [3]. Classical game theory suffers from several shortcomings, such as the need for perfect information about strategies of other players, or about the probability distribution of their strategies. Such assumptions are infeasible in an environment of competing service providers (SPs), which are the players in the game-theoretic problem, hence the need for alternative ways to solve this game, such as Machine Learning [4].

Machine Learning is a branch of artificial intelligence that encompasses areas such as Neural Networks, Genetic Algorithms, Ant Colony Optimization, and Reinforcement Learning (RL) [5]. RL will be used to enable the decision makers, in this case the competing SPs, to optimize their operation using trial-and-error interactions with the external environment, in order to steer the operation of the network infrastructure towards the greater good for both themselves and for their customers, without the need to share any information with other SPs.

The closest work to this paper is presented by Wang and Li [6]. In their approach, concepts from control theory are used to help selfish nodes in a service overlay network incrementally adapt to the market, by making optimized strategic decisions based on past experiences. While the techniques they use are comparable to those adopted in this paper, their application is drastically different. This paper involves a different negotiation mechanism since some customers specify the rate required instead of only having a Best Effort service as is the case in the work of Wang and Li. The complexity of the problem changes as well since this paper uses a hierarchical architecture. Furthermore, this paper attempts to improve the utilization of the network infrastructure's virtual resources by SPs while satisfying customer requirements, whereas Wang and Li are attempting to force selfish nodes in a service overlay network towards more cooperation.

# 3   Autonomic Service Architecture Overview

The main task of the Autonomic Service Architecture (ASA) is to automate the delivery of services offered by a service provider (SP) to its customers in next generation networks. ASA achieves this goal through the interaction of self-managing entities, called Autonomic Resource Brokers (ARBs), which autonomically handle provisioning, management, and termination of offered services.

The layered structure of ARBs in ASA is shown in Fig. 1. When customers activate service instances they have bought from SPs, these service instances are managed by the SPs using Service Instance ARBs (SIARBs). The multiple service instances of a particular service offered by a SP are managed by Composite ARBs (CARBs). The different services offered by a SP (managed by CARBs) are managed by a Global ARB (GARB), which handles all the resources available at this SP's disposal. Physical resources are virtualized into virtual resources to deal with heterogeneity, using concepts similar to those in [7].

Resource management in next generation networks using ASA could be seen as a market where virtual resources are exchanged between customers and SPs. This view is becoming a reality with architectures such as the one used by Amazon [8], or with the proliferation of Grids [9]. Virtual resources can be assimilated to commodities with prices that vary depending on the demand. The market consists of several competing SPs owning the different virtual resources and services which are offered to customers. In the upcoming sections, we elaborate on how the market model applies for hierarchical resource management in ASA.

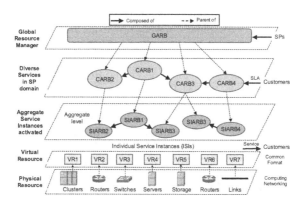

**Fig. 1.** Autonomic Resource Brokers Hierarchy in the Autonomic Service Architecture

# 4   Hierarchical Resource Management Algorithm

For each virtual resource in the network infrastructure, we run the proposed market-based hierarchical resource management algorithm with Machine Learning, according to the autonomic loop shown in Fig. 2. This algorithm, which will

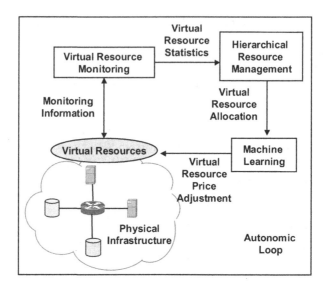

**Fig. 2.** Autonomic Hierarchical Resource Management Algorithm

**Table 1.** Notations for the market-based hierarchical resource management algorithm

| | |
|---|---|
| $R_{req}^{r}$ | Amount of Virtual Resource $r$ requested by QoS customers |
| $R_{BE}^{r}$ | Amount of Virtual Resource $r$ offered to BE customers |
| $R_{miss}^{r}(ARB_i)$ | Missing amount of Virtual Resource $r$ at ARB $i$ |
| $R_{thr}^{r}(ARB_i)$ | Threshold amount of Virtual Resource $r$ at ARB $i$ |
| $RC(VR_r, ARB_i)$ | Residual Capacity of Virtual Resource $r$ at ARB $i$ |
| $A_{upst}(VR_r, ARB_i)$ | Total upstream amount of Virtual Resource $r$ at ARB $i$ |
| $A_{dnst}(VR_r, ARB_i)$ | Total downstream amount of Virtual Resource $r$ at ARB $i$ |
| $A_{QoS}(VR_r, ARB_i)$ | Total QoS amount of Virtual Resource $r$ allocated at ARB $i$ |
| $U^r(ARB_i)$ | ARB $i$ utility for Virtual Resource $r$ |
| $\Delta U^r(ARB_i)$ | ARB $i$ differential utility for Virtual Resource $r$ |
| $p_{QoSi}^{r}$ | QoS price for Virtual Resource $r$ at ARB $i$ |
| $p_{BEi}^{r}$ | BE price for Virtual Resource $r$ at ARB $i$ |
| $TRev(VR_r, ARB_i)$ | Total revenue from Virtual Resource $r$ at ARB $i$ |
| $TCost(VR_r, ARB_i)$ | Total cost for Virtual Resource $r$ at ARB $i$ |
| $\epsilon_1(t)$ | Time varying scaling factor for utility function |

be detailed next, is performed by the Autonomic Resource Brokers (ARBs) of the aforementioned Autonomic Service Architecture (ASA). The notations used in the rest of this paper are shown in Table 1.

The detailed hierarchical model of ARBs at a given SP is shown in Fig. 3. Initially, the SP reserves a fraction of the available capacity at its GARB for a given virtual resource. The CARBs will share this fraction of the capacity proportionally to the needs of the service that each CARB manages, while the remaining capacity is kept to remedy for any virtual resources shortages. Service

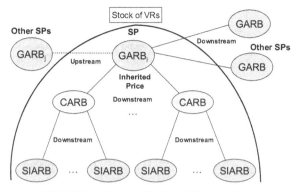

Within SP: Several commodities (Virtual Resources)

**Fig. 3.** Detailed Hierarchical Resource Management Model

requests arrive from customers at random times for the different services offered by this SP which use this virtual resource. Thus, a given amount of it is allocated to each activated service instance. These requests consist of two main tuples of interest for the management of a given virtual resource: <Amount, Duration>. The virtual resource amounts are allocated if available, and if not, a new request is triggered for additional virtual resources to be bought from other SPs.

The interaction between the different ARBs is shown in Fig. 4. At level 0, the GARB which is the global manager of a given SP, interacts with the GARBs of other SPs in a peer-to-peer (P2P) fashion. The SPs can therefore exchange virtual resources when needed. Initially, each SP has a maximum capacity array of the virtual resources $[MC(VR_1), \ldots, MC(VR_N)]$. At level 1, the CARB which manages a given service is allocated an array of virtual resource amounts $[A(VR_1), \ldots, A(VR_N)]$. This allocation is performed by the GARB to its children CARBs, i.e. the CARBs corresponding to the services offered by this SP. The price of a virtual resource is inherited at the CARB from its parent GARB. We assume that a separate price is set by a SP for each virtual resource, one for BE requests and one for QoS requests. The price for a service composed of several virtual resources is a combination of these virtual resources' prices, according to service pricing approaches beyond the scope of this paper.

The negotiation algorithm, shown in Algorithm 1, works as follows: For QoS customers, the SP needs to guarantee that the virtual resource amounts delivered to the customers are equal to those requested. For BE customers, the SP does not guarantee delivery of any virtual resource amounts to the customers. An issue for the algorithm is to determine an appropriate utility function to maximize in order to determine the amount of virtual resources allocated to BE customers. The choice of the utility function was based upon the needs of an efficient management system. The higher the amount allocated, the greater the revenue for the SP. However, the amount allocated should not be too high, since it limits the number of additional customers that could be served in the future. One key requirement of the utility function is to be concave up. Due to these

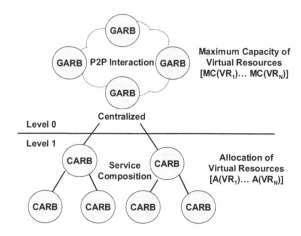

**Fig. 4.** Autonomic Resource Brokers Interaction

conflicting needs, we use two terms in the utility function: one relates to the revenue of the SP, and the other to the amount of resources allocated. Therefore, the chosen utility function for virtual resource $r$ at $CARB_i$ is given by:

$$U^r(CARB_i) = \epsilon_1(t) \times log\left(1 - \frac{A_{dnst}(CARB_i) - A_{upst}(CARB_i)}{A_{dnst}(CARB_i) + RC(VR_r, CARB_i)}\right)$$
$$+ p^r_{BEi}(t) \times A_{dnst}(CARB_i) \qquad (1)$$

The amount $\epsilon_1(t)$ is time-dependent and set to $p_{BEi}(t) \times (A_{dnst}(CARB_i) + RC(VR_r, CARB_i))$. In the rest of this paper, we are concerned with the additive utility, that is the utility added to the SP by allocating an amount $R^r$ of virtual resource $r$ to a customer, which is given by:

$$\Delta U^r(CARB_i) = \epsilon_1(t) \times log\left(1 - \frac{A_{dnst}(CARB_i) - A_{upst}(CARB_i) + R^r}{A_{dnst}(CARB_i) + RC(VR_r, CARB_i) + R^r}\right)$$
$$- \epsilon_1(t) \times log\left(1 - \frac{A_{dnst}(CARB_i) - A_{upst}(CARB_i)}{A_{dnst}(CARB_i) + RC(VR_r, CARB_i)}\right) + p^r_{BEi}(t) \times R^r \quad (2)$$

The aforementioned utility function was chosen for the following reasons:

– The first derivative has a point of inflection where it changes signs.

$$\frac{dU^r(CARB_i)}{dR^r} = -\epsilon_1(t) \times \frac{1}{R^r + A_{dnst}(CARB_i) + RC(VR_r, CARB_i)} \qquad (3)$$
$$+ p^r_{BEi}(t) = 0$$

This point of inflection corresponds to the rate $R^r_{BE}$ offered to the customer.

$$R^r_{BE} = \frac{\epsilon_1(t)}{p^r_{BEi}} - (A_{dnst}(CARB_i) + RC(VR_r, CARB_i)) \qquad (4)$$

---

**Hierarchical Resource Management Algorithm**

*Service Instance activation for Service j by QoS Customer i from Service Provider k*

**QoS Customers-Service Providers**
```
Service Instance of Service j activated;
```
Amount $R^r_{req}$ of virtual resource $r$ requested;

if $R^r_{req} < RC(VR_r, CARB_j)$ then
|     Accept request for the amount $R^r_{req}$ of virtual resource $r$;
|     Update CARB $j$ and SIARB $i$ accordingly;

else
|     Find missing amount $R^r_{miss}(CARB_j) = R^r_{req}$ of virtual resource $r$ at
|     CARB $j$;
|     Trigger internal flow between CARB $j$ and GARB $k$ for missing amount
|     $R^r_{miss}(CARB_j)$ of virtual resource $r$;

end

*Service Instance activation for Service j by BE Customer i from Service Provider k*

**BE Customers-Service Providers**
```
Service Instance of Service j activated;
Find amount that maximizes the differential utility for virtual
```
resource $r$ at CARB $j$: $R^r_{BE} = argmax(\Delta U^r(CARB_j))$;

if $R^r_{BE} > R^r_{th}(CARB_j)$ then
|     Accept Best-Effort request for amount $R^r_{BE}$ of virtual resource $r$;

else
|     Find missing amount $R^r_{miss}(CARB_j) = R^r_{BE}$ of virtual resource $r$ at
|     CARB $j$;
|     Trigger internal flow between CARB $j$ and GARB $k$ for missing amount
|     $R^r_{miss}(CARB_j)$ of virtual resource $r$;

end

**CARB-GARB (Triggered)**

Missing amount $R^r_{miss}(CARB_j)$ of virtual resource $r$ requested between CARB $j$ and its parent GARB $k$

if $R^r_{miss}(CARB_j) < RC(VR_r, GARB_k)$ then
|     Accept request for the missing amount $R^r_{miss}(CARB_j)$;
|     Update CARB $j$ and GARB $k$ accordingly;

else
|     Trigger external flow between GARB $k$ and other GARB $l$ for missing
|     amount $R^r_{miss}(GARB_k) = R^r_{miss}(CARB_j)$ of virtual resource $r$;

end

**Between GARBs (Triggered)**

Missing amount $R^r_{miss}(GARB_k)$ of virtual resource $r$ requested between GARB $k$ (or downstream GARB) and GARB $l$ (or upstream GARB)

if $R^r_{miss}(GARB_k) < RC(VR_r, GARB_l)$ then
|     Accept request for the missing amount $R^r_{miss}(GARB_k)$;
|     Update GARB $k$ and GARB $l$ accordingly;

else
|     Reject triggered request, and original customer request;

end

---

**Algorithm 1.** Pseudo Code for Hierarchical Resource Management Algorithm

- The second derivative is always positive, so the proposed utility function is concave up, as required.

$$\frac{d^2 U^r(CARB_i)}{dR^{r2}} = \frac{\epsilon_1(t)}{(R^r + A_{dnst}(CARB_i) + RC(VR_r, CARB_i))^2} \quad (5)$$

- In addition, the chosen utility function achieves our goal. An increase in the upstream amount is not desirable as this triggers external exchanges with other SPs, which is costly. When the residual capacity and the upstream amount both reach zero, the first utility term is equal to zero (its highest possible value), which means all the residual capacity is being used, but there is no need for additional resource amounts to be bought from other SPs.

## 5   Strategy Improvement Using Learning

Reinforcement Learning (RL) represents a class of Machine Learning problems where an agent explores its environment, observes its current state $s$, and takes a subsequent action $a$, according to a decision policy $\pi : s \rightarrow a$. The RL model consists of a set of states $S$ and a set of actions $A$. RL aims to find a control policy that will maximize the observed rewards over the lifetime of the agents, in our case the Global Autonomic Resource Brokers (GARBs) corresponding to the different service providers (SPs) in the network. To do so, a GARB will incrementally adjust its virtual resources' prices based on the feedback (or reinforcement) received from the environment. An optimal decision policy is to incur the highest accumulated reinforcement values.

Prior to defining the RL model, we need to clarify the goal that the network infrastructure aims to achieve. Ideally, no SP should monopolize the network, as customers should be tempted to buy from all SPs. However, SPs need to make as much profit as possible. By increasing their prices without boundary, SPs will be at a disadvantage if customers are looking for the cheapest service to buy and activate. In addition, customer demands should also be satisfied to the best of a SP's ability as long as no detrimental performance effects are observed.

In our approach, we used two different prices based on whether we are dealing with QoS or BE customers. The approach taken for each price adjustment method using RL could be different for the QoS and BE cases, but we assume a similar approach for both. Hence, in what follows, we will only show the QoS price adjustment approach. The BE price adjustment approach is similar, where BE prices are varied using BE virtual resource amounts instead of QoS virtual resource amounts to calculate the reinforcement value. Table 2 lists the variables used in the proposed RL method to improve hierarchical resource management.

RL operates on a virtual resource basis at a given GARB. In the discrete-time domain, RL models the interaction between a GARB and the environment as a Markov Decision Process. Suppose the GARB is in state $s^r$ at time step $(t)$, then the GARB performs action $a$ and shifts to state $s^{r'}$ at the next time step $(t+1)$. In our case, the states are chosen as the ratio of the GARB's residual capacity for the given virtual resource, and the sum of the GARB's residual capacity

Table 2. Variables used in Reinforcement Learning method

| $Q^r(s^r, a)$ | Q-value function for state $s^r$ and action $a$ |
|---|---|
| $P(a/s^r)$ | Probability of taking action $a$ when in state $s^r$ |
| $rl^r$ | Reinforcement value received by GARB |
| $\psi^r$ | Positive constant to control exploration vs. exploitation |
| $\gamma^r$ | Discounting factor |
| $\zeta^r$ | Learning rate |
| $\epsilon_2(t)$ | Time varying scaling factor for reinforcement |

and the delivered downstream QoS virtual resource amounts. The actions taken are variations of the QoS price $p_{QoSi}^r(t)$ charged by the upstream ARB to its downstream ARBs for QoS amounts of Virtual Resource $r$ at time step $(t)$, to steer the performance towards the desired goals.

In this paper, we will adopt the Q-learning algorithm to iteratively approximate the state-action value function, $Q^r(s^r, a)$, which represents the expected return when taking action $a$ in state $s^r$ and then following the current policy to the end. The action $a$ in state $s^r$ is taken with a probability $P(a/s^r)$, and the GARB receives a reinforcement value $rl^r$. The actions are picked according to their Q-values, following a Boltzmann distribution, as follows:

$$P(a/s^r) = \frac{\psi e^{Q^r(s^r, a)}}{\sum_{a'} \psi e^{Q^r(s^r, a')}} \tag{6}$$

The standard updating rules for Q-learning are given as follows:

$$Q^r(s^r(t+1), a) = (1 - \zeta^r) Q^r(s^r(t), a) + \zeta^r (rl^r + \gamma^r max_{a'} Q^r(s^r(t), a')) \tag{7}$$

At each GARB, the QoS price is dynamically adjusted over time to maximize its economic revenue and minimize its empirical loss due to the decrease of its residual capacity because of demands by downstream ARBs. Therefore, we choose the following reinforcement value for node $i$ at time step $(t+1)$:

$$rl^r = \epsilon_2(t) \times (TRev(VR_r, GARB_i) - TCost(VR_r, GARB_i))$$
$$+log\left(1 - \frac{A_{QoS}(VR_r, GARB_i)}{A_{QoS}(VR_r, GARB_i) + RC(VR_r, GARB_i)}\right) \tag{8}$$

The value $\epsilon_2(t)$ is chosen to be time-dependent in order to constantly adjust the reinforcement value as time elapses. In order to obtain similar orders of magnitude of the two terms of the reinforcement value, we set $\epsilon_2(t)$ to $500 \times p_{QoSi}^r(t)$. The reinforcement value is supposed to steer the SP towards the aforementioned goals, increasing its revenue, but also taking the residual capacity and the delivered rate into account. In order to ensure that the shortcomings which are usually encountered in RL models are avoided, and to guarantee convergence to global optima, the following conditions, satisfied in our RL model, are required:

1. Each state-action pair is visited an infinite (i.e. large) number of times
2. Learning rate is decreased with time
3. Rewards are incremented as the goal is approached

## 6   Simulation Results

The proposed approach is tested using extensive simulations. To emulate the desired environment of service providers (SPs), of physical and virtual resources, of services offered, of customers and the service instances they activate, we built a custom simulator using the Java programming language. We create customer entities connecting to the network infrastructure through physical resources to activate the service instances. Services are composed using other component services and several virtual resources. The candidate component services for the composition process are equally considered to avoid bias towards a given service.

The parameters used in the simulation were the same for all experiments. We generated several component services, as well as physical and virtual resources, which were owned by 10 SPs. For each virtual resource, random amounts were available in the infrastructure and distributed in the available physical resources. We allowed several customers to buy services from different SPs and to activate instances of such services. The service instances were activated according to a different Poisson process for each service bought, and were kept active for exponentially distributed service times which were different for each service instance.

Fig. 5 shows how the utility function chosen to service Best Effort (BE) customers works for a given SP. As can be seen in the figure, the rate offered varies depending on the virtual resource's residual capacity at this SP. When this residual capacity increases, the rate offered increases, and vice versa. This shows that the utility function is performing as desired, adapting the rate offered by this SP to BE customers according to its available capacity.

We now show the instantaneous variation of the QoS prices for 5 randomly chosen SPs for 2 cases where the Reinforcement Learning (RL) method is applied. In the Random Choice case (Fig. 6), the prices vary around their starting point. The interesting observation is that one SP's price tends to devi-

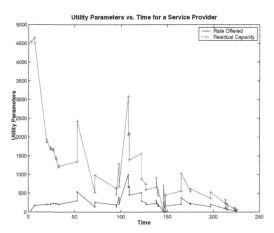

**Fig. 5.** Utility: Variation of Rate Offered with Residual Capacity

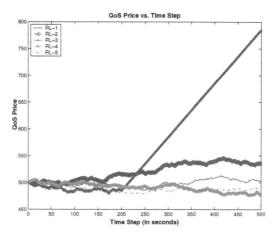

**Fig. 6.** QoS Price Variation for Random Choice Scenario

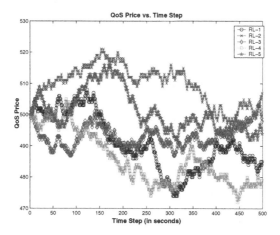

**Fig. 7.** QoS Price Variation for Least Cost Scenario

ate from the others. This is due to the fact that in this experiment, the upstream SP when external flows are triggered is randomly chosen. There is therefore no reward for a SP offering a lower price for a given virtual resource, and it is not harmful in this case to deviate from the general consensus of keeping prices under control. The RL method is not totally suitable in this case. In the Least Cost case (Fig. 7), the prices vary around their starting point. The interesting observation is that no SP's price tends to deviate from the others. If it does, it is re-adjusted by the RL method. This is due to the fact that in this experiment, the upstream SP when external flows are triggered is chosen according to the least cost offered by other SPs for that virtual resource. There is therefore a reward for a SP offering a lower price for a given virtual resource, and it is harmful in this case to deviate from the

**Table 3.** Average Virtual Resource Goodput for the three pricing approaches

| Traffic | Fixed | Varying Random Choice | Varying Least-Cost Choice |
|---|---|---|---|
| All Traffic | 0.3083 | 0.2867 | 0.0657 |
| QoS Traffic | 0.2842 | 0.2441 | 0.0555 |

general consensus of keeping prices under control. This is much more likely to be the case in real-world environments. In such environments, the proposed RL method for market-based hierarchical resource management performs as desired.

To further measure the performance of the proposed reinforcement learning approach, we propose a new metric which we refer to as the Virtual Resource Goodput (VRG). The VRG is calculated as the ratio of the total downstream rate of the SP over the revenue of that SP. Therefore, the goal of a SP is to bring the VRG down, so that less virtual resources are needed for more revenues. The value of his unit of virtual resource increases when the VRG decreases. Table 3 shows the average VRG for the three approaches: Fixed Price, Varying Price Random Choice, and Varying Price Least-Cost. We also compute the VRG for the QoS downstream rate only. As seen in the table, the average VRG is highest (worst performance) for the Fixed Price approach, followed by the Varying Price Random Choice approach, and the best performance is achieved by the Varying Price Least Cost approach. Also, note that the VRG of the QoS traffic is better than the VRG of the entire (QoS and BE) traffic, as the QoS traffic gives the SP more value per unit virtual resource.

# 7   Conclusion

In this paper, we presented a market-based hierarchical resource management algorithm using machine learning to autonomically learn prices and adjust them as time evolves in order to improve the service providers' performance, keep the customers satisfied, and avoid monopolies by preventing service providers' price deviation. The paper proposed a negotiation algorithm using a carefully chosen utility function to serve BE customers, and providing QoS customers with the the rate requested. It also proposed a learning method to adjust virtual resource prices according to the environment. Results have shown that the utility function operates as expected, that the learning mechanism avoids price deviation and keeps prices under control, and that the virtual resource amount needed by a given service provider for a unit of revenue decreases when learning is used. Future work will consider other similar hierarchical resource management algorithms, as well as variations to the utility functions and reinforcement learning methods. The paper has shown the potential of reinforcement learning when competing service providers wish to steer their operation towards a desired goal.

# References

1. Kephart, J., et al.: The vision of autonomic computing. IEEE Computer Magazine, 41–50 (2003)
2. Farha, R., et. al.: Towards an Autonomic Service Architecture. LNCS, pp. 58–67 (2005)
3. Osborne, M.: An introduction to Game Theory. Oxford University Press, Oxford (2002)
4. Alpaydin, E.: Introduction to Machine Learning. MIT Press, Cambridge (2004)
5. Kaelbling, L., et al.: Reinforcement Learning A Survey. Journal of Artificial Intelligence Research, 237–285 (1996)
6. Wang, W., Li, B.: Market-based self-optimization for autonomic service overlay networks. IEEE Journal on Selected Areas in Communications, 2320–2332 (2005)
7. Leon-Garcia, A., et al.: Virtual Network Resource Management for Next-Generation Networks. IEEE Communications Magazine, 102–109 (2003)
8. Garfinkel, S.: Commodity Grid Computing with Amazon's S3 and EC2. Usenix (2007)
9. Minoli, D.: A networking approach to Grid Computing. Wiley, Chichester (2004)

# Probabilistic Fault Diagnosis Using Adaptive Probing*

Maitreya Natu and Adarshpal S. Sethi

Dept. of Computer and Information Science,
University of Delaware, Newark, DE, USA, 19716,
{natu,sethi}@cis.udel.edu

**Abstract.** Past research on probing-based network monitoring provides solutions based on preplanned probing which is computationally expensive, is less accurate, and involves a large management traffic. Unlike preplanned probing, adaptive probing proposes to select probes in an interactive manner sending more probes to diagnose the observed problem areas and less probes in the healthy areas, thereby significantly reducing the number of probes required. Another limitation of most of the work proposed in the past is that it assumes a deterministic dependency information between the probes and the network components. Such an assumption can not be made when complete and accurate network information might not be available. Hence, there is a need to develop network monitoring algorithms that can localize failures in the network even in the presence of uncertainty in the inferred dependencies between probes and network components. In this paper, we propose a fault diagnosis tool with following novel features: (1) We present an adaptive probing based solution for fault diagnosis which is cost-effective, failure resistant, more accurate, and involves less management traffic as compared to the preplanned probing approach. (2) We address the issues that arise with the presence of a non-deterministic environment and present probing algorithms that consider the involved uncertainties in the collected network information.

## 1 Introduction

Modern network environments impose several challenges on the fault localization problems which include (1) presence of multiple failures, (2) incomplete and inaccurate information about the network, (3) non-determinism in the system structure and its observed state, (4) the demand for fault diagnosis with minimal management traffic etc.

One promising approach to effective and efficient fault diagnosis is *adaptive probing*. Probing based approaches perform network monitoring by sending

---

* Prepared through collaborative participation in the Communications and Networks Consortium sponsored by the U.S. Army Research Laboratory under the Collaborative Technology Alliance Program, Cooperative Agreement DAAD19-01-2-0011. The U.S. Government is authorized to reproduce and distribute reprints for Government purposes notwithstanding any copyright notation thereon.

A. Clemm, L.Z. Granville, and R. Stadler (Eds.): DSOM 2007, LNCS 4785, pp. 38–49, 2007.
© IFIP International Federation for Information Processing 2007

probes to determine if the components are in good health. Since probes generate additional traffic in the network, it is important to carefully select probes such that the desired diagnostic capability can be achieved with less traffic overhead. Adaptive probing addresses this concern by adapting the probe set to the observed network conditions by sending less probes in the healthy areas of the network and more probes where a failure is detected.

The past work on probing relies on a complete, accurate, and deterministic information about the underlying dependencies between the end-to-end probes and the probed components. A non-deterministic model is needed to address the issues that arise when the causal relationships among the system elements cannot be learned with certainty. For instance, if the dependencies change dynamically, or when the information about these dependencies provided to the management system is not guaranteed to be accurate.

A fault diagnosis solution for modern communication systems should have the following properties: (1) Ability to perform reasoning under uncertainty about the underlying dependencies, (2) Diagnosis of multiple failures, (3) Low management traffic overhead, (4) Small deployment cost, (5) High accuracy and low computational complexity.

With adaptive probing, we attempt to meet the above stated requirements of a fault diagnosis tool. We provide adaptive probing solutions assuming the availability of non-deterministic dependency information. We attempt to find multiple failures. Adaptive probing attempts to minimize overhead of probe traffic. Unlike the traditional way of deploying passive monitors over a large part of the network, probing solutions reduce the instrumentation overhead by requiring instrumentation of a smaller number of nodes as probe stations. Adaptive probing is computationally much less complex that the preplanned approach of probe selection. We show through simulation results that the adaptive probing approach provides a high detection ratio and low false positive ratio as compared to preplanned probing.

This paper is structured as follows. We present the related work in Section 2. We introduce the probabilistic dependency model and the system architecture in Section 3. We then present an adaptive and preplanned probing algorithm in Section 4. We present an experimental evaluation of the proposed algorithms in Section 5 followed by conclusion in Section 6.

## 2   Related Work

Network probing with low overhead has prompted development of many monitoring approaches. Due to space reasons, we survey only those approaches that directly relate to probe selection.

Probing tools proposed in the past consist of connectivity, latency and bandwidth measurement tools such as [3], [4], [5] etc. Li et. al. in [6] propose to use source routed probes to measure end-to-end performance metrics. Bejarano et. al. [1] propose a probe selection algorithm for monitoring network links based on a greedy heuristic of selecting a probe that covers maximum number of uncovered

network components. In the past, Rish et. al. [10] have proposed adaptive probing approach for fault localization. In our previous work, we have presented algorithms for adaptive probe selection in [8], [9] assuming a deterministic
environment.

Most of the work proposed in the past suffer from two main limitations: (1) a
preplanned approach is used to build a probe set to localize all possible failures
in the network. (2) an assumption of availability of deterministic dependency
information is made. An important contribution in this paper is to propose
an adaptive probing approach for localizing faults while considering the non-
determinism present in the system. We present algorithms for probe selection in
a non-deterministic environment where the dependencies between the probes and
network components are represented using a probabilistic dependency model.

## 3   System Architecture

Figure 1 presents the proposed system architecture. The two main components
of the architecture are probe station selection and probe selection. The probe
station selection module finds suitable locations in the network where probe
stations should be deployed. As part of our ongoing research, we are working on
the probe station selection problem. The probe selection module refers to the
selection of probes such that faults in the network can be detected and localized.
Using adaptive probing, we divide the probing task into two sub-tasks which we
call *Failure Detection* and *Fault Localization*. Through the *Failure Detection*
module, we first send a small number of probes that can only detect the presence
of a failure in the network. They might not be able to localize the exact failure.
Once a failure is detected in the network, we perform *Fault Localization* by
sending additional probes over the selected area of the network in an interactive
manner to localize the exact cause of failure.

The *Probe Station Selection* and *Probe Selection* modules of the architecture use the dependencies between probes and the nodes through which these
probes pass which are stored in a dependency model. To address the uncertainties involved in the dependency information, we propose to use a probabilistic
dependency model. Each node n is associated with a probability of its independent failure $p(n)$. The dependency between a probe-path $p$ and a node $n$ is
represented with the probability of the causal implication, $P(p|n)$, which rep-
resents the probability that the failure of node $n$ may cause failure of probe $p$.
The causal probabilities can be computed in a variety of ways. For instance, in
a scenario of multi-path routing, the probabilities could be based on the policy
that the routers or load balancers use to select the next hops. In the presence
of mobility, if different dependency models are available for different times, then
probabilities could be based on the temporal closeness of the failure time of a
path and the built time of the dependency models [7]. We represent the fault-
symptom dependencies using a matrix where each column represents a fault and
each row represents a symptom. In our case, a fault represents a node failure
and a row represents a probe. A *cell(i,j)* in the matrix represents the probability

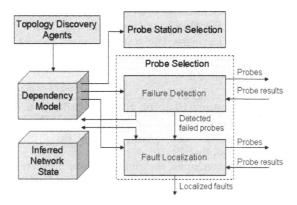

**Fig. 1.** System architecture for fault diagnosis using adaptive probing

that the node failure represented by column $j$ can cause failure of probe $j$. In other words, it represents the probability that the probe represented by row $j$ passes through node represented by column $j$.

# 4   Probe Selection

In this section, we present algorithms for probe selection using preplanned and adaptive probing. Preplanned probing involves a high computational complexity and we later show through simulation results that preplanned probing is less accurate and requires much larger number of probes as compared to adaptive probing.

## 4.1   Preplanned Probing

The preplanned probing approach proposes to select a set of probes such that all possible fault scenarios can be uniquely diagnosed. As explained in Section 3, we represent the fault-symptom relationships using a dependency matrix. For the preplanned probing, we extend the dependency matrix such that, along with single-node failures, columns also represent states of combinations of more than one faults that can occur in the system. The algorithm assumes a limit on total number of failures than can be diagnosed, which decides the number of fault combinations that are represented in the matrix. Thus, a $cell(i, j)$ in the matrix represents the probability that failure of fault combinations represented by column $j$ can cause failure of probe $i$. In other words, it represents the probability that the probe $j$ passes through the nodes represented by column $j$. For a particular system state corresponding to a column $j$, the vector of probe outcomes of success or failure would be based on dependency of the probes on the faults represented by the column $j$. That is, a probe $i$ with high probability value in cell(i, j) is more likely to fail in the given system state as compared to the probe with a smaller probability value. Thus each system state can be represented by a vector of probe outcomes. The problem of probe selection can then be formulated as finding the smallest set of probes such that each state can be represented by a unique probe vector. In that case, the state of failure can be determined by observing the vector of probe outcomes. In this section, we present a heuristic based algorithm to select such a probe set.

---

**Algorithm PPFL: Preplanned-Probing Fault Localization Algorithm**

---

Initialize partition $statePartition$ = all non-probe-station nodes; set SP = Null;
**while** $statePartition$ *does not consist of singleton sets* **do**
    Compute $splitOverhead(statePartition, p)$ and
    $splitBelief(statePartition, p)$ for each unused probe $p$, where
    $splitOverhead(statePartition, p) = \sum_{\forall set S \in statePartition} splitOverhead(S, p)$
    $splitBelief(statePartition, p) =$
    $(\sum_{\forall set S \in statePartition}(splitBelief(S, p)))/|statePartition|$
    where
    $splitOverhead(S, p) = ((|S^-|/|S|)log(|S^-|)) + ((|S^+|/|S|)log(|S^+|))$
    $splitBelief(S, p) = (\prod_{s \in S^+} P(p|s)).(\prod_{s \in S^-} 1 - P(p|s))$
    where $S^-$ and $S^+$ are the subsets of the set $S$ such that
    $\forall_{n \in S}(P(p|n) > dependencyThreshold) \rightarrow (n \in S^+)$, and
    $\forall_{n \in S}(P(p|n) <= dependencyThreshold) \rightarrow (n \in S^-)$;
    Select a probe $p_{min}$ that minimizes the value
    $0.5.splitOverhead(statePartition, p_{min}) + 0.5.(1 -$
    $splitBelief(statePartition, p_{min}))$;
    Add $p_{min}$ to the set $SP$;
    $totalSplitBelief(statePartition, SP) = splitBelief(statePartition, p_{min})$;
    **while** $totalSplitBelief(statePartition, SP) < splitBeliefThreshold$ **do**
        Select a probe $q$ that maximizes the $splitBelief(statePartition, q)$, where
        $S^-$ and $S^+$ are the sets built by probe $p_{min}$ on splitting each set
        $S \in statePartition$;
        $totalSplitBelief(statePartition, SP) =$
        $totalSplitBelief(statePartition, SP) + splitBelief(S, q) -$
        $(splitBelief(S, q).totalSplitBelief(statePartition, SP))$;
        Add $q$ to $SP$;
    **end**
    Divide each set $S \in statePartition$ into subsets $S^-$ and $S^+$ as computed by
    the probe $p_{min}$;
**end**

---

The algorithm starts with partition P consisting of a single set of all possible system failure states under consideration. With each new probe selected, each set in the partition P gets split into two subsets keeping the states that are less likely to fail in one set and those that are more likely to fail in the other set. In the past, work has been done by Brodie et. al. [2] to select probes for fault localization for a deterministic environment (where the dependency matrix only has 0 or 1 values). In this section, we consider a non-deterministic environment and incorporate the probabilistic dependency information in computing the probe set. In what follows, we describe our approach to probe selection for preplanned probing in a non-deterministic environment.

---

**Algorithm GFD: Greedy Failure Detection Algorithm**

---

Initialize the $NodeCoverage(n) = 0$ for each node $n$; $UncoveredNodes = \{N - ProbeStationNodes\}$;

**while** $|UncoveredNodes| > 0$ **do**

    **foreach** $node\ n \in UncoveredNodes$ **do**

        $Entropy(n) = \sum_{(p \in AvailableProbes)\&(P(p|n)>0)} -P(p|n)log(P(p|n))$;

    **end**

    Select the node $target$ with smallest $Entropy(target)$;

    **foreach** $(probe\ p \in AvailableProbes)and(P(p|target) > 0)$ **do**

        $InformationGain(p) =$

        $0.5 * (P(p|target) - P(p|target) * Coverage(target)) + 0.5 *$
        $\sum_{m\in\{UncoveredNodes-target\}}(P(p|m) - P(p|m) * NodeCoverage(m))$;

    **end**

    Select the probe $p$ with maximum $InformationGain(p)$; Add $p$ to $FDProbes$; Remove probe $p$ from $AvailableProbes$;

    **foreach** $node\ n \in UncoveredNodes$ **do**

        $NodeCoverage(n) =$
        $NodeCoverage(n) + P(p|n) - P(p|n) * NodeCoverage(n)$;

        Remove $n$ from $UncoveredNodes$ if
        $NodeCoverage(n) > coverageThreshold$;

    **end**

**end**

---

*Algorithm PPFL* assumes a *dependencyThreshold* value to consider a probe to be dependent or independent of the failure represented by a certain system state. Thus the dependencies below a *dependencyThreshold* are considered zero and those above the *dependencyThreshold* are considered one. Based on this criteria, a metric can be computed to represent the overhead of the split that can be obtained from a probe. If a probe $p$ splits a set $S$ into subsets $S^-$ and $S^+$, then the *splitOverhead* for $S$ obtained from $p$ can be computed as:

$$splitOverhead(S,p) = ((|S^-|/|S|)log(|S^-|)) + ((|S^+|/|S|)log(|S^+|)) \qquad (1)$$

where $|S^-|/|S|$ and $|S^+|/|S|$ represent the probability that the failure lies in the set $S^-$ and $S^+$ respectively. $log(|S^-|)$ and $log(|S^+|)$ represent estimates of the number of additional probes required for localization within the subsets $S^-$ and $S^+$ respectively.

However, since the model is probabilistic, it can not be declared with absolute certainty that failure of nodes represented by some state will not cause failure of probes that have dependencies less than the *dependencyThreshold* value and will surely cause failure of probes with dependency greater than the *dependencyThreshold* value. Hence together with *splitOverhead* we also compute a metric *splitBelief* to indicate our confidence in the set split obtained by selecting a probe:

$$splitBelief(S,p) = \prod_{s\in S^+} P(p|s). \prod_{s\in S^-} (1 - P(p|s)) \qquad (2)$$

The metric represents the belief that a probe does not pass through the nodes represented by states in the set $S^-$ and does pass through the nodes represented by states in the set $S^+$.

The partition $P$ starts with a single set, and splits into multiple sets in subsequent iterations. Thus the *splitOverhead* and *splitBelief* obtained from a probe $p$ is computed over all the sets of the partition to compute a *splitBelief* and *splitOverhead* value for a partition $P$ obtained by a probe $p$ as follows:

$$splitOverhead(P,p) = \sum_{S_i \in P} splitOverhead(S_i,p) \tag{3}$$

$$splitBelief(P,p) = (\sum_{S_i \in P} splitBelief(S_i,p))/|P| \tag{4}$$

Based on these two metrics, the algorithm selects the probe that minimizes the *splitOverhead* and maximizes the *splitBelief* of the current partition $P$.

Note that because of the involvement of both factors, the selected probe might not provide an acceptable belief value for the splits of the sets of partition $P$. That is, failure of $p_{min}$ might not state with enough confidence the success of states in set $S^+$ and failure of states in set $S^-$. Hence, we select additional probes to strengthen the belief in the splits. Probes are selected that maximize the *splitBelief* and thus maximize the confidence in obtaining the partition performed by the probe $p_{min}$. If the probe $p_{min}$ splits a set $S$ into two subsets $S^-$ and $S^+$, then the *splitBelief* for a set $S$ and thus for the partition $P$ obtained by a probe $p$ in obtaining the same split is also computed using the Equation 2 and 4. Note that the subsets $S^+$ and $S^-$ derived from the set $S$ are obtained by the split performed by $p_{min}$. Probe $p$ simply reinforces the belief of getting the same split as defined by $p_{min}$.

Let $SP$ represent the set of probes selected in the current iteration. We denote as $TSP(P,SP)$ the total belief of getting the split of partition $P$ by the probes in the set $SP$. Set $SP$ is initialized to $p_{min}$ and $TSP(P,SP)$ is initialized to $splitBelief(P,p_{min})$ When a probe $p$ is added to the set $SP$, the $TSP(P,SP)$ is updated as:

$$TSP(P,SP) + splitBelief(P,p) - (TSP(P,SP).splitBelief(P,p)) \tag{5}$$

*Algorithm PPFL* selects additional probes until the $TSP(P,SP)$ value reaches the desired acceptable *splitBeliefThreshold*. At the end of each iteration, each set $S$ in the partition $P$ is split into subsets $S^+$ and $S^-$ as divided by the probe $p_{min}$. This new partition is further split in further iterations till all sets in the partition become singleton sets or no probes are left for selection.

## 4.2   Adaptive Probing

In this section, we present adaptive probing based algorithms for failure detection and fault localization for a non-deterministic environment.

**Failure detection.** The algorithm is based on identifying the nodes where the uncertainty in selection is minimum, and then applying the Greedy approach of selecting a probe that gives maximum coverage of nodes among all the probes that pass through this node.

Consider a case where a node $n$ is probed by only one probe. In this case, the only probe probing node $n$ must always be selected in the probe set for failure detection. In a non-deterministic scenario, consider a case where a node $n1$ is probed by 2 probes with probability 0.9 and 0.1 respectively, and another node $n2$ is also probed by 2 probes with probability 0.5 and 0.5. In this scenario, the case of node $n1$ involves less uncertainty making it an easier choice to select the probe that probes node $n1$ with probability 0.9. Hence the algorithm would first choose node $n1$ to cover. In a deterministic environment, a node with minimum probe selection uncertainty can be identified as the node through which least number of probes pass. However, with a probabilistic dependency model, we identify the node with minimum probe selection uncertainty by computing the entropy of the probabilities by which the node is probed by probes [2]. The entropy for a node $n$ is computed as follows:

---

**Algorithm GFL: Greedy Fault Localization Algorithm**

---

**foreach** *Probe $p \in PassedProbes$* **do**
    **foreach** *Node $n \in SuspectedNodes$* **do**
        if $P(p|n) = 1$, SuspectedNodes -= $n$; PassedNodes += $n$;
        if $P(p|n) > 0$, $belief(n)* = \alpha * (1 - P(p|n))$;
    **end**
**end**
**foreach** *Probe $p \in FailedProbes$* **do**
    **foreach** *Node $n \in SuspectedNodes$* **do**
        *PathSuspectedNodes = ProbePathNodes($p$) $\cap$ SuspectedNodes*;
        Remove the node $\in PathSuspectedNodes$ from *SuspectedNodes* and add
        to *FailedNodes* if $|PathSuspectedNodes| = 1$;
        if $P(p|n) > 0$, $belief(n)* = \beta * P(p|n)$;
    **end**
    **foreach** *Node $n \in SuspectedNodes$* **do**
        **if** $belief(n) > failureBeliefThreshold$ **then**
            Remove the node $\in PathSuspectedNodes$ from *SuspectedNodes*;
            Add the node $\in PathSuspectedNodes$ to *FailedNodes*;
        **end**
    **end**
**end**
**foreach** *node $s \in SuspectedNodes$* **do**
    Select a probe $p \in AvailableProbes$ that maximizes the *probeWorth($p$)*:
    $probeWorth(p) = 0.5P(p|s) + 0.5(\prod_{n \in \{SuspectedNodes-s\}} (1 - P(p|n)))$;
    Remove probe $p$ from *AvailableProbes*; Add probe $p$ to *FLProbes*;
**end**
Return (FLProbes, PassedNodes, FailedNodes);

---

$$H(n) = \sum_{(p \in AvailableProbes)\&(P(p|n)>0)} -P(p|n)log(P(p|n)) \qquad (6)$$

where $P(p|n)$ represents the probability that probe $p$ passes through node $n$. The node with minimum entropy is chosen as the next node to cover.

Once a node $n$ is selected, of all the probes that probe this node, the probe that gives maximum coverage is selected. In a deterministic environment, of all the probes that pass through node $n$, the probe that passes through maximum number of other nodes can be selected. However, in a non-deterministic environment, two factors decide the probe selection for failure detection: (1) probability gain obtained in covering node $n$, and (2) probability gain obtained in covering other nodes. For each node $m$, we maintain a value $Coverage(m)$ to represent the probability that the node $m$ has been covered by the probes selected so far. For probe selection, we compute a metric to identify the improvement that can be obtained in the probability of covering node n and probability of covering other nodes by selecting a certain probe. We represent this metric as:

$$0.5 * P(p|n)(1 - Coverage(n)) + 0.5 * \sum_{m \in \{N-n\}} P(p|m)(1 - Coverage(m)) \quad (7)$$

After selecting the probe $p$, it is removed from the available probes and the value $Coverage(n)$ is updated for each node as follows:

$$Coverage(n) = Coverage(n) + P(p|n) - P(p|n) * Coverage(n) \quad (8)$$

Any node $n$ with $Coverage(n)$ greater than a $coverageThreshold$ is considered covered and is removed from the node set. The process of probe selection continues till all nodes are covered. Algorithm GFD presents this Greedy algorithm for failure detection.

**Fault localization.** In this section, we present Algorithm GFL for probe analysis and selection in a non-deterministic environment.

### Probe analysis

We use a belief metric to express the confidence associated with a given node failure relative to the failure of other nodes. The belief value is initialized to the probability of independent failure of the node, which we represent by $P(n)$. We update this belief value on observing probe successes and failures. This belief value should not be interpreted as the probability of failure of a node, given the observed probe successes and failures. The belief metric only encodes the relative confidence in the failure of a node in the space of all considered explanations.

On observing the $i^{th}$ probe failure, the belief value of failure of node $n$, $b(n)$, is expressed using the probability of failure of node $n$ and the probability that node $n$ explains the failure of observed failed probes that have a non-zero dependency on node $n$. The belief value can be represented as follows:

$$b_{new}(n) = \beta b_{old}(n).P(p|n) \quad (9)$$

where $b_{new}(n)$ and $b_{old}(n)$ represent the new and old belief values for failure of node $n$ respectively.

On observing a successful probe $p$, we incorporate the probe success information in the belief computation as follows:

$$b_{new}(n) = \beta b_{old}(n).(1 - P(p|n)) \quad (10)$$

The component $(1 - P(p|n))$ provides the probability that failure of node $n$ has not caused failure of probe $p$. This multiplier decreases the value of the belief metric associated with failure of node $n$.

**Probe selection**

After the probe analysis, appropriate probes need to be selected that can give best information for further localization. We build a set of *SuspectedNodes* that consist of all nodes that have non-zero probability of being on the failed probe paths. In Algorithm GFL, for each suspected node $s$, a probe is chosen that is (1) most likely to pass through node $s$, and (2) least likely to pass through any other suspected nodes. Such a probe set can quickly localize the health of its target node, due to high probability of passing through the target node and less number of possible explanations of probe success or failure. For each probe $p$ under consideration, we compute a metric *probeWorth(p)* considering these factors.

$$probeWorth(p) = 0.5P(p|s) + 0.5( \prod_{n\in\{ShadowNodes-s\}} (1 - P(p|n))) \qquad (11)$$

where $P(p|s)$ represents the probability that probe $p$ passes through node $s$, and the term $\prod_{n\in\{ShadowNodes-s\}} (1 - P(p|n))$ represents the probability that the probe $p$ does not pass through other suspected nodes. The probe $p$ with maximum value for *probeWorth(p)* is selected to probe suspected node $s$.

# 5    Experimental Evaluation

## 5.1    Simulation Model

We simulated various network topologies with different network sizes and node degrees. Let MD, AD, and N represent the maximum node degree, average node degree, and the total number of nodes in the network respectively. Given these three parameters, we create a network of N nodes, randomly introducing N*AD links such that no node has a degree greater than MD, and also ensuring that the network is connected. We conducted experiments on network sizes ranging from 10 to 50 nodes with an average node degree of 4, and maximum node degree set to 10. Because of the involved computational and memory requirements of the preplanned probing approach, we were not able to run the preplanned probing algorithm on larger network sizes. We use a probabilistic dependency model to represent dependencies between the probes and the nodes used on these probes. We build this dependency model by computing multiple paths between nodes and assigning probabilistic dependency weights to nodes on these paths. The nodes on the longer path are assigned lower weight, while the nodes on the smaller paths are assigned higher weight. We try to find two paths between every end-to-end node by running a shortest path and a second shortest path algorithm. We assume that a probe station can always probe the neighbors that are directly connected to it. We present results to localize node failures in the network.

## 5.2    Simulation Results

Figure 2(a) shows the number of probes sent by both approaches to localize the failure. The probe counts for the two algorithms are almost the same. Note that,

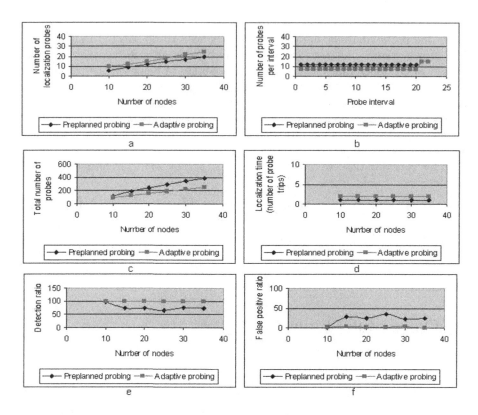

**Fig. 2.** Comparison of (a) Number of localization probes, (b) Number of probes sent per interval, (c) Total number of probes sent, (d) localization time, (e) detection ratio, and (f) false positive ratio obtained by adaptive and preplanned probing

preplanned probing sends these probes at all times. On the other hand, adaptive probing sends these probes only after detecting a failure. Consider a scenario where a failure occurs in the $20^{th}$ interval. As shown in Figure 2(b), preplanned probing sends the localization probes in all intervals, where as adaptive probing sends a much smaller set of probes for first 20 intervals, and then sends the larger set of localization probes. As can be seen from the graph in Figure 2(c) which shows the total number of probes sent by both approaches over a period of 20 intervals, the adaptive approach sends significantly less number of probes than the preplanned probing.

Figure 2(d) compares the localization time taken by the two algorithms. Figure shows that adaptive probing is able to localize a failure in almost 2 probe trip intervals which is an acceptable localization time with the amount of decrease in the required number of probes. Moreover, we show through graphs in Figure 2(e) and Figure 2(f), that adaptive probing delivers a higher detection ratio and smaller false positive ratio as compared to the preplanned probing. This improvement can be attributed to the property of adaptive probing that it can infer the network health from previous probe results to select most suitable new probes, which avoids incorrect diagnosis.

## 6   Conclusion

In this paper, we presented failure-resistant adaptive probing solutions to monitor a network in a non-deterministic environment. We presented a preplanned probing algorithm to select a set of probes such that all possible failures can be diagnosed. We then proposed adaptive probing based algorithms to select probes for localizing faults in an interactive manner. We showed through simulation results that the adaptive probing approach provides significant improvement in the probe traffic and accuracy of detection over the preplanned probing approach.

The views and conclusions contained in this document are those of the authors and should not be interpreted as representing the official policies, either expressed or implied of the Army Research Laboratory or the U.S. Government.

## References

1. Bejerano, Y., Rastogi, R.: Robust monitoring of link delays and faults in IP networks. In: IEEE INFOCOM, San Francisco, CA (March 2003)
2. Brodie, M., Rish, I., Ma, S.: Optimizing probe selection for fault localization. In: Distributed Systems Operations Management, pp. 1147–1157 (2001)
3. Downey, A.B.: Using pathchar to estimate Internet link characteristics. In: ACM SIGCOMM, Cambridge, MA (1999)
4. Huffaker, B., Plummer, D., Moore, D., Claffy, K.: Topology discovery by active probing. In: Symposium on Applications and the Internet, Nara, Japan (January 2002)
5. Lai, K., Baker, M.: Measuring bandwidth. In: IEEE INFOCOM 1999, New York City (March 1999)
6. Li, F., Thottan, M.: End-to-end service quality measurement using source-routed probes. In: 25th Annual IEEE Conference on Computer Communications (INFOCOM), Barcelona, Spain (April 2006)
7. Natu, M., Sethi, A.S.: Adaptive fault localization in mobile ad-hoc battlefield networks. In: MILCOM 2005, Atlantic City, NJ (2005)
8. Natu, M., Sethi, A.S.: Active probing approach for fault localization in computer networks. In: E2EMON 2006, Vancouver, Canada (2006)
9. Natu, M., Sethi, A.S.: Efficient probing techniques for fault diagnosis. In: ICIMP 2007. International Conference on Internet Monitoring and Protection, Silicon Valley, CA (to appear, 2007)
10. Rish, I., Brodie, M., Ma, S., Odintsova, N., Beygelzimer, A., Grabarnik, G., Hernandez, K.: Adaptive diagnosis in distributed systems. IEEE Transactions on Neural Networks 6(5), 1088–1109 (2005)

# Fault Representation in Case-Based Reasoning

Ha Manh Tran and Jürgen Schönwälder

Computer Science, Jacobs University Bremen, Germany
{h.tran,j.schoenwaelder}@jacobs-university.de

**Abstract.** Our research aims to assist operators in finding solutions for faults using distributed case-based reasoning. One key operation of the distributed case-based reasoning system is to retrieve similar faults and solutions from various online knowledge sources. In this paper, we propose a multi-vector representation method which employs various *semantic* and *feature* vectors to exploit the characteristics of faults described in semi-structured data. Experiments show that this method performs well in fault retrieval.

**Keywords:** Case-based Reasoning (CBR), Fault Retrieval, Fault Management, Semantic Search.

## 1 Introduction

Fault management involves detecting, reporting and solving faults in order to keep the communication networks and distributed systems operating effectively. Managing faults in small and homogeneous networks requires not much effort. However, this task becomes a challenge as networks grow in size and heterogeneity. Proposing solutions for faults not only costs much time and effort but also degrades related network services. Artificial intelligence methods introduce some promising techniques for fault resolution.

The Case-based Reasoning (CBR) [1] approach seeks to find solutions for similar problems by exploiting experience. A CBR system draws inferences about a new problem by comparing the problem to similar problems solved previously. The system either classifies a given problem into a group of already known and already solved problems or proposes new solutions by adapting solutions for related problems to the new circumstance of the problem. Existing CBR systems for fault management usually cooperate with trouble ticket systems to take advantage of the trouble ticket database as the case database. These systems only function on the local case database, and thus limit the capability of exploring fault-solving knowledge present at other sites. Using shared knowledge sources, however, not only provides better opportunities to find solutions but also propagates updates in case databases that otherwise frequently become obsolete in environments where software components and offered services change very dynamically.

Search engines like Google [2] today furnish information search with global data sources and powerful search techniques. It has become common practice for

A. Clemm, L.Z. Granville, and R. Stadler (Eds.): DSOM 2007, LNCS 4785, pp. 50–61, 2007.

people to "google" for a piece of information. Operators are unexceptional; they use fault messages or keywords to search for fault resolution in indexed public archives. Observations have shown that "googling" takes quite some time to find suitable solutions for a given fault. Furthermore, these solutions are typically found in indexed discussion forums, bug tracking and trouble ticket systems, or vendor provided knowledge bases. While some of these data sources maintain some structured information (e.g., bug tracking and trouble ticket systems), this information cannot be exploited due to the usage of a generic search engine which does not understand the meta information readily available.

To deal with this problem, we have proposed a distributed case-based reasoning system [3] which first exploits various fault knowledge sources in a distributed environment to discover similar faults, and then reasons on the retrieved solutions to provide new solutions adapting to the circumstances of new faults. In this paper, we focus on a multi-vector representation method to describe faults as cases in an expressive format, thus allowing the CBR system to retrieve more relevant cases. Intuitively, similar faults can probably be found if they are represented in comparable formats. The paper is organized as follows: in Section 2, we provide

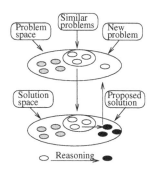

**Fig. 1.** Case-based reasoning

some background information about CBR systems and semantics-based search mechanisms. Section 3 explains a novel method to represent faults for case retrieval in the CBR system. The evaluation of this method is presented in Section 4. The related work describes the existing systems in Section 5 before the paper concludes with future work in Section 6.

## 2   Background

This section provides an overview of the CBR system and the semantics-based search mechanisms (also known as semantic search). A CBR system basically contains four processes: *case retrieval* to obtain similar cases, *case reuse* to infer solutions, *case revision* to confirm solutions and *case retaining* to update new cases. The first process concerns case representation and similarity evaluation; whereas the remaining processes are more related to case reasoning and maintenance. The main focus here is on case representation, similarity functions and semantic search.

### 2.1   Case Representation and Similarity Functions

A case representation method expresses a case in a formal format to reveal hidden properties and to facilitate case evaluation. Moreover, the representation method also has an influence on the performance of case retrieval. Research in CBR has proposed several representation methods for various domains. The bag of words (BOW) used for law cases tokenizes a text into single words; i.e., a form of term vectors. The XML-based case representation language (CBML) used for travel markets describes cases in XML format. A review of these methods has been reported in [4]. In addition, other proposals [5,6] in fault management have explored field-value pairs to present faults; i.e., a form of feature vectors. Note that the terms "feature vectors" and "field-value vectors" are used interchangeably throughout this paper.

The structure of trouble tickets [5,6] has been used to represent cases in CBR systems. An example ticket encompasses fields such as "Device name", "Device type", "IP address", "Trouble", "Additional data", "Resolution" plus other fields used for management purposes (e.g., "Owner", "Status", "Time"). Cases are represented as {*field:value*} pairs, where *value* is either numeric or symbolic. Case similarity is measured by the number of pairs matched.

Knowledge management systems [7,8] and practical CBR applications [6,9] express cases in *feature* vectors $<f_1:v_1,\ldots,f_n:v_n>$, where $n$ is number of features; $f_i$ is a domain-specific feature pre-defined in knowledge sources; $v_i$ is a value of the respective feature, which avoids using natural language. This representation not only supports semantic search, but can also be used to represent cases in CBR systems.

Case similarity is calculated by various methods. The *global similarity* method [9,7] takes the significance of features into account:

$$sim(q, c) = \sum_{i=1}^{n} w_i sim(q_i, c_i) \tag{1}$$

$n$ is the number of features; $q_i$ and $c_i$ are features of cases $q$ and $c$ respectively; $sim(q_i, c_i)$ is the distance between $q_i$ and $c_i$, which are expressed in binary, numeric or symbolic values; $w_i$ is a weight of the $i^{th}$ feature such that $\sum_{i=1}^{n} w_i = 1$ with $w_i \in [0, 1]$ $\forall i$. A weight is a user-defined value which exhibits the significance of a certain feature.

The *logical match* method [8] uses a logical model to express a case in a set of *predicates* $<f_1=v_1,\ldots,f_n=v_n>$, where each predicate $\{f_i=v_i\}$ is a field-value pair. A case $C_i$ *matches* a case $C_j$, denoted $C_i \subseteq C_j$, if $C_j$ holds for all predicates in $C_i$:

$$\forall k\{f_k = v_k\} \in C_i, \{f_k = v_k\} \in C_j \implies C_i \subseteq C_j \tag{2}$$

This method supports a *partial match* for the heterogeneous cases that contain different numbers of features.

The *word similarity* method [10,11] compares cases using the hierarchical word structure, namely the taxonomy tree.

$$sim_{Topic}(q, c) = \begin{cases} e^{-\alpha l} \frac{e^{\beta h} - e^{-\beta h}}{e^{\beta h} + e^{-\beta h}} & \text{if } q \neq c \\ 1 & \text{otherwise} \end{cases} \tag{3}$$

$l$ is the length of the shortest path between the topics of $q$ and $c$ in the taxonomy tree, $h$ is the depth level of subsumer in the taxonomy tree, and $\alpha \geq 0$ and $\beta > 0$ are parameters scaling the contribution of shortest path length $l$ and depth $h$, respectively.

## 2.2   Semantic Search

Resources and queries in semantic search are expressed in formal formats semantically understandable to search engines. Knowledge management systems
describe resources in feature or semantic vectors and evaluate the similarity
between vectors using similarity functions. Existing systems have employed different methods including the schema-based method [11,12] for resources related
to structured, domain-specific data, and the Latent Semantic Indexing method
(LSI) [13] for resources described textually.

**Fulltext-Based Search.** The LSI method brings the essential abstract concepts of a document or query to a semantic vector. To generate this vector, a
document or a query is first represented in a term vector. The Vector Space
Model (VSM) [14] weights each term, denoted by $w(t)$, in the term vector by
calculating the appearance frequency of this term in the document and the appearance frequency of this term in other documents, as follows:

$$w(t) = \frac{n_{t \in d}}{N_d} \log \frac{N}{n_{d \supset t}} \qquad (4)$$

$n_{t \in d}$ is number of term $t$ in document $d$; $N_d$ is number of terms in document $d$;
$N$ is number of documents; $n_{d \supset t}$ is number of documents containing term $t$. A
high frequency of a term indicates the significance of the term in the document,
but its significance is compensated if the term also appears in many other documents. LSI deals with noise and synonyms in a document by transforming a term
vector into a semantic vector. To carry out the transformation, LSI represents all
documents and terms in the documents in a $t \times d$ matrix $A$, where each element
$a_{ij}$ computed by Eq. 4 denotes the significance of term $i$ in document $j$. Using
singular value decomposition (SVD) [14], $A$ is decomposed into the product of
three matrices: $A = U \Sigma V^T$, where $\Sigma = diag(\sigma_1, \dots, \sigma_r)$ is an $r \times r$ diagonal matrix, $r$ is the rank of $A$ and $\sigma_i$ is the singular value of $A$ with $\sigma_1 \geq \sigma_2 \geq \dots \geq \sigma_r$.
LSI eliminates noise and synonyms by picking up the $s$ largest singular values
resulting in reducing the rank of $A$; e.g., $A_s = U_s \Sigma_s V_s^T$. The optimal value of $s$
is chosen depending on $r$; e.g., between 50 and 350. Semantic vectors of documents in $A$ are indexed by the rows of $V_s$. Semantic vectors of new documents or
queries are computed by using $U_s$, $\Sigma_s$ [14]. The similarity between two vectors is
measured by the cosine of the angle between these vectors. Formally, given two
vectors $q = (q_1, q_2, \dots, q_s)$ and $c = (c_1, c_2, \dots, c_s)$ normalized with $\|q\| = 1$ and
$\|c\| = 1$, the similarity between $q$ and $c$ is computed by the following equation:

$$cos(q, c) = \sum_{i=1}^{s} q_i c_i \qquad (5)$$

**Schema-Based Search.** The schema-based method (also known as metadata-
based or ontology-based search) maps the properties of resources in a pre-defined
schema into feature vectors. A schema here denotes the structure of data; e.g.,
a schema of a digital document consists of title, author, abstract, etc. A query

is also expressed in a feature vector using a schema. Fig. 2 plots the process of the schema-based search. This method works based on knowledge sources that globally define concepts and their relationships related to some domain of interest. These concepts are employed to specify the structured data of resources or queries in schemas. The similarity evaluation of feature vectors has been discussed in 2.1.

### 2.3   Case Reasoning

While case retrieval is only responsible for producing similar cases, case reasoning deduces from the retrieved cases relevant solutions for the problem, see Fig.1. The deductive capability of case reasoning lies upon an intelligent process named *case adaptation*. This process basically carries out two tasks: the first task distinguishes a retrieved case from the problem to clarify key differences, then the second task modifies the retrieved case following the differences. Instructions from opera-

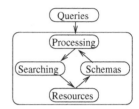

**Fig. 2.** Schema-based search

tors take vital roles in these tasks, thus improving the self-adapting capability is the major challenge of case reasoning. Furthermore, case reasoning also undertakes the process of *case retaining* that submits the changes of the adapted cases to the case base after processing case adaptation. It is essential that the process of case learning verifies the results of applying the adapted solutions to a real system before case databases are updated. However, this process is difficult to be performed because real test systems are sometimes unavailable in decentralized environments.

## 3   Fault Retrieval

This section proposes a multi-vector representation method to represent faults. Evaluating the similarity between faults involves several functions corresponding to the represented vectors and an aggregation function to calculate the final similarity value.

### 3.1   Multi-vector Representation

The heterogeneity of describing cases leads to difficulties in representing cases resulting in vectors with various dimensions and features. The comparison of these vectors thus becomes troublesome and imprecise. A feature vector is either limited by the pre-defined features or composed of the unpredictable user-defined features. It is also difficult to use this vector to explore the properties of the textual cases. On the other hand, a semantic vector exploits the textual cases, but neglects the importance of the case features. This vector only works with the local case database; e.g., two cases retrieved from two different case bases by comparing their vectors are possibly semantically different.

The proposed multi-vector representation method describes cases using a set of vectors instead of a single vector. This method deals with the above problems by breaking a case into various semantic and feature vectors resulting in both expressing cases more effectively and facilitating the comparison of these vectors. In addition, this method is suitable for faults which usually contain hierarchical fields, parameters, textual symptoms. The set of vectors takes advantage of these factors to discover the properties of cases. Nevertheless, introducing several vectors requires an aggregation function to evaluate the similarity between vectors. A network fault is anatomized by the following concerns:

- Field-value pairs classify a fault into the smaller groups of network faults. As described in [6], these groups are related to connectivity, communication performance, authentication service, hardware and software configuration. A case contains several pre-defined field-value pairs such as problem type and area, hardware, platform, and other user-defined field-value pairs. To represent $n$ pairs, we employ the field-value vector: $v_f = <f_1:v_1,\ldots, f_k:v_k,\ldots,f_n:v_n>$, where $k$ is the fixed number of pre-defined pairs.
- Other field-value pairs specify symptoms and typical parameters such as port number, cache buffer, packet loss, error messages depicted in domain-specific terminology. These pairs are represented by another field-value vector $v_p = <p_1:v_1,\ldots,p_m:v_m>$, where $m$ is number of symptoms and parameters. Symptoms are either binary, numeric or symbolic values. This vector is useful for faults with diagnosis information.
- Textual descriptions including effects, symptoms, debugging message and additional information are represented by the semantic vector $v_s$ using LSI. This high-dimension vector exhumes the properties of a case hidden in the natural language, thus distinguishing the case from other cases. Indexing fault cases and generating query vectors only work with local case databases.

A case, in fact, contains problem and solution parts. A set of vectors $\{v_f, v_p, v_s\}$ can be used to represent the problem part (of a network fault). It is natural to extend the set of vectors to the solution part resulting in more vectors added to the set; the similarity between cases possibly becomes more precise. However, to make the proposed method simple and feasible, we only insist on using the vector set of the problem part for retrieving similar faults; the extended vector set of the solution part related to reasoning the retrieved cases and providing the best case is not discussed in this paper. The following example is a fault extracted from a networking forum [15]:

*Problem*: Hub connectivity not functioning
*Description*: The WinXP network contains many machines obtaining an address from a DHCP server. The network is extended to 3 more machines by unplugging the LAN cable from one of the machine's and plugging it to a hub with the intention to add the 3 new machines. From the hub, none of the machines successfully obtains an IP address from the DHCP server; an error message shows "low or no network connectivity".

To make this fault case understandable and comparable to CBR engines, vector $v_f$ contains <problem_type: connectivity, problem_area: hardware configuration, hardware: PC, platform: WinXP>. Vector $v_p$ comprises <network: LAN, error-message: low or no network connectivity, ip-address: false, DHCP: true>. Using LSI, several terms are considered to build the vector $v_s$.

### 3.2 Similarity Evaluation

A similarity evaluation function measures the essential properties of cases to conclude the degree of similarity between cases. This function usually depends on the representation method, and therefore has an impact on the performance of case retrieval. For the proposed representation method, the field-value vectors $v_f$ and $v_p$ are evaluated by Ordered Weighted Averaging (OWA) [16,9], which is an aggregation function for multi-criteria decision making, see Eq. 6. This function is suitable for a scenario where the information of the importance of features is unknown, but the order of the importance of features is possibly exploited. It means that the pre-defined features are considered more important than user-defined features, thus receiving higher weight values.

$$sim(q, c) = \sum_{i=1}^{n} w_i sim_{\sigma(i)}(q_i, c_i) \tag{6}$$

where $n$, $q_i$ and $c_i$ are already discussed in Eq. 1; $sim_{\sigma(i)}(q_i, c_i)$ is a distance between $q_i$ and $c_i$ expressed in binary, numerical or symbolic values. $\sigma(i)$ is a permutation of 1,...,n such that $sim_{\sigma(i)}(q_i, c_i) \geq sim_{\sigma(i+1)}(q_{i+1}, c_{i+1}) \; \forall i = 1, \ldots, n - 1$. We compute a weight value $w_i$ using the following function:

$$w_i = \begin{cases} \frac{2}{n+2i} & \text{if } i < \frac{n}{2} \\ \frac{1}{2i} & \text{if } i \geq \frac{n}{2} \end{cases} \tag{7}$$

This monotonic function decreases from $\frac{2}{n+2}$ to $\frac{1}{2n}$, corresponding to the importance of features, as $i$ increase 1 to $n$; besides, the function guarantees $\sum_{i=1}^{n} w_i \approx 1$. The similarity between semantic vectors $v_s$ is evaluated by the inner product of vectors, see Eq. 5. In summary, given a case $c$, a query $q$ and the similarity values $sim_{v_f}(q, c)$, $sim_{v_p}(q, c)$, $cos_{v_s}(q, c)$ for the corresponding vectors $v_f, f_p, v_s$, the similarity $\mathcal{S}$ between $c$ and $q$ is measured by the aggregation function Eq. 1:

$$\mathcal{S}(q, c) = \alpha sim_{v_f}(q, c) + \beta sim_{v_p}(q, c) + \gamma cos_{v_s}(q, c) \tag{8}$$

Parameters $\alpha$, $\beta$ and $\gamma$ specify the significance of vectors provided by users; for instance: $\alpha = 0.4$, $\beta = 0.2$ and $\gamma = 0.4$.

## 4    Evaluation of Multi-vector Representation

The goal of this evaluation is to show the performance of the multi-vector representation method in terms of retrieving relevant documents. We focus on two methods: (1) the LSI method using the single semantic vector (*lsi* for short), and (2) the combined method using the two semantic and field-value vectors (*lsi+fvv* for short). We have used the CISI and MED bibliographic datasets [17] with 1460 and 1033 titles and abstracts (*documents* for short) respectively. These datasets provides the textual queries and the corresponding numbers of relevant documents for evaluating document retrieval; besides, the keyword-based queries are also included, as the following example:

> A *textual query*: How can actually pertinent data, as opposed to references or entire articles themselves, be retrieved automatically in response to information requests?
> A *keyword-based query*: and (*or* ("data", "information"), *or* ("pertinent", "retrieved", "requests", "automatically", "response", *not* (*or* ("articles", "references"))));

These two queries are the same, but the keyword-based query specifies main keywords and their importance using operators: *and, or, not*. Therefore, the query could be employed as a field-value vector by assigning different weight values to keywords. Each term possesses a weight value of $\frac{1}{\eta\theta}$, where $\eta$ is number of *or* groups, $\theta$ is number of terms in the group containing the term. Terms in *not* groups receive negative values. For the above example, "data", "pertinent" and "articles" possesses weight values of 0.25, 0.08 and -0.04 respectively. Sum of weight values for a query is 1 except for queries with *not* operators.

The core component of *lsi* is to compute SVD for the large term-document matrix built on the dataset. We have implemented the Jacobi algorithm [18] for computing SVD. The advantage of this algorithm is high accuracy, which is very crucial for resolving this large, sparse matrix with small elements. The issue of *lsi+fvv* is to determine the importance of specific keywords similar to features in field-value vectors; we simply use the same method as Eq. 4 for documents and the additional operators: *and, or, not* for queries. We experimentally choose $\alpha = 0.4$ for semantic vectors and $\beta = 0.6$ for field-value vectors in the aggregation function Eq. 8; i.e., given a query, the similarity value for each document is aggregated by cosine and global similarity values.

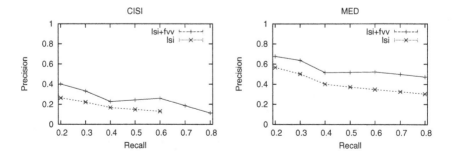

**Fig. 3.** Precision by various recall rates for the CISI and MED datasets

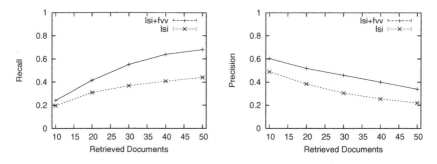

**Fig. 4.** Recall and precision by various numbers of retrieved documents for the MED dataset

We have considered two popular metrics to evaluate the performance of document retrieval in the experiments: *recall rate* $(r_c)$ and *precision rate* $(r_p)$ [13]. The recall rate is the ratio of the number of relevant documents retrieved to the pre-defined number of relevant documents. The precision rate is the ratio of the number of relevant documents retrieved to the total number of documents retrieved $(R_d)$. Intuitively, the former only concerns the capability of obtaining many relevant documents regardless $R_d$; whereas, the later involves the capability of achieving relevant documents in the limited number of documents retrieved. These two rates are usually opposed as $R_d$ increases.

We have used 40 queries for CISI and 30 queries for MED. The first experiment evaluates the precision of *lsi+fvv* and *lsi* over the recall rate; i.e., we keep retrieving documents until recall rates are reached, then count the number of documents retrieved and compute precision rates. Fig. 3 shows that $r_p$ decreases as $r_c$ (and also $R_d$) increases. In the CISI plot, both methods perform poorly for CISI; *lsi* cannot go over the recall rate of 0.6 because the similarity values of retrieved documents go down below 0; *lsi+fvv* performs slightly better. We found the same performance of *lsi* for CISI in [13]. According to this paper, the homogeneous distribution of CISI and the vague description of queries cause the unreliable judgment of the evaluation function. In the MED plot, both methods perform better for MED; *lsi+fvv* slowly reduces the precision rate and remains 0.48 as the recall rate reaches 0.8; whereas, *lsi* acquires 0.3 at the recall rate of 0.8, which is relatively low compared to the precision of *lsi+fvv*. An observation shows that choosing the size of semantic vectors influences the precision of *lsi*; i.e., the reduced rank of the matrix, and choosing the $\alpha$ and $\beta$ values affects the precision of *lsi+fvv*.

Since the MED dataset provides more reliable results, the second experiment uses this dataset to calculate the accumulative recall and precision rates for different numbers of retrieved documents; i.e., 10, 20, ..., 50. Fig. 4 indicates that *lsi+fvv* outperforms *lsi* in both recall and precision. An observation shows that several relevant documents could be obtained by *lsi+fvv*, while they possess low similarity values in *lsi*; thus, the field-value vector plays a vital role in *lsi+fvv*. Another observation is that *lsi* tends to be misled by queries with *not* operators,

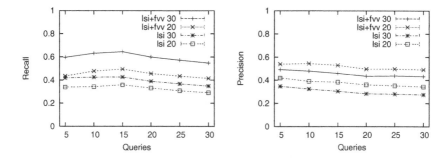

**Fig. 5.** Recall and precision by various numbers of queries for 20 and 30 documents of the MED dataset

while *lsi+fvv* tends to perform well for queries with distinguished keywords. The precision rate quickly reduces because some queries possess the small number of relevant documents compared to 40 or 50 retrieved documents; for example, a query with 20 relevant documents acquires 16 relevant documents for 40 retrieved documents and 17 relevant documents for 50 retrieved documents, its precision reduces from 0.4 (16/40) to 0.34 (17/50).

To further investigate these methods, we choose 20 and 30 retrieved documents to observe how they perform since the average number of relevant documents per a query is 23.3. Fig. 5 also displays the accumulative recall and precision rates for different numbers of queries; i.e., 5, 10, ..., 30. These rates are relatively stable, thus all queries acquire the similar ratios of relevant documents to the number of retrieved documents (precision) and to the pre-defined number of relevant documents (recall).

## 5   Related Work

So far several attempts have been given to CBR in fault management. Most of the existing approaches focus on using trouble tickets to represent cases. The work in [5] improves fault management by extending the trouble ticket system (TTS) to CBR. The proposed system can learn from previous experience and offer solutions to novel faults. This work employs trouble tickets as cases for CBR. Likewise, the DUMBO system [6] takes advantage of the knowledge hoarded in TTS to propose solutions for problems. The system not only contains six types of features to express cases but also provides both similarity and reliability measurements for evaluating features between cases. However, these systems are relatively limited by two aspects: (1) the representation of trouble tickets is only suitable for simple feature matching mechanisms, thus restricting the exploitation of features; (2) the knowledge source is limited by using local case databases. Another interesting work [9] uses sets of pre-defined case attributes and preferences of users to improve case representation in recommendation systems. This paper involves using the multi-vector representation and the advanced similarity evaluation to improve fault retrieval, which is the core component of the proposed distributed CBR system.

Other research activities have concentrated on knowledge management systems working on both multiple case databases and semantic search on peer-to-peer (P2P). Shlomo et al. [7] proposes an approach to retrieving cases on a structured P2P network with the hypercube topology. The approach employs the schema-based method, namely unspecified ontology, to maintain the case base on P2P environment. Case retrieval is based on the approximated search algorithm for feature vectors only, and the focal domain is e-commerce advertisement. The Bibster or SWAP system [11] supports bibliographic data storage and ontology-based search on a super-peer network. The Piazza system [8] deals with the problem of sharing semantically heterogeneous data on a P2P network. These two systems also use the schema-based method to define shared data and retrieve data by evaluating the similarity between feature vectors. The proposed distributed CBR system associates the semantics-based search mechanism with CBR to support not only fault retrieval but also fault-solving capability.

## 6   Conclusion

Our research aims at building a distributed CBR system to assist operators in finding solutions for faults. The system is more relevant than general search engines because it enables not only searching for similar faults described in semi-structured data but also producing new solutions for new faults. In this paper, we address the problem of retrieving similar faults in the CBR system. By studying the description of fault cases, we propose a multi-vector representation method which uses several feature and semantic vectors to express faults. These vectors not only exploit better the characteristics of faults described in semi-structured data but also provide facilities for evaluating the similarity between faults, thus ameliorating fault retrieval.

We have tested the performance of the proposed method using the CISI and MED bibliographic datasets whose documents contain semi-structured data. The evaluation results show that the combination of semantic and feature vectors outperforms the use of single semantic vectors in terms of document retrieval. Future work will focus on using real fault datasets whose diversity may demand various vectors instead of two vectors. In addition, the proposed method will be extended to case reasoning, which infers the best case from the vector sets of the retrieved cases.

## Acknowledgement

The work reported in this paper is supported by the EC IST-EMANICS Network of Excellence (#26854).

# References

1. Aamodt, A., Plaza, E.: Case-based reasoning: foundational issues, methodological variations, and system approaches. AI Communications 7(1), 39–59 (1994)
2. Google search engine. Accessed in (May 2007), http://www.google.com/
3. Tran, H.M., Schönwälder, J.: Distributed case-based reasoning for fault management. In: Proc. 1st Conference on Autonomous Infrastructure, Management and Security, pp. 200–203. Springer, Heidelberg (2007)
4. Weber, R.O., Ashley, K.D., Brüninghaus, S.: Textual case-based reasoning. The Knowledge Engineering Review 20(3), 255–260 (2005)
5. Lewis, L.M.: A case-based reasoning approach to the resolution of faults in communication networks. In: Proc. 3rd International Symposium on Integrated Network Management (IFIP TC6/WG6.6), North-Holland, pp. 671–682 (1993)
6. Melchiors, C., Tarouco, L.M.R.: Fault management in computer networks using case-based reasoning: DUMBO system. In: Proc. 3rd International Conference on Case-Based Reasoning and Development, pp. 510–524. Springer, Heidelberg (1999)
7. Berkovsky, S., Kuflik, T., Ricci, F.: P2P case retrieval with an unspecified ontology. In: Proc. 6th International Conference on Case-Based Reasoning, pp. 91–105. Springer, Heidelberg (2005)
8. Tatarinov, I., Ives, Z., Madhavan, J., Halevy, A., Suciu, D., Dalvi, N., Dong, X., Kadiyska, Y., Miklau, G., Mork, P.: The piazza peer data management project. SIGMOD Record 32(3), 47–52 (2003)
9. Montaner, M., López, B., de la Rosa, J.L.: Improving case representation and case base maintenance in recommender agents. In: Proc. 6th European Conference on Advances in Case-Based Reasoning, pp. 234–248. Springer, Heidelberg (2002)
10. Li, Y., Bandar, Z.A., McLean, D.: An approach for measuring semantic similarity between words using multiple information sources. IEEE Transactions on Knowledge and Data Engineering 15(4), 871–882 (2003)
11. Haase, P., Broekstra, J., Ehrig, M., Menken, M., Mika, P., Plechawski, M., Pyszlak, P., Schnizler, B., Siebes, R., Staab, S., Tempich, C.: Bibster — a semantics-based bibliographic peer-to-peer system. In: Proc. 3rd International Semantic Web Conference, pp. 122–136. Springer, Heidelberg (2004)
12. Nejdl, W., Wolf, B., Qu, C., Decker, S., Sintek, M., Naeve, A., Nilsson, M., Palmér, M., Risch, T.: EDUTELLA: a P2P networking infrastructure based on RDF. In: Proc. 11th International Conference on World Wide Web, pp. 604–615. ACM Press, New York (2002)
13. Deerwester, S., Dumais, S., Landauer, T., Furnas, G., Harshman, R.: Indexing by Latent Semantic Analysis. JASIST 41(6), 391–407 (1990)
14. Berry, M.W., Drmac, Z., Jessup, E.R.: Matrices, vector spaces, and information retrieval. SIAM Review 41(2), 335–362 (1999)
15. Networking forum. Accessed in (March 2007), http://www.computing.net/
16. Yager, R.R.: On ordered weighted averaging aggregation operators in multi-criteria decision making. IEEE Transactions on SMC 18(1), 183–190 (1988)
17. Latent semantic indexing. Accessed in (March 2007), http://www.cs.utk.edu/~lsi/
18. Demmel, J.W.: Applied numerical linear algebra. In: Society for Industrial and Applied Mathematics, Philadelphia, PA, USA (1997)

# Fault Detection in Autonomic Networks Using the Concept of Promised Cooperation

Remi Badonnel[1,2] and Mark Burgess[1]

[1] Faculty of Engineering, Oslo University College
Pb 4 St. Olavs Plass, 0130 Oslo, Norway
[2] LORIA - INRIA, Nancy University
BP 239, 54506 Vandœuvre, France

**Abstract.** Fault detection is a crucial issue in autonomic networks for identifying unreliable nodes and reducing their impact on the network availability and performance. We propose in this paper to improve this situation based on the concept of promised cooperation. We exploit the promise theory framework to model voluntary cooperation among network nodes and make them capable of expressing the trust in their measurements during the detection process. We integrate this scheme into several distributed detection methods in the context of ad-hoc networks implementing the OLSR routing protocol. We quantify how the fault detection performances can be increased using this approach based on an extensive set of experimentations performed under the ns-2 network simulator.

**Keywords:** Fault Detection, Autonomic Networks, Promise Theory.

## 1 Introduction

Autonomic networks are self-organized networks capable of managing themselves and adapting to changes in accordance with high-level policies and objectives [17]. These networks are typically formed from a distributed set of nodes that are themselves autonomic, just as an organism is a collection of autonomous cells. They can also interact with other autonomic networks in order to provide extended services in a cooperative manner. Fault detection is a crucial issue in autonomic networks for detecting and isolating unreliable nodes that may impair the network performance.

A typical example of autonomic networks can be given with ad-hoc networking. Ad-hoc networks are spontaneously deployed from a set of mobile devices (laptops, personal digital assistants, mobile phones, sensors) without requiring any preexisting infrastructure. The deployment of an ad-hoc network is performed dynamically by the mobile devices themselves: each device is both a terminal that communicate with the others and a router that can forward packets on behalf of the other devices through multi-hop communications. The network topology can therefore be highly dynamic, since nodes might come and go based

A. Clemm, L.Z. Granville, and R. Stadler (Eds.): DSOM 2007, LNCS 4785, pp. 62–73, 2007.

on user mobility, out-of-reach conditions and energy exhaustion. The network resources are scarce because the network is self-maintained by devices that usually operate under bandwidth and energy constraints.

Detection mechanisms are required in such autonomic networks for identifying a large range of faults including faults at the physical layer (due to physical errors), at the routing layer (due to misconfiguration) and from the energy viewpoint (due to battery failures). We designed and evaluated in [3,4] a distributed fault detection scheme for ad-hoc networks, where we infer network faults by analysing the intermittence of nodes. The nodes observe themselves in a cooperative manner: they monitor the behaviour of the neighbour nodes based on routing layer information, then share and synthesize the measurements among them. A local node implementing the detection service can identify faulty nodes in the direct neighbourhood, but the service may generate biased local views in this configuration. We addressed this issue by defining several distributed detection methods in order to improve the detection performances. These methods correlate the measurements performed by different observer nodes so that such biased local views are discarded. However, we considered in this distributed scheme that the measurements are of equal importance during the detection process, whatever the observer node generating the measurements is, and whatever the trust the observer node has in its own measurements.

We propose in this paper to extend this fault detection scheme using the concept of promised cooperation. Promise theory [10] defines a graph theoretical description of autonomous agents that are independent and have private knowledge. These agents can learn about each other only if each agent promises to make information about itself (and its local view) available, and they promise to use such information. Each interaction by this voluntary cooperation therefore requires a set of promises to give and receive information [6]. Our objective is to model and instantiate the detection service as a set of promises among the network nodes, so that each node can express the trust it has in its local detection service. In that manner, a node is capable of voluntarily reducing the relative importance of its detection measurements in the distributed scheme when it considers the measurements may deteriorate the detection performances. The main issue that we address can be stated in three simple questions: how can the network nodes define the detection service using promise theory and express the trust in their local measurements? How can we integrate these parameters into distributed detection methods? How does this promise-based scheme impact on the whole performances of the detection?

The paper is structured as follows: we overview in Section 2 a distributed fault detection scheme for autonomic networks based on the analysis of routing plane information to detect faulty nodes. Section 3 describes how this fault detection scheme can be extended using the promise theory so that the network nodes can voluntarily tune their importance during the detection process in a beneficial manner. We detail how these promise properties can be expressed by the nodes and can be coupled with trust and reputation mechanisms. We evaluate the performance of our extended detection scheme through an extensive set of experimentations in Section 4. A survey of related work is given in Section 5. Finally, Section 6 concludes the paper and presents future research efforts.

## 2   Fault Detection in Autonomic Networks

Detection of faults in autonomic networks is performed by the nodes themselves based on a self-management scheme. Fig. 1 illustrates an example scenario with a network composed of 4 nodes $V = \{v_1, v_2, v_3, v_4\}$. Each node $v_i \in V$ locally monitors the behaviour of the direct neighbor nodes in order to detect misbehaving nodes. The monitoring data can be shared among the network nodes using

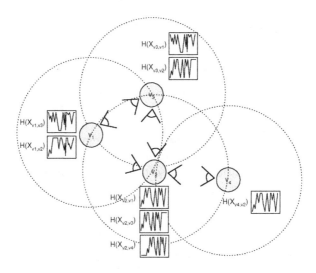

**Fig. 1.** Fault detection in an autonomic network where nodes observe themselves

a distributed detection scheme. In that case, the detection process takes into account and synthesizes a set of measurements performed by different network nodes to detect faulty elements.

### 2.1   Local Detection

The first step for designing a fault detection scheme is to define what a faulty behavior corresponds to and how the nodes can observe it locally. The example scenario illustrated in Fig. 1 corresponds to the fault detection scheme that we designed in [3] based on the analysis of node intermittence in an ad-hoc network. Intermittence is a relatively normal condition due to causes that are inherent to such an autonomic network, e.g. node mobility. However, intermittence might have also different causes related to faulty behavior such battery failures, errors at the physical layer, routing misconfiguration. In our context, the faulty behavior is defined in terms of node intermittence and is detected by analysing the information already available at the routing plane. Each network node $v_i$

observes the intermittence of the direct neighbor nodes by monitoring the number $X_{v_i,v_j}$ of periodic hello messages received from another node $v_j$ during a time interval. An entropy-based metric $H(X_{v_i,v_j})$ is then applied to the random variable $X_{v_i,v_j}$ (see Eq. 1).

$$H(X_{v_i,v_j}) = \sum_{k=0}^{b_{max}} P(X_{v_i,v_j} = k).log(\frac{1}{P(X_{v_i,v_j} = k)}) \qquad (1)$$

Based on a Markov chain-based analytical model, we approximated this entropy-based metric asymptotically via analytic depoissonization (see Eq. 2 where $b_{max}$ is the maximal number of packets that can be received during the measurement interval and $p_{up}$ is the state probability that the given node is up) and showed that this metric can be used to locally characterize a faulty intermittent node.

$$H(X_{v_i,v_j}) \asymp \frac{1}{2}ln(b_{max}) + ln\sqrt{2\pi p_{up}(1 - p_{up})} + \sum_{k \geq 1} a_k b_{max}^{-k} \qquad (2)$$

## 2.2   Distributed Detection

The second step is typically extending the detection scheme in a distributed manner, so that the measurements performed by different nodes are synthesized at the network scale, in order to drop out any local biased views. In particular, we have defined three distributed detection methods based on thresholding in [3].

A threshold-based detection consists in (1) ranking the network nodes according to a criterion $c$ and then (2) identifying faulty nodes according to a threshold value $\lambda$ (faulty nodes are those presenting a criterion value $c(v_j) > \lambda$). We briefly overview below these three detection methods:

- The first detection method $m_1$ (also called majority voting) ranks the network nodes based on the number of observer nodes that locally observed and detected the node as a faulty one.
- The second method $m_2$ (also called sum of values) takes into account the number of observer nodes, but also the measurement values generated by these nodes by ranking the network nodes in function of the sum of measurement values at the network scale.
- The last method $m_3$ (also called average of values) consists in ranking the network nodes based on the average of measured values. $m_3$ does not focus on the number of observing nodes, but favors the measurement values at the network scale.

These methods can increase the detection performances by correlating the measurements performed by different observer nodes.

## 3   Fault Detection with Promises

We propose in this paper an extended fault detection scheme based on the concept of promised cooperation. Biased measurements impact on the performances

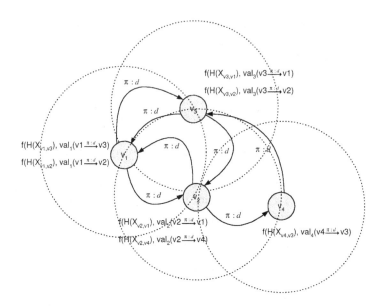

**Fig. 2.** Fault detection in an autonomic network with promises

of fault detection schemes, it would be valuable if network nodes could voluntarily decrease the relative importance of their measurements when they consider these measurements have a high probability to be biased. Of course, a simple solution would be that network nodes only report measurements when they consider them to be trusted. However, this solution may lose substantial information.

The objective of our approach is to report all measurements, but to enhance them with a trust factor: the importance of a measurement given by a detection service should be proportional to the trust the observer node has in this measurement. We consider the logical framework of promise theory which provides support for specifying the interactions and constraints among autonomous agents (see Fig. 2). The concept of voluntary cooperation is central to this modeling and is clearly appropriate in the context of autonomic networks. The framework defines a service view of interactions. We consider the local detection service as the service promised by an autonomic agent that is not externally controllable, to another agent. In the promise logical graph, a promise (notation $\pi$) corresponds to a labeled edge of the form $v_i \xrightarrow{\pi:s} v_j$ where $v_i$ and $v_j$ are agents and $s$ is the type of promise. We introduce the type of promise $d$ corresponding to the local detection service. Each promise of giving the service (plotted on Fig. 2) is implicitly completed by a promise of receiving it.

Trust (notation $\tau$) is closely coupled to the concept of promises and can be defined as a judgment, or more specifically as a valuation of a service promise [6]. The general notation to define that agent $S$ trusts agent $R$ to ensure that agent $T$ keeps a promise of type s to agent $U$ is given by Eq. 3.

$$S[T] \xrightarrow{\tau:s} R[U] \qquad (3)$$

In our context, we propose that a network node $v_i$ can express its own trust in the detection service it provides to another node $v_j$ i.e. the trust in keeping the promise $v_i \xrightarrow{\pi:d} v_j$ true. This trust (see Eq. 4) can be quantified by a valuation $\text{val}_i$ made by node $v_i$ to determine the trust in the measurements generated by its detection service.

$$v_i[v_i] \xrightarrow{\tau:d} v_i[v_j] \leftrightarrow \text{val}_i(v_i \xrightarrow{\pi:d} v_j) \tag{4}$$

The valuation $\text{val}_i(v_i \xrightarrow{\pi:d} v_j)$ corresponds to a normalized value and takes therefore values between 0 (trustless detection service) and 1 (trustful detection service). We consider that the default value for a promise of type $d$ is the maximum value i.e. 1, so that a network node can only reduce the relative importance of its measurements in the distributed detection process. In our scenario, the network nodes share the intermittence measurements $H(X_{v_i,v_j})$, but also specify the trust $\text{val}_i(v_i \xrightarrow{\pi:d} v_j)$ valuation in the local detection service. The promise logical graph is exploited during the distributed fault detection in order to improve its performances.

### 3.1 Integration into Distributed Detection Methods

These valuations are then integrated into the distributed detection methods. Let's consider the three threshold-based detection methods previously presented, the measurements $H(X_{v_i,v_j})$ can be weighted in function of the trust valuation provided by the promise graph: $f(H(X_{v_i,v_j}), \text{val}_i(v_i \xrightarrow{\pi:d} v_j))$. In that manner, the threshold-based detection methods can be refined as follows:

- The first detection method $m_1$ (majority voting) is then defined by the sum of observer nodes that locally detected the node as a faulty node, weighted by the trust valuations $\text{val}_i(v_i \xrightarrow{\pi:d} v_j)$. The importance of an observer node in this detection method is thus equal to the trust value. This means that the vote of an observer node is not taken into account when the trust is equal to 0.
- The second method $m_2$ (sum of values) is now defined by a new criterion $c_2(v_i)$ corresponding to the sum of $H(X_{v_i,v_j})$ weighted by the trust valuations $\text{val}_i(v_i \xrightarrow{\pi:d} v_j)$ by varying the $j$ value.
- The last method $m_3$ (average of values) consists in ranking the network nodes based on the average of measured values. As previously done with the two first detection methods, the measure values are weighted by the trust factor as follow: $H(X_{v_i,v_j}) \times \text{val}_i(v_i \xrightarrow{\pi:d} v_j)$.

The trust valuations are defined by the nodes themselves in a voluntary manner based on the promise graph. As a consequence, malicious or faulty nodes may parameterized false values. However, as previously mentioned, the trust normalized value is by default set to the maximum value, so that a network node can only decrease its participation in the fault detection process i.e. decrease the relative importance of its measurements.

## 3.2 Trust and Reputation

In our application scenario, promises permit network nodes to express the trust in the measurements they have performed: $v_i[v_i] \xrightarrow{\tau:d} v_i[v_j]$. A local node can typically detect bias by analysing and comparing the set of local measurements. For instance, if a node detects all the other nodes as intermittent, there is a high probability that these measurements are biased and that the node itself is intermittent. This endogenous factor (how the node perceives itself) is complementary to the exogenous factor (how the node perceives the other nodes). The trust valuations of other nodes $v_i[v_j] \xrightarrow{\tau:d} v_i[v_i]$ can be performed in an indirect manner by exploiting the detection results. In particular, the network nodes detected as faulty nodes by the distributed detection methods should be dynamically discarded from the detection process, as they may introduce biased information data and may significantly deteriorate the detection performances. A two-phase scheme can typically be instantiated in order to drop out the measurements performed by nodes that are suspected to be faulty and to determine if the detection results are unchanged when we discard these nodes from the detection scheme. During a first phase, a node can change from the normal state to the potential faulty state. In that case, the node is not considered as faulty, but the measurements generated by it are not taken into account during the following of the detection process. During a second phase, a node can change from the potential faulty state to the faulty state if the node is still selected by the detection method.

# 4   Experimental Results

We evaluated the performance of our fault detection scheme through an extensive set of experimental results, and we determined to what extent promising nodes can improve the detection in an autonomic network. The simulations were performed with the discrete event network simulator ns-2 [1]. We simulated an ad-hoc network composed of a set of 50 nodes moving in a 1500 m x 300 m rectangular area during a time period of 900 simulated seconds. We considered the IEEE 802.11 MAC protocol at the data link layer. The routing protocol is the OLSR ad-hoc network protocol (implementation of the NRL [2]).

The node mobility corresponds to the wide-spread (RWP) random waypoint model (individual mobility of nodes) [7]. Each network node moves at a constant speed less than *speed* m/s to a destination point selected uniformly in the rectangle area and then waits during a pause time *pause* before moving to a new destination. The RWP model may generate initialization discrepancy issues [18] , we therefore used the steady-state mobility model generator *mobgen-ss* to guarantee an immediate convergence and obtain reliable simulation results.

For each experiment, we have randomly chosen a set $F$ of faulty nodes (from 0 to 5 nodes) and a set $P$ of promising nodes (from 0 to 50 nodes). The faulty nodes follow a two-state Markov chain faulty behavior model that we proposed in [3]. The promising nodes express the trust they have in the measurements they

**Table 1.** Simulation parameters

| Parameter | Value |
|---|---|
| Simulator | ns-2 |
| Simulation time | 900 s |
| Simulation area | 1500 m x 300 m |
| Network nodes | 50 nodes |
| Faulty nodes | 0 - 5 node(s) |
| Promising nodes | 0 - 50 node(s) |
| Cooperative method | average of values |
| Mobility model | random waypoint *mobgen-ss* |
| Speed | 0 - 10 m/s |
| Pause time | 0 - 120 s |
| Physical Layer | FSP / 2-RGR |
| MAC layer | IEEE 802.11 |
| Routing layer | NRL OLSR |

provide to the other nodes. We arbitrarily considered that the trust valuations are set to 50% for the promising nodes that are faulty, and are set to 100% for the promising nodes that are regular, as defined by Eq. 5 and 6.

$$\forall v_i \in P \cap F, \forall v_j \in V, \mathrm{val}_i(v_i \xrightarrow{\pi:d} v_j) = 0.5 \tag{5}$$

$$\forall v_i \in P \cap \bar{F}, \forall v_j \in V, \mathrm{val}_i(v_i \xrightarrow{\pi:d} v_j) = 1 \tag{6}$$

We quantified the performances (sensitivity and specificity) of the detection scheme with promises by comparing the initialized set of faulty nodes to the the the set of nodes identified by the detection scheme. A detection scheme can be seen as a diagnostic test, where we test if a network node is a faulty node (positive test) or a regular node (negative test). By comparing the initialized set of faulty nodes to the set of positive-tested nodes, it is possible to determine if the test provides true or false results.

We compared the performances of our detection (method $m_3$) with different percentages of promising nodes in the network (0%, 25%, 50%, 75% and 100%). We plotted the Receiver Operating Characteristic (ROC) [21], a graphical plot of sensitivity (Sn) versus 1-specificity (1 - Sp) for each scenario. The sensitivity quantifies how well the method picks up true cases, by defining the proportion of cases having a positive test result of all positive samples tested, while the specificity quantifies how well it detects false cases, by comparing the proportion of true negatives of all the negative cases tested. A diagnostic test is always a tradeoff between specificity and sensibility. The ideal diagnostic test shows a plot that is a point in the upper left corner of the ROC space.

We were interested in analysing the performances of method $m_3$ (that showed the best performances in [3]) but in that case by considering the concept of promises. As we are looking for a low positive false positive rate, we limited the plotting of ROC curves to a false positive rate no more than 20%. The comparison of ROC curves clearly depicts that the percentage of promising nodes impact on the detection performances. We did not know a priori to what extent the promises will impact on the cooperative methods. The experimental results

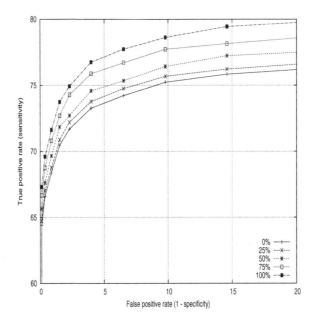

**Fig. 3.** Detection performances based on the percentage of promising nodes

shows that the detection performances can be improved of up to 4% in our configuration. The performances could be further improved by considering lower trust valuations: the lowest trust valuations (nodes part of $P \cap F$) were of 50% in our simulation scenarios. Moreover, reputation mechanisms could be integrated in the detection process in order to evaluate the ability of promising nodes to keep their promises. The detection is done in a lightweight manner based on information available at the routing plane, and management information are propagated using the extensible OLSR messages. Scalability and overhead are therefore directly dependent on the OLSR routing protocol performances.

## 5 Related Work

Among the pioneering approaches of fault management, Jakobson introduced in [12] an approach for correlating events and faults with temporal constraints. Conceptual anomaly detection in distributed environments is proposed in [5] using an analytical method based on principal component analysis. The method does not address a specific deployment, but relates to the distributed detection methods that we defined. In both cases, distributed data from different hosts are correlated to provide an importance ranking of anomalies.

Detection schemes permit to identify misbehaving nodes based on different criteria in the context of network management. In particular, such a management approach was proposed in [15] by analysing the packet forwarding behavior of nodes in an ad-hoc network. We have proposed in [3] a detection scheme based on the analysis of the distribution of routing packets and complete it in this paper using the concept of promises. Failures detection algorithms based on keep-alive messages were also experimented in [20] and their performance are evaluated in overlay networks. Moreover, an active mechanism is detailed in [8] to characterize dynamic dependencies and to determine the root-causes of an anomaly at the application layer. Research efforts in ontology-based knowledge representation [11] contribute also to improve automated reasoning in this context.

The problem of distributed network monitoring and of its optimization has been addressed by [14] where heuristics are defined in order to optimize instrumentation location in bandwidth constrained environments. To a certain extent, these heuristics can be adapted to autonomic networks and systems. The DAMON architecture [16] defines a distributed monitoring system for ad-hoc networks, supporting multiple data repositories and including an auto-discovery mechanism of data repositories by the agents. This generic architecture is not dedicated to specific network parameters and could therefore be appropriate for the storage of fault detection data. A multi-tier architecture for efficient monitoring and management is proposed in [19] where nodes are grouped to ensure that they can be reached via a member of its group and is applicable to autonomic networks where network ressources are also constrainted. Finally, an excellent overview of trust and reputation issues in autonomic networks is given in [13].

## 6    Conclusions and Future Work

Fault detection is a management activity of crucial importance in autonomic networks for increasing network availability and reliability. This activity is performed by the nodes themselves in a self-organized manner in order to identify and isolate unreliable nodes. We propose in this paper to apply the concept of promised cooperation to fault detection methods in autonomic networks. The objective is to improve the detection performances by modeling voluntary cooperation among nodes and making them capable of expressing the trust they have in the measurements they provide to the other nodes.

We have shown in this paper how the network nodes can express this trust based on the framework of promise theory. We have specified a promise $d$ for the local detection service: $v_i \xrightarrow{\pi:d} v_j$ and defined the trust in the measurements given by a node as a normalized valuation $\mathrm{val}_i(v_i \xrightarrow{\pi:d} v_j)$. We then have integrated these parameters into several threshold-based cooperative detection methods, so that a network node can voluntarily reduce the relative importance of its measurements in the distributed scheme. Promise theory therefore served as a support to bring an endogenous factor (how the node perceives itself) complementary to an exogenous factor (how the node perceives the others). We have evaluated these detection methods with promises in the context of ad-hoc networks by using our entropy-based intermittence measure. We have quantified the performances in terms of sensitivity and specificity by plotting the corresponding ROC curves. The intermittence measure also provides a practical and inexpensive approach to classifying the observed behaviour of nodes in keeping their promises, and does not require any kind of centralized management.

Our future work will consist in experimenting our extended fault detection methods with more complex fault models with higher order Markov chains and more developed internal chain architectures. We will also use the promise logical graph to evaluate the performances of the detection methods coupled with reputation mechanisms in an analytical manner. While our scheme mainly focuses on fault management, it would be interesting to extend it to security management and, in particular, to determine how collaborative attacks can affect the solution. Finally, the entropy-based intermittence measure is a complementary metric to that already used in cfengine [9] (*last seen time*). We have now implemented the present method into cfengine and are testing it in a variety of networks.

## Acknowledgments

We would like to gratefully acknowledge Radu State and Olivier Festor for their helpful discussions and comments. This work is supported by IST-EMANICS Network of Excellence #26854.

## References

1. Ns-2 network simulator. http://www.isi.edu/nsnam/ns/
2. OLSR Extension for Ns-2. Navy Research Laboratory OLSR Project, http://pf.itd.nrl.navy.mil/projects/olsr/
3. Badonnel, R., State, R., Festor, O.: Fault Monitoring in Ad-Hoc Networks Based on Information Theory. In: Boavida, F., Plagemann, T., Stiller, B., Westphal, C., Monteiro, E. (eds.) NETWORKING 2006. LNCS, vol. 3976, Springer, Heidelberg (2006)
4. Badonnel, R., State, R., Festor, O.: Self-configurable Fault Monitoring in Mobile Ad-Hoc Networks. Elsevier Journal of Ad-Hoc Networks (to be published, 2007)
5. Begnum, K., Burgess, M.: Principle Components and Importance Ranking of Distributed Anomalies. Machine Learning Journal 58(2), 217–230 (2005)
6. Bergstra, J., Burgess, M.: Local and Global Trust Based on the Concept of Promises. Technical report, Oslo University College, Norway (2006)
7. Le Boudec, J.-Y., Vojnovic, M.: Perfect Simulation and Stationarity of a Class of Mobility Models. In: INFOCOM 2005. Proc. of IEEE International Conference on Computer Communications, Miami, FL, USA (March 2005)
8. Brown, A., Kar, G., Keller, A.: An Active Approach to Characterizing Dynamic Dependencies for Problem Determination in a Distributed Application Environment. In: IM 2001. Proc. of the 7th IFIP/IEEE International Symposium on Integrated Network Management, Seattle, WA, USA (May 2001)
9. Burgess, M.: A site configuration engine. USENIX Computing systems 8(3) (1995)
10. Burgess, M., Fagernes, S.: Promise theory - A Model of Autonomous Objects for Pervasive Computing and Swarms. In: ICNS 2006. Proc. of the International Conference on Networking and Services, Silicon Valley, USA (June 2006)

11. Lehtihet, E., Strassner, J., Agoulmine, N., Foghlu, M.O.: Ontology-Based Knowledge Representation for Self-governing Systems. In: State, R., van der Meer, S., O'Sullivan, D., Pfeifer, T. (eds.) DSOM 2006. LNCS, vol. 4269, Springer, Heidelberg (2006)
12. Jakobson, G., Weissman, M.D.: Real-time Network Management: Extending Event Correlation with Temporal Constraints. In: IM 1995. Proc. of the 4th IFIP/IEEE International Symposium on Integrated Network Management, Santa Barbara, CA, USA (1995)
13. Buttyan, L., Hubaux, J.-P.: Security and Cooperation in Wireless Networks. Cambridge Press, Cambridge (2007)
14. Li, L., Thottan, M., Yao, B., Paul, S.: Distributed Network Monitoring with Bounded Link Utilization in IP Networks. In: INFOCOM 2003. Proc. of IEEE International Conference on Computer Communications, San Francisco, USA (2003)
15. Duque, O.G., Pavlou, G., Howarth, M.: Detection of Packet Forwarding Misbehavior in Mobile Ad-Hoc Networks. In: WWIC 2007. Proc. of the 5th International Conference on Wired/Wireless Internet Communications, Coimbra, Portugal (May 2007)
16. Ramachandran, K., Belding-Royer, E., Almeroth, K.: DAMON: A Distributed Architecture for Monitoring Multi-hop Mobile Networks. In: SECON 2004. Proc. of IEEE International Conference on Sensor and Ad Hoc Communications and Networks, Santa Clara, CA, USA (October 2004)
17. Murch, R.: Autonomic Computing. IBM Press (2004)
18. Yoon, J., Liu, M., Noble, B.: Random Waypoint Considered Harmful. In: INFOCOM 2003. Proc. of IEEE International Conference on Computer Communications, San Francisco, CA, USA, pp. 1312–1321 (April 2003)
19. Younis, M., Munshi, P., Al-Shaer, E.: Architecture for Efficient Monitoring and Management of Sensor Networks, E2EMON Workshop. In: Marshall, A., Agoulmine, N. (eds.) MMNS 2003. LNCS, vol. 2839, Springer, Heidelberg (2003)
20. Zhuang, S.Q., Geels, D., Stoica, I., Katz, R.H.: On Failure Detection Algorithms in Overlay Networks. In: INFOCOM 2005. Proc. of IEEE International Conference on Computer Communications, Miami, FL, USA (March 2005)
21. Zweig, M.H., Campbell, G.: Receiver-Operating Characteristic (ROC) Plots. Clinical Chemistry 29(4), 561–577 (1993)

# On Fully Distributed Adaptive Load Balancing

David Breitgand[1], Rami Cohen[2], Amir Nahir[1], and Danny Raz[2]

[1] IBM Haifa Research Lab, Israel
[2] CS Department, Technion, Haifa

**Abstract.** Monitoring is an inherent part of the management loop. This paper studies the problem of quantifying utility of monitoring in a fully distributed load balancing setting. We consider a system where job requests arrive to a collection of $n$ identical servers. The goal is to provide the service with the lowest possible average waiting time in a fully distributed manner (to increase scalability and robustness).

We present a novel adaptive load balancing heuristic that maximizes utility of information sharing between the servers. The main idea is to forward the job request to a randomly chosen server and to collect load information on the request packet as it moves on. Each server decides, based on that information, whether to forward the job request packet to another server, or to execute it locally. Our results show that in many practical scenarios this self-adaptive scheme, which does not require dedicated resources for propagating of load information and decision making, performs extremely well with respect to best known practice.

## 1 Introduction

To maximize value of Information Technology (IT), its low level management policies have to be aligned with the high level business goals, which in many cases impel systematic reduction of management overheads. In this paper, we concern ourselves with the monitoring overhead present in any management loop. Consequently, it is important to maximize the utility of monitoring in order to improve the utility of the overall management process.

Consider for example a service that is being provided by a set of servers over the network. The goal of the service provider is to provide the best service (say, minimizing the response time) given the amount of available resources (*e.g.*, the number of servers). The provider can add a load sharing system (for example as suggested in RFC 2391 [1]) and improve the response time. However, the same resources (budget) can be used to add additional servers to the system and thus provide better service to end customers. The dilemma here is between adding more computational power and adding management abilities, where the goal is to achieve the best improvement in the overall system performance.

Simple load balancing schemes, such as random selection or Round Robin are oblivious to actual server load when making job assignment decisions. This may work well for workloads with low variability. However, load-oblivious algorithms lack adaptiveness and therefore may perform poorly for workloads exhibiting

A. Clemm, L.Z. Granville, and R. Stadler (Eds.): DSOM 2007, LNCS 4785, pp. 74–85, 2007.

medium to high variability. In order to considerably improve expected response time in such cases, load-aware algorithms are required. These algorithms need updated load information from the servers. Handling such load information requests requires small but nonzero resources (*e.g.*, CPU) from each server. Thus, it is not easy to predict the actual amount of improvement expected from preferring a specific configuration. It is thus important to identify just the right amount of resources that should be allocated to management tasks (such as monitoring) in order to maximize the overall system performance.

Typically, load balancing is implemented via a centralized dedicated entity that receives all requests and assigns servers to the requests. This option requires additional resources and limits the system's scalability and robustness. In [2] we extensively studied quantifying of monitoring utility in such environment. As shown in [2], for each service request rate, there exists an optimal number of servers that should be monitored in order to maximize utility of monitoring or reducing the total service time. This is a very generic result, which is applicable to any management scheme that employs explicit monitoring components.

In this paper, we extend these results and develop a very efficient fully distributed and self-adaptive load balancing scheme. The main idea behind the scheme is as follows. When a new job request arrives at an idle server, the server executes it locally. Otherwise, it adds its local load information to the job request packet and forwards the request to a randomly chosen peer in the cluster. A peer server that receives the packet with the senders' load information on it, compares it to its own load and makes a decision whether to execute the job locally, or to further forward it to another peer. This way, the load information on the request packet is collected *en-route*. When the $d$-th server receives the job request packet, the latter contains information about the load of other $d - 1$ servers. As $d$ grows, this information becomes more out of date and the waiting time prior to execution grows linearly with $d$. Thus, there is a tradeoff between the number of hops a job request may travel before getting executed at the least loaded server and both the delay it spends and the quality of load information that is used to determine the least loaded server.

We study several heuristics for optimizing this tradeoff and evaluate their performance using extensive simulations and an implementation on a real testbed. The primary results are represented by the self-adaptive heuristics, in which the system adapts to the changing environmental conditions (i.e., load, type of requests and their service time, *etc.*) in a fully distributed scheme. It turns out that in many realistic scenarios self-adaptiveness performs extremely well, resulting in significant performance gains.

The rest of this paper is organized as follows. In Section 2 we formally define the model for the framework. In Section 3 we describe two advanced heuristics, that are self-adaptable to the load conditions and compare them to the optimally configured Centralized Monitoring (CM scheme). In Section 4 we describe the implementation of the scheme and present its performance evaluation on a real set of servers. Section 5 describes related work. We conclude in Section 6 with a short discussion of our results.

## 2  Model

In this section we describe our model and provide intuitive motivation for selecting the main factors that influence the total performance of any distributed load balancing mechanism.

As described in the previous section, we consider a fully distributed server system in which client requests arrive in a set of Poisson streams of traffic intencity (load) $\lambda$ to a set of $n$ identical servers. The total load in the system is $n \cdot \lambda$. We assume a *non preemptive* load sharing model, in which a job that started executing at a server cannot move to another server. For the sake of simplicity we assume a single FCFS queue for job requests at each server. When such a request arrives at a server, the server has to decide whether to serve the job request locally or forward it to another server. The information available to the server when making this decision includes local information and information attached to the job request. The local information contains the server current queue length and statistics describing the workload parameters computed from the local execution history. These statistic information include job request frequency and average job service time. The information provided by the job request itself contains client based information, an estimation of service time, and information added by other servers in the system if the request was forwarded from another server and not directly received from a client.

In order to make the algorithmic decision of whether to accept the request or forward it and to which server to forward it, the server has to stop serving the current job (if the server is not idle), and to allocate resources (CPU) to the management process. It has to examine local data and data provided with the request, run the decision algorithm, and, if needed, forward the request. This delays the execution of the current job and of all jobs that wait for execution in the local queue. Note that in case of a multi-CPU server, the situation is essentially the same, since dedicating a full separate CPU just to serve control requests is wasteful. Thus, preemption of client requests will be unavoidable under high load conditions. To verify this point, we implemented a CPU intense server as described in Section 4. This multithreaded server was executed on a a blade server containing Dual PowerPC machines, each having a 2.2GHz 64-bit CPU, with 4GB of RAM. Figure 1 depicts the average normalized execution time (from the time the job started to be executed until it terminated) as a function of the number load queries per job. The net service time (measured in a setting without load) was about 165 milliseconds, but as can be seen clearly from the figure, the actual time increases linearly with the number of monitoring requests. This shows that even in an advanced architectures, the monitoring overhead is not negligible.

Therefore, the ratio between the time it takes a server to handle such job request and the expected mean service time is a critical factor that affects the overall performance of the system. This *overhead efficiency ratio*, denoted by $C$, reflects the amount of impact  the distributed management task has on the actual service. In this intense CPU setting, where a user request takes about 165 milliseconds, each load request takes about 0.33-0.5 milliseconds so $C$ is between 0.002 and 0.004.

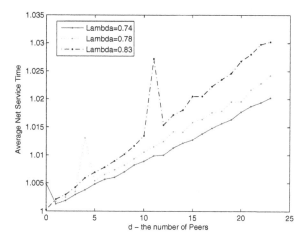

**Fig. 1.** Execution time as a function of the number peers' load requests

When a job request is forwarded, it takes time until it arrives to the next server, and this time is added to the overall response time. Thus, another important factor is the ratio between the communication time between servers and the mean expected service time of a job, called *communication ratio*. This ratio is denoted by $CT$. When a server examines a job request, the load information piggybacked in it may be staled due to communication delay. If the delay is small relatively to the service time, the affect of the delay may be negligible, but otherwise it may have a detrimental affect on the total performance. As an example of the former case consider servers communicating over a Gbit Ethernet and an average service time of 300 milliseconds. As an example of the latter case consider servers distributed throughout the Internet and an average service time of about 100 milliseconds; in this case communication time is in the same order as service time and the load information piggybacked on the job request may be totally out of date.

Both the communication ratio and the overhead efficiency ratio depend on physical aspects of the system such as the communication delay and the CPU and memory abilities, and on the service provided that determines the distribution of jobs' service time.

Let $d$ be the number of hops (the number of servers) an incoming job request travels before it is being admitted to a local FCFS queue of some server. Effectively, this is the number of servers being implicitly monitored by this job request. Let $\frac{1}{\mu}$ denote the mean service time. Then the expected mean response time in the system $E(R)$ is given by Equation 1, where $\bar{L}$ is the average queue length.

$$E(R) = \frac{1}{\mu}(\bar{L}(1 + d \cdot C) + d \cdot CT) \tag{1}$$

The first factor is due to the queue and the fact that on the average $d$ job requests arrive during the service of a job, each consumes $C$ fraction of the job service time. The second factor is due to the time it takes to move from one server to another.

## 3   Self Adaptive Heuristics

In Basic heuristic that is used for baselining, if the server is idle or the server receives a job request that traveled more than $d$ hops, the server serves the request. Otherwise, if the job request traveled less than $d$ hops, the server forwards the request to a random new server. If the job request traveled exactly $d$ hops, the server finds a server with the shortest queue among these $d$, according to information on the request, and forwards the job to this server. This heuristic basically says that as long as we did not examine $d$ servers we stop only if we find an idle server. After examining $d$ servers, we execute the job on the least loaded (the one with the shortest queue) server among these $d$.

The important factor is, of course the choice of $d$. The dependency of the average queue length (and thus the average time in the system) on $d$ is rather complex. On the one hand, as $d$ increases we have a higher probability of finding an idle server (or a server with a small queue) and thus reducing the average queue length. On the other hand, as $d$ increases more and more servers have to forward the same job request thus "paying" a portion of $C$ resources and slowing down the actual service.

The optimal value of $d$ depends on the system parameters such as the load, the overhead efficiency ratio $C$, and the communication ratio $CT$. While $C$ and $CT$ are almost an invariant for a given system, the load of the system may change often. Thus monitoring a constant number of servers $d$ (explicitly or via piggybacking) is not optimal. In this section, we present two self adaptive heuristics in which the number of examined servers dynamically changes with the system load.

In the centralized model, in which one dispatcher receives all the jobs, the mean time between jobs arrival together with the mean service time and the number of servers, determine the load in the system. Updating the load can be done dynamically by considering the mean time between job arrivals measured so far and the new time between consecutive job arrivals, every time a new job arrives. Thus, if two consecutive jobs arrive to the dispatcher at $t^+$ and $t^-$ ($t^+ > t^-$), the new mean time between job arrivals, calculated at time $t^+$ is:

$$mtba(t^+) = \alpha \cdot mtba(t^-) + (1 - \alpha) \cdot (t^+ - t^-), \qquad (2)$$

where $0 < \alpha < 1$ is a parameter that defines the speed in which the system adapts to the new settings. When the distributed model is considered, each server receives only a small part of all the jobs. Thus, the load measured by computing the mean time between job arrivals locally at each server can be biased and may not reflect the actual load of the entire system. To overcome this problem, each server computes the load by considering the mean time between job arrivals using only the population of jobs that served by this server, but not those forwarded to other servers. This estimation is much more robust since the served jobs are distributed more evenly due to the load balancing mechanism that is used, and the mean time between local job assignments approximates the actual mean inter-arrival time of the jobs in the system.

The theoretical analysis in [2] provides a way to determine an optimal number of servers that should be monitored for each set of values of load and $C$. These values can be used to estimate the optimal value of $d$. In our first self adaptive heuristic, each server maintains a lookup table that contains an optimal value of $d$ for different values of load and $C$. When a new job arrives to a server it can locally determine (based on its local estimation of the load) what the optimal value of $d$ is. Then, using *Basic* heuristic, it decides whether to accept the job or to forward it to a different random server.

Forwarding a job from one server to another can reduce the waiting time of the job if the queue length in the next server is shorter than the current queue length. However, there is also a cost associated with this process. This cost includes the communication cost and the processing time it takes to monitor the next server. In the second self adaptive heuristic we present, every server that receives a job, evaluates the cost associated with forwarding the job to another server and compares it with the expected benefit. If the benefit is greater than the cost, the server forwards the job, otherwise, the server assigns the job to the server with the shortest queue among all servers that were visited by this job request so far.

Forwarding a job to another server increases the response time of that job by $CT$. Moreover, the new server has to invest CPU in order to handle this job request. This increases the service time of all jobs waiting to be served at this new server by $C$ times the mean service time. Thus, the cost of forwarding a job in terms of the mean service time is $CT + \bar{L} \cdot C$, where $\bar{L}$ is the average queue length at the new server.

If the queue length of the new server is shorter than the minimum queue length found so far, then it is beneficial to forward the job to the new server. Denote by $p(i)$ the probability that the queue length in the new server is equal to $i$ and by $\mathcal{Q}(min)$ the minimum queue length among servers visited so far. The expected benefit from forwarding a job to a new server in terms of the mean service time is:

$$\mathcal{B} = \sum_{i=0}^{\mathcal{Q}(min)} (\mathcal{Q}(min) - i) \cdot p(i). \tag{3}$$

In [3] the author shows that the probability that a queue length is greater than or equal to $i$ is $s(i) = \lambda^{\frac{d^i - 1}{d - 1}}$. Considering the overhead efficiency ratio $C$, the effective load is increased by $\frac{1}{1 - a \cdot C \cdot d}$, where $a$ is some constant (see [2]), therefore we use $\lambda = \lambda' \cdot \frac{1}{1 - 2C \cdot d}$ for the system load, where $\lambda'$ is the incoming load. Thus,

$$p(i) = s(i) - s(i+1) = \lambda^{\frac{d^i - 1}{d - 1}} - \lambda^{\frac{d^{i+1} - 1}{d - 1}}. \tag{4}$$

The current load in the system $\lambda$ can be estimated using the same technique discussed in the first heuristic, and $d$ the number of peers is the average number

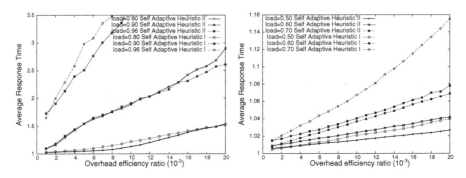

**Fig. 2.** Average service time as a function of the overhead efficiency ratio

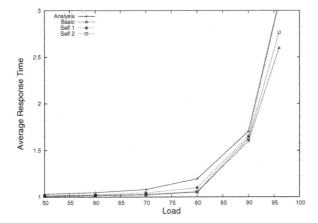

**Fig. 3.** Performance of the self adaptive heuristic as a function of the system load - Simulation results

of peers visited so far. Using the above formulae and these estimations, each server can compute the expected cost and benefit and forwards the job only if the expected benefit exceeds the cost.

Figure 2 depicts the average response time vs. the overhead efficiency ratio $C$ for a different values of load, obtained by simulating the two self adaptive heuristics over a LAN environment. In most cases, especially when the load is relatively low, the second heuristic achieves better results compared to the first heuristic, while in high load their performance is similar. This is due to the fact that while the first heuristic uses a general model to derive the optimal $d$, the second heuristic is more sensitive to the actual queue lengths found so far.

Figure 3 demonstrates average response time of the self-adaptive heuristics, for $C = 5 \cdot 10^{-3}$ and a very small communication ratio. For comparison we also plot the average service time of the Basic heuristic, where for each run $k$ is set to be the optimal value for this load value, and the expected average service time in the centralized model of [2]. As one can see, the adaptive methods (without any tuning) perform as good as the algorithms optimally configured for the specific load level and the basic distributed heuristic.

## 4  Practical Implementation and Evaluation

In order to study the practical performance of a distributed load sharing system as described in this paper and the actual usefulness of the theoretical results, we implemented such a server based system and tested its performance on a testbed network.

Each server is comprised of two main components:

1. **Service Component:** this is the component which performs user requests. When no user requests exist, this component is idle. When a new user request arrives (queued by the main component see below), the Service Component is interrupted, it deques the user request and processes it. Processing of a request is implemented as a busy-wait loop emulating CPU intensive service, where the service duration depends on a tunable parameter and the servers CPU power. Upon completion, a response is sent to the originating user, and if additional user requests exist, the Service Component proceeds with the processing of the next request.

2. **Main Component:** this component listens for job requests (received directly from the user or forwarded from another server). Whenever a job request is received, this component determines whether to process the request locally, or to forward it to another server. If the server is idle the request is processed locally. Otherwise, the specific logic implementing the heuristic is deployed and the decision is made.

The load estimation mechanism required for both adaptive heuristics is implemented based on Equation 2. Whenever a server queues a job request, it calculates the length of the time interval between the previous job request's

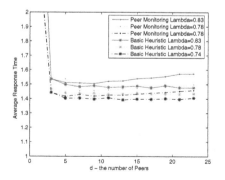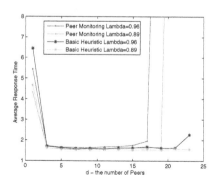

**Fig. 4.** Performance of the scheme on a testbed

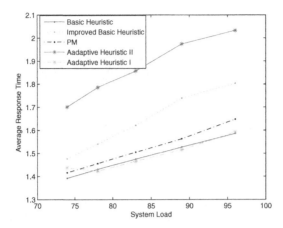

**Fig. 5.** Performance of the self adaptive heuristic as a function of the system load

arrival time and the current one's, and updates its load estimation. For the purpose of testing, $\alpha = 0.9$ was used. The average queue length, $\bar{L}$, needed for the implementing the scond heuristic is estimated locally in a similar manner.

The entire server is implemented in Java. Each component is implemented as a Java thread. The Main Component acts as the producer in a consumer-producer relationship between the Main and Service Components. Jobs received by the Main Component which are queued locally are consumed by the Service Component. To simplify the implementation, service requests are implemented using UDP.

In order to test the performances of our scheme, a system containing distributed copies of the above described server component, 24 copies of this server were deployed on 12 Dual PowerPC machines, each of which has a 2.2GHz 64-bit CPU, with 4GB of RAM. These machines are part of a Blade Center. Therefore CT in our setting is negligible and implicitly accounted by C. A client was created to generate all requests, to collect all answers from the servers and to produce logs that were processed to create the system statistics. The average service time in all test runs was set up to be around 165 milliseconds.

In order to compare our method to distributed load balancing alternatives, which employ dedicated monitoring, we implemented a scheme called Peer Monitoring (PM). This scheme is depicted in Figure 6. In PM, the server actively queries $k$ peer servers for their load (where $k$ is a parameter of the scheme), using a dedicated monitoring algorithm, and assigns the job to the least loaded server among these peers. Essentially, PM is a straightforward distributed version of CM, in which each server acts in two capacities: a regular server and a centralized dedicated monitor for a neighborhood of size $k$. From testing the service time for different values of $d$ (number of peers to query) we conclude that the overhead efficiency ratio $C$ was approximately 0.003 in our setting.

For each $d$ value and each load parameter (load is achieved by tuning the average inter arrival time at the client) we performed several runs of over 20000

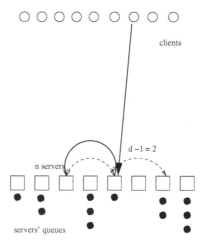

**Fig. 6.** A basic distributed scheme with explicit monitoring: Peer Monitoring

job requests each, and computed the average response time. The average response time for five load values as a function of $d$ is depicted in Figure 4. One can see that the basic hop count scheme performs better than the PM scheme. This is because the Basic heuristic incurs less management overhead on the server, since the data needed to perform management decision is conveyed via the job request packet, and not by direct load queries. It is worth noting that the results of the Basic heuristic are quite similar in the low and medium load (when $d \geq 3$), this is due to the fact that in such loads, the probability of finding an idle server within a few hops is high.

Figure 5 depicts the performance of the two adaptive heuristics with respect to Basic PM, where each is assumed to use the *best* parameters for that load. One can see that Self Adaptive Heuristic I outperforms both the PM scheme as well as the basic hop count scheme. The second Adaptive Heuristic does not perform as well. This indicates that this heuristic is more sensitive to parameter tuning. Note again that neither of the adaptive heuristics uses any tuning, and the process is self adaptable to the current load. Also note that even for a relatively small set of servers, the load balancing performs very well for all load values.

## 5   Related Work

Load balancing mechanisms were extensively studied in a variety of contexts over the last twenty years. Proliferation of highly dynamic research and industrial efforts caused the "load balancing" term to become a somewhat overloaded concept. Load balancing (sometimes referred to as "load sharing") may have slightly different meanings when different computer science communities are concerned. Interested reader are encouraged to read [4] for the load balancing taxonomy and fully specified positioning of our monitoring overhead-aware approach to load balancing.

The cost of monitoring is an integral part of the overall cost of the load balancing algorithm. Clearly, a trade-off exists between the quality of monitoring and the cost of acquiring the monitoring data. On the one hand, the more updated the monitoring data is, the higher is the total quality of load balancing [5,6,7,2]. On the other hand, since monitoring takes small but non-zero amount of computational and communication resources, its inherent cost becomes a limiting factor for scalability. Although this trade-off has been long noticed, no formal study of it was performed until recently [2]. Some insightful empiric studies have been carried out, though [7,5].

Our approach is fully distributed and is close in spirit to *Direct Neighbor Repeated (DNR)* policy [8] used in *diffusive*. Our solution is different from the DNR-like strategies since it does not use explicit monitoring to evaluate the load distribution in the neighborhood, but rather collect the monitoring information *en-route*, while a new job travels a few hops before settling for execution. In addition, we use a randomly selected dynamic logical neighborhood, while the DNR-like solutions use a physical static neighborhood.

A novel approach to Load Evaluation and Task Migration sub-policies was presented in [9]. In this solution a unified cost model for heterogenous resources was presented. Using this cost model, the "marginal cost" of adding a task to a given destination is computed. A task is dispatched to the destination which minimizes the total marginal cost. In a sense, it is a variation of a greedy algorithm. However, thanks to its sophisticated cost model, it outperforms simple greedy algorithms.

Another innovative approach that combines a threshold-based approach with the greedy strategy in an interesting way was presented in [10]. The primary goal of this work is to achieve an autonomic adaptable strategy for peer-to-peer overlay maintenance with QoS guarantees in spite of possible server crashes.

In contrast to other load balancing mechanisms, our solution explicitly takes monitoring costs – which is an integral part of any load balancing solution – into account following the footsteps of [2]. In contrast to [2], in this work we concentrate on a fully distributed setting. The distribution, however, brings about a problem of staleness of the load data acquired at different points in time as new job requests travel among different randomly selected servers. It turns out that closed form solution of the average response time in presence of staleness is unlikely even for the Poisson traffic model [5,2]. We, therefore, use mainly simulations and emulation to study the behavior of our proposed heuristics.

## 6   Conclusions and Future Work

The ability to quantify the benefits of a system management tool and the overhead associated with it is an important step toward developing cost effective self enabled systems. This paper provides one building block in the strive to rigorously quantify the effectiveness of management systems. We consider a distributed service setting where the goal is to minimize the total average time required to provide the service to the customers. Much of the overhead associated with load balancing systems in such a setting is due to the need to monitor the load on the different servers in order to assign job requests to sub-utilized servers.

In order to understand the exact benefit of this explicit monitoring, we compare the benefit of explicit monitoring systems with the best possible "no monitoring" solution. Note that a simple random assignments of servers to jobs in our setting results in an average waiting time of $\frac{1}{1-\lambda}$, which yields a total time of 2.5 times the service time in 80% load. Our schemes reduces this factor considerably (to $1.2 - 1.5$).

These results indicate the importance of identifying the exact cost and benefit associated with system and network management. The same methods could be used to understand this tradeoff in different networking settings (such as routing) that involve dissemination of local information through the network.

# References

1. Srisuresh, P., Gan, D.: Load Sharing using IP Network Address Translation (LSNAT) (August 1998)
2. Breitgand, D., Cohen, R., Nahir, A., Raz, D.: Cost aware adaptive load sharing. In: IWSOS 2007. The 2nd International Workshop on Self-Organizing Systems, English Lake District, UK (September 2007)
3. Mitzenmacher, M.: The power of two choices in randomized load balancing. IEEE Transactions on Parallel and Distributed Systems 12(10), 1094–1104 (2001)
4. Breitgand, D., Nahir, A., Raz, D.: To know or not to know: on the needed amount of management information, Tech. Rep. H-0242, IBM T.J. Watson Research Center (2006)
5. Mitzenmacher, M.: How useful is old information? IEEE Transactions on Parallel and Distributed Systems 11(1), 6–20 (2000)
6. Hui, C.-C., Chanson, S.T.: Improved Strategies for Dynamic Load Balancing. IEEE Concurrency 7(3), 58–67 (1999)
7. Othman, O., Balasubramanian, J., Schmidt, D.C.: Performance Evaluation of an Adaptive Middleware Load Balancing and Monitoring Service. In: 24th IEEE International Conference on Distributed Computing Systems (ICDCS), Tokyo, Japan (May 2004)
8. Corradi, A., Leonardi, L., Zambonelli, F.: On the Effectiveness of Different Diffusive Load Balancing Policies in Dynamic Applications. IEEE Concurrency 7(1), 22–31 (1999)
9. Amir, Y., Awerbuch, B., Barak, A., Borgstrom, R.S., Keren, A.: An Opportunity Cost Approach for Job Assignment in a Scalable Computing Cluster. IEEE Transactions on Parallel and Distributed Systems 11(7), 760–768 (2000)
10. Adam, C., Stadler, R.: Adaptable Server Clusters with QoS Objectives. In: IM 2005. 9th IFIP/IEEE International Symposium on Integrated Network Management, Nice, France (May 2005)

# Smart Dimensioning of IP Network Links

Remco van de Meent[1], Michel Mandjes[2], and Aiko Pras[1]

[1] University of Twente, Netherlands
{r.vandemeent,a.pras}@utwente.nl
[2] University of Amsterdam & Centre for Mathematics and Computer Science, Netherlands
mmandjes@science.uva.nl

**Abstract.** Link dimensioning is generally considered as an effective and (operationally) simple mechanism to meet (given) performance requirements. In practice, the required link capacity $C$ is often estimated by rules of thumb, such as $C = d \cdot M$, where $M$ is the (envisaged) average traffic rate, and $d$ some (empirically determined) constant larger than 1. This paper studies the viability of this class of 'simplistic' dimensioning rules. Throughout, the performance criterion imposed is that the fraction of intervals of length $T$ in which the input exceeds the available output capacity (i.e., $C \cdot T$) should not exceed $\varepsilon$, for given $T$ and $\varepsilon$.

We first present a dimensioning formula that expresses the required link capacity as a function of $M$ and a variance term $V(T)$, which captures the burstiness on timescale $T$. We explain how $M$ and $V(T)$ can be estimated with low measurement effort. The dimensioning formula is then used to validate dimensioning rules of the type $C = d \cdot M$. Our main findings are: (i) the factor $d$ is strongly affected by the nature of the traffic, the level of aggregation, and the network infrastructure; if these conditions are more or less constant, one could empirically determine $d$; (ii) we can explicitly characterize how $d$ is affected by the 'performance parameters', i.e., $T$ and $\varepsilon$.

## 1 Introduction

In order to meet the users' performance requirements on an Internet connection, two approaches seem viable, see, [1,2]. The first approach relies on the use of protocols that enforce certain service levels, for instance by prioritizing some streams over other streams, by performing admission control, or by explicitly dedicating resources to connections; examples of such techniques are DiffServ [3] and IntServ [4]. The second approach does not use any traffic management mechanisms, but rather relies on allocating sufficient network capacity to the aggregate traffic stream. In this approach the link capacity should be chosen such that it is always large enough to satisfy the performance requirements of *all* flows. This approach, which is often called *overdimensioning*, is commonly used by network operators for their backbone links; some studies found that such links generally have a capacity which is '30 times the average traffic rate' [5].

As described in [6,7], it has several advantages to guarantee the users' performance requirements (agreed upon in a service level agreement, or SLA) by relying on link dimensioning. Perhaps the most significant advantage is that dimensioning is (operationally) *simple*; it eliminates the need for network systems and network management

A. Clemm, L.Z. Granville, and R. Stadler (Eds.): DSOM 2007, LNCS 4785, pp. 86–97, 2007.

to support relatively complex (and therefore error-prone) techniques for enforcing the SLA parameters.

Although the idea of link dimensioning is simple, still the question remains of *how much* link capacity is needed to guarantee the parameters agreed upon in the SLA. Without sufficient capacity, the performance, as experienced by the users, will drop below the required levels. If the link is dimensioned too generously, however, then the performance does not improve anymore, and hence resources are essentially wasted. This trade-off leads to the concept of *smart dimensioning*, which we define as the lowest link capacity at which the SLA is met.

When determining this link capacity, a specific question is for instance: is there, for a given performance target, a fixed ratio between the required capacity and the *average* traffic rate? If there would be, then we would evidently have a simple and powerful dimensioning rule. A more detailed question concerns the dependence of $d$ on the performance requirement imposed: when making the performance target more stringent, evidently $d$ should increase, but can this dependence be quantified?

*Approach and organization.* The idea in this paper is to study smart dimensioning, as introduced above; the main question is 'what is the link capacity that is minimally required?' Throughout, the performance criterion imposed is that the fraction of intervals of length $T$ in which the input exceeds the available output capacity (i.e., $CT$) should not exceed $\varepsilon$, for given $T$ and $\varepsilon$.

There are various possible approaches to answer this question. For instance, one could follow a fully empirical approach. Then one experimentally increases (or decreases) a network link's capacity, and evaluates the performance as experienced by the users, so as to determine the minimally required link capacity.

We opt, however, for a different approach: we first derive an analytical link dimensioning formula; this gives the required link capacity to achieve a certain performance target, for given input traffic (in term of a mean rate and a variance term that expresses the traffic aggregate's burstiness). Then we explain how these traffic parameters can be estimated with minimal measurement effort. We prefer this approach, mainly because of its *systematic* nature: it explicitly shows which parameters of the underlying traffic process essentially determine the required link capacity, and how it is affected by the performance requirement.

The present paper builds upon previous work on traffic modeling and network link dimensioning [8,9,11,12]. Section 2 recapitulates our findings on the modeling of real network traffic (based on our measurements at 5 representative networking environments); importantly, these measurements indicate that under fairly general circumstances the Gaussian traffic model applies. We also derive a link dimensioning formula, which greatly simplifies under Gaussianity; this formula shows how the 'performance parameters' $T$ and $\varepsilon$ affect the required link capacity. Section 3 reviews approaches to estimate the Gaussian traffic model's parameters, i.e., mean and variance. In Section 4 it is discussed how to apply the link dimensioning formula from Section 2 in practice, through an evaluation of its performance in different scenarios. Section 5 systematically assesses the amount of link capacity required; interestingly, it is also shown how one could explicitly predict the impact of changing $T$ and/or $\varepsilon$ on the required link capacity. Concluding remarks are provided in Section 6.

## 2   Link Dimensioning Formula

As argued in the introduction, an important prerequisite for dimensioning is a formula that determines, for given characteristics of the offered traffic and performance target, the minimum required link rate. Preferably, such a dimensioning formula has minimal requirements on the 'nature' of the traffic offered; for instance, we do not want to impose any conditions on its correlation structure. In this section, we present a formula that relies on only weak conditions on the traffic process, i.e., stationarity and Gaussianity:

- *Stationarity* means that, with $A(s,t)$ denoting the amount of traffic arrived in the time interval $[s,t)$, the distribution of $A(s+\delta,t+\delta)$ does not depend on $\delta$ (but just on the interval length $t - s$). In the sequel we use the abbreviation $A(t) := A(0,t)$.
- *Gaussianity* refers to the probability distribution of $A(t)$. It is supposed that $A(\cdot)$ is a Gaussian process with stationary increments, i.e., $A(s,t)$ is normally distributed, with mean $M \cdot (t - s)$ and variance $V(t - s)$, for some mean rate $M \in \mathbb{R}$ and variance curve $V(\cdot) : \mathbb{R}^+ \to \mathbb{R}^+$.

Stationarity is a common assumption in traffic modeling; it usually applies on timescales up to, say, hours. In earlier work, we have thoroughly investigated the Gaussianity of real Internet traffic, in various representative settings (in terms of types of users, network infrastructure, timescales, etc.) — see [8,9]. We found that a Gaussian traffic model accurately describes real traffic, particularly when the level of aggregation was sufficiently high. We note that this Gaussianity issue was the subject of a number of other studies, see for instance Fraleigh *et al.* [6] and Kilpi and Norros [10]; similar conclusions were drawn.

*Derivation of link dimensioning formula for Gaussian traffic.* Given the observation that a real Internet traffic stream can be accurately approximated by a Gaussian process, we now develop a formula that estimates the minimally required link capacity to cater for that traffic stream.

First, however, we specify what 'to cater for a traffic stream' means. In this paper we rely on the notion of *link transparency* that was introduced in [11]. Its main objective is to ensure that the links are more or less 'transparent' to the users, in that the users should not (or almost never) perceive any performance degradation due to a lack of bandwidth. Clearly, this objective will be achieved when the link rate is chosen such that only during a small fraction of time $\varepsilon$ the aggregate rate of the offered traffic (measured on a sufficiently small time scale $T$) exceeds the link rate: $\mathbb{P}(A(T) \geq CT) \leq \varepsilon$. The values to be chosen for the parameters $T$ and $\varepsilon$ typically depend on the specific needs of the application(s) involved. Clearly, the more interactive the application, the smaller $T$ and $\varepsilon$ should be chosen; network operators should choose them in line with the SLAs they agreed upon with their clients.

Now, given the criterion $\mathbb{P}(A(T) \geq CT) \leq \varepsilon$, we can derive a formula for the minimal link rate needed (without assuming Gaussian input at this point). Relying on the Markov inequality $\mathbb{P}(X \geq a) \leq \mathbb{E}(X)/a$ for a non-negative random variable $X$, we have for $\theta \geq 0$ that $\mathbb{P}(A(T) \geq CT) \leq \mathbb{E}\exp(\theta A(T))\exp(-\theta CT)$, and hence we obtain the celebrated Chernoff bound

$$\mathbb{P}(A(T) \geq CT) \leq \min_{\theta \geq 0} \left( e^{-\theta CT} \mathbb{E}e^{\theta A(T)} \right).$$

Rewriting this expression, it is not hard to see that, in order to be sure that $\mathbb{P}(A(T) \geq CT) \leq \varepsilon$ it suffices to take the link's bandwidth capacity $C$ at least

$$C \equiv C(T, \varepsilon) = \min_{\theta \geq 0} \frac{\log \mathbb{E} \exp(\theta A(T)) - \log \varepsilon}{\theta T}. \tag{1}$$

Finally, imposing some additional structure on $A(\cdot)$ simplifies the general dimensioning formula of (1). When assuming traffic is Gaussian, with $\delta := \sqrt{-2 \log \varepsilon}$, the dimensioning formula (1) reduces to

$$C = M + \frac{\delta}{T} \cdot \sqrt{V(T)}; \tag{2}$$

here it is used that $\mathbb{E} \exp(\theta A(t)) = M\theta t + \theta^2 V(t)/2$. The important consequence of this, is that for the application of the dimensioning formula (2) in this Gaussian context it is required to have estimates for the mean rate $M$ and the variance $V(T)$.

## 3  Estimating Traffic Parameters

In the previous section we concluded that, in order to dimension a network link by applying dimensioning formula (2), an accurate estimate of the traffic offered (both in terms of the mean traffic rate $M$, as well as its fluctuations, expressed through $V(T)$) is required. Estimating $M$ is relatively straightforward, and can be done through standard coarse traffic measurements, e.g., by polling Interfaces Group MIB counters via SNMP (Simple Network Management Protocol) every 5 minutes.

Estimating the variance $V(T)$ (which could be interpreted as 'burstiness'), however, could be substantially harder: particularly on smaller timescales $T$, it is hard to do accurate measurements through SNMP. The standard way to estimate $V(T)$ (for some given small interval length $T$) is what we refer to as the 'direct approach': perform traffic measurements for disjoint intervals of length $T$, say $a_i(T)$ for $i = 1, \ldots, N$, and compute their sample variance

$$(N-1)^{-1} \sum_{i=1}^{N} (a_i(T) - MT)^2.$$

An important drawback to this direct approach, however, is that it requires substantial measurement effort to accurately measure $a_i(T)$ for small $T$. This drawback is countered by our so-called 'indirect approach', which is briefly discussed next — we refer to [12] for an in-depth description.

*Indirect estimation of* $V(T)$. The 'indirect approach' to estimate $V(T)$ relies on (coarse-grained) measurements of the buffer occupancy, as follows. By regular polling the occupancy $B$ of the buffer in front of the to-be-dimensioned network link, the probability distribution $\mathbb{P}(Q > B)$ of the buffer occupancy is estimated. Interestingly, as shown in [12], for Gaussian inputs, the distribution of the buffer occupancy uniquely determines the variance function $V(\cdot)$ of the input process, for given mean rate $M$; in particular, it was shown that it does so through the following relation:

$$V(t) \approx \inf_{B \geq 0} \frac{(B + (C - M)t)^2}{-2 \log \mathbb{P}(Q > B)}.$$

**Table 1.** Measurement locations

| Location | Short description | # traces | Mean rate (Mbit/s) |
|---|---|---|---|
| U | university residential network (1800 hosts) | 15 | 170 |
| R | research institute (250 hosts) | 185 | 6 |
| C | college network (1500 hosts) | 302 | 35 |
| A | ADSL access network (2000 hosts) | 50 | 120 |
| S | server hosting provider (100 hosts) | 201 | 12 |

In other words: when knowing $\mathbb{P}(Q > B)$ (or an accurate estimate), we can infer $V(t)$ for any timescale $t$. As our numerical and experimental evaluation in [12] shows, the above 'indirect approach' to obtain $V(\cdot)$ from coarse-grained measurements, yields estimates of the variance that are remarkably close to the actual values.

Hence, we can estimate both $M$ and $V(T)$ with relatively low measurement effort. In the next section we demonstrate how these can be used to support finding an accurate estimate of the required link capacity.

## 4  Dimensioning

In Section 2 we developed a link dimensioning formula (2) for Gaussian network traffic, which has the input parameters the mean $M$ and variance $V(T)$, and is supposed to meet the performance target $\mathbb{P}(A(T) \geq CT) \leq \varepsilon$. In Section 3 we then explained how $M$ and $V(T)$ could be estimated through coarse measurements. In the present section, the estimates of $M$ and $V(T)$ are inserted into the dimensioning formula (2) to estimate the minimally required link capacity. We can then verify whether the performance criterion imposed is actually met. We will do so through a number of case studies — a sizable collection of traffic traces of 15 minutes each, from various representative locations, see Table 1; for more detailed information, see [9, Section 2.3].

We evaluate the accuracy of the dimensioning formula (2). It requires knowledge of $M$ and $V(T)$, which we estimate as described in Section 3; in particular, $V(T)$ is estimated through the 'indirect approach'. This indirect approach requires an estimate of $\mathbb{P}(Q > B)$ (as a function of $B \geq 0$); this was enabled by a simple simulation environment that 'replays' the real traffic trace through a simulated buffer and link. The resulting estimates are inserted into (2), yielding the estimated minimally required link capacity for a chosen $\varepsilon$ and $T$. In the present experiments, we set $\varepsilon$ to 1%, and set $T$ to 1 sec, 500 msec and 100 msec. These are timescales that are, for various applications, important to the perception of quality by (human) users, and thus are relevant when striving for link transparency. Now it is interesting to validate whether, under the estimated minimally required link rate, the performance requirement would be met.

A first validation result is presented in Fig. 1. It shows the estimated required bandwidth for three different values of $T$, with $\varepsilon = 0.01$, for location A. It is noted that the fluctuations of the traffic rate in this specific example are relatively low compared to the mean traffic rate. This is because at this location a large number of relatively small (ADSL) access links are multiplexed on a large (1 Gbit/sec) backbone, and therefore a single user cannot have a strong impact on the aggregate traffic stream.

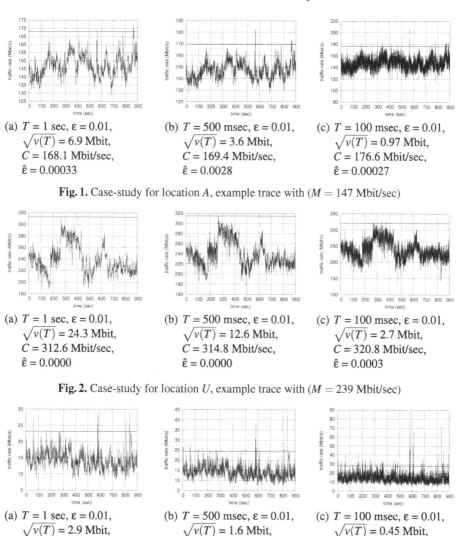

**Fig. 1.** Case-study for location $A$, example trace with ($M = 147$ Mbit/sec)

(a) $T = 1$ sec, $\varepsilon = 0.01$,
$\sqrt{v(T)} = 6.9$ Mbit,
$C = 168.1$ Mbit/sec,
$\hat{\varepsilon} = 0.00033$

(b) $T = 500$ msec, $\varepsilon = 0.01$,
$\sqrt{v(T)} = 3.6$ Mbit,
$C = 169.4$ Mbit/sec,
$\hat{\varepsilon} = 0.0028$

(c) $T = 100$ msec, $\varepsilon = 0.01$,
$\sqrt{v(T)} = 0.97$ Mbit,
$C = 176.6$ Mbit/sec,
$\hat{\varepsilon} = 0.00027$

**Fig. 2.** Case-study for location $U$, example trace with ($M = 239$ Mbit/sec)

(a) $T = 1$ sec, $\varepsilon = 0.01$,
$\sqrt{v(T)} = 24.3$ Mbit,
$C = 312.6$ Mbit/sec,
$\hat{\varepsilon} = 0.0000$

(b) $T = 500$ msec, $\varepsilon = 0.01$,
$\sqrt{v(T)} = 12.6$ Mbit,
$C = 314.8$ Mbit/sec,
$\hat{\varepsilon} = 0.0000$

(c) $T = 100$ msec, $\varepsilon = 0.01$,
$\sqrt{v(T)} = 2.7$ Mbit,
$C = 320.8$ Mbit/sec,
$\hat{\varepsilon} = 0.0003$

**Fig. 3.** Case-study for location $S$, example trace with ($M = 14.3$ Mbit/sec)

(a) $T = 1$ sec, $\varepsilon = 0.01$,
$\sqrt{v(T)} = 2.9$ Mbit,
$C = 23.2$ Mbit/sec,
$\hat{\varepsilon} = 0.0056$

(b) $T = 500$ msec, $\varepsilon = 0.01$,
$\sqrt{v(T)} = 1.6$ Mbit,
$C = 24.3$ Mbit/sec,
$\hat{\varepsilon} = 0.0083$

(c) $T = 100$ msec, $\varepsilon = 0.01$,
$\sqrt{v(T)} = 0.45$ Mbit,
$C = 27.8$ Mbit/sec,
$\hat{\varepsilon} = 0.0100$

Because of the rather small fluctuations, the amount of extra bandwidth required to cater for the peak traffic rates (which is desirable under the link transparency criterion imposed), compared to the mean traffic rate, is also relatively small: some 20% at the 100 msec timescale. Later on in this paper we will see that in other scenarios, the extra required bandwidth can be as high as hundreds of percents.

Figs. 2 and 3 present similar results for locations U and S, respectively. Fig. 2 shows an interesting example of a heavily loaded network: it can be shown that the peak traffic rates in this example trace, even at small timescales, are lower than may be expected from a Gaussian traffic stream with the estimated mean and variance. As a result of this,

**Table 2.** Required bandwidth: estimation errors ($\varepsilon = 0.01$)

| Location | $T$ | avg. $|\varepsilon - \hat{\varepsilon}|$ | stderr $|\varepsilon - \hat{\varepsilon}|$ |
|---|---|---|---|
| U | 1 sec | 0.0095 | 0.0067 |
| | 500 msec | 0.0089 | 0.0067 |
| | 100 msec | 0.0077 | 0.0047 |
| R | 1 sec | 0.0062 | 0.0060 |
| | 500 msec | 0.0063 | 0.0064 |
| | 100 msec | 0.0050 | 0.0053 |
| C | 1 sec | 0.0069 | 0.0047 |
| | 500 msec | 0.0066 | 0.0043 |
| | 100 msec | 0.0055 | 0.0041 |
| A | 1 sec | 0.0083 | 0.0027 |
| | 500 msec | 0.0083 | 0.0024 |
| | 100 msec | 0.0079 | 0.0020 |
| S | 1 sec | 0.0052 | 0.0050 |
| | 500 msec | 0.0049 | 0.0055 |
| | 100 msec | 0.0040 | 0.0059 |

the 'realized performance' (in terms of the $\hat{\varepsilon}$ that will be defined below) is well below the anticipated $\varepsilon = 0.01$. This might be caused by the relatively high average traffic rate (compared to the other parts in this same trace), from the approximately 280 th to 420 th second.

Fig. 3 illustrates the importance of looking at small timescales when dimensioning network links: the peak rates at small timescales, in this particular example, are sometimes as much as 6 times the average traffic rate. Evidently, also the setting of $\varepsilon$ is of importance when determining the required bandwidth capacity. It can clearly be seen from Fig. 3 that when $\varepsilon$ is set smaller than the 0.01 chosen here, the estimated required bandwidth capacity increases significantly, as then a larger number of the traffic peaks should be catered for.

The above experiments already gave a rough impression about the performance of our dimensioning procedure. In order to further validate how well the estimated bandwidth capacity $C$ corresponds to the required bandwidth, we introduce the notion of 'realized exceedance', denoted with $\hat{\varepsilon}$. We define the 'realized exceedance' as the fraction of (disjoint) intervals of length $T$, in which the amount of offered traffic $a_i(T)$ exceeds the estimated required capacity $CT$ — we stress the fact that 'exceedance' in this context does not correspond to 'packet loss'. In other words:

$$\hat{\varepsilon} \equiv \hat{\varepsilon}(C) := \frac{\#\{i \in \{1,\ldots,N\} \mid a_i(T) > CT\}}{N}.$$

If $C$ is properly estimated, then 'exceedance' (as in $a_i(T) > CT$) may be expected in a fraction $\varepsilon$ of all intervals. There are, however, (at least) two reasons why $\hat{\varepsilon}$ and $\varepsilon$ may not be equal in practice. (i) Firstly, (2) assumes 'perfectly Gaussian' traffic, which is not always the case [8]. Evidently, deviations of 'perfectly Gaussian' traffic may have an impact on the estimated $C$. (ii) Secondly, to obtain (1), an upper bound (viz. the

Chernoff bound) on the target probability has been used, and it is not clear upfront how far off this bound is.

To assess to what extent the dimensioning formula for Gaussian traffic is accurate for real traffic, we compare ε and ê. We do this comparison for the hundreds of traces that we collected at measurement locations {U, R, C, A, S}. Table 2 presents the average differences between the targeted ε and the 'realized exceedance' ê at each location (where the averaging is done over all traces collected at that location), as well as the corresponding standard deviations, for three different timescales $T$ (1 sec, 500 msec and 100 msec). The table shows that differences between ε and ê are small. Hence, we conclude that our approach accurately estimates the required bandwidth to meet the pre-specified performance target.

## 5 Dimensioning Factors

In this section we address the question whether there is, for a given performance target, a fixed ratio between the required capacity $C$ and the average traffic rate $M$. We start this section, however, with a quantification of this ratio as a function of the parameters $T$ and ε (i.e., the parameters that determine the performance requirement).

*Dimensioning for various parameter settings.* As indicated earlier, the required bandwidth should increase when the performance criterion (through ε and $T$) becomes more stringent. To give a few examples of the impact of the performance parameters $T$ and ε on the required bandwidth capacity, we plot curves for the required bandwidth capacity at $T = 10, 50, 100$ and 500 msec, and ε ranging from $10^{-5}$ to 0.1, in Fig. 4. In these curves, $M$ and $V(T)$ are estimated from an example traffic trace collected at each of the locations {U, R, C, A, S}.

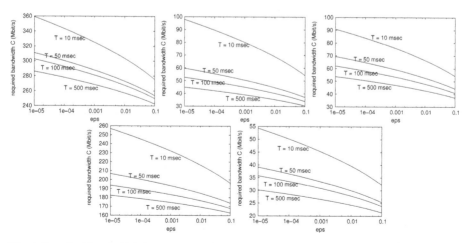

**Fig. 4.** Required bandwidth for other settings of $T$ and ε for locations {U, R, C, A, S}, with $M = \{207, 18.9, 23.4, 147, 14.3\}$ Mbit/s, respectively

Figure 4 shows that the required bandwidth $C$ decreases in both $T$ and $\varepsilon$, which is intuitively clear. The figures show that $C$ is more sensitive to $T$ than to $\varepsilon$ — take for instance the top-left plot in Figure 4, i.e., location U; at $\varepsilon = 10^{-5}$, the difference in required bandwidth between $T = 10$ msec and $T = 100$ msec, is some 20%. At $T = 100$ msec, the difference in required bandwidth between $\varepsilon = 10^{-5}$ and $\varepsilon = 10^{-4}$ is just 3% approximately. For other examples, the precise differences may change but the impression stays the same: a tenfold increase in stringency with respect to $T$ requires (relatively) more extra bandwidth, than a tenfold increase in stringency with respect to $\varepsilon$ (of course, this could already be expected on the basis of the required link rate formula).

We have verified whether the required link rate is accurately estimated for these case-studies with different settings of $T$ and $\varepsilon$. The estimation errors in these new situations are similar to the earlier obtained results (cf. Table 2). It should be noted however, that we have not been able to verify this for all possible combinations of $T$ and $\varepsilon$: for $\varepsilon = 10^{-5}$ and $T = 500$ msec for instance, there are only 1800 samples in our traffic trace (which has a length of 15 minutes) and hence, we cannot compute the accuracy of our estimation. Another remark that should be made here, is that for locations with only limited aggregation in terms of users (say some tens concurrent users), combined with a small timescale of $T = 10$ msec, the Gaussianity assumption may become questionable. Consequently, the accuracy of our required bandwidth estimation decreases.

*Impact of changing performance parameters on required bandwidth.* As illustrated in Fig. 4, it is possible to express the estimated required bandwidth capacity as function of $\varepsilon$ and $T$. Having such a function at our disposal, and one or two actual estimates of the required bandwidth, it is possible to 'extrapolate' such estimates to other settings of $\varepsilon$ and $T$. This allows for investigation of the impact of, say, a more stringent performance target on the required capacity. We first assess the impact of a change in $\varepsilon$ and then of a change in $T$.

Suppose that, for a given $T$, a proper required bandwidth estimate $C(T,\varepsilon_1)$ is known, for some $\varepsilon_1$ and estimated $M$. From (2) it follows that $C(T,\varepsilon_1) = M + \delta_1 \cdot \Psi$, where $\delta_1 := \sqrt{-2\log\varepsilon_1}$. Evidently, we can estimate $\Psi$ by $(C(T,\varepsilon_1) - M)/\delta_1$. Then, to find the required bandwidth estimate for some *other* performance target $\varepsilon_2$, it is a matter of inserting these $M$ and $\Psi$ into

$$C(T,\varepsilon_2) = M + \Psi\sqrt{-2\log\varepsilon_2}.$$

We give an example application hereof using the top-left graph (location U) in Fig. 4. At the $T = 100$ msec timescale, taking $\varepsilon_1 = 0.01$, $M = 207$ Mbit/s, it follows that $C(T,\varepsilon_1) \approx 266$ Mbit/s. Thus, $\Psi \approx 19.4$. Suppose we are interested in the impact on the required bandwidth capacity if we reduce $\varepsilon$ with a factor 1000, i.e., $\varepsilon_2 = 10^{-5}$. Estimating the new required bandwidth capacity through the formula above yields that $C(T,\varepsilon_2) \approx 300$ Mbit/s, which indeed corresponds to the required bandwidth as indicated by the curve in Fig. 4. Hence, informally speaking, the additional bandwidth required to cater for 1000 times as many 'traffic peaks' is, in this scenario, just some 34 Mbit/s.

Secondly, we look at the impact of a change in $T$ on the required bandwidth. Compared to the above analysis for $\varepsilon$, we now have the extra complexity of the variance $V(T)$ in (2), which evidently changes with various $T$. We therefore impose the additional assumption that traffic can be modeled as fractional Brownian motion (fBm); this

Table 3. Required bandwidth: dimensioning factors ($\varepsilon = 0.01$)

| Location | U | | | R | | | C | | | A | | | S | | |
|---|---|---|---|---|---|---|---|---|---|---|---|---|---|---|---|
| $T$ (sec) | 1.0 | 0.5 | 0.1 | 1.0 | 0.5 | 0.1 | 1.0 | 0.5 | 0.1 | 1.0 | 0.5 | 0.1 | 1.0 | 0.5 | 0.1 |
| $d$ | 1.33 | 1.35 | 1.42 | 2.91 | 3.12 | 3.82 | 1.71 | 1.83 | 2.13 | 1.13 | 1.14 | 1.19 | 1.98 | 2.10 | 2.44 |
| $\sigma_d$ | 0.10 | 0.09 | 0.09 | 1.51 | 1.57 | 1.84 | 0.44 | 0.49 | 0.67 | 0.03 | 0.03 | 0.03 | 0.78 | 0.87 | 1.01 |

special case of the Gaussian model has found widespread use in modeling network traffic. Under fBm, the variance satisfies $V(T) \approx \sigma \cdot T^{2H}$, where $H$ is the so-called Hurst parameter, and $\sigma$ is some positive scaling constant. Using this variance function, (2) can be rewritten as $C = M + \delta \cdot \Phi(T)$, with $\Phi(T) = \sqrt{\sigma} \cdot T^{H-1}$.

Now suppose that for two different time intervals, namely $T_1 = T$ and $T_2 = \beta T$ (for some $\beta > 0$; $\varepsilon$ is held fixed), the required bandwidth is known. This enables us to compute $\Phi(T)$ and $\Phi(\beta T)$, as above. But then

$$\frac{\Phi(\beta T)}{\Phi(T)} = \frac{\sqrt{\sigma} \cdot (\beta T)^{H-1}}{\sqrt{\sigma} \cdot T^{H-1}} = \beta^{H-1},$$

or, in other words, $g := (\log \beta)^{-1} \cdot \log(\Phi(\beta T)/\Phi(T))$ is constant in $\beta$ (and has value $H - 1$). Again we consider, as an example, location U, with $\varepsilon = 10^{-3}$. For $T = 100$ msec we obtain from $C(T, \varepsilon) \approx 279$ that $\Phi(T) = 19.37$. Now take $\beta = 0.5$; from $C(\beta T, \varepsilon) \approx 290$ we obtain $\Phi(\beta T) = 22.3$ It follows that $g = -0.20$. Suppose we now wish to dimension for $T_3 = \beta' T$ with $\beta' = 0.1$ (i.e., $T = 10$ msec), we obtain $\Phi(\beta' T) = \Phi(T)(\beta')^g \approx 30.7$, so that $C(\beta' T, \varepsilon) = M + \sqrt{-2 \log \varepsilon} \cdot \Phi(\beta' T) \approx 321$. It is easily verified that this corresponds to the required bandwidth as indicated by the curve in Fig. 4.

*Dimensioning factors.* Link dimensioning formula (2) requires knowledge of $M$ and $V(T)$ to estimate the minimally required link capacity, for specified $\varepsilon$ and $T$. It is common practice to measure $M$, for instance through the popular MRTG tool [13]. Operators then look at the 'busy hour' to estimate the load at the busiest time of the day. It is less common to also estimate $V(T)$, which reflects the fluctuations of the traffic rate at the (usually rather small) timescale $T$ — this could be done through the method described in Section 3 of this paper. It would be interesting though to know whether there is a common *dimensioning factor*, say $d$, which yields the required bandwidth (taking into account fluctuations at small timescales), just on the basis of the mean traffic rate. If there would be such a common dimensioning factor, one could easily estimate the required bandwidth through a simple formula of the type $C = d \cdot M$.

In order to study this dimensioning factor, the required bandwidth and mean traffic rates are compared, by computing $d := C/M$, for each trace at all locations. These dimensioning factors, averaged over all traces at each location, as well as their respective standard deviations, are given in Table 3.

Table 3 shows, for instance, that at location U, some 33% extra bandwidth capacity would be needed on top of the average traffic load $M$, to cater for 99% ($\varepsilon = 0.01$) of all traffic peaks at a timescale of $T = 1$ sec. At location R, relatively more extra bandwidth is required to meet the same performance criterion: about 191%. Such differences between those locations can be explained by looking at the network environment: at location R, a single user can significantly influence the aggregated traffic, because of the relative low aggregation level (tens of concurrent users) and the high access link speeds (100 Mbit/sec, with a 1 Gbit/sec backbone); at location U, the user aggregation level is much higher, and hence, the traffic aggregate is 'more smooth'. Conclusion is that simplistic dimensioning rules of the type $C = d \cdot M$ are inaccurate, as the $d$ is all but a universal constant (it depends on the nature of the traffic, on the level of aggregation, the network infrastructure, and on the performance target imposed). The table does, however, show, that *within a location* in some situations (in particular locations U and A) the standard deviation of $d$ is rather low; in these cases one could empirically determine $d$ (for fixed $T, \varepsilon$), and dimension through $C = d \cdot M$.

## 6   Concluding Remarks

This paper introduced the concept of 'smart dimensioning'. We derived a dimensioning formula that gives the minimally required bandwidth capacity for a network link. We evaluated this formula using an extensive number of traffic traces collected at different locations. It turned out that the formula accurately predicts the required bandwidth, which is of valuable help when considering link dimensioning as approach to meeting the performance targets agreed upon in the Service Level Agreement.

The main question we posed is that of *how much* additional bandwidth is required, on top of the average rate traffic rate $M$. From our evaluation, we may conclude that there is no universal multiplicative factor $d$ that would support a statement like 'a bandwidth of $d \cdot M$ suffices'. It is clear that the factor $d$ depends heavily on the performance requirement imposed, but also on the nature of the traffic, the level of aggregation, and the network infrastructure. We have seen that in some scenarios, as low as 13% extra bandwidth (on top of $M$) is enough, while in others almost this percentage was around 300% (but, evidently, these numbers should be not seen as universal boundaries). Clearly, the '30 times the average traffic rate', as observed by [5] in several real scenarios, seems highly overdone.

*Acknowledgments.* This paper was supported in part by the EC IST-EMANICS Network of Excellence (#26854) (RvdM & AP) and the EC IST-EURO-FGI Network of Excellence (#28022) (MM).

## References

1. Zhao, W., Olshefski, D., Schulzrinne, H.: Internet Quality of Service: an Overview. Technical report, Columbia University, CUCS-003-00 (2000)
2. Pras, A., van de Meent, R., Mandjes, M.: QoS in Hybrid Networks - An Operator's Perspective. In: de Meer, H., Bhatti, N. (eds.) IWQoS 2005. LNCS, vol. 3552, pp. 388–391. Springer, Heidelberg (2005)
3. Blake, S., Black, D., Carlson, M., Davies, E., Wang, Z., Weiss, W.: An Architecture for Differentiated Services. IETF RFC 2475 (1998)
4. Braden, R., Clark, D., Shenker, S.: Integrated Services in the Internet Architecture: An Overview. IETF RFC 1633 (1994)

5. Odlyzko, A.M.: Data networks are lightly utilized, and will stay that way. Review of Network Economics 2, 210–237 (2003)
6. Fraleigh, C., Moon, S., Lyles, B., Cotton, C., Khan, M., Moll, D., Rockell, R., Seely, T., Diot, C.: Packet-Level Traffic Measurements from the Sprint IP Backbone. IEEE Network 17 (2003)
7. Fraleigh, C., Tobagi, F., Diot, C.: Provisioning IP Backbone Networks to Support Latency Sensitive Traffic. In: Proceedings of IEEE Infocom, San Francisco, USA (2003)
8. van de Meent, R., Mandjes, M., Pras, A.: Gaussian traffic everywhere? In: ICC 2006. Proceedings of the 2006 IEEE International Conference on Communications, Istanbul, Turkey (2006)
9. van de Meent, R.: Network link dimensioning: a measurement & modeling based approach. PhD thesis, University of Twente (2006)
10. Kilpi, J., Norros, I.: Testing the Gaussian approximation of aggregate traffic. In: Proceedings of the 2nd ACM SIGCOMM Internet Measurement Workshop, Marseille, France, pp. 49–61. ACM Press, New York (2002)
11. van den Berg, J., Mandjes, M., van de Meent, R., Pras, A., Roijers, F., Venemans, P.: QoS-aware bandwidth provisioning of IP links. Computer Networks 50, 631–647 (2006)
12. Mandjes, M., van de Meent, R.: Inferring traffic characteristics by observing the buffer content distribution. In: Boutaba, R., Almeroth, K.C., Puigjaner, R., Shen, S., Black, J.P. (eds.) NETWORKING 2005. LNCS, vol. 3462, pp. 303–315. Springer, Heidelberg (2005)
13. Oetiker, T.: MRTG: Multi Router Traffic Grapher (2003), available from http://people.ee.ethz.ch/~oetiker/webtools/mrtg/

# Managing Performance of Aging Applications Via Synchronized Replica Rejuvenation*

Artur Andrzejak[1], Monika Moser[1], and Luis Silva[2]

[1] Zuse Institute Berlin (ZIB)
Takustraße 7, 14195 Berlin, Germany
{andrzejak,moser}@zib.de
[2] Dep. Engenharia Informática
Univ. Coimbra, Portugal
luis@dei.uc.pt

**Abstract.** We investigate the problem of ensuring and maximizing performance guarantees for applications suffering software aging. Our focus is the optimization of the minimum and average performance of such applications in virtualized and non-virtualized scenario. The key technique is to use a set of simultaneously active application replica and to optimize their rejuvenation schedules. We derive an analytical method for maximizing the minimum "any-time" performance for certain cases and propose a heuristic method for maximization of minimum and average performance for all others. To evaluate our method we perform extensive studies on two applications: aging profiles of Apache Axis 1.3 and the aging data of the TPC-W benchmark instrumented with a memory leak injector. The results show that our approach is a practical way to ensure uninterrupted availability and optimize performance for even strongly aging applications.

## 1 Introduction

**Problem statement.** Software aging or rather *software running image aging* is the phenomenon of progressive degradation of running software image which might lead to performance reduction, hang ups or even crashes [1]. The primary causes are exhaustion of systems resources, like memory-leaks, unreleased locks, non-terminated threads, shared-memory pool latching, storage fragmentation, or data corruption. This undesirable phenomenon has been observed in enterprise clusters [2], telecommunications systems [1], web servers as well as other software. It is most likely to manifest itself in long-running or always-on applications such as web and applications servers, components of web services, and complex enterprise systems.

The primary method to fight aging is software rejuvenation, i.e. a restart of the aging application periodically or adaptively. While a lot of a research has

* This research work is carried out in part under the FP6 Network of Excellence Core-GRID funded by the European Commission (Contract IST-2002-004265) and the SELFMAN project funded by the European Commission.

A. Clemm, L.Z. Granville, and R. Stadler (Eds.): DSOM 2007, LNCS 4785, pp. 98–109, 2007.

been devoted recently to adaptive software rejuvenation [2,3,4,5], the remaining negative and serious side effect of a rejuvenation is the temporarily outage of service. Initiatives such as Recovery Oriented Computing (ROC) [6] and research on micro-reboots could reduce the rejuvenation time considerably. However, they require changes of the original applications and still cannot ensure uninterrupted service.

Due to their long running times service-oriented applications are especially prone to aging. We focus on this type of software and assume that invocations are triggered by external requests (we do not cover software whose invocations are triggered by timers or internal events). For such SOA-based IT-infrastructures an approach to eliminate completely the outage due to rejuvenation has been presented in [7]. The idea is to maintain in a stand-by mode an exact replica of the running application and perform an instantaneous migration in the situation when the original application is about to be rejuvenated. During the migration no requests are dropped - it is completely transparent for the users. This approach uses virtual machines as containers for the replica in order to avoid the need for additional hardware. The study [7] used one active replica at a time only and un-optimized performance thresholds as rejuvenation triggers. This causes two shortcomings: a large variation of the application performance and wasted application capacity due to non-optimal rejuvenation schedules.

**Paper idea and contributions.** The idea proposed in this paper is to hold multiple *active* replicas of the aging application, and trigger the rejuvenation of each one according to an *optimized schedule*. We implement this schema by simulating the system of multiple replicas and using a genetic algorithm to find such schedules. The optimization can maximize either the "any time" cumulative performance (minimum performance), the average cumulative performance (averaged over many rejuvenation phases), or a mix of both. Our approach can be used equally well in a virtualized environment on a single-server or in a cluster of native deployed applications.

Compared with the approach used in [7] our work ensures higher levels of "any time" cumulative performance, better overall utilization levels and higher resilience to unexpected performance changes or failures of individual replica. Another benefit is a smaller variation of the instantaneous performance, as with $k$ active replicas the cumulative performance during rejuvenation is roughly $(k-1)/k$ of the maximum. Furthermore, for the case of our data running $k$ replicas in parallel slows down the aging progress by a factor of $k$. As for drawbacks, our approach is more involved as it requires a rejuvenation scheduler and models of the aging processes [8].

This paper provides following contributions:

- we obtain analytically the optimized rejuvenation schedules for the minimum cumulative performance for the case of two identical replicas
- we propose and implement a heuristic method for finding optimized schedules for equal or different aging profiles of the replicas based on simulating the chains of rejuvenations and optimization via genetic algorithms

- we perform an extensive set of experiments to investigate the optimized rejuvenation schedules for a multitude of scenarios using the following data:
  - a TPC-W benchmark coupled with a fault injector to produce memory leaks (512, 768 or 1024 bytes) at each request
  - Apache Axis 1.3/1.4 server which suffers under severe "natural" aging problems
- we show that for our datasets the virtualization overhead does not depend on the number $k$ of replicas and that using $k$ replicas slows down the aging process by a factor of $k$.

**Paper structure.** Section 2 discusses related work. In Section 3 we introduce definitions and derive an analytical method to maximize the minimum performance of two replicas. In Section 4 we describe the idea and implementation of the heuristic optimization method. Section 5 is devoted to the experimental results, and we conclude with Section 6.

## 2   Related Work

The major tool to combat the problems related to software aging is software rejuvenation. There are two major approaches in this domain: *periodical rejuvenation* based on time or work performed, and *adaptive* or *proactive rejuvenation* [2,3,4,5] where the time to resource depletion or performance degradation is estimated. Countless studies have shown that the latter approach is more efficient, resulting in higher availability and lower cost.

Among the methods to apply proactive software rejuvenation two are dominant: analytic-based approach, and the measurement-based approach. The first method attempts to obtain an analytic model of a system taking into consideration various system parameters such as workload, MTTR and also distributions of failure. On this basis, an optimized rejuvenation schedule is obtained. The tools used here include continuous-time Markov chain models [9], semi-Markov models [10], and others [11].

The measurement-based approach the goal is to collect some data from the system and then quantify and validate the effect of aging in system resources [3]. The work presented in [2] considers several algorithms for prediction of resource exhaustion, mainly based on curve-fitting algorithms. Our previous work [8] used spline-based aging models to obtain optimized rejuvenation schedules. While these results are related to this work, the focus in [8] is on a single server or application.

The Recovery Oriented Computing (ROC) [6,12] project form Stanford and Berkeley focuses on minimizing the negative side effects of the rejuvenation or in general recovery phases. While the ROC-based approaches can substantially increase the up time, they require modifications of the application code.

Object and process-level migration are very well-studied techniques for providing fault-tolerance in distributed systems [13,14]. However, they add substantial cost to the software development and increase the overall system complexity.

Moreover, they do not guarantee resilience against aging, as the faulty process/object state might be migrated as well. Checkpointing-based schemes [15] suffer from similar drawbacks. In contrast, the approach discussed here does not require code modifications and can be used with legacy or black-box software.

Virtualization has proved as a successful tool for management of complex IT-environments and it is emerging as a technique to increase system reliability [16,7]. It has been exploited in [16] for proactive migration of MPI tasks from health-deteriorating to healthy hardware nodes. Work presented in [7] uses virtual machines with application replica to completely eliminate the service outage during the rejuvenation. Contrary to this work we consider a scenario of multiple simultaneously active replicas and optimize the rejuvenation schedules.

## 3   Maximizing Performance of Aging Applications

In the following we use the terms performance and throughput interchangeably, where latter is the number of served requests per second. We consider the scenario of an application consisting of two or more *replicas* which provide the same service. The term *cumulative* is used when all replicas are involved, otherwise we speak of an *individual* replica. The *instantaneous performance* $P_X$ of a replica $X$ is defined as the maximum number of requests per time unit which it can handle. An analogous performance definition is assumed for the cumulative case and is denoted as $P_{cum}$.

If $k$ replicas are running simultaneously we can rejuvenate one of them without interruption of availability. During rejuvenation the instantaneous performance (throughput) decreases by about $1/k$. The choice of a proper rejuvenation schedule is critical to guarantee the cumulative performance characteristics. We are especially interested in the *minimum (cumulative) performance* $P_{min}$ and the *average (cumulative) performance* $\bar{P}$ over longer time intervals (many rejuvenation cycles). The earlier is defined as the minimum instantaneous performance accumulated over all $k$ replicas during the whole considered operation interval. The latter is the number of requests served cumulatively divided by the total time in which they have been served.

Due to aging effects the individual instantaneous performance is not constant and so it is represented as a function called *aging profile*. Following the study in [8] we assume that an aging profile is as a function of the number $w$ of served requests since the last rejuvenation, i.e. $P_X = P_X(w)$.

An essential parameter is the number of requests dropped during the rejuvenation by an individual replica. We denote this number by $D$. Its value depends on the actual (and unknown) service rate distribution. However, it can be bound from above as the product of the rejuvenation time and the maximum instantaneous performance of a replica.

### 3.1   Optimizing the Minimum Performance

We consider in the following the problem of maximizing $P_{min}$ for the case of two replicas running simultaneously. When replica $A$ is rejuvenating, $B$ is completely responsible for the cumulative performance, and so the rejuvenation phase of $A$ should be chosen during the highest performance of $B$. This implies that the start of $A's$ rejuvenation should be dependent on the current state of performance of $B$. Since the latter is determined by $P = P(w)$ and $w$, we introduce $d_A$ as the number of requests served by $B$ (since $B's$ rejuvenation) which we count until $A$ should be rejuvenated. We call $d_A$ the *delay* of $A$, and define $d_B$ analogously for $B$. Since both replicas are identical, we might assume that the best solution is symmetric, and so $d_A = d_B$.

Our experience shows that the aging profiles usually consists of a *build-up phase* when the performance goes from 0 to a peak, and the *decay phase* when a performance drops monotonically from the peak until a complete crash, see Figure 1. This type of behavior is typical for aging processed caused by successive depletion of resources and widely encountered in software systems, see discussion at the end of Section 5.1. Sometimes secondary aging effects or inherent system characteristics can cause the profile to

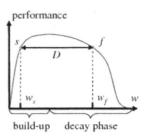

**Fig. 1.** Computing optimal rejuvenation schedule for the case of two identical replicas

be more "random", e.g. exhibit multiple performance "jumps" before crash. Our approach does not work if this randomness is too large. To eliminate these cases, we use the aging modeling schema developed in [8] which provides a test whether the aging behavior is sufficiently "deterministic" and so our assumptions are applicable.

Based on these aging properties, the idea is to schedule the rejuvenation of $A$ such that $B$ is performing at the "top" of its aging profile while $A$ is not available. It is not hard to see that for reasonably small values of $D$ there always exist two unique points $s = (w_s, P_s)$, $f = (w_f, P_f)$ on the aging profile with the following conditions, see Figure 1:

- $s$ is in the build-up phase, and $f$ is in the decay phase,
- their horizontal distance $w_f - w_s$ is exactly $D$,
- their respective performance level is the same, i.e. $P_s = P_f$.

Obviously the solution of finding $P_{min}$ is to set the rejuvenation start of $A$ (i.e. shut down $A$) such that it coincides exactly with $s$, i.e. $d_A = w_s$, and put $A$ into function exactly after $B$ served $D$ requests. With a reasonable value of $D$ this is always possible. Since $B's$ performance does not drop below $P_s = P_f$ during the rejuvenation, $P_{min}$ has at least this value. Moreover, there is no segment of the aging curve of "horizontal length" $D$ s.t. the performance inside the segment is strictly higher than $P_f$, and so this is also the optimum.

After this rejuvenation the roles of the replica are switched, i.e. $B$ is rejuvenated after $A$ has served $d_B = d_A$ requests since its restart. The points $s$ and $f$ can be found via a binary search on the performance ($y$) axis of the aging curve with the curve peak as the upper bound. The reader might note that the value of $d_A$ determines the length of the rejuvenation phase, and so the average number of requests. Therefore, optimization of $P_{min}$ might conflict with the optimization of the average performance.

Figures 2 show that that the build-up phase might not exist. This is a special case of the above discussion, and here the solution is obviously to rejuvenate $B$ right at the start of the other replica. Other types of aging profiles (especially with several local maxima) require further refinement of this approach. Intuitively, such a pair of points can be found via a "sweep" with a horizontal line from above until the intersections of the aging curve with the line form at least one segment whose endpoints fulfill the conditions analogous to those shown in Figure 1.

For $k > 2$ replicas (even identical) finding the solution is even more involved. One approach would be to perform the above "sweep" for any delay combination of the $k - 1$ replicas remaining active. Since this is not feasible, we propose a heuristic optimization described in Section 4.

# 4    Heuristic Optimization of Rejuvenation Schedules

In this section we describe the design of the heuristic rejuvenation scheduler and explain the policies used in our simulations. The basic idea is to use a simulation which evaluates the scheduling policy in combination with a genetic algorithm which searches for optimal policy parameters. Genetic algorithm optimization is a well-known technique which essentially performs a parallel hill climbing [17].

The major case specific part of the this optimization is the evaluation of a candidate scheduling policy by means of a simulation. It emulates the performance behavior of the full set of application replicas over a large number of rejuvenations. The simulation progresses over the number of cumulatively served requests and not over time, i.e. each step corresponds to a change caused by serving a fixed number of requests. In each step the requests are first distributed in the round-robin fashion according to the instantaneous performance of each simulated replica. Then the counters of the number of served requests are updated, and finally the new instantaneous performance levels are computed from the spline-based aging models.

After each step, the new state of the system is essentially determined by the number of requests served by each replica since each rejuvenation. Usage of the spline-represented aging profiles allows for determining the instantaneous performance levels for individual replicas and for the cumulative view. During the simulation the minimum cumulative performance and the average cumulative performance are recorded and later returned as the results.

The implementation has been done in Matlab 2006b. In the genetic optimization the maximum number of generations was 100 and the population size was set to 40. The running time of a single optimization was always below 1 minute on single core of an Intel Core Duo T2600 processor. These parameters were chosen to keep the running time low without affecting the quality of results.

### 4.1    Rejuvenation Policies

In this process each rejuvenation is initiated according to the current policy and its parameters. We tested two classes of policies:

- *delay based*: the least performing replica $X$ (usually "oldest") is rejuvenated when the most recently restarted ("youngest") replica has served at least $d_X$ requests,
- *performance based*: the least performing replica $X$ is rejuvenated when the cumulative performance drops below a certain level $Q_X$.

Each policy is thus determined by its type and the vector of parameter values which are subject to optimization. We have also experimented with the variation that the parameters $d_X$ and $Q_X$ depend both on the replica $X$ to be rejuvenated and the "youngest" replica $Y$, i.e. we have then $d_{X,Y}$ and $Q_{X,Y}$. However, the used profiles and the request distribution scheduling implied that the order of rejuvenation of the replicas remain the same, and so the pairs $X$, $Y$ are uniquely determined by $X$ or $Y$.

At the start of the simulation the replicas are added (or "started") subsequently. In the delay based case the second replica is added after the first has served $d_1$ requests, the third is started after the second has served $d_2$ requests etc. For the performance based policy the next replica is started after the previously started replica has served 10.000 requests (in the subsequent rejuvenations these shifts adjust according to the cumulative performance level). In the simulation we do not consider the initial phase and start recording performance levels when all replicas are up.

## 5    Experimental Studies

### 5.1    Experimental Setup

For our study we used data from two web service applications. Table 1 summarizes these datasets and their characteristics. For each case or a combination of settings we performed a run until complete crash to model aging by sending service requests with a constant rate exceeding the capacity of the server. The un-served requests have been dropped by the server and were not counted. We recorded the throughput (of served requests) as a function of time and as the number of served requests.

The first application is Apache Axis 1.3. We have conducted two sets of studies for this case. The first is used for observing the virtualization overhead (datasets $V_1, \ldots, V_4$), see Section 5.2. Here we run several replica ($k = 1, \ldots, 4$ in $V_k$) of the Axis server simultaneously, each in a separate virtual machine. Details on the parameters of the servers, virtual machines and the replicas can be found in Section 4.2.5 of [7]. The second set of experiments ($A1$ and $A2$) with Apache Axis 1.3 has been performed to record the consistency of the aging behavior and the aging profile of this server. These experiments used a non-virtualized scenario.

Depending on the maximum number of total connections the collected data gives rise to datasets $A1$ and $A2$, where the maximum number of connections for $A1$ was 20 and 25, whereas for $A2$ it was 50 and 100. The time needed for rejuvenation of a replica was about 10 seconds for this application. For more details see [8].

The second type of application was a Java implementation [18] of the TPC-W benchmark which created datasets $T1$, $T2$ and $T3$. This benchmark has been run with XEN virtual machines on top of Linux

**Table 1.** Used datasets and their characteristics (VM = operated in a virtual machine)

| Name | Application | VM | Aging | # Runs |
|------|-------------|-----|-------|--------|
| $V_1$-$V_4$ | Axis 1.3 | yes | natural | 5 |
| $A1,A2$ | Axis 1.3 | no | natural | 6 |
| $T1,T2,T3$ | TPC-W | yes | memory leak | 5 |

2.6.16.21-0.25-smp. Since the original TPC-W implementation did not show any visible aging problem, we implemented a small fault-injector that works as a resource parasite: it consumes system resources in competition with the application [19]. The only difference between each setting was the size of the memory leak injected at every request, namely 1024 bytes ($T1$), 768 bytes ($T2$) and 512 bytes ($T3$). The rejuvenation time for the TPC-W software ranged between 12 and 15 seconds, with 13.6 seconds on average. Further information on the configuration values can be found in Section 4.1.3 of [7].

To obtain spline-based models of aging we followed the approach presented in [8], and obtained models accurate within at most 8% tolerance. The accuracy of these models confirm that the studied aging process depend essentially on the *number* of served requests, and are independent on the request rate distribution or its burstiness [8]. While not all aging processes has this property, those caused by unreleased resources (such as memory leaks) are very likely to exhibit this behavior. This is a large class of aging processes (all processes encountered by the authors are of this type) which supports the experimental validity of the approach.

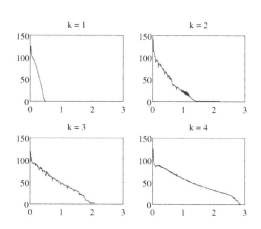

**Fig. 2.** Average cumulative throughput for different number of replicas as a function of time (x-axis: time in hours, y-axis: throughput in requests / second)

## 5.2   Virtualization Overhead and Delaying the Aging Process

According to the results in [7] running the Axis server on top of XEN virtual machine introduced a 12% overhead compared to its performance directly on Linux. We evaluate here the overhead of running different numbers of replicas in a virtualized environment by considering the throughput of $k$ virtualized replicas of datasets $V_1, ..., V_4$ ($k = 1, ..., 4$). Table 2 implies that the overhead is not dependent on $k$. Simultaneously Figure 2 shows that using more replicas delays the aging process: if an application without replicas crashes after $x$ requests, the replicated case crashes after $k\,x$ requests. This is the case as the aging behavior for the Axis application depends on the number of served requests. When using $k$ replicas in parallel, each of them has to serve around $1/k$ requests per time and therefore it lives $k$−times longer.

**Table 2.** Performance measures for different number $k$ of replicas

|       | # served req. (in 100s) in interval $[min, min]$ | | | | | | peak throughput $[req./sec]$ | time to crash $[min]$ |
|-------|---------|---------|---------|---------|----------|------|------|------|
|       | [5, 10] | [5, 15] | [5, 30] | [5, 60] | [5, 120] | all  |      |      |
| $k = 1$ | 280   | 510     | 790     | 790     | 790      | 790  | 126  | 30   |
| $k = 2$ | 279   | 525     | 1173    | 1852    | 2026     | 2026 | 141  | 84   |
| $k = 3$ | 275   | 540     | 1244    | 2299    | 3258     | 3264 | 119  | 124  |
| $k = 4$ | 260   | 521     | 1261    | 2480    | 4059     | 4075 | 126  | 171  |

## 5.3   Schedules with Optimized Minimum and Average Performance

In this section we present the results of the optimization. We distinguish between policies with one parameter and policies with different parameters. Policies with one parameter represent the most common case, as normally all application replicas should have the same aging profile.

We have first performed the optimization of the minimal performance by the analytical approach from Section 3. The values of $d$ are as follows: $A1+A1$: 21600, $A2 + A2$: 197500, $T1 + T1$: 13000, $T2 + T2$ and $T3 + T3$: both 0. They agree within a reasonable error with the results obtained from the heuristic approach for policies with one parameter (Table 3 - case $T2 + T2$ is not included there). This verifies that the simulation is correct. The latter table does not include cases with the performance based scheduling policy as this approach turned out to be more sensitive to parameter variations (see discussion below).

**Table 3.** Optimization results by the simulation approach using 1-parameter policies (objective: ave = average performance, min = minimum performance)

| Cases | $A1 + A1$ | | $T1 + T1$ | | $T3 + T3$ | | $A1 + A1 + A1$ | | $T1 + T1 + T1$ | | $A1 + A1$ | |
|-------|-------|-------|-------|-------|-------|------|-------|-------|-------|-------|------|------|
| Policy |       | | | delay | | | | | | | perf. | |
| Objective | ave | min | ave | min | ave | min | ave | min | ave | min | ave | min |
| $P_{min}$ | 422 | 433 | 55 | 56 | 56 | 57 | 833 | 839 | 111 | 112 | 302 | 297 |
| $P_{ave}$ | 760 | 746 | 110 | 109 | 110 | 57 | 1138 | 1122 | 165 | 164 | 682 | 710 |
| $d$ or $Q$ | 29771 | 20260 | 35688 | 14139 | 17813 | 0 | 18946 | 12726 | 25682 | 9810 | 600 | 610 |

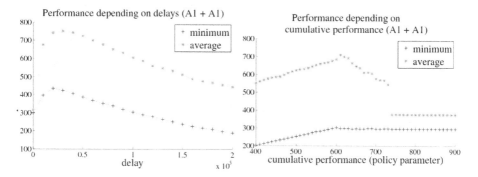

**Fig. 3.** Average and minimum performance plots for dataset A1 with two replicas. Left: delay based policy, right: performance based policy.

Table 4 contains the results from the heuristic approach for policies with different parameters. It shows that an optimization for the average or minimum performance results in different delays.

The heuristic optimization and simulation are illustrated by two different kind of plots: simulation plots and range plots. Simulation plots show the performance history of the individual replica and the cumulative performance history depending on the number of processed requests. Contrary to this, range plots show the minimum and average performance depending on the parameter value of the rejuvenation policy.

Figure 3 shows a range plot with the performance of two identical replicas depending on either a delay based or a performance based scheduling policy. The peaks of the curves show that the optimized policy parameters are different for the optimized minimum performance and the optimized average performance. An optimization for both performance measures at the same time is not possible in this case. The results of the range plot with a performance based scheduling policy show that choosing the right value for rejuvenation is more important than with the delay based policy. If the chosen value is too high the performance of the replicas drops fast. Also this policy is less resilient to variations in the system than a delay based policy.

As an example we show a simulation plot for a combination of different replicas (Figure 4). This is a simulation run with a delay based policy. The delays are

**Table 4.** Optimization results by the simulation approach using 2 or 3-parameter policies

| Cases | $A1 + A2$ | | $T1 + T3$ | | $T2 + T3$ | | $T1 + T2 + T3$ | |
|---|---|---|---|---|---|---|---|---|
| Objective | ave | min | ave | min | ave | min | ave | min |
| $P_{min}$ | 420 | 431 | 54 | 56 | 54 | 56 | 108 | 110 |
| $P_{ave}$ | 761 | 752 | 78 | 106 | 109 | 59 | 164 | 137 |
| $d_1$ | 38552 | 22819 | 45111 | 0 | 51438 | 0 | 44357 | 0 |
| $d_2$ | 21434 | 22334 | 7337 | 12733 | 14243 | 1 | 28157 | 1 |
| $d_3$ | - | - | - | - | - | - | 823 | 1 |

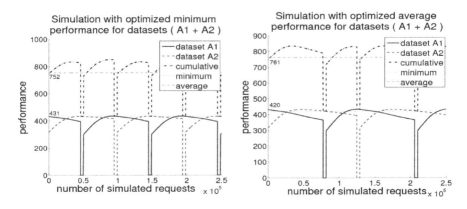

**Fig. 4.** Simulated performance of individual replicas (lower part) and cumulative performance (upper part). Left: delays optimized for minimum performance, right: delays optimized for average performance (each with two different replica $A1 + A2$).

those which were gained from the optimization described in Section 4. In settings with identical replicas, the delays have the same values. The plots confirm the results from the range plots. Optimization for the minimum performance lead to different delays than an optimization for the average performance.

## 6   Conclusions

Our results show that optimization of the rejuvenation schedules of simultaneously active application replicas is a practical and effective approach to combat software aging without sacrificing availability and performance. Since this approach does not require software changes, it offers a simple and non-intrusive way to reducing management costs of aging application in SOA-based environments.

Future work will include experiments with an implementation under real-world conditions to verify the practical efficacy of the approach. Furthermore, we plan to extend the approach to non-deterministic aging profiles and transient failures.

## References

1. Avritzer, A., Weyuker, E.: Monitoring smothly degrading systems for increased dependability. Empirical Software Engineering 2(1), 59–77 (1997)
2. Castelli, V., Harper, R., Heidelberg, P., Hunter, S., Trivedi, K., Vaidyanathan, K., Zeggert, W.: Proactive management of software aging. IBM Journal Research & Development 45 (2001)
3. Garg, S., van Moorsel, A., Vaidyanathan, K., Trivedi, K.: A methodology for detection and estimation of software aging. In: 9th International Symposium on Software Reliability Engineering, pp. 282–292 (1998)

4. Vaidyanathan, K., Trivedi, K.S.: A measurement-based model for estimation of resource exhaustion in operational software systems. In: 10th IEEE International Symposium on Software Reliability Engineering, pp. 84–93. IEEE Computer Society Press, Los Alamitos (1999)
5. Vaidyanathan, K., Trivedi, K.S.: A comprehensive model for software rejuvenation. IEEE Trans. Dependanble and Secure Computing 2, 1–14 (2005)
6. Brown, A.B., Patterson, D.A.: Embracing failure: A case for recovery-oriented computing. In: High Performance Transaction Processing Symposium (2001)
7. Silva, L.M., Alonso, J., Silva, P., Torres, J., Andrzejak, A.: Using virtualization to improve software rejuvenation. In: IEEE International Symposium on Network Computing and Applications, IEEE Computer Society Press, Los Alamitos (2007)
8. Andrzejak, A., Silva, L.: Deterministic models of software aging and optimal rejuvenation schedules. In: 10th IFIP/IEEE Symposium on Integrated Management, IEEE Computer Society Press, Los Alamitos (2007)
9. Huang, Y., Kintala, C., Kolettis, N., Fulton, N.: Software rejuvenation: Analysis, module and applications. In: FTCS-25 (1995)
10. Dohi, T., Goseva-Popstojanova, K., Trivedi, K.S.: Statistical non-parametric algorithms to estimate the optimal software rejuvenation schedule. In: Pacific Rim International Symp. Dependable Computing, pp. 77–84 (2000)
11. Garg, S., Puliafito, A., Telek, M., Trivedi, K.S.: Analysis of preventive maintenance in transactions based software systems. IEEE Transactions on Computers 47, 96–107 (1998)
12. Candea, G., Kiciman, E., Zhang, S., Fox, A.: Jagr: An autonomous self-recovering application server. In: 5th Int Workshop on Active Middleware Services (2003)
13. Chakravorty, S., Mendes, C.L., Kalé, L.V.: Proactive fault tolerance in MPI applications via task migration. In: 13th HiPC (2006)
14. Douglis, F., Ousterhout, J.K.: Transparent process migration: Design alternatives and the sprite implementation. Software — Practice and Experience 21, 757–785 (1991)
15. Stellner, G.: Cocheck: Checkpointing and process migration for MPI. In: 10th IPPS 1996, pp. 526–531 (1996)
16. Nagarajan, A., Mueller, F., Engelmann, C., Scott, S.: Proactive fault tolerance for HPC with xen virtualization. In: ICS 2007 (2007)
17. Man, K.F., Tang, K.S., Kwong, S.: Genetic Algorithms: Concepts and Designs. Springer, Heidelberg (1999)
18. Manjhi, A.: TPC-W in Java on Tomcat and MySQL. Carnegie Mellon University (2005)
19. Gross, K., Bhardwai, V., Bickford, R.: Proactive detection of software aging mechanisms in performance critical computers. In: 27th Anual IEEE/NASA Software Engineering Symposium (2002)

# Dependency Detection Using a Fuzzy Engine

Dimitrios Dechouniotis[1], Xenofontas Dimitropoulos[2], Andreas Kind[2],
and Spyros Denazis[1]

[1] University of Patras, Rion Patras 26500, Greece
[2] IBM Zurich Research Laboratory, 8803 Rueschlikon, Switzerland
{ddexouni,sdena}@ece.upatras.gr, {xed,ank}@zurich.ibm.com

**Abstract.** The discovery of dependencies between components of a network can reveal relationships among components of multi-tier applications and the underlying IT infrastructure, such as servers and databases. Knowledge of these dependencies is thus important for the management of large distributed, heterogeneous and virtualized systems, where it is difficult to maintain an accurate view of how network assets are functionally connected. In this paper we present a passive method that uses attributes of traffic flow records and derives traffic dependencies among network components using a flexible fuzzy inference mechanism. Simulations and evaluation with real traffic traces show the applicability of the approach for flow-based dependency detection.

## 1 Introduction

In the past several years, a result of the rapid growth of the Internet is the development of distributed, heterogeneous and virtualized networks. Monitoring and management of such systems have become a critical issue. The purpose of a management system is to monitor vital attributes of network in an automatic manner and to take action whenever needed. Furthermore, with the rapid evolution of enterprise networks, many different applications and services are being developed. Most of them are distributed and consist of different components. Availability and performance of these services are important for revenue-generating business processes, so enterprises enter service level agreement (SLA) with Internet service providers (ISPs). The monitoring of the performance of the services, according to the SLA, is a crucial issue of network management.

Due to the financial impact of SLAs, there is great research interest in service management and integrated management tools that automatically monitor the performance of multi-tier applications and that can also autonomously handle arising problems. A functional and structural model of a service or application is a powerful tool for the maintenance, expansion and performance analysis of the service. It helps administrators to detect which component of a service is responsible for a possible failure and which other business processes will be affected. These two problems are known as root cause analysis and business impact analysis, respectively. The first step in building an operational model of a service is to completely understand the interaction of the network components that comprise an integrated application. Because of the complexity and the heterogeneity

A. Clemm, L.Z. Granville, and R. Stadler (Eds.): DSOM 2007, LNCS 4785, pp. 110–121, 2007.
© IFIP International Federation for Information Processing 2007

of enterprise networks, there are many types of relationships and dependencies between the parts of multi-tier applications. In [1], Keller et al. presents a good definition and classification of the different types of dependencies among service components. This classification is based on many characteristics, such as locality, domain, component type and activity as well as dependency detection method and strength.

Our work focuses on the problem of detecting dependencies between IT components by examining attributes of flow records in enterprise networks. This is particularly useful for administrators in order to predict the impact of low service performance and to detect which network component is at the root of a problem. It potentially reduces recovery time and is useful to predict the impact of maintenance operations on the performance of the entire system. Furthermore, it is a powerful designing tool for expanding the IT infrastructure, reducing operational costs and complexity as well as decoupling the various parts of different services and business processes.

This work investigates the problem of detecting dependencies between network components in order to reveal relationships between parts of multi-tier applications and, more generally, of business processes. We present a novel method of discovery using attributes of traffic records and a fuzzy inference engine. A fuzzy inference mechanism is appropriate for dependency detection for two major reasons. First, there are many quantitative features so that it is more natural to use a modelling approach in terms of fuzziness than based on sharp boundary intervals. Second, the fuzziness employed in representing these features helps to smooth the strict separation of dependency versus non-dependency.

The remainder of the paper is structured as follows. The next section discusses related work. Section 3 contains an analytical description of our algorithm, which is based on collecting traffic attributes of network and analyzing them with the help of a fuzzy system. Section 4 describes the implementation and evaluation of the approach using real data as well as some simulations. In Section 5, we discuss the limitations of our method. The paper finishes with the conclusions and an outlook in Section 6.

## 2   Related Work

Kind et al. [2] present an ad hoc passive method that uses NetFlow records and the start and end timestamps to discover relationships between network assets. A similar approach is presented in [3], which uses the start and end timestamps of a flow record to produce dependency graphs between network components. Chen et al. provide a framework in [4] to identify which components are used to satisfy each individual request by instrumenting the middleware and the communication layer between network components. Brown et al. [5] present an active dependency discovery method to determine the dynamic relationships between parts of a service. Kar et al. [6] use data collected from system information repositories, such as the IBM AIX Object Data Manager (ODM), which keeps track of the installed software package, file sets and their versions to enable a dependency analysis for managing application services. Another ad hoc technique is proposed in [7], the authors use Leslie graphs to represent the relationships between components of IT systems. A passive statistical approach based on the timestamps of flow records is presented in [8]. It provides a direct dependency estimation method that calculates the probability with which a transaction of a flow is contained in at least one other transaction. Kashima et al. propose a concrete modelling method for discovering direct dependencies by calculating the service call frequency matrix and the service call ratio (SCR) matrix, which reveal dependency values regardless of the work load intensity. In [9], a neural network approach is used for automated generation of service dependency models. The behaviour of hosts was monitored repeatedly by collecting time series of their activities, such as CPU activity of a host, communication bandwidth used by a system. The neural networks are fed with these time series to determine whether there is a dependency. Finally a data-mining technique exists that can be used to discover correlation between data of databases. In [10], the author proposes a method of detecting time correlations in time-series data streams in order to discover service relationships and analyze the business impact analysis.

## 3    Dependency Discovery

We consider the problem of detecting dependencies between IT elements by examining attributes of flow records in enterprise networks. These relationships can be classified into intra-system and inter-system dependencies. Intra-system dependencies are the dependencies between components of an enterprise network located within a single site. Inter-system dependencies describe the relationships between components of an enterprise network that are distributed across more than one site. The existing approaches for identifying relationships can be classified into active and passive methods. The basic idea of active discovery methods is to generate traffic flows from a starting point and use an iterative algorithm to explore the entire network up to an end point. Passive mapping performs the collection and analysis of traffic characteristics without generating any kind of traffic. The collection of the necessary information can be done by any traffic meter that exports NetFlow/IPFIX flow information, such as many routers and switches (see [11]). NetFlow provides flow-based traffic information, such as source/destination IP address, protocol and source and destination ports. Apart from the tuple that defines a flow, we can collect other attributes such as packet and octet volumes. In our approach, we are interested in detecting dependencies by examining the attributes of flow records. The most important characteristics are the start and end timestamps of flows. By examining these time stamps we would like to decide whether a flow triggers the start of another flow. This trigger can be interpreted on the functional level of a service as the connection of two different components to execute a specific task that is part of the same service or business process. By identifying all these relationships between network components of a service, we can obtain a clear overview in terms of which elements of network infrastructure are responsible for the provision of a particular service and business process. Before we formalize what a flow dependency is, it is essential for our algorithm to introduce a formal definition of the flow concept.

### 3.1 Flows and Events

We define a flow $f$ as a 3-tuple of the following basic traffic attributes

$$f = (srcIP, dstIP, dstPort) \in F,$$

where $srcIP$ and $dstIP$ are the IP address of source and destination host, respectively, and $dstPort$ is the TCP/UDP service port of destination host. The set of all flows is denoted by $F$. We only use $dstPort$ because it can be assumed that in most TCP-based server environments the destination port is identical to the service port. The source port is, however, randomly chosen and thus not useful for further analysis. If we had used source port for flow definition, then two different requests from the same source host to the same destination would create two different flows. This is not desirable because these two flows are related with the same task. An event—typically a NetFlow record—is defined as

$$e = (f, t_s, t_e, octs, pkts) \in E,$$

where $f$ is the flow as defined and $t_s$ and $t_e$ are the start and end timestamps of a flow event respectively, $octs$ and $pkts$ are the number of bytes and packets of a flow respectively. The set of all events is denoted as $E$. Finally we denote the set of all events of a given flow $f$ as

$$E(f) = \{e \in E \mid f_e = f\}.$$

The $dstPort$ cannot be assigned to an application but it can be only an indication of it, because nowadays many applications use unpublished or dynamically assigned ports. By the definitions of flow and event and analyzing the event attributes, we can easily distinguish whether a specific host acts as server or client. As a server always accepts requests in a specific port, all requests from the same source host are represented by the same flow. This fact can be exploited for focusing our attention on some entities, such as server and databases, which are integral components of multi-tier distributed services and applications. Running our algorithm for extended time periods many dependencies that are not so obvious will reveal such as the use of a secondary or backup server.

### 3.2 Flow Pair and Event Pair

An event can present the attributes of a connection between two hosts, but it cannot reveal any relationship among many hosts that are integral parts of a process or service. Nowadays, most of the applications and services are multi-tier. This means that they are based on different individual components, which are distributed and strongly depended one on the other. Hence, the main goal of our algorithm is to identify network assets that are parts of a multi-tier application and to measure the strength of their dependency. The basic principle of our approach is to identify which flow pairs (or chains of flows) occur more often than other pairs do. The existence of specific frequent flow pairs can show a functional dependency between specific hosts. For the aforementioned reason we must define what a flow pair is. We consider that any two flows in $F$ define a flow pair if the following two conditions are satisfied:

- the destination IP address of the first flow is identical to the source IP address of the second flow.
- the destination of the second flow is not identical to the source of the first flow.

We exclude the case that the destination IP of second flow is identical to the source IP of the first flow, because this reveal a client-server relationships. Since we are interested in detecting relationship between more than two hosts that are components of multi-tier services, client-server relationships cannot reveal such kind of dependencies. Assuming any two different flows $f_i$ and $f_j$ in $F$, where

$$f_i = (srcIP_i, dstIP_i, dstPort_i)$$

$$f_j = (srcIP_j, dstIP_j, dstPort_j)$$

the flow pair function is defined as

$$f_p(f_i, f_j) = \begin{cases} 1 \ if \ dstIP_i = srcIP_j \ \wedge \\ \quad srcIP_i \neq dstIP_j \\ 0 \ \text{otherwise.} \end{cases}$$

After the definition of the flow-pair function, we define the set of all event pairs for any two different flows $f_i$ and $f_j$ in $F$. Assuming any two different events $e_k, e_l$ in $E$,

$$e_k = (f_i, t_{sk}, t_{ek}, octs_k, pkts_k) \in E(f_i).$$

$$e_l = (f_j, t_{sl}, t_{el}, octs_l, pkts_l) \in E(f_j).$$

the set of all event pairs $P$ for any two flows $f_i$ and $f_j$ in $F$, with $f_i \neq f_j$, is defined as

$$P(f_i, f_j) = \{(e_k, e_l) \mid 0 \leq t_{sl} - t_{sk} < t_{max} \ \wedge \ f_p(f_i, f_j) = 1\}.$$

As shown in the above definition, two events are considered an event pair if they satisfy the flow-pair function and the difference of their start timestamps is less than $t_{max}$. The main idea of using this time difference as a criterion of dependency is that flow events close in time are likely to be really dependent. The value of $t_{max}$ is critical for the success of the algorithm. If it is too small, then dependencies between heavily-loaded servers can not be identified. On the other side, if it is too large, then it is possible to identify false dependencies between hosts that they do not have any operational relationship. Also $t_{max}$ depends mostly on the time that a server or a database needs to process a request and reply. This processing time varies and depends on the complexity of the request and the work-load of the server. From our experience a logical value for $t_{max}$ can be 10 seconds.

### 3.3   Confidence Variables

The time difference of the start timestamps of two events cannot be a safe metric of dependency by itself. In heavily-loaded networks there is high probability of discovering many erroneous event pairs, which were created by chance. To reduce the erroneously recognized dependencies between hosts, we use a metric to express how confident we are that an event pair is real. We define two confidence variables based on the following concepts:

- If a specific event pair occurs many times, then our confidence for this pair is high.
- Assume that there is a set of event pairs between any two flows $f_1$ and $f_2$. If the ratio between the number of these event pairs and the number of events $e_1$ and $e_2$ that do not belong to any of these event pairs is high, then we are more confident that the event pair exhibits a dependency.

We encode the previous considerations in the math expressions of two confidence variables $c_1(f_1, f_2)$ and $c_2(f_1, f_2)$:

- $c_1(f_1, f_2) = \frac{|P(f_1, f_2)|}{\mu}$,

where $|P(f_1, f_2)|$ is the number of event pairs and $\mu$ is the average number of elements of all sets of all event pairs described by the expression:
$$\mu = \frac{\sum_{i=1..m} \sum_{j=1..m} P(f_i, f_j)}{m}$$

- $c_2(f_1, f_2) = \frac{|P(f_1, f_2)|}{|P(f_1, f_2)| + |E(f_{1w})| + |E(f_{2w})|}$

where $|P(f_1, f_2)|$ is the same as before, $|E(f_{1w})|$ and $|E(f_{2w})|$ are the numbers of sets $E(f_{1w})$ and $E(f_{2w})$, respectively, which are defined, given a $P(f_1, f_2)$, as follows:
$$E(f_{1w}) = \{e_1 \mid e_1 \epsilon E(f_1) \ and \ e_1 \notin P(f_1, f_2)\}$$
$$E(f_{2w}) = \{e_2 \mid e_2 \epsilon E(f_2) \ and \ e_2 \notin P(f_1, f_2)\}.$$

In other words, $|E(f_{1w})|$ and $|E(f_{2w})|$ represent how many events of flows $f_1$ and $f_2$, respectively, do not participate in the creation of an event pair that is an element of set $P(f_1, f_2)$. We can also define different confidence variables or a combination of the variables defined above.

### 3.4   Fuzzy System

Fuzzy systems have demonstrated their ability to solve different kinds of problems in various applications. Our method of discovering relationships between network hosts and service components is based on fuzzy logic. We can build a fuzzy inference engine that can determine how strong or weak the dependency of an event pair is. The advantages of a fuzzy inference mechanism are that it has a simple and flexible structure and can be used in different networks. In addition, it can describe, in an intuitive and user-friendly manner, the problem of detecting relationships without making assumptions about the nature of the

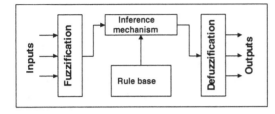 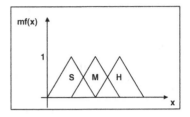

**Fig. 1.** Structure of a fuzzy system and membership functions

correlated traffic. But, in fact, these assumptions may not be valid or absolutely correct. Also, fuzzy logic helps to smooth the strict separation of dependency and non-dependency and the quantitative features (e.g., time and confidence variables) can be modelled in terms of fuzziness rather than using hard boundary intervals. The fuzzy system is based on the transformation of our knowledge into a set of fuzzy rules. Input and output of the fuzzy system are expressed by the linguistic values of the fuzzy variables of the system. A fuzzy system [12] (Fig. 1) is composed of the following four elements:

- A fuzzification interface, which converts the inputs into fuzzy information that the inference mechanism can easily use to activate and apply rules.
- A rule base (a set of If-Then rules), which contains a fuzzy logic quantification of the linguistic description of our knowledge.
- An inference mechanism which emulates the expert's decision making in interpreting and applying knowledge about how to compute the correct output.
- A defuzzification interface, which converts the conclusions of the inference mechanism into numerical output.

Note that the fuzzification and defuzzification interfaces of a fuzzy system have to be described in greater detail. Each input and output of the system is described by linguistic values and their membership functions (Fig. 1). Linguistic values are terms, such as LOW, HIGH, MEDIUM, that intuitively describe the fuzzy input/output parameters. Membership functions of a linguistic value describe the *degree of certainty* of the numeric value of an input or output to be classified under the specific linguistic value. Typical membership functions can be triangular, such as that at the right side in Fig. 1, but can also have different shapes, like Gaussian or trapezoid. One interesting property of membership functions is that a numerical input can be converted into two linguistic values simultaneously. This feature is appropriate for modelling quantitative attributes that do not use hard boundary intervals like time and confidence variables.

### 3.5   Fuzzy System for Dependency Detection

In our approach, we build a fuzzy system with three input parameters and one output parameter. The input parameter are the following

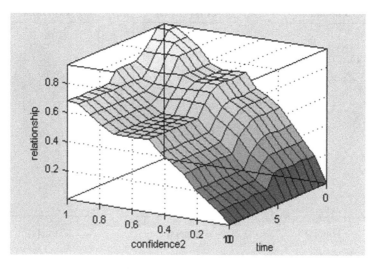

**Fig. 2.** Dependency surface

- The difference between the start timestamps of two event of a event pair, $dt = t_{s2} - t_{s1}$.
- The confidence variable $c_1(f_1, f_2)$ of an event pair, as defined above, which represents our confidence to the most frequent event pairs.
- The confidence variable $c_2(f_1, f_2)$ of an event pair, as defined above, which is used to separate correctly correlated from wrongly identified event pairs.

The output of the fuzzy system is the degree of dependency for every event pair, $dep(f_1, f_2)\epsilon[0, 1]$. Each of the three input/output parameter are described by five linguistic values (VERY SMALL, SMALL, MEDIUM, HIGH, VERY HIGH) with triangular membership functions. We select triangle membership functions because they are simple and can represent the fuzziness of input and output parameter in a effective manner. The rule base consisted of 125 rules, which can describe all possible combinations of the input parameters. Furthermore, rules can be merged into a smaller set because some of them can be merged into a single rule. Another interesting feature of fuzzy systems, which illustrates their ability of describing complex systems, is the *control surface*. The name comes from the use of fuzzy system to control complex industrial systems and processes. In our approach, we can call it *dependency surface* because it presents all possible values of a dependency according to input values. Fig. 2 depicts the dependency surface for $c_1(f_1, f_2) = 85$ and every possible value of time difference and confidence variable $c_2(f_1, f_2)$. This figure reveals that a fuzzy system can convert our knowledge -expressed in linguistic terms- into a non-linear surface that represents the inference mechanism of extracting dependencies between events. We can easily adapt our fuzzy inference engine and its dependency surface by changing the rule-base and the membership functions of linguistic values. This feature allows us to change the properties of our fuzzy mechanism and adapt it according to the various attributes of enterprise networks. This surface is more

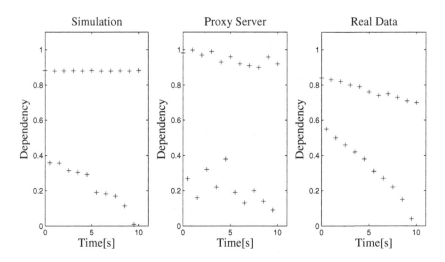

**Fig. 3.** Dependency using known event pairs, a proxy server and real data

flexible and effective than an assumption that the correlation between flows and events can be modelled by a specific time distribution.

## 4    Implementation and Evaluation

The dependency algorithm was tested in three different scenarios. Firstly, we ran some simulations generating random events and mixed them with a known number of related events. In the second evaluation test, some hosts were connected to a network through a proxy server. The hosts generated events by browsing on the Internet. Our algorithm analyzed these flow events with the aim to discover the known relationships. We use flow-based network profiling system developed in the IBM Aurora project [13] for the collection and processing of flow events. The system can collect, store, and analyze NetFlow/IPFIX records. Finally we tested our algorithm using real flows from a high-speed enterprise network to discover relationships between servers. The steps in the algorithm for dependency detection are the following,

i Parse NetFlow records and sort events by start timestamps.
ii Walk through events with a time window of $t_{\max}$ and compute confidence variables for each event pair.
iii Walk through events and compute the output of the fuzzy system (dependency) for each event pair.
iv Sort event pairs by their dependency.
v Generate a file of event pairs having a high dependency.

In the first evaluation test, we generate files containing a large number of random events and inject it events that create specific event pairs. We analyze these data with our algorithm to test whether it can identify and separate the known event pairs from wrongly identified event pairs. The results show that the algorithm identifies all correct event pairs and distinguishes them correctly from the false event pairs produced. The left part of Fig. 3 illustrates the results of simulation using $5x10^4$ random events mixed with events which create 10 known event pairs. The correlated events are produced by random Gaussian distributions with a mean value between 0 and $t_{max} = 10$ and unitary standard deviation. The dependency for correct event pairs is around 0.9. The dependency of flow event pairs that were randomly generated ranges between 0 and 0.36. This means that our algorithm managed to identify successfully all real pairs, assign them large dependency values and distinguish them from the false pairs having lower dependency values. Furthermore we compared our method with the algorithm presented in [2]. We used exactly the same simulation data to test the two algorithms. The results in Table 3 show that our algorithm is more accurate. The algorithm in [2] failed to identify event pairs, if the difference of their start timestamp is large ($\geq 7s$). Also the correlation confidence value in [2] was very low, almost zero, for the pre-known event pairs and it was impossible to separate them from the erroneously generated. On the contrary the fuzzy inference engine identified successfully all the real event pairs and assigned them high dependency value. Table 1 illustrates the comparison of the two methods.

**Table 1.** Accuracy of Fuzzy Inference Engine and Time Correlation Algorithm

|  | Fuzzy Inference Engine | Time Correlation Algorithm |
|---|---|---|
| identified known event pairs | 10 | 7 |
| dependency value of known pairs | 0.9 | 0 |

In the second test, we used a network setup with client machines in a subnet that is connected to the Internet using a proxy server. The machines produce ca. $10^5$ events per hour when browsing on the Internet. The algorithm for discovering dependencies processed the collected events in order to identify the relationship between individual hosts, proxy server and web server. On the middle of Fig. 3, the graph shows the highest dependent event pairs ($dep \epsilon [0.9, 0.99]$), which correspond to the events that represent the connections between 10 hosts to the proxy server and the connections between the proxy server and the web server. Many wrong event pairs were produced, but their dependency was low. Fig. 3 also shows the 10 false event pairs having the highest dependency. It clearly visible that their dependency is significantly lower than the correct event pairs. Also another advantage of fuzzy system is that the dependency of false event pairs continuously decreased as the time passed.

Finally our algorithm was tested with real data, collected from an enterprise network of 700 hosts. We collect $2.2x10^5$ flow records, which corresponds to one hour of data traffic in a larger enterprise. We applied the fuzzy inference mechanism to detect the relationships between network components of multi-tier services and applications. Most of the event pairs produced (i.e, 96%) were false pairs having a low and very low dependency value. There are about 20 event pairs with a dependency value higher than 0.7. Some of them represent relationships between DNS servers, whereas the remaining event pairs reveal relationships between servers and databases of specific applications. As we can see on the right side of Fig. 3, there is a clear distinction of correct and false pairs. Our algorithm succeeds in identifying real pairs and assigning high dependency value to them. Moreover, it produces low dependency values for wrongly generated event pairs. Also it is not surprising that our algorithm identified few (about 20) event pairs with high dependency value, since correlated flows represent usually a small percentage of the overall traffic load of an enterprise network.

The results of all tests were successful for our algorithm of relationship discovery. In every case, the fuzzy inference mechanism succeeded in identifying all correct event pairs and assigned them high dependency values. Additionally it separated correctly the correct event pairs by assigning low dependency values to the randomly generated event pairs. For the first two tests, the accuracy of the detection algorithm was 100%. The accuracy of our algorithm is also high for the third test. The event pairs with the highest dependency value correspond to correct dependencies between network assets like DNS servers and servers of particular applications. It would be useful to define a threshold value of dependency in order to decide if an event pair correctly represent a dependency. This threshold can vary for different networks, but it should be high (i.e., $\geq 0.7$).

## 5    Limitations

The major limitation of the algorithm is the generation of a large number of false event pairs($\geq 95\%$). Most of them have very low dependency value. However, there are some pairs with high values, because they represent some network components that are used by more than one application or they are not frequently used. Another limitation is that if the traffic load is very heavy, the number of flow records we have to process can increase the processing time and the computational resources necessary. To reduce the vast amount of data, we can use some NetFlow techniques, like flow aggregation or sampling.

## 6    Conclusion and Future Work

This paper presented an algorithm for discovering relationships between network components using a fuzzy inference engine. Dependencies between certain network assets can correspond to operational relationships between parts of a specific service or application. A fuzzy inference mechanism is appropriate for dependency detection for two major reasons. First, there are many quantitative features, such as time correlation, for which it is more natural to be modelled in terms of fuzziness than using sharp boundary intervals. Second, the fuzziness employed in representing these features helps to smooth the strict separation between dependency and non-dependency. Another advantage of the proposed method is that it is passive so that it does not produce any additional traffic load. To increase the flexibility of our method and reduce the generation of false dependencies, our future work will focus on using fuzzy adaptive and learning techniques based on neural networks and genetic algorithms.

# References

1. Keller, A., Blumenthal, U., Kar, G.: Classification and computation of dependencies for distributed management. In: Proc. of the 5th IEEE Symposium on Computers and Communications ISCC, pp. 78–83. IEEE Computer Society Press, Los Alamitos (2000)
2. Kind, A., Gantenbein, D., Etoh, H.: Relationship discovery with netflow to enable business-driven it management. In: Proc of the First IEEE/IFIP International Workshop on Business-Driven IT Management, BDIM, pp. 63–70 (2006)
3. Gupta, M., Neogi, A., Agarawal, M.K., Kar, G.: Discovering dynamic dependencies in enterprise enviroments for problem determination. In: Proc. of the 14th IEEE/IFIP International Workshop on Distributed Systems: Operations and Management (2003)
4. Chen, M., Kiciman, E., Fratkin, E., Fox, A., Brewer, E.: Pinpoint:problem determination in large,dynamic internet services. In: Proc. of the International Conferance on Dependable Systems and Networks DSN, pp. 595–604 (2002)
5. Brown, A., Kar, G., Keller, A.: An active approach to characterizing dynamic dependencies for problem determination in a distributed environment. In: Proc. of the International IFIP/IEEE Symposium on Intergrated Network Management, pp. 377–390. IEEE Computer Society Press, Los Alamitos (2001)
6. Kar, G., Keller, A., Calo, S.: Managing application services over service provider networks: Architecture and dependency analysis. In: Proc. of the 7th International IFIP/IEEE Network Operations and Management Symposium NOMS, pp. 61–74. IEEE Computer Society Press, Los Alamitos (2000)
7. Bahl, P., Barham, P., Black, R., Chandra, R., Goldszmidt, M., Isaacs, R., Kandula, S., Li, L., MacCormick, J., Maltz, D., Mortier, R., Wawrzoniak, M., Zhang, M.: Discovering dependencies for network management. In: Proc. of the 5th Workshop on Hot Topics in Networks HotNets V, pp. 97–102 (2006)
8. Kashima, H., Tsumura, T., Ide, T., Nogayama, T., Etoh, R.H.H., Fukuda, T.: Network-based problem detection for distributed systems. In: Proc. of the 21th International Conference on Data Engineering ICDE, pp. 978–989 (2005)
9. Ensel, C.: New approach for automated generation of service dependency models. In: Proc. of the 2th Latin American Network Operation and Management Symposium LANOMS (2001)
10. Sayal, M.: Detecting time correlations in time-series data streams. In: HP Technical Report HPL-2004-103 (2004)
11. CISCO: Netflow (2007), http://www.cisco.com/en/US/products/ps6601/product ios protocol group home.html
12. Passino, K., Yurkovich, S.: FUZZY CONTROL. Addison-Wesley, Reading (1998)
13. IBM: Aurora-network traffic analysis and visualization (2007), http://www.zurich.ibm.com/aurora

# Bottleneck Detection Using
# Statistical Intervention Analysis

Simon Malkowski[1], Markus Hedwig[1], Jason Parekh[1], Calton Pu[1], and Akhil Sahai[2]

[1] CERCS, Georgia Institute of Technology,
266 Ferst Drive, Atlanta, GA 30332
{simon.malkowski,markus.hedwig,jason.parekh,
calton}@cc.gatech.edu
[2] HP Laboratories, Palo-Alto, CA
akhil.sahai@hp.com

**Abstract.** The complexity of today's large-scale enterprise applications demands system administrators to monitor enormous amounts of metrics, and reconfigure their hardware as well as software at run-time without thorough understanding of monitoring results. The Elba project is designed to achieve an automated iterative staging to mitigate the risk of violating Service Level Objectives (SLOs). As part of Elba we undertake performance characterization of system to detect bottlenecks in their configurations. In this paper, we introduce our concrete bottleneck detection approach used in Elba, and then show its robustness and accuracy in various configurations scenarios. We utilize a well-known benchmark application, RUBiS (Rice University Bidding System), to evaluate the classifier with respect to successful identification of different bottlenecks.

**Keywords:** Bottleneck detection, statistical analysis, enterprise systems, perforance analysis

## 1 Introduction

Pre-production configuration testing of complex n-tier enterprise application deployment, or *staging*, can be as demanding and complex as the production system itself. System analysts and administrators monitor and analyze a large number of application-specific metrics such as the number of active threads and the number of EJB entity bean instances, along with system-level metrics like CPU usage and disk I/O rate. Any of these resources may cause the system to violate performance service level objectives (SLO), usually specified as service level agreements (SLA). Significantly lower cost and results at higher confidence levels may be produced by automated staging. The latter is an iterative process in the Elba project [11] whereby an application configuration is gradually refined.

The main contribution of this paper is an automated bottleneck detection scheme based on a statistical intervention model. This approach is distinct from our previous work that used machine learning [4]. We introduce a deterministic algorithm, which has proven to be very effective in the Elba environment. The process automatically examines and analyzes the entire metric data derived from the staging experiment

A. Clemm, L.Z. Granville, and R. Stadler (Eds.): DSOM 2007, LNCS 4785, pp. 122–134, 2007.

trials. A limited set of interesting metrics is identified very fast without the need of an extensive training or configuration phase. This set is then ordered according to the degree of correlation with the high-level system performance. We also show that we are able to accurately determine potential bottlenecks in different scenarios. Moreover, the resulting output is easily interpretable due to the intuitive model structure.

The remainder of this paper is organized as follows. Section 2 describes our approach to bottleneck detection using intervention analysis. Section 3 presents the evaluation environment and our results utilizing RUBiS. Section 4 discusses related work, followed by the conclusion.

## 2 Intervention Analysis

An effective staging phase assures system administrators that a hardware/software configuration is capable of handling workloads to be seen during production. Starting at an initial configuration, this phase augments resources allowing the configuration to better satisfy the SLOs. So far our bottleneck detection approaches consisted of a multi-step analysis. If a SLA was not met (SLO-satisfaction drops significantly) in a certain scenario, a three-step detection process began: staging the system with varying workloads and collecting performance data from system-level and application-specific metrics, training a machine learning classifier with the data, and finally querying the trained machine learning classifier to identify potential bottlenecks. Please refer to [4] for more details. While our three-step methodology proved to be successful, it mainly relies on machine learning algorithms to execute the final performance modeling and classification. This implies two typical shortcomings that lie in the nature of the modeling scheme. Firstly, the machine learning classifiers require a training phase. This can be cost-intensive since certain accuracy and robustness levels might be defined *a priori*. Secondly machine learning classifiers produce a model that is not necessarily interpretable in a trivial manner. We discussed suitable interpretations in [4]. Nevertheless, this led to a residual degree of uncertainty in the interpretation of the analysis results.

In this article we propose a novel approach based on statistical techniques, which results in an improvement of our bottleneck detection process in a consistent manner. We introduce an intuitive statistical model, which eliminated the need of machine learning on the one hand. And on the other, we observe that our approach achieves the same high accuracy level at a lower cost (fewer staging trials). Therefore we greatly increase the efficiency of the detection process and enhance the clarity of the final results at the same time.

### 2.1 Assumptions

The following assumptions form the basis of our automated bottleneck methodology. They emphasize the general issues that need to be addressed by any satisfactory detection method and are reflected in previous Elba efforts.

- A single experiment trial is not sufficient to record a conclusive metric vector and thus several trials of varying workloads are required.

- Non-obvious interactions between resources make observation based bottleneck detection a hard problem. Nontrivial correlations have to be examined and the detection method needs to be able to produce a probabilistic result ranking.
- The number of recorded monitoring metrics is very high. It is critical to device an approach that is able to sort through copious metric data automatically.
- The nature and appearance of metrics can vary significantly and they are typically categorized as either system-level or application-specific.
- High utilization of a resource implies high demand from an application while it may not necessarily be indicative of a bottleneck. A detection mechanism has to be capable of distinguishing bottlenecking behavior in terms of resource saturation.
- Especially trend changes in metric graphs are of high importance. In fact we found in our previous work that it was highly effective to examine first derivative approximations instead of the actually recorded values.

## 2.2  The Detection Model

These assumptions together with observations from empirical data analysis suggest a simple performance model. We formulate the latter in terms of statistical intervention analysis, which allows us to formalize the characteristic bottleneck behavior of the system accurately.

First we need to define an exogenous crossover point ($c \in WS$). This specific number of concurrent user sessions can be seen as an intervention point that divides our workload span ($WS$) into two disjunctive intervals:

$$I := \{w \in WS : w < c\} \tag{1}$$

$$I' := \{w \in WS : w \geq c\} \tag{2}$$

In this notation $I$ represents the set of workloads that result in high levels of SLO satisfaction of the system, whereas the satisfaction levels drop significantly when exposed to workloads in $I'$ (intervention effect).

For our purposes we also need to adapt the standard transfer functional model formulation [1]. For any workload $w \in WS$ an impact assessment model for the first difference of any metric value $Y_w$ can be formulated in terms of Equation 3. Note that we use the first difference as approximation of the first derivative consistently with our findings in [4].

$$\nabla Y_w := f(I_w) + N_w + \mu \tag{3}$$

$$I_w := \begin{cases} 1 & \text{for } w \geq c \\ 0 & \text{else} \end{cases} \tag{4}$$

In this formulation $N_w$ is the noise component, and $\mu$ denotes the constant term. The effect of the intervention variable $I_w$ on the metric trend is defined as $f(I_w)$. Following the standard notation, $I_w$ is defined as an indicator function (Equation 4). We can now subtract the noise component from both sides of Equation 1. Since we only have to deal with abrupt and permanent intervention effects we can assume linearity in the metric values. Based on this linearity assumption we introduce $\delta$ as the constant term of the intervention effect, which yields the following formulation:

$$\nabla Y_w - N_w = \delta I_w + \mu \tag{5}$$

In order to characterize the final model in a convenient manner, we define $\mu'$ in Equation 6 which leads to the final model formulation in Equation 7.

$$\mu' = \mu + \delta \tag{6}$$

$$\nabla \tilde{Y}_w = \nabla Y_w - N_w = \begin{cases} \mu & \text{for } w < c \\ \mu' & \text{for } w \geq c \end{cases} \tag{7}$$

This notation emphasizes the importance of the potential change in the trend of the metric value $Y_w$ as the system progresses from $I$ to $I'$ with increasing workload. Moreover, it allows us to establish causality between the model parameters of the low level metric and the high level system performance in an intuitive manner.

### 2.3 Determining an Intervention Point

Since the crossover point ($c$) between $I$ and $I'$ needs to be defined *a priori*, we define an iterative algorithm for our automated analysis scheme. The main idea is to asses the workload when the SLO-satisfaction ($SAT_w$) looses its stability and starts to deteriorate significantly upon further workload increase (i.e. we assume Property 8 and 9). Although the model formulation requires an exact transition point, it is sufficient for our method to approximate $c$ in a qualitative manner (refer to Table 4).

$$\forall_{i \in I} : SAT_i \approx \text{const} \tag{8}$$

$$\forall_{i \in I'} : SAT_i << \frac{1}{|I|} \sum_{j \in I} SAT_j \tag{9}$$

We start at the lowest workload in our dataset and iteratively increase the value by the smallest possible step. In every iteration we calculate a simple heuristic approximation of the ninety-five percent confidence interval of the SLO satisfaction values seen so far. We consider $n_0$ values which resulted from a workload smaller or equal to $w_0 \in WS$ (the workload currently examined).

$$90\% \leq \frac{1}{n_0} \sum_{0 \leq i \leq w_0} SAT_i - \frac{1.96}{\sqrt{n_0 - 1}} \sqrt{\sum_{0 \leq i \leq w_0} (SAT_i - \frac{1}{n_0} \sum_{0 \leq j \leq w_0} SAT_j)^2} \tag{10}$$

We continue to the next iteration as long as the lower bound of the confidence interval is not below ninety percent (Equation 10). Thus we characterize the satisfaction level for the first interval in a binary fashion as suggested by our observations. Once the lower bound of the confidence interval drops below ninety percent we exit the algorithm. The exit point $w^* \in WS$ is a heuristic approximation of the crossover point $c$. We can assume that the SLO satisfaction has deteriorated significantly from its stable level for all workloads greater or equal to $w^*$, which yields the following formulation:

$$\hat{I} := \{w \in WS : w < w^*\} \tag{11}$$

$$\hat{I'} := \{w \in WS : w \geq w^*\} \tag{12}$$

## 2.4 Metrics Selection Scheme

We can now turn to the process of selecting a set of potential bottleneck metrics and discarding all metrics that do not indicate a high resource saturation level. Given a known intervention (SLO begins to deteriorate) we identify all metrics that show evidence of a corresponding plateau (i.e. significant and permanent shift in average value) and a variability change in their first derivative (further evidence for a saturated resource). To identify the candidate set we perform a basic hypothesis-testing scheme adapted from [10]. We define a rule-based analysis process for testing the null hypothesis (13) of constant mean $\mu$ and variance $\sigma$ between the two intervals.

$$H_0 : \quad \hat{\mu} \approx \hat{\mu}' \ \wedge \ \hat{\sigma} \approx \hat{\sigma}' \tag{13}$$

Empirical testing revealed that we have to account for the high variability of the metric data as well as adjust the analysis to specifically detect abrupt plateau shifts. Thus we deviate from the traditional intervention analysis methodology and devise a different testing scheme. We calculate representative quantiles for each interval and metric. The latter characterize the filtered behavior of the data in a more stable manner. We proceed to apply two selection rules in order to limit the group of candidate bottleneck metrics.

$$q_{0.5} > q'_{0.5} \ \wedge \ |q_{0.2} - q_{0.8}| > |q'_{0.1} - q'_{0.9}| \tag{14}$$

Rule 14 accounts for all limited metrics that will saturate at a level of hundred percent. We choose all metrics where the median has decreased as well as where the distance between ten- and ninety-quantile in the second interval is smaller than the distance between twenty- and eighty-quantile in the first interval. If this rule is satisfied we have significant evidence to reject the null hypothesis and assign the metric to a set of potential bottlenecks.

$$q_{0.9} < q'_{0.1} \ \wedge \ q_{0.9} < q'_{0.5} \ \wedge \ q_{0.9} < q'_{0.9} \tag{15}$$

Rule 15 accounts for all metrics that are not limited and show an exponential behavior when the resource saturates. We select all metrics, where all three quantiles of the second interval have increased above the ninety quantile of the first one. Again we reject the $H_0$ if the rule applies. In this manner we have eliminated all metrics that do not show strong indications of bottlenecking behavior near the intervention point and narrowed our attention to potentially interesting resources. Note that the complete empirical derivation of the two decision rules is omitted due to space restrictions. Nevertheless it is based on standard statistical methods and our analysis experience.

## 2.5  Impact Assessment

Once we have identified the set of candidate bottlenecks we can perform a ranking to describe the magnitude of the change. The magnitude reveals the correlation with the intervention and specifically accounts for the exact time when the change in the metric occurred. Hence we design a normalizing ranking function $R$ by calculating the quotient of the absolute mean values of the two intervals:

$$R \coloneqq \left| \frac{\hat{\mu}}{\hat{\mu}'} \right| \qquad (16)$$

This mechanism has two implications. Firstly, we assess how well the crossover point was chosen for each particular metric (temporal ranking). If the split is not exact, the resulting quotient will have a value closer to one. Furthermore, we have to rank how large the relative shift in plateau levels is for each particular metric. We expect bottlenecked metrics that were chosen with Rule 14 (limited metric) to display a very high-ranking value potentially approaching infinity. The slope of the metric values drops from a linear increase to a stable value near zero. Metrics chosen by Rule 15 (unlimited metrics) will show a very low ranking value that is close to zero on the other hand. This means that a moderate positive slope changes to a very strong (exponential) growth. In the following evaluation we will subdivide the candidate set into set one and two. This will simplify the analysis for limited and unlimited metrics, respectively.

# 3  Experimental Evaluation

Rice University Bidding System, is a multi-tiered e-commerce application with 26 interaction types, such as browsing, bidding, buying, or selling items; registering users; and writing or reading comments. RUBiS provides two workload transition matrices describing two different user behaviors: a browsing transition consisting of read-only interactions and a bidding transition, including 15% write interactions. In our experiments the write ratio is extended adding additional variability as explained in [6]. We utilize the bidding transition as well as neighboring write ratios of 10% and 20% in our evaluation since these transitions are better representatives of an auction site workload [2] and provide a more accurate picture [6]. Our system reuses and extends a recent version of RUBiS from ObjectWeb [13]. Generally, experiments show that RUBiS is application-server tier intensive. In other words, it is characteristically constrained by performance in the EJB container tier as introduced in [2].

To execute the staging phase with RUBiS, we employ Apache 2.0.54 as an HTTP server, MySQL max-3.23.58 as a database server with type 4 Connector/J 3.0.11 as a JDBC driver, and JOnAS4.4.6-Tomcat5.5.12 package as an EJB-Web container. Apache HTTP server is equipped with mod_jk so that it can be used as a front-end server to one or several Tomcat engines, and it can forward servlet requests to multiple Tomcat instances simultaneously via AJP 1.2 protocols. We increase the number of the maximum processes of Apache to avoid connection refusals from the server when numerous clients simultaneously request services. We also set the automated increment option on every primary key of the RUBiS databases to prevent duplication errors when clients simultaneously attempt to insert data into a table with the same key. Finally, we adjust JOnAS to have an adequate heap memory size for preventing out-of-memory exceptions during staging.

For gathering system-level metrics, we wrote a shell script to execute Linux/UNIX utilities, sar and ps, with monitoring parameters such as staging duration, frequency, and the location of monitored hosts. We also use JimysProbing 0.1.0 for metrics generated from JOnAS-Tomcat server, apachetop 0.12.5 for Apache HTTP server, and mysqladmin for MySQL database server. We slightly modified apachetop to generate XML encoded monitoring results. The client workload generator is designed to simulate remote Web browsers that continuously send HTTP requests, receiving corresponding HTML files, and recording response time as a performance metric during staging. Sysstat 7.0.2 was used for system resource utilization tracking.

The experimental setup was deployed on two different clusters. Our initial data set (used in Section 3.1) was collected on the Georgia Tech Warp Cluster. This cluster is comprised of 56 Intel Blade Servers with Red Hat Enterprise Linux 4, with Linux kernel version 2.6.9-34-i386 as operating system. Each server is equipped with two Xeon 64-bit 3.06 GHz CPUs, 1 or 2 GB main memory, 1 Gbps network adapter, and a 5400 RPM disk with 8 MB cache. The second cluster used for the data generation was the Emulab [12], which provides more than 200 servers of different types. Emulab also allows the physical separation of experiments by simulating a local network topology for each experiment. The results detailed in Section 3.3 incorporate two types of servers. Primarily we employed a high end system with one Xeon 3.0Ghz 64 bit CPU, 2 GB main memory , six 1 Gbps network adapters, and a 10000 RPM disk. In order to change the bottleneck pattern we also used low end machines with a Pentium P3 600 MHz processor, 256 MB main memory, five 100 Mbps network adapters, and 7200 RPM disk. Both server types ran with Red Hat Enterprise Linux 4, with Linux kernel version 2.6.9-34-i386.

### 3.1 Bottleneck Detection in the 1/1/1 configuration

In this section we present a walk-through of our bottleneck detection process for a 1/1/1 configuration (no server replication in the tiers). The RUBiS benchmark was set to use the bidding transition matrices and the workload was incremented in steps of two.

The graphs in Fig. 1 show two different representative metrics in all tiers. The SLO satisfaction is graphed against the CPU usage in (a) and against the memory usage in (b). The depicted satisfaction level needs to be calculated by for each trial. This is conveniently resolved by the policy specific SLO-evaluator that is generated by Mulini. Individual satisfaction levels are determined for each of the SLO components. Interested readers can refer to [4] and [11] for more details. For simplicity reasons we solemnly use the response time of the system from the SLO-evaluator in the presented analysis. It is clearly visible that the satisfaction level meets our assumptions. It remains very stable up to around one hundred and fifty users, and decreases rapidlyonce this point is crossed. The CPU usage of the application server increases linearly and saturates at 100% when the SLO satisfaction drops down to around 85%. Furthermore, it is evident that the variability of CPU usage strongly decreases at the same time, signifying the maximal saturation level. The trends of other CPU utilizations

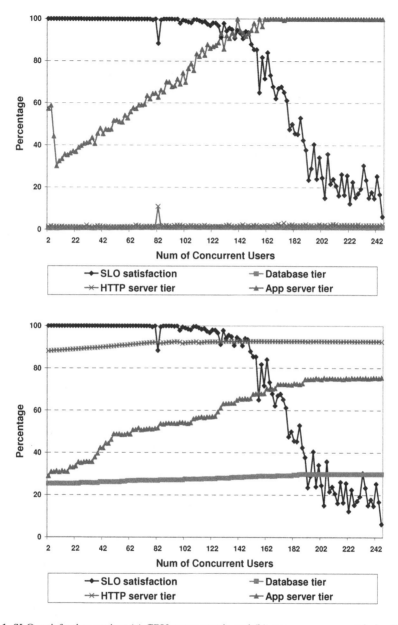

**Fig. 1.** SLO satisfaction against (a) CPU usage metric and (b) memory usage metric in all tiers

remain linear and stable on the contrary. In Fig. 1 (b) we can see that the memory of the application server and database server is underutilized. Both show a fairly stable linear trend. Although the memory usage of the HTTP server is somewhat high its trend is almost flat. The variability of all other metrics stays fairly constant throughout the whole experiment. Following the argument in [4] we can regard the

**Table 1.** Heuristic approximation of the intervention point

| AVG [%] | ST-DEV | CI-LB | WL |
|---------|--------|-------|-----|
| 98.39 | 2.37 | 93.75 | 148 |
| 98.31 | 2.46 | 93.49 | 150 |
| 98.17 | 2.72 | 92.84 | 152 |
| 98.09 | 2.81 | 92.58 | 154 |
| 97.79 | 3.83 | 90.28 | 156 |
| **97.63** | **4.05** | **89.70** | **158** |
| 97.40 | 4.53 | 88.52 | 160 |
| 97.26 | 4.66 | 88.12 | 162 |

application server CPU a typical representative of a single bottlenecked resource that will show a strongly non-stationary behavior in its delta values (first difference normalized by the step-width). All other delta series will retain a stable behavior throughout the entire workload span.

We can now turn to the actual detection process. Table 1 contains the output of the algorithm used to determine the intervention as described in Section 2.3. We performed the analysis on a dataset consisting of one hundred and seventy-five staging trials. The number of concurrent users ranged from two to three hundred and fifty. The lower bound of the confidence interval drops below ninety percent for a workload of one hundred and fifty-eight. According to Section 2.3 this defines our heuristic approximation of the crossover point $c$.

The final outcome of our heuristic testing scheme (2.4) and the impact assessment (2.5) for a limited dataset (first one-hundred and twenty-five trials) are summarized in Table 2.

The two delta value intervals $I$ and $I'$ are [4-156] and [158-250] respectively. While Rule 14 returns six hits, Rule 15 results in an empty set of candidate bottlenecks. All other metrics are discarded automatically. The values in the last column reveal the application tier CPU as most likely bottleneck. Thus our model has correctly detected the bottleneck in this scenario. For further understanding of the table it is important to note that we map all related values to its resource for the final interpretation. Therefore the $R$-value of the APP_CPU can result from more than one metric (e.g. the overall usage or the system usage) for instance.

We now proceed to demonstrate the robustness of our method when subjected to various configuration settings. We show that our approach is highly robust with regard to variations in the width of the intervals (Table 3), the position of the crossover

**Table 2.** Results of the bottleneck detection process

| Metric | $q_{0.1}$ | $q_{0.5}$ | $q_{0.9}$ | $q'_{0.2}$ | $q'_{0.5}$ | $q'_{0.8}$ | $R$ |
|--------|-----------|-----------|-----------|------------|------------|------------|-----|
| APP_CPU | -1.01 | 0.05 | 0.74 | -0.62 | -0.02 | 0.58 | 70.05 |
| DB_KBCached | -3.80 | 4.63 | 12.39 | -3.56 | 3.26 | 11.46 | 11.72 |
| APP_KBBuffers | 7.40 | 53.00 | 170.60 | 0.00 | 0.00 | 39.00 | 3.33 |
| DB_CPU | -0.03 | 0.00 | 0.04 | -0.03 | 0.00 | 0.03 | 2.81 |
| APP_Memory | -0.15 | 0.08 | 1.04 | -0.14 | 0.03 | 0.38 | 2.26 |
| WWW_CPU | -0.07 | 0.00 | 0.06 | -0.05 | 0.00 | 0.06 | 1.08 |

**Table 3.** Ranking function value against interval width

| $I$ | $I'$ | $R*$ | Pred Acc |
|---|---|---|---|
| [4;156] | [158;206] | 6.94 | 1 |
| [4;156] | [158;256] | 68.32 | 1 |
| [4;156] | [158;350] | 13.92 | 1 |
| [58;156] | [158;206] | 3.83 | 1 |
| [58;156] | [158;256] | 7.66 | 1 |
| [58;156] | [158;350] | 15.01 | 1 |
| [108;156] | [158;206] | 4.33 | 1 |
| [108;156] | [158;256] | 8.67 | 1 |
| [108;156] | [158;350] | 17.11 | 1 |

point (Table 4), and the step-width between the different workloads (Table 5). Table 3 shows the value of the ranking function depending on the length of the two input intervals. Our model predicted the bottleneck correctly each time. We see that the width of the second interval influences the magnitude of the $R$-value strongly.

We now examine the impact of different choices of crossover point values, which are summarized in Table 4. Within certain intuitive limits the model predicts correctly. This is of special importance since the determination of the intervention point is the result of the algorithm in Section 2.3. We see that its heuristic character is justified in the nature of the data.

Finally we turn to Table 5 and the analysis of the robustness of the choice of step-width. The table contains the ranking function values for different step-widths. At first it looks surprising that the ranking values increase almost monotonically as the

**Table 4.** Ranking function value against different crossover points

| $I$ | $I'$ | $R*$ | Pred Acc |
|---|---|---|---|
| [16;114] | [116;214] | - | 0 |
| [26;124] | [126;224] | - | 0 |
| [36;134] | [136;234] | 5.09 | 1 |
| [46;144] | [146;244] | 6.86 | 1 |
| [56;154] | [156;254] | 7.93 | 1 |
| [66;164] | [166;264] | $\infty$ | 1 |
| [76;174] | [176;274] | 59.43 | 1 |
| [86;184] | [186;284] | 0.93 | 0 |

**Table 5.** Ranking function value against the step width

| $I$ | $I'$ | Step | # Trials | $R*$ | Pred Acc |
|---|---|---|---|---|---|
| [4;156] | [158;350] | 2 | 174 | 13.92 | 1 |
| [4;156] | [160;348] | 4 | 87 | 12.58 | 1 |
| [4;156] | [164;348] | 8 | 44 | 188.60 | 1 |
| [4;148] | [164;340] | 16 | 22 | 112.17 | 1 |
| [4;132] | [164;324] | 32 | 11 | $\infty$ | 1 |

step-width increases. Nevertheless, this is due to the stochastic nature of our data and the fact that with increased step width the two intervals are separated farther apart. By increasing the observable change in the bottleneck metric the results become clearer. This proves the robustness of our method and reveals its effectiveness when exposed to data of higher step-width.

### 3.2 Performance Comparison of the Analysis

In this section we present the results of our experiments across a wide range of configurations to show how the method evaluates a changing bottleneck pattern. This data was collected on Emulab [12] with different write ratios (WR0.1 and WR0.2) and server configurations (H and L).

Table 6 lists the top candidate bottleneck metrics and their $R$-value in the last two columns. We also applied a simple heuristic filtering mechanism to discard uninteresting ranking values. The latter eliminates the problematic behavior of some utilization values for instance, which was detailed in our previous work. We automatically discard values if the utilization does not cross a certain threshold (90% in our case) [4]. The table shows that our methodology is able to detect the shifting bottleneck as we progress to higher replication levels of the application server tier.

**Table 6.** Top candidate bottleneck metrics

| Config | WR | $WS$ | # Trials | $c$ | S1/S2-Sz | Result Metric | $R*$ |
|--------|------|----------|------|------|------|------------|-------|
| H/2H/H | 20% | 100-600 | 51 | 440 | 11/2 | APP_CPU | 73.02 |
| H/4H/H | 20% | 540-1040 | 51 | 844 | 4/1 | APP_CPU | 16.61 |
| H/6H/H | 20% | 1040-1448 | 51 | 1264 | 7/0 | APP_CPU | 13.10 |
| H/8H/L | 10% | 1300-1820 | 51 | 1490 | 4/0 | DB_Memory | 10.22 |
| H/8H/2L | 10% | 1400-1920 | 51 | 1640 | 5/1 | APP_CPU | 7.82 |

In order to make the performance limitation appear faster we employed a lower write ratio and lower end DBs in the last two data sets. At a replication level of eight application servers the bottleneck has shifted to the database tier. Our algorithm identifies the DB memory as a potentially saturated resource. Now we examine the effect of replicating the bottlenecked DB. This again results in a shift of the bottleneck towards the application tier and is successfully detected by our algorithm. It is also evident that we are able to perform our detection process accurately with a significantly lower number of trials than other approaches.

## 4  Related Work

The area of performance modeling in multi-tier enterprise systems has been subjected to substantial research efforts in the recent time. Many of the well-documented approaches use machine learning or queuing theory.

Cohen et al [3] apply a tree-augmented Naïve Bayesian network to discover correlations between system-level metrics and performance states, such as SLO satisfaction and SLO failure. Powers et al [5] also use machine learning techniques to analyze performance. However, rather than detecting bottlenecks in the current system, they predict whether the system will be able to withstand load in the following hour. Similarly, we have performed a comparative study of machine learning classifiers to investigate performance patterns [11]. Our goal was to compare the performance of several well-known machine learning algorithms as classifiers in terms of bottleneck detection, and finally to identify the classifier that best detects bottlenecks in multi-tier applications. Several other studies are based on dynamic queuing models combined with predictive and reactive provisioning as in [9]. Their contribution allows an enterprise system to increase capacity in bottleneck tiers during flash crowds in production.

Elba, in addition to being oriented towards avoiding in-production performance shortfalls, emphasizes fine-grained reconfiguration. By identifying specific limitations such as low-level system metrics (CPU, memory, etc.) and higher-level application parameters (pool size, cache size, etc.) configurations are tuned to the particular performance problem at hand. Another fundamental difference of our work is that in addition to correlating metrics to performance states, we focus on the detection of actual performance-limiting bottlenecks. We employ a unique procedure to analyze the change in trends of metrics. Finally, our set of metrics for bottleneck detection includes over two hundred application-level metrics as well as system-level metrics.

## 5  Conclusion

Our detection scheme based on intervention analysis has proven to be very effective with our experimental data. The method is able to characterize the potential change in metric graph trends automatically and assess its correlation with SLO violations. Our statistical modeling approach eliminates the previously necessary data filtering (e.g. correlation analysis) and model calibrating phases (e.g. classifier training). The results are clear and intuitive in the interpretation. We showed that our new method yields these general as well as practical advantages in our evaluation. Potential bottlenecks are identified accurately in different scenarios. As future work this method could be extended with a maximization/minimization scheme for the ranking function. This would allow a more thorough root-cause analysis in the case of multiple bottlenecks. We also plan to employ our results as input for a regression model that will be able to predict actual SLO satisfaction levels.

## Acknowledgment

This research has been partially funded by National Science Foundation grants CISE/IIS-0242397, ENG/EEC-0335622, CISE/CNS-0646430, AFOSR grant FA9550-06-1-0201, IBM SUR grant, Hewlett-Packard, and Georgia Tech Foundation through the John P. Imlay, Jr. Chair endowment.

## References

1. Brockwell, P., Davis, A.: Introduction to Time Series and Forecasting. Springer Inc., New York (1996)
2. Cecchet, E., Chanda, A., Elnikety, S., Marguerite, J., Zwaenepoel, W.: Performance comparison of middleware architectures for generating dynamic Web content. Middleware (2003)

3. Cohen, I., Goldszmidt, M., Kelly, T., Symons, J., Chase, J.: Correlating instrumentation data to system states: A building block for automated diagnosis and control. In: OSDI 2004 (2004)
4. Jung, G., Swint, G., Parekh, J., Pu, C., Sahai, A.: Detecting Bottlenecks in n-Tier IT Applications through Analysis. In: State, R., van der Meer, S., O'Sullivan, D., Pfeifer, T. (eds.) DSOM 2006. LNCS, vol. 4269, Springer, Heidelberg (2006)
5. Powers, R., Goldszmidt, M., Cohen, I.: Short Term Performance Forecasting in Enterprise Systems. In: KDD 2005 (2005)
6. Pu, C., Sahai, A., Parekh, J., Jung, G., Bae, J., Cha, Y., Garcia, T., Irani, D., Lee, J., Lin, Q.: Observation-Based Approach to Performance Characterization of Distributed n-Tier Applications (submitted for publication)
7. Quinlan, J.R.: C4.5: Programs for Machine Learning. Morgan Kaufmann, San Francisco (1993)
8. Raghavachari, M., Reimer, D., Johnson, R.D.: The Deployer's Problems: Configuring Application Servers for Performance and Reliability. In: ICSE 2003 (2003)
9. Urgaonkar, B., Shenoy, P., Chandra, A., Goyal, P.: Dynamic Provisioning of Multi-tier Internet Applications. In: ICAC 2005 (2005)
10. Wu, C., Hamada, M.: Experiments: Planning, Analysis, and Parameter Design Optimization. Wiley & Sons Inc., New York (2000)
11. Elba project. http://www-static.cc.gatech.edu/systems/projects/Elba
12. Emulab/Netlab. http://www.emulab.net/
13. RUBiS distribution. http://forge.objectweb.org/project/showfiles.php?group_id=44

# Mitigating the Lying-Endpoint Problem in Virtualized Network Access Frameworks

Ravi Sahita, Uday R. Savagaonkar, Prashant Dewan, and David Durham

Intel Corporation
2111 NE 25th Ave, Hillsboro, OR, USA
{ravi.sahita,uday.r.savagaonkar,prashant.dewan,david.durham}@intel.com
http://www.intel.com

**Abstract.** Malicious root-kits modify the in-memory state of programs executing on an endpoint to hide themselves from security software. Such attacks negatively affect network-based security frameworks that depend on the trustworthiness of endpoint software. In network access control frameworks this issue is called the lying-endpoint problem, where a compromised endpoint spoofs software integrity reports to render the framework untrustworthy. We present a novel architecture called Virtualization-enabled Integrity Services (VIS) to protect the run-time integrity of network-access software in an untrusted environment. We describe the design of a VIS-protected network access stack, and characterize its performance. We show that a network access stack running on an existing operating system can be protected using VIS with less than 5% overhead, even when each network packet causes protection enforcement.

**keywords:** Network Access Framework, Lying Endpoint, Virtualization, Memory Protections.

## 1 Background and Introduction

With increased use of mobile platforms, the effectiveness of perimeter defenses has decreased. Additionally, malicious software has become increasingly stealthier and complex to detect. To counter these threats, a number of network-access control models [1,2] have been proposed. Before allowing an endpoint to connect to a network, these models require it to present its software-integrity information (this is in addition to the existing user authentication). Most integrity-based access models work as shown in Fig. 1. An access-client on the endpoint (a real or virtual machine) requests access to the network, triggering access negotiation with a server. The client and server mutually authenticate each other, and then the access-client sends its integrity posture to the server. This posture information is based on reports from local security services such as firewall, anti-virus, and anti-intrusion. The server uses verification services that match the client security services to ensure that the client posture is acceptable. The server pushes the access decision to the enforcement point, which typically allows, disallows,

A. Clemm, L.Z. Granville, and R. Stadler (Eds.): DSOM 2007, LNCS 4785, pp. 135–146, 2007.

or partially allows the client access. The fundamental weakness of this model is that a compromised lying-endpoint could spoof its posture and gain full access to the network compromising the entire framework.

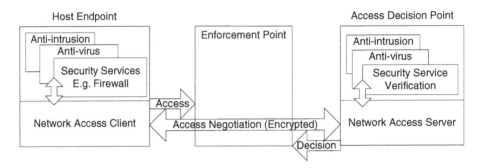

**Fig. 1.** Generalized Network Access Control Model

To this end, we describe a platform service called Virtualization-enabled Integrity Services (VIS) to overlay run-time memory access-control on programs running in an untrusted environment. VIS leverages hardware virtualization to provide memory protections at a page-level granularity. Our approach differs from other virtualization-based techniques [3,4,5] in that, we protect programs within a shared linear address space from peer programs in the same address space, allowing tamper-resistant conversation between a remote server and a VIS-protected access stack, even in un-trusted OS environment. Such trusted communication can then be leveraged to address the lying-endpoint problem. We focus on protection of network access stacks since they are a key attack point [6] for network access frameworks.

The rest of the paper is organized as follows. In Sec. 2, we present related work. Sec. 3 outlines the threat model. Sec. 4 presents the architecture. Sec. 5 presents the application. In Sec. 6, we present threat coverage analysis. In Sec. 7 we evaluate the overhead, followed by conclusion in Sec. 8.

## 2    Related Work

Two fundamental approaches related to our work exist in literature. The first is to verify and load only trusted programs at the highest privilege [7]. Even though this approach can reduce threat exposure, it entails validation of a large body of legacy code against a multitude of run-time vulnerabilities, many of which may not even have been identified. Additionally, any unidentified vulnerability can expose this approach to zero-day attacks. The second approach is to run untrusted code in restricted conditions, and monitor/prevent policy violations. Examples of such include Terra [3], Denali [4], and Tahoma [5], which allow programs to run in isolated Virtual Machines (VMs). Terra leverages properties similar to those provided by Intel® Trusted Execution Technology (TXT) [8] to create isolated partitions. Denali uses special-purpose VMs crafted for the application. Tahoma uses Dom0 of Xen* to proxy all web queries for browsers running in isolated VMs. However, most untrusted programs are legacy components, and are typically beyond control of the network access stack writers. Thus, in reality, such programs pose significant challenges in terms of making them work in restricted environments. Additionally, running security services in separate VMs is not always possible, since some security services (e.g., intrusion prevention) need some presence on the endpoint to function properly. VIS uses a combination of these two approaches.

A number of other related approaches exist in literature. Engler *et al.* [9] advocate a model where applications manage their own resources with the help of libraries. Witchel *et al.* [10] propose a word-level memory access control matrix. Chen and Morris [11] propose code and data validation for every cache access. Unlike VIS, these approaches require changes to existing hardware and software. Miller *et al.* [12] overlay protection domains on physical memory for capability operating systems that do not support process separation. Bhatkar *et al.* [13] extend address-space randomization techniques to provide probabilistic protections against memory exploits. Arbaugh *et al.* [14] propose a secure bootstrap mechanism similar to TXT. Kiriansky *et al.* [15] use an approach that has similar goals as VIS. They prevent execution of malware by validating code at run-time and putting it in a secure cache. McCune *et al.* [16] propose a minimal code execution model using TXT for running code in isolation.

Our main contributions of this paper are: 1. We describe a novel way to provide inline memory protections to legacy software within a shared address space, without modifying OS infrastructure. 2. We describe a novel method to increase efficiency of protecting software using VIS to mitigate the lying endpoint problem for network access.

## 3   Threat Model

We assume that the attack has compromised the privilege-level separation and installed itself at the highest privilege level in the OS (e.g., see [17]). Consequently, the malware has full access to the OS state. The following types (or combination) of attacks can now be launched to lie about the integrity state of the endpoint.

**Circumvention:** A malicious program can jump into the code of a security service to bypass software checks. For example, a rootkit could prepare a false posture report and jump to the "sign-and-send" function of the network-access client. Examples of such attacks can be found in [6] and [18].

**Tampering:** A malicious program can modify the in-memory contents of a program. For example, a rootkit could modify the conditional branches of a local security service to report a false health report. Examples include Shadow Walker [19] (hooks system handlers and modifies page tables), and tamper of data in transit using function hooking [6].

**Eavesdropping:** A malicious program may read memory containing secrets that are owned by security services. For example, a rootkit could hijack a secure session with the authentication severely simply reading the access-client's memory. Examples of password-stealing malware abound [20].

**Disk-image Modification:** On-disk rootkits, such as Direct Masquerades [21], either modify binaries or completely replace them with malicious binaries.

In Sec. 6 we discuss how each of these threats is mitigated in our proposal.

## 4    Virtualization-Enabled Integrity Services

### 4.1    Software Integrity for Lying-Endpoint Problem

VIS leverages Intel® Virtualization Technology or VT-x [8] to overlay memory protections from the hypervisor onto software running in a VM. In the context of this paper, the network endpoint is running in a VM, and the network-access client and other security services on the client would be protected using VIS. Below we provide a brief overview of hardware-based virtualization, and then describe the VIS architecture in detail. We assume that the hypervisor is a small body of code that is measured on launch thereby reducing the attack surface.

### 4.2    Hardware Virtualization Overview

*Virtualization* refers to the technique of partitioning a machine into Virtual Machines (VMs). Different virtualization techniques have been discussed in literature [4,22,23]. A hypervisor manages VMs by operating at the highest software privilege level (VMX-root mode in VT-x). A control transfer into the hypervisor is called a VMExit and transfer of control to a VM is called a VMEntry. A VM can explicitly force a VMExit by using a VMCall instruction (a hypercall). A Guest OS runs in VMX-non-root mode which ensures that critical OS operations cause a VMExit, which allows the hypervisor to enforce isolation policies. The hypervisor manages launch/shutdown of VMs, memory/device isolation, control register/MSR accesses, interrupts and instruction virtualization.

VIS leverages the hypervisor to control use of physical memory. The hypervisor manages parallel page tables for each VM running on the platform. Each guest OS maintains its own page tables, called the Guest Page Tables (GPTs). The parallel page tables are called the Active Page Tables (APTs) and are used by the processor for address translation. The hypervisor synchronizes APTs with GPTs using a family of algorithms called the Virtual Translation Look-aside Buffer (VTLB) algorithms which emulate the processor TLB. The algorithms leverage VMX-root mode to trap on page-faults and execution of certain instructions such as INVLPG, MOV CR3 that are used by an operating system to manage virtual memory. A discussion of VTLB can be found in [24].

### 4.3    VIS Architecture

VIS comprises of three components–a VIS Registration Module (VRM), an Integrity Measurement Module (IMM), and a Memory Protections Module (MPM).

These modules are isolated from the guest OS. A program (e.g., the access-client) in the guest OS requests protection via a registration hypercall to the VRM. The VRM uses the APT to identify the physical page locations for the program in memory and uses the IMM to verify the integrity of the contents of these pages. If the program passes integrity verification, the VRM uses the MPM to protect the program memory using page-table modifications. Fig. 2 shows these components pictorially.

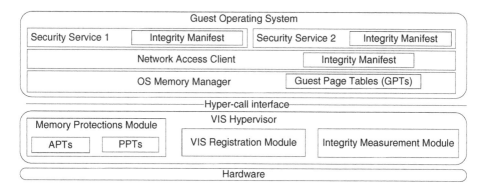

**Fig. 2.** Virtualization-enabled Integrity Services Architecture

**VIS Registration Module:** The VRM is implemented in the hypervisor (see Fig. 2) interacts with programs in the guest OS via hypercall interfaces. It validates the registration requests, coordinates the IMM-MPM interaction, and notifies the program of the registration outcome.

**Integrity Measurement Module:** The IMM is implemented in the VIS hypervisor (see Fig. 2) and has direct access to the guest OS physical memory via page table translations provided by the hypervisor. To facilitate measurement, each program seeking protection is required to provide a vendor-signed reference measurement called an Integrity Manifest or a vendor-signed disk image that can be used to create the Integrity Manifest. The Manifest is cryptographically signed by an entity whose authenticity can be verified by the IMM directly or through a chain of trust. In this respect, the Integrity Manifest is similar to an X.509 certificate. The Manifest contains cryptographic hashes of the program-section's in-memory contents, relocation fix-up information per-section, and exported entry-points per-section. At program load, the OS loader may apply relocation fix-ups to the program image, consequently modifying the in-memory image. The IMM reverses relocation fix-ups using information from the Manifest and with the relocation-reversed copy of the image, can perform meaningful hash verification. Note that, to ensure unrestricted IMM access to the program's memory, VIS requires that the program being protected be pinned in guest OS's physical memory. Most OSes allow such pinning via various application programming interfaces.

**Memory Protections Module:** The MPM is implemented in the hypervisor (see Fig. 2) provides memory protection for each IMM-measured program's code/data sections. As described in Sec. 4.2, the hypervisor maintains shadow APTs corresponding to the OS GPTs. To institute protection on measured physical pages for programs, the MPM creates Protected Page Tables (PPTs) in addition. The MPM populates the PPTs with references to the measured physical pages corresponding to the program's linear address space, and removes references to the program's protected pages from the APTs (or marks them read-only) and flushes the TLBs. All data pages that are mapped to both the APTs and the PPTs are marked execute-disable (XD). Due to this setup, code/data accesses from the APTs to the PPTs or vice versa lead to page-faults that invoke the hypervisor. Depending on the policy defined for the programs, the hypervisor either allows/restricts the access. Fig. 3. shows an example setup for the network access stack from Fig. 2.

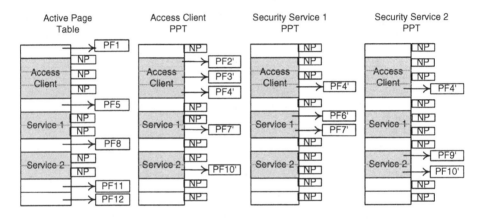

**Fig. 3.** Page Table Setup for a Simple Network Access Stack

## 5    Applying VIS to the Lying-Endpoint Problem

### 5.1    Registration of Access-Client and Security Services

Each access-client and security service program loaded in the guest OS provides the following information in a registration hypercall to the hypervisor: 1. The run-time linear address of the program's integrity manifest. 2. The start and end linear addresses for each program section. 3. The entry points into the programs expressed as offsets into code sections. 4. The type of protection (shared or protected) required for the data sections.

We create a special data section in the access-client and each security service for protected message passing. In the access-client, this section has at least one page for each security service expected. In each security service, this data section must be at least one page long. For example, in Fig. 3, PF 3' and 4' represent the data section pages in the access-client, and PF 7' and 10' represents the data section in security services 1 and 2 respectively. A protected type will be requested for the data section reserved for communication with the access server.

The MPM verifies that a) the physical memory corresponding to the region is page-aligned and paged-in, b) the physical page is not already protected in another PPT (unless policy-specified), and c) there is no existing alias mapping for that physical frame in any other context. To prevent race conditions, the MPM write-protects the program's pages as program contents are copied for reversing relocation fix-ups. During the measurement phase the MPM does not allow any accesses to occur into the code/data sections. The IMM measures the program as described in Sec. 4.3. If the program passes the IMM check, the MPM creates a new PPT, adds the references for the protected pages into the PPT, and removes them from the APT described in Sec. 4.3. The MPM . To prevent the malware from bypassing registration, the hypervisor disallows any network access until it receives a successful registration and verification of the access-client and a set of security services.

The next phase of registration is to bind the security services to the access-client so that they can communicate securely. A security service does not respond to any access-client request for posture information until it gets a bind success from the hypervisor. Note here that the hypervisor is provisioned with the manifests of the expected security services. After the access-client and the expected security services have been verified, the VRM uses the MPM to associate the security services with the measured access-client. The hypervisor does this by modifying the page table entries corresponding to the reserved data section for the access-client. The hypervisor modifies the page table entries in the access-client PPT to refer to the individual data sections reserved for communication in each of the security service PPTs. This setup is shown in Fig. 3. Page frame pairs 4', 7', and 3', 10' are the protected memory channels from the access-client to security service 1 and security service 2 respectively.

## 5.2   Memory Protected Operation

As noted earlier, the hypervisor grants only restricted network access from the endpoint until it has verified and protected the access-client and the other security services. Additionally, due to the VMExits seen during protected program execution, the hypervisor can also verify that the protected programs are not disabled at run-time. Execution can further be enforced by making the network driver and the memory-mapped network hardware a part of the access stack. In such a setting, a packet must traverse the access stack before it can be sent out onto the network. Alternately, the firewall can cryptographically tag operational data to demonstrate that correct operations were applied to the network packets.

As the packets enter the access stack, execution of the protected sections of the access stack results in a page-fault VMExit. If faulting address corresponds to a valid entry-point into the access stack, the MPM modifies the CR3 register to point to the access-stack's PPT, and resumes execution. Interrupts received during execution of protected stack are handled as follows. On an interrupt, the hypervisor notes down the linear address of the interrupted instruction, switches

CR3 to point to APTs, and jumps into the interrupt service routine (ISR). When the ISR returns, the hypervisor checks the return address against the recorded address, and resumes execution in the protected domain if there is a match.

If the unprotected code attempts to access protected data, the MPM receives a VMExit, and denies/redirects this access. If protected code attempts to access unprotected data, the MPM may map that page to the PPTs with XD permission, and allow the access. Even though such accesses are architecturally allowed, they should be kept to a minimum. Additionally, all posture data exchanged between the security services and access-client should be transferred via the protected data channels setup in the PPT.

The access-client and the security services interact through VIS-enforced entry-points (for code interactions) and protected data channels (for data interactions), and as such, this interaction is tamper-resistant. However, to prevent spoofing, the remote access-server must be able to verify that the access-client is in fact VIS-protected. Such verification can be achieved by requiring the access-client and remote-server maintain a security association using platform-derived keys. These could be stored in the Trusted Platform Module (TPM) on the client, and made available to the hypervisor only if the platform boots with a trusted hypervisor. The hypervisor, in turn, can use these keys to perform crypto operations on behalf of the VIS-protected components. A detailed discussion of a similar model can be found in work by Goldman et al. [25].

# 6    Threat Analysis

## 6.1    Threat Mitigation

**Circumvention:** VIS mitigates instruction-flow circumvention by enforcing entry-points into the protected programs. Additionally, protecting the channels between the access-client and services prevents malware from inserting spurious posture data into the protected network-access stack.

**Tampering:** Protected code/data pages belonging to the protected access stack cannot be accessed by external programs, ensuring that malware cannot tamper with the operation of network-access stack.

**Eavesdropping:** Since the protected data of the network-access stack is not mapped into APTs, any access to that data by external entities can be monitored/redirected by VIS. It is responsibility of the security software to ensure that the secrets are not exposed beyond the protected sections.

**Disk-image Modification:** VIS protects a program from tamper after registration. However, on-disk modification may stop the access-client from registering with the hypervisor. However, an unregistered access client would not get access to the platform-derived keys, enabling the access server to detect the attack.

## 6.2    Attack Vectors

VIS does not address hardware attacks from DMA devices, which can largely be addressed by device I/O virtualization [26]. VIS also does not address buffer-overflow attacks within protected programs. However, a variety of techniques (e.g., XD bit) exist to eliminate such vulnerabilities, and consequently a carefully designed access stack should not suffer from such vulnerabilities. Most commercial OSes force the protected programs to share their stack with rest of system services. However, such an attack can be mitigated by carefully designing the protected program to use private stack/data segment for its critical operations, and verifying the data passed on the stack. Finally if a protected program uses services from an unprotected program, then a malicious program can modify the unprotected program to change the behavior of the protected programs. Similarly, any unprotected data pages accessed by protected programs potentially create an attack vector. VIS cannot inherently protect against such threat vectors. However, for controlled programs such as those in the network-access stack, the interaction with the unprotected programs can be minimized/eliminated. We have a working prototype of network device driver that does not rely on OS services.

# 7   Performance Overhead Analysis

We described how VIS can be used to protect the network-access stack. However, VIS uses VMExits to enforce memory protections, which are extremely CPU-intensive. In this section, we quantify and propose ways to reduce the performance overhead of such protections. Firewalls typically require most frequent protection-domain switching–typically on each packet–and consequently incur the most overhead. Other components of the access stack (e.g., the access-client) typically require much less frequent switching. Hence, we protect a firewall driver that is in the path of the network traffic. Below, we focus only on instruction fetch page faults, as the data-fetch page faults can be eliminated by sharing pages (marked XD) in the PPTs (see Sec. 5.1). We quantified the VIS overhead by measuring the cycles spent by the CPU transferring each byte of network data. A low cycles-per-byte (CPB) indicates an efficient protected program. We derived CPB measurement using NTttcp tests between our prototype (sender) directly connected to an Intel® Xeon™-based receiver. Our test system has an integrated PCIe gigabit Ethernet controller, 1GB of memory, and a VT-x enabled 1.83 GHz Intel® Core™ Solo T1400 processor. We used an internally developed hypervisor and used a Windows* XP* OS. We describe our experiments with software and hardware-assist methods to reduce VIS overhead below.

**Software Assist:** The VMExit cost incurred by an access-stack component can be reduced by mapping the services frequently used by that component into the PPTs. Of course, such services must be mapped read-only in the APTs to protect the access-stack component from code-injection attack. Our firewall frequently called NDIS which results in two VMExits per call. We expanded the scope of the PPT to share NDIS (and other known kernel programs) into the PPT of the firewall service. However, to make NDIS available to other networking programs, it was also mapped to the APTs as a write-protected program. A similar case can be made for the other security services to reduce the instruction fetch VMExits. As can be seen from Fig. 4, protecting the firewall incurs an overhead of 140 CPB. However, adding other measured components brings the CPB down to less than 90.

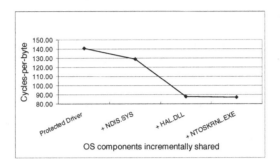

**Fig. 4.** Effect of PPT Expansion on Page-table Transition Cost

**Hardware-assist:** As described in Sec. 4.2, when a VM attempts to modify the value of the CR3 register, it incurs a VMExit. However, VT-x allows the hypervisor to define a "cheat list" of known good CR3 values. If the new CR3 value is included in this list, the VM does not incur a VMExit. We modified our firewall service to leverage this feature. To elaborate, all registered entry-points into the firewall were placed on a read-only page shared between the APTs and the PPTs. The code on this page changes the CR3 value to point to the PPTs, and then calls the protected firewall function. On return from the function, the shared code changes the CR3 to point it back to APTs, and then returns to the caller. The hypervisor is responsible for keeping the CR3 "cheat list" up-to-date with correct addresses of the APTs/PPTs. It should be noted that, to successfully move from APTs to PPTs, the code modifying the CR3 value must be mapped to both the APTs and the PPTs. Consequently, without support from the hypervisor, this feature cannot be attacked by the malware.

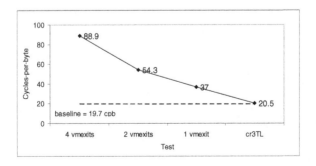

**Fig. 5.** Reducing the Cost of hypervisor Round-trips Using Hardware Assist

Fig. 5 shows the reduction in CPB as the VMExits are reduced. With the use of the cheat list, we experienced no VMExits and recorded a CPB of 20.5 with VIS protections, versus a baseline CPB of 19.7 without any protections (4% overhead). The throughput measured was 715 Mbps (protected) versus 745 Mbps (unprotected). The overhead is due to disabling interrupts at the transition points and the cost of MOV CR3 instructions.

# 8   Conclusion and Future Work

In this paper we demonstrated how virtualization can be used to protect programs operating in a shared linear address space. We used the architecture to protect the network access-client stack to address the lying end-point issue. We implemented the architecture in a hypervisor, and described an OS-independent method to protect software. We outlined software and hardware based techniques to reduce the performance overhead of such protections to negligible levels. For our future work, we are working towards providing case studies of other applications and addressing the attacks not mitigated by VIS.

# References

1. Cisco*: Cisco* Network Admission Control. http://www.cisco.com/go/nac
2. Microsoft*: Microsoft* Network Access Protection.
   http://www.microsoft.com/nap
3. Garfinkel, T., Pfaff, B., Chow, J., Rosenblum, M., Boneh, D.: Terra: A virtual machine-based platform for trusted computing. Special Interest Group on Operating Systems: Operating Systems Review 37, 193–206 (2003)
4. Whitaker, A., Shaw, M., Gribble, S.D.: Scale and performance in the Denali isolation kernel. In: OSDI 2002. Proceedings of the Fifth Symposium on Operating System Design and Implementation, Boston, MA (December 2002)
5. Cox, R.S., Gribble, S.D., Levy, H.M., Hansen, J.G.: A safety-oriented platform for web applications. In: SP 2006. Proceedings of the 2006 IEEE Symposium on Security and Privacy (S&P'06), pp. 350–364. IEEE Computer Society Press, Washington, DC, USA (2006)
6. Thumann, M., Roecher, D.J.: NACATTACK–hacking the cisco* NAC framework. In: Blackhat Europe (2007)
7. Microsoft*: Digital signatures for kernel modules on x64-based systems running windows* vista* (2006),
   http://www.microsoft.com/whdc/system/platform/64bit/kmsigning.mspx
8. Intel Corporation: IA-32 Intel® Architecture Software Developers Manual.
   http://www.intel.com/products/processor/manuals/index.htm
9. Engler, D.R., Kaashoek, M.F., James O'Toole, J.: Exokernel: an operating system architecture for application-level resource management. In: Proceedings of the Fifteenth ACM Symposium on Operating Systems Principles, pp. 251–266. ACM Press, New York (1995)
10. Witchel, E., Cates, J., Asanović, K.: Mondrian memory protection. In: Proceedings of the Tenth International Conference on Architectural Support for Programming Languages and Operating Systems, San Jose, CA (October 2002)

11. Chen, B., Morris, R.: Certifying program execution with secure processors. In: 9th Workshop on Hot Topics in Operating Systems (2003)
12. Miller, F.W.: Simple memory protection for embedded operating system kernels. In: Proceedings of the FREENIX Track: 2002 USENIX Annual Technical Conference, pp. 299–308. USENIX Association, Berkeley, CA, USA (2002)
13. Bhatkar, S., Sekar, R., DuVarney, D.C.: Efficient techniques for comprehensive protection from memory error exploits. In: SSYM 2005. Proceedings of the 14th conference on USENIX Security Symposium, pp. 17–17. USENIX Association, Berkeley, CA, USA (2005)
14. Arbaugh, W.A., Farber, D.J., Smith, J.M.: A secure and reliable bootstrap architecture. In: SP 1997.: Proceedings of the 1997 IEEE Symposium on Security and Privacy, p. 65. IEEE Computer Society Press, Washington, DC, USA (1997)
15. Kiriansky, V., Bruening, D., Amarasinghe, S.P.: Secure execution via program shepherding. In: Proceedings of the 11th USENIX Security Symposium, pp. 191–206. USENIX Association, Berkeley, CA, USA (2002)
16. McCune, J.M., Parno, B., Perrig, A., Reiter, M.K., Seshadri, A.: Minimal TCB code execution. In: IEEE Symposium on Security and Privacy, pp. 267–272. IEEE Computer Society Press, Los Alamitos (2007)
17. Kaslin, K.: Kernel malware: The attack from within. In: Association of anti-Virus Asia Researchers (AVAR) International Conference, New Zealand (2006)
18. Kapoor, A., Sallam, A.: Rootkits part 2: A technical primer (2006), http://www.mcafee.com/us/local_content/white_papers/wp_rootkits_0407.pdf
19. Naraine, R.: Shadow walker pushes envelope for stealth rootkits (2005), http://www.eweek.com/article2/0,1895,1841266,00.asp
20. Symantec*: Symantec* internet security threat report: Trends for july-dec 2006 (March 2007)
21. Thimbleby, H., Anderson, S., Cairns, P.: A framework for modelling trojans and computer virus infection. The Computer Journal 41(7), 445–458 (1998)
22. Devine, S., Bugnion, E., Rosenblum, M.: Virtualization system including a virtual machine monitor for a computer with a segmented architecture (1998)
23. Barham, P., Dragovic, B., Fraser, K., Hand, S., Harris, T., Ho, A., Neugebauer, R., Pratt, I., Warfield, A.: Xen and the art of virtualization. In: Proceedings of the Nineteenth ACM Symposium on Operating Systems Principles, pp. 164–177. ACM Press, New York (2003)
24. Smith, J.E., Uhlig, R.: Virtual Machines: Architectures, Implementations, and Applications. In: HOTCHIPS: A Symposium on High Performance Chips (2005)
25. Goldman, K., Perez, R., Sailer, R.: Linking remote attestation to secure tunnel endpoints. Technical Report RC23982, IBM Corporation (June 2006)
26. Hiremane, R.: Intel® Virtualization Technology for Directed I/O (Intel® VT-d). Technology@Intel Magazine 4(10) (May 2007)

*Other names and brands may be claimed as the property of others.

# On the Risk Exposure and Priority Determination of Changes in IT Service Management

Jacques P. Sauvé, Rodrigo A. Santos, Rodrigo R. Almeida, and J. Antão B. Moura

Federal University of Campina Grande, Brazil
{Jacques,almeida,rodrigor,antao}@dsc.ufcg.edu.br

**Abstract.** This paper deals with the Change Management process within IT Service Management. Change Management includes several activities, some of which need to evaluate the risk exposure associated with changes to be made to the infrastructure and services. We present a method by which risk exposure associated with a change can be evaluated and the risk exposure metric is applied to the problem of automatically assigning priorities to changes. A formal model is developed to this end; the model captures the business perspective by using financial metrics in the evaluation of risk. A case study, performed in conjunction with a large IT service provider, is reported and provides good results when compared to decisions made by human managers.

**Keywords:** Change Management, Risk, Change Prioritization, IT Service Management, Business-Driven IT Management.

## 1 Introduction

**The context.** Information Technology Service Management (ITSM) has been the object of concentrated study over the past decade due to the ever-growing importance of IT to corporate activity. As a result, best practice collections for ITSM such as the Information Technology Infrastructure Library (ITIL)[2] and Control Objectives for Information and related Technology (COBIT) [1] are becoming popular. In this paper, ITIL vocabulary is used, although the work applies in general settings. ITIL divides IT management processes in several areas, one of which is Service Support, which includes such processes as Service Desk, Incident Management, Problem Management, Configuration Management, Change Management and Release Management. This paper focuses on the Change Management (CM) process.

Changes are made to *Configuration Items* (CIs) that are part of the IT infrastructure. CIs include servers, communication equipment, systems software, embedded software in, for example, routers, middleware, application software and so on. The CM process aims to ensure that efficient and prompt handling of all changes to the IT infrastructure is performed using standard procedures, in order to minimize the impact of changes on the services supported by the infrastructure. Change Management is a very important process as is attested to by the following assessment by Stephen Elliot, Research Manager, IDC: "Over 80% of business-critical service disruptions can be attributed to poor change control processes including flawed

A. Clemm, L.Z. Granville, and R. Stadler (Eds.): DSOM 2007, LNCS 4785, pp. 147–158, 2007.

change impact assessment." It is for this reason that, when an enterprise initiates the implementation of ITIL management processes, one of the first to be included is CM.

The CM process includes several activities including change initiation where a Request for Change (RFC) describing the required change is registered, change filtering, priority allocation, categorization ("minor", "significant", "major"), planning, testing, implementation and review. Significant or major changes must go through the Change Advisory Board (CAB) for analysis and approval. The CAB is a group of people capable of analyzing changes from a technical as well as from a business point of view. This paper looks into the *prioritization of change* activity in greater detail. When prioritizing a change, the change manager (or the CAB) must evaluate the *impact* on the business of *not* implementing the change as well as the *urgency* to the business. In ITIL terms, impact is usually associated with a degradation of service levels and urgency is associated with a business perspective of the change. The urgency can be partially estimated by examining the deadline specified by the business by which it needs the change to be implemented. Penalties are frequently paid by the service provider if the deadline is overstepped. For each change, the change manager must therefore ask: "How long can I delay to handle this change?" The answer is given as a priority level, say one of: "Immediate", "High priority", "Medium priority" or "Low priority". These priority levels and the semantics behind them are company policy.

Observe that assigning priorities does not schedule changes. Scheduling is an activity that is performed further down the line when plans are ready, changes have been tested and when changes must be allocated to *change windows*, chosen according to business convenience. Change prioritization is performed very early in the CM process, before plans are ready and before very much is known about change implementation.

How is prioritization done? Many dimensions must be taken into account by the change manager, including the business impact of service down time, the business urgency (deadline), the complexity of the change and risks associated with the change implementation. Risk itself is a complex dimension that includes change complexity, whether the activities have been performed before, the probability of a change being unsuccessful, etc. Uncertainty in the time needed to perform the change activities causing possible delays and service disruption, crossing deadlines with consequent penalties are a major source of risk.

**The problem.** Whether performed by the change manager or by the CAB, the change prioritization activity is difficult. At that early stage in the process, little information is known about the change, business impact must somehow be evaluated and risk must be accounted for. All of these difficulties are compounded by the sheer scale of the problem (the number of changes to be dealt with); for example, cases are known where a large service provider must deal with hundreds of changes *per week* for a single customer. How can be prioritization activity be performed adequately?

**Our objective.** This paper provides a method through which priorities can be automatically (or semi-automatically) assigned to changes. We use a Business-Driven IT Management (BDIM) approach to capture the business impact of service disruption due to changes. The impact is estimated by evaluating the risk exposure of service disruption due to delays caused by uncertainties in time when performing change activities. In an ITIL context, the resulting method can be packaged as a tool, used by a change manager whenever change prioritization need to be calculated. This would typically be done whenever inputs to the tool change, for example, whenever a new Request For Change is submitted.

The rest of the paper is structured as follows: section 2 proposes a new risk-based impact model; this model is used in section 3 to automate the assignment of priorities to changes; section 4 discusses a real case study that validates the approach; section 5 summarizes related work; finally, section 6 offers a brief summary, conclusions and discussion of further possible work.

## 2   Estimating Change Impact Through Risk

Our objective in this section is to calculate the business impact associated with a change; risk will be used in the formulation. Let us first describe what we intend to do informally. A formal treatment will follow. We want to estimate the business impact caused by a set of changes to be applied to IT infrastructure. Since a BDIM approach is being used, one wants to estimate this impact using a metric understood by business people and a financial measure of impact is thus chosen. Assume that these changes affect a single IT service; it is straightforward to extend the formal treatment to cover several services affected by the changes. Several sources of impact are considered:

1. As soon as the RFC is submitted, there is already a need felt for the change to be implemented. The business is somehow suffering until the change has been implemented; in other words, there is a business impact right from the start. This may be due to a service being down, for example, as would happen if the change were requested as a result of a problem that disrupted the service. There may be other impact causes, say lost opportunities such as would occur for a change meant to bring up a completely new service.
2. While the change is being implemented, assume that the service is down. Thus the impact due to service unavailability will be captured. Change windows negotiated with the business, during which unavailability is not counted against the provider, are not considered here for the sake of brevity; they can easily be accommodated.
3. When the deadline associated with the change is crossed, a penalty may be paid by the service provider and new, more severe, business impact is felt until the change is implemented.

The change implementation time is subject to statistical variations and the resulting uncertainty in the time needed to complete a change can affect the impact. Also, the more one waits to *start* change implementation, the higher the business impact will be, since the probability of completing change implementation before the deadline will decrease. Since the impact is closely tied to the time-related risks associated with changes, we will call the numerical impact calculated for a change the (financial) *risk exposure* of that change. The risk exposure of a change is defined as the expected value (in a probabilistic sense) of the business losses accrued as a result of waiting to implement the change and then implementing it using activities of uncertain time duration (but with known distribution). Observe that we are borrowing a fairly standard definition of risk (see section 6): risk is typically calculated by taking into account the probability of occurrence of certain events and the impact resulting from each event. The expected value of impact is the risk exposure value.

Let us now formalize these concepts: our goal is to find an expression for the risk exposure, $R_n(t)$, associated with the $n^{\text{th}}$ change if the change implementation starts at time $t$. Time $t=0$ is *now*, the time at which the change manager is performing the risk calculation; time $t$ thus indicates how far in the future one expects to start implementing the change. Let the set of changes for which one needs to calculate risk exposure be $C = \{c_1, \ldots, c_n, \ldots, c_{|C|}\}$.

Several parameters will be associated with change $c_n$:

- The change is initiated at time $t_n^I$ (superscript $I$ means "Initial"). Choosing this value is obviously of critical importance and will be considered in the next section when change prioritization is analyzed.
- The duration of implementation for the change is the random variable $\tilde{t}_n$ with cumulative probability distribution: $F_n(t) = P[\tilde{t}_n \leq t]$. Let $M_n(t) = 1 - F(t)$ be the complementary cumulative distribution function.
- A deadline $t_n^D$ (superscript $D$ means "Deadline") exists before which the change must be implemented. Different impact calculations may be performed before and after the deadline. Although a change can have its own deadline, frequently, the deadline will be imposed by a Service Level Agreement (SLA) associated with the service affected by the change; in that case, the change simply inherits the SLA-specified deadline.
- Before a change is implemented, non-obedience to contractual clauses or the loss of business opportunities may cause business impact. Assume that, while the change remains unimplemented, financial loss is accrued at a rate $\varphi_{n,BD}^c$, before the deadline (in the interval $[0, t_n^D)$) and at a rate $\varphi_{n,AD}^c$ after the deadline (in the interval $[t_n^D, \infty]$). To help the reader, observe that superscript $c$ means "Change" and subscripts $BD$ and $AD$ mean "Before Deadline" and "After Deadline", respectively.
- Recall that the service is assumed to be down during change implementation activities. Let $\varphi_{n,BD}^S$ (superscript $S$ means "Service") be the rate of financial loss due to service unavailability during the time interval $[t_n^I, t_n^D)$, when $t_n^I < t_n^D$ (unavailability before the deadline). After the deadline, the cost of service unavailability may be higher and we let financial loss accrue at a rate of $\varphi_{n,AD}^S$ during the interval $[t_n^I, \infty]$, when $t_n^I \geq t_n^D$.

The crucial observation in calculating the expected value of loss can now be stated: if, at time $t$, change $c_n$ has not yet been completed and loss is accumulated at rate $\varphi$, then, over the time interval $[t, t + dt]$, the accumulated loss is $\varphi \cdot dt$. Now, consider two time instants $t_1$ and $t_2$ occurring *before* a change has started; the total loss over the period is simply $\int_{t_1}^{t_2} \varphi \cdot dt = (t_2 - t_1)\varphi$. If, however, the change implementation has already started, loss will only accumulate until the implementation is completed. The probability distribution of $\tilde{t}_n$ must therefore be taken into account to calculate loss. At time $t$, loss accumulates with probability $P[\tilde{t}_n > t] = 1 - F_n(t) = M_n(t)$. Thus, between time instants $t_1$ and $t_2$, the accumulated financial loss will be $\int_{t_1}^{t_2} M_n(t) \cdot \varphi \cdot dt$.

We are now ready to combine these concepts to calculate risk exposure (expected value for impact). The expression depends on whether implementation starts before or after the deadline:

$$R_n(t_n^I) = \begin{cases} t_n^I \cdot \varphi_{n,BD}^c + \int_0^{t_n^D - t_n^I} (\varphi_{n,BD}^c + \varphi_{n,BD}^s) M_n(t) dt + \int_{t_n^D - t_n^I}^\infty (\varphi_{n,AD}^c + \varphi_{n,AD}^s) M_n(t) dt & \text{if } t_n^I < t_n^D \\ t_n^D \cdot \varphi_{n,BD}^c + (t_n^I - t_n^D)\varphi_{n,AD}^c + \int_0^\infty (\varphi_{n,AD}^c + \varphi_{n,AD}^s) M_n(t) dt, & \text{if } t_n^I \geq t_n^D \end{cases}$$

(1)

Figures 1 and 2 show which loss rate is in effect at which time and will help the reader understand the above equation. Figure 1 applies when the change implementation starts before the deadline and Figure 2 when it starts after the deadline.

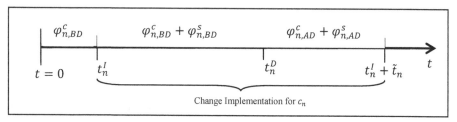

**Fig. 1.** – Change implementation starts before deadline

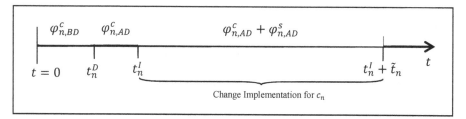

**Fig. 2.** – Change implementation starts after deadline

## 3    Assigning Priorities to Changes

The risk exposure measure given in Equation (1) can be used in several manners. In this section, we show how to calculate a change's priority level ("Immediate", etc.) from it, indicating how quickly the change should be dealt with. Priority thus influences the order of implementation; it also influences whether the CAB gets involved or even whether a CAB meeting is called to consider a very high-risk change.

How can the priority level be chosen? ITIL recommends that priority be chosen after evaluating service impact and business urgency (through the deadline and financial loss, for example). Since both these dimensions are captured in the above risk exposure measure, it should be useful in establishing priority. From Equation (1), risk depends on the time $t_n^I$ at which the change implementation starts. How is this time to be chosen and how can the risk exposure measure be translated to a priority level?

A naïve algorithm can calculate risk exposure at $t_n^I = 0$ (now) and use risk thresholds for each priority level. This algorithm is not adequate. Consider, for example, the case of a change with very high penalty starting tomorrow, or next week. Merely evaluating risk at $t = 0$ does not reveal just how close the precipice really is!

Informally, the algorithm we propose is as follows. Company policy sets a *tolerance limit to risk exposure* (or a pain threshold), say $10,000.00. Risk is evaluated assuming the change implementation will start at several instants in time, one for each priority level. Intuitively, this time instant captures "how long implementing changes with this priority can be delayed". For example, *now* is the instant associated with "Immediate", "this weekend" is associated with level "High", "two weeks from now" is associated with level "Medium", and so on. Now, the priority level chosen for a change is that which initiates change implementation furthest in the future but which does *not* cause risk exposure to cross the tolerance limit. Thus, if a change has $1,000.00 risk exposure at $t_n^I = 0$ and $50,000.00 at $t_n^I =$ "this weekend", then the change would be "Immediate" since delaying till the weekend makes risk exposure cross the pain threshold.

Let us formalize the concepts. Let $P = \{p_1, \dots, p_{|P|}\}$ be the set of priority levels, where level $p_i$ is more urgent than level $p_{i+1}$. Time instant $t_i$ is associated with priority level $p_i$. Further, let the tolerance level to risk be $\eta$, as set by corporate policy. Let $e_n$ be the priority level associated with change $c_n$. Here is the result we were seeking:

$$e_n = \begin{cases} p_1 & \text{if } R_n(t_1) \geq \eta \\ p_{|P|} & \text{if } R_n(t_{|P|}) < \eta \\ p_i & \text{if } R_n(t_i) < \eta \ \text{ and } R_n(t_{i+1}) \geq \eta, 1 \leq i < |P| \end{cases}$$

Prioritizing a single change can be done in time $O(|P|)$, which is constant in the number of changes, making the algorithm adequate to prioritize very many changes with no performance restrictions.

## 4    Case Study and Validation

A case study was undertaken in conjunction with a large multinational IT service provider in Brazil. A scenario (also used in [5], but in the context of change scheduling) was set up in conjunction with the service provider and all parameters used here were furnished by the provider. We first describe the scenario and then discuss how validation of the models and methods presented in this paper was performed.

**The services and infrastructure.** Please refer to Figure 3. The IT infrastructure supports a credit card payment service and must be extended to support a new e-commerce service. Each service is subject to an SLA that specifies service level objectives, penalties, deadlines, etc. Configuration items supporting the services are as follows: two servers support the credit card payment service, a database server and an application server. Firewall B controls traffic to both servers. The e-commerce service will be supported by the e-commerce server, the router and Firewall A. Furthermore, other service (whose exact nature was not specified by the provider) also and may be affected by maintenance activity to IT infrastructure components.

**The SLAs.** The three services are subject to SLA clauses as follows.

- General clauses for all SLAs: Any security-related RFC costs $1000/hour until the change is implemented. Any service affected by security issues must be brought down.
- Credit-card service SLA: Downtime costs $9000/hour before the deadline and $12000/hour from the deadline onward; deadlines are negotiated per incident. By default, RFCs raised due to incidents cost $1500/hour before the deadline and $2500/hour from the deadline onward; deadlines are negotiated per incident. Performance-related problems are penalized at the rate of $300/hour before the deadline and $400/hour from the deadline onward; deadlines depend on the severity of the performance problem.
- New e-commerce service. The service must be up by a certain date, 18 days in the future. From that point on, a penalty of $18000/hour is exacted from the provider.
- Other services. Performance-related penalties amount to $4000/hour before the deadline and $5000/hour from the deadline onward; deadlines depend on the severity of the performance problem.

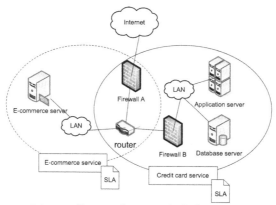

**Fig. 3.** Case study scenario infrastructure

**The changes.** Four changes were included in the scenario:

- Change $c_1$: Bring the new e-commerce service online. Since the Internet Connection used for the service is already being paid for even before the service is up, a link cost of $25/hour applies.
- Change $c_2$: Because of change $c_1$, new firewall rules must be installed in firewall A. Since this is tied to bringing up the e-commerce service, it must be done by the same deadline (18 days). The e-commerce service cannot come up until this change is performed.
- Change $c_3$: An incident occurring in the credit card service forces maintenance on the database server which will bring down the service. This change was negotiated to be performed within 20 days.

- Change $c_4$: Due to traffic overload, communication technology used for "other services" needs to be tweaked. This will have heavy performance impact and degrade service quality while the change is being done.

Data from the service SLAs and the changes described above are summarized in Table 1. Observe that $\varphi^s_{1,AD}$ (associated with the service) has value zero since, in this case, the service is down right from the start (RFC submission) and the impact is already included in $\varphi^c_{1,AD}$ associated with the change.

Table 1. Changes and their parameters

| # | Change | $t^D_n$ (days) | Affected service | $\varphi^c_{n,BD}$ | $\varphi^c_{n,AD}$ | $\varphi^s_{n,BD}$ | $\varphi^s_{n,AD}$ |
|---|--------|----------------|------------------|---------------------|---------------------|---------------------|---------------------|
| $c_1$ | Provision e-commerce service | 18 | e-comm | $25/h | $18000/h | $0/h | $0/h |
| $c_2$ | Firewall configuration | 18 | e-comm | $1000/h | $1000/h | $0/h | $18000/h |
| $c_3$ | Maintenance to database server | 20 | Credit Card | $1500/h | $2500/h | $9000/h | $12000/h |
| $c_4$ | Maintenance to infrastructure | 13 | Others | $300/h | $400/h | $4000/h | $5000/h |

**Cumulative probability functions.** In order to complete the risk model, the service provider supplied a historical log of 977 changes performed over 1 month from which probabilistic parameters were obtained. This log provided the RFC registration time, change implementation start time and implementation duration. Still, there were not enough changes of all types to extract a meaningful distribution from the data. We therefore extracted the mean $\mu_n$ and standard deviation $\sigma_n$ from changes of the same type as the ones considered in the scenario and assumed a normal (Gaussian) distribution for the implementation time $\tilde{t}_n$. The appropriateness of this assumption can be argued as follows: a change implementation consists of several activities and the duration of each activity is a random variable with its own probability distribution. Since $\tilde{t}_n$ is simply the sum of several such random variables, we can use the Central Limit Theorem (see, e.g., [4]) which states that the distribution of a sum of independent random variable will tend to the normal distribution. We therefore use the normal distribution: $M_n(t) = 1 - \frac{1}{2}\left(1 + \text{erf}\left(\frac{t-\mu_n}{\sigma_n\sqrt{2}}\right)\right)$. Finite values for $\mu_n$ and $\sigma_n$ guarantee that the infinite integrals of Equation (1) will converge.

The parameters shown in Table 2 were obtained from the historical change log.

Table 2. Mean and standard deviation for change duration

| # | $\mu_n$ (hours) | $\sigma_n$ (hours) |
|---|-----------------|--------------------|
| $c_1$ | 5.6840 | 6.2520 |
| $c_2$ | 8.1421 | 7.4317 |
| $c_3$ | 6.1018 | 6.1852 |
| $c_4$ | 9.0152 | 7.3802 |

**The case study scenario.** These 4 changes must be prioritized by the change manager now (at $t = 0$). Let us use the following common priority levels: P = {"Immediate", "High", "Medium", "Low"}. The time instants used to evaluate risk exposure are *now* and the end of next three change windows, which occur weekly. Thus, $t_1=0$, $t_2=7$

Table 3.  Priority levels when evaluating at t=0

| # | $R_n(0)$ | $R_n(7)$ | $R_n(14)$ | $R_n(21)$ |
|---|---|---|---|---|
| $c_1$ | \$0 | \$4,000 | \$9,000 | \$1,520,000 |
| $c_2$ | \$8,700 | \$176,000 | \$344,000 | \$1,100,000 |
| $c_3$ | \$76,000 | \$496,000 | \$916,000 | \$2,021,000 |
| $c_4$ | \$29,000 | \$72,000 | \$257,000 | \$325,000 |

(days), $t_3$=14, $t_4$=21. Company policy set the pain threshold at $\eta$ =\$200,000. Table 3 shows the results of the risk exposure calculation.

Recall that the algorithm sets the priority according to the largest time before the pain threshold is crossed. This would set change priorities as: {"Medium", "High", "Immediate", "High"}. For example, change $c_1$ crosses threshold between $t$=14 (medium) and $t$=21 (low), which makes it a medium-priority change. The time $t$=14 does not mean that this change should be implemented 14 days from now; it means that leaving it till the next change window ($t$=21) is too painful. Ideally, it can be done much ahead of that time limit. This will depend on the set changes to be performed, resources available, etc. The change scheduling problem is studied in [5].

Priority levels change with time as can be seen in Figure 4. Let us assume that time passes and we are now one week later. Deadlines are now closer by 7 days and, if evaluating priorities again, yields {"High", "Immediate", "Immediate", "Immediate"}. If the change manager waits a further 7 days, all changes are tagged as "Immediate".

**Validation.** The case study scenario described above was configured with the help of an experienced change manager working at a large multinational IT service provider in Brazil. In order to validate our method, we asked this manager to prioritize the changes using his current approach. The manager typically uses proximity to deadlines and loss rate before the deadline to assign priorities. His final priorities were: {"Medium", **"Medium"**, "Immediate", "High"}. We then ran our algorithm and obtained the results shown previously: {"Medium", **"High"**, "Immediate", "High"}. There is only one difference in priority. We showed our results, the model used and

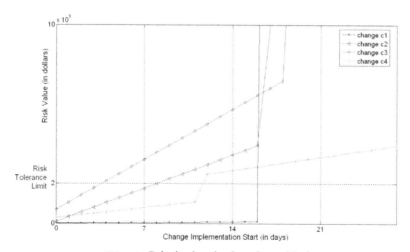

**Fig. 4.** Priority levels changing with time

the graph in Figure 4 and the manager agreed that "High priority" is more adequate for change $c_2$, since risk exposure would be too high if the change were left till later.

**Discussion.** Several points concerning the proposed method for evaluating risk exposure and assigning priorities need clarification. A model is no better than the parameters fed into it. The model used here has several inputs such as loss rates and the probability distribution functions for change duration. Where do these come from?

Loss rates can either come from SLAs (as we did here) or can come from a business impact model such as used in BDIM models. As an example, for e-commerce applications, business process throughput (monetary transactions per second) can be used to estimate loss due to downtime (see, e.g., [17]).

To obtain probability distributions for change duration, we suggest two alternatives: historical information can be used as we did here; furthermore, if historical information is available for individual change implementation activities, then distributions for each activity can be used to estimate distribution for change duration using the central limit theorem. A second alternative is to ask change implementers to specify minimum and maximum values for expected change implementation times and use a Weibull distribution; a distribution with negative skew is more likely to match reality since experience shows that actual change duration is more likely to edge closer to the maximum value.

## 5  Related Work

This section reviews some past work concerning risk that bears some relationship to our own work. The discussion progresses from the general to the more specific.

**Work concerning risk in general.** Risk management is a well-studied subject in various areas of human endeavor. The definition of risk itself varies according to the area of application. For example, in *Statistics*, risk is taken as a probability of some event that is seen as undesirable. More frequently used is the definition from *Probabilistic Risk Analysis* (PRA) whereby risk is characterized by two quantities: the severity of the possible adverse consequence(s), and the probability of occurrence of each consequence. In *Finance*, risk is the probability that an investment's actual return will be different than expected. In *Information Security*, risk is a similar to the PRA definition but considers two separate probabilities: that there are threats and that there are vulnerabilities to be exploited by threats. Our work is based on the PRA definition of risk (see, for example, [3]).

**Risk in IT.** In the world of IT, risk has been used in project management [6], software development, security [7, 8], and other areas [12]. Most risk assessment methodologies use probabilistic analysis. All of these approaches were instrumental in helping reach the model we propose here. However, whereas the approaches listed here calculate numerical values of risk, they use ad hoc weights and impact measures that are not direct business metrics; by contrast, our method carefully defines risk parameters and calculates values for risk exposure in terms of metrics that are directly understandable by business people. Also, our approach uses historical information to estimate model parameters.

**Risk in change management.** Some tools are commercially available that claim to help in managing changes, although no details are given that can be used to evaluate and compare methods [9, 10]. Several papers have presented approaches to qualitatively evaluate risk (e.g., [11, 13]). These studies do not provide quantitative risk analysis. On the other hand, most of these methods evaluate more dimensions than our analysis which limits itself to the risks associated with the uncertainty in change implementation duration.

Keller and others, in [14, 15], present the CHAMPS system to automate some steps in the execution of changes. Even though the authors try to solve a different problem in Change Management, this work was one of the first to model changes formally and influenced our own work.

Finally, some of our own past work in change scheduling led to the model developed and presented here [16, 5]. Our past work in change management dealt with scheduling and business impact. The similarity with our past work is that *business loss* is a basic metric used to solve the scheduling (past work) and prioritization (this work) problems. However, our present work deals with another change management process activity (prioritization) and includes risk (due to uncertainties) in the model formulation; both of these things are completely new.

**Assigning priority to changes using risk.** To our knowledge, this is the first formal, quantitative, business-driven method to automatically quantify risk and to assign priorities to a set of changes in ITSM.

## 6   Conclusions and Future Work

**Summary.** This paper has dealt with the Change Management process within IT Service Management. Change Management includes several activities, some of which need to evaluate the risk associated with changes to be made to the infrastructure and services. We presented a method by which risk exposure associated with a change can be evaluated and the risk metric was applied to the problem of automatically assigning priorities to changes. A formal model was developed to this end; the model captures the business perspective by using financial metrics in the evaluation of risk exposure. A case study was performed in conjunction with a large IT service provider and provides good results when compared to decisions made by human managers. To the best of our knowledge, this is the first such automatic solution published in the literature. The method is scalable and can be applied to evaluate risk exposure and prioritize hundreds or thousands of changes.

**Conclusions.** The validation exercise has shown the method to be useful. Risks associated with changes can be calculated and changes prioritized in an automatic fashion. We understand that we have not concluded full validation and that more extended use is required to reach final conclusions regarding the worth of the approach. Still, preliminary results are very encouraging and the change manager participating in the study wholeheartedly supports our continued efforts. Observe also that our method need not altogether substitute human managers or claim to "do better" than human managers: it claims to help managers handle a larger scale of changes by automating some of the risk and priority calculations and provides better visibility into the possible impact of changes from a business (financial) perspective.

**Future work.** We would like to improve the following deficiencies: model parameters may be difficult to obtain if SLAs are deficient, the business impact models used may not be applicable in all type of business processes affected by IT services, the model only considers risk due to uncertainties in time and lateness in implementing changes; other risk dimensions such as change complexity and the presence of back-out plans can be investigated.

Finally, the risk metric proposed here can be applied to other change management activities such as change scheduling and also to other ITSM processes.

**Acknowledgments.** This work was developed in collaboration with HP Brazil R&D. We thank contributions by A. Christodoulou, J. A. Cerqueira and C. Paraizzo.

# References

1. IT Governance Institute, Cobit 3rd edn. (2000), www.isaca.org/cobit.htm
2. IT Infrastructure Library, ITIL Service Delivery and Support, OGC, UK (2003)
3. Kaplan, S., Garrick, B.J.: On the Quantitative Definition of Risk. Risk Analysis 1, 11–27 (1981)
4. Rohatgi, V.K.: An Introduction to Probability Theory and Math. Statistics. Wiley, Chichester (1976)
5. Rebouças, R., Sauvé, J., Moura, A., Bartolini, C., Trastour, D.: A Decision Support Tool for Optimizing Scheduling of IT Changes. In: 10th IFIP/IEEE Symp. on Integrated Mgmt., IEEE Computer Society Press, Los Alamitos (2007)
6. PMBOK - Project Management Book of Knowledge, http://www.pmi.org
7. http://www.cert.org/octave/
8. http://www.cramm.com/
9. Cisco IT Balances Innovation and Risk With Change Management Process, http://www.cisco.com/web/about/ciscoitatwork/case_studies/business_management_dl2.html
10. IT Service Management - Change and Configuration Management: Reducing Risk by understanding your infrastructure, http://www-03.ibm.com/solutions/itsolutions/doc/content/bin/itsol_it_service_management_change_and_configuration_management.pdf
11. Goolsbey, J.: Risk-Based IT Change Management, http://web.reed.edu/nwacc/programs/awards/excellence_award/pnnl_submissions_07/pnnl_risk-based_it_change_management.pdf
12. Benoit A., Rivard S., Patry M.: Managing IT Outsourcing Risk, Cirano, Montreal (2001)
13. Mosier, S., Gutenberg, S., Raphael, R.: The Relationship of Technology Change Management to Risk Management, Engineering Management Society (2000)
14. Keller, A., Hellerstein, J.L., Wolf, J.L., Wu, K.-L., Krishnan, V.: The CHAMPS system: change management with planning and scheduling. In: Network Operations and Management Symposium, pp. 395–408 (2004)
15. Brown, A.B., Keller, A., Hellerstein, J.L.: A model of configuration complexity and its application to a change management system. In: IM 2005, pp. 631–644 (2005)
16. Sauvé, J., Rebouças, R., Moura, A., Bartolini, C., Boulmakoul, A., Trastour, D.: Business driven support for change management: planning and scheduling of changes. In: DSOM 2006. 17th IFIP/IEEE International Workshop on Distributed Systems: Operations and Management, Dublin, Ireland (October 23–25, 2006)
17. Menascé, D., Almeida, V.A.F., Fonseca, R., Mendes, M.A.: Business-Oriented Resource Management Policies for e-Commerce Servers, Performance Evaluation 42, pp. 223–239. Elsevier Science, Amsterdam (2000)

# Assessing Operational Impact in Enterprise Systems by Mining Usage Patterns

Mark Moss and Calton Pu

CERCS, Georgia Institute of Technology
801 Atlantic Drive, Atlanta, GA 30332
{markmoss,calton}@cc.gatech.edu

**Abstract.** Performing impact analysis involves determining which users are affected by system resource failures. Understanding when users are actually using certain resources allows system administrators to better assess the impact on enterprise operations. This is critical to prioritizing system repair and restoration actions, and allowing users to modify their plans proactively. We present an approach that combines traditional dependency analysis with resource usage information to improve the operational relevance of these assessments. Our approach collects data from end-user systems using common operating system commands, and uses this data to generate dependency and usage pattern information. We tested our approach in a computer lab running applications at various levels of complexity, and demonstrate how our framework can be used to assist system administrators in providing clear and concise impact assessments to executive managers.

**Keywords:** operational impact analysis, system management, data mining.

## 1 Introduction

An important question in system management is determining which users are affected by system resource failures [1]. System administrators are often tasked to assess the impact of system resource failures on business operations, which we refer to as *assessing the operational impact*, and to present this assessment to management executives. Administrators must present this information in a manner that is clear and operationally relevant to the executives. An example assessment is: "The purchasing department users will not be able to access their invoice applications for the next two hours because our application server has failed", which connects the effects of the technical event clearly to one or more business operations. It also captures the concept that an *operational* impact occurs only if the purchasing department needs to access the invoice application during the outage period. Taking this usage information into account makes the impact assessment significantly more effective.

Consequently, producing effective operational impact assessments requires: (1) connecting lower-level technical events to their impacts on higher-level, user-relevant resources; and, (2) integrating an understanding of when the higher-level resources

A. Clemm, L.Z. Granville, and R. Stadler (Eds.): DSOM 2007, LNCS 4785, pp. 159–170, 2007.

are actually needed by the enterprise's users. Most users are aware of the applications that they use to manage their local and remote data. We categorize these resources – programs, data files, and web sites – as higher-level because they are generally well understood by users in the context of allowing them to achieve the enterprise objectives. These resources can vary in importance based on timing considerations. As one example, having access to certain financial files may be important to the enterprise only near the end of a fiscal quarter or year. In this case, we say that there is a *schedule-based usage pattern* for the users accessing those files. As a different example, consider a special application that is accessed only when a certain combination of other resources are accessed – perhaps in response to a rare customer request. These requests might not occur at regularly scheduled times, as in the schedule-based example. However, we may still be able to determine that the application is always accessed within a certain amount of time after the customer request is placed, and we say that there is a *demand-based usage pattern* for the users accessing this special application. We believe that this information can be collected, processed and integrated to assist system administrators in producing effective operational impact assessments.

The main contribution of the paper is an operational impact assessment system that integrates events from all system and application components. These events are clustered through simple data mining and statistical techniques to infer usage patterns needed for assessment. By integrating events from all relevant components, our system is able to translate a low level event (e.g., failure of a device or router) into user level impact assessments meaningful to system administrators and managers. We demonstrate our approach by collecting and analyzing operational data at Georgia Tech for 35 days. Our experimental results show promising results in providing quantitative statistical support for operational impact analysis.

The rest of the paper is organized as follows. We define our key goals and definitions in Section 2. We highlight how our approach is distinguished from previous work in Section 3. We cover our approach in Section 4, and examine how we collect, process and integrate the topology and usage pattern data. We provide our experimental data in Section 5, including an example scenario of how we would produce the impact assessment from a specific technical event. Finally, we consider some possible extensions of our work in Section 6.

## 2 Problem Goals and Definitions

Our goal is to present a framework that helps system administrators assess the operational impact by determining the users affected by a component failure. This framework supports assessments in the current time period, and also provides a predictive capability by leveraging the information generated from usage pattern mining to infer the likelihood of impacts during future time periods. We don't expect this approach to assess the operational impact perfectly; the intent is that it will provide clear, operationally focused, and timely feedback that assists system administrators in assessing the operational impact for the executive users of the system. Our approach is based on collecting operating system data from selected end-systems to construct a model of the intra-system and inter-system resource dependencies. This information is then aggregated to construct a dependency model for the overall enterprise system. The data is also time-stamped, and data mining techniques are applied to detect usage patterns. The dependency topology and usage pattern information is then used to assess operational impacts.

We define an *Enterprise System* as a distributed system of components that are used in combination in pursuit of one or more functional objectives. We model an enterprise system as a directed graph of its' distributed resources, where the nodes represent the system's resources, and the edges represent the functional dependencies between resources. An edge from a source node to a sink node implies that the failure of the sink node would likely prevent the source node from completing its tasks successfully. Fig. 1 presents our terminology and definitions.

*Enterprise System = {Resources, Dependencies}*
   where *Dependencies = {$d_{i,j}$ | $r_i$, $r_j \in$ Resources and $r_i \rightarrow r_j$}, source(dependency $d_{i,j}$) = $r_i$*
*sink(dependency $d_{i,j}$) = $r_j$*, and *RealUsers $\subset$ Resources*

*Technical Event = <Failed, $t_{failure}$, duration, Status>*
   where *Failed $\subset$ Resources, Status = { d:active(d, $t_{failure}$) | d $\in$ Dependencies }*
and *active(dependency d, time t) = { 1 if d occurs at t; 0 otherwise }*

*Impact Assessment = { <Path, $t_{start}$, $t_{stop}$, $p_{impact}$> }*
   where *Path = { $d_{(1)}$, $d_{(2)}$, ..., $d_{(k)}$ }, source($d_{(1)}$) $\in$ RealUsers, sink($d_{(k)}$) $\in$ Failed,*
*$\forall$ i sink($d_{(i)}$) = source($d_{(i+1)}$), and $t_{failure} \leqslant t_{start} \leqslant t_{stop} \leqslant$ ($t_{failure}$ + duration)*

**Fig. 1.** Operational Impact Terminology and Definitions

We define a *Technical Event* as a 4-tuple which represents the instance where a certain set of resources have *Failed* at time $t_{failure}$, and will not be repaired or restored until ($t_{failure}$ + *duration*). In most cases, the average repair time (i.e. MTTR) can be used as an approximate duration value. *Status* captures the operational status of the system resources at the time of failure. Capturing all system status data might not be possible in some environments, but even partial status data can be useful in assessing impact. We then define an operational *Impact Assessment* as a set of 4-tuples. Each tuple represents how one user will be affected by one of the failed resources along a given *Path*, during the period from $t_{start}$ to $t_{stop}$, with a likelihood of $p_{impact}$. The path information is generated from the topology data, while the $t_{start}$, $t_{stop}$ and $p_{impact}$ values are generated from the usage pattern data.

## 3  Related Research

There has been significant research in the areas of impact analysis, dependency discovery and data mining. Two main factors distinguish our approach from previous research: (1) a focus on the subset of the topology with a directly traceable impact to one or more users; and (2) close integration of the resource dependency and resource usage data. Both of these factors help increase the operational relevance of the resulting assessments.

**Impact Analysis.** There are still a significant number of administrators and executive users who perform impact analysis manually, based on best practices and rules of thumb [2][3]. Other automated, dynamic approaches have been proposed [4][5][6][7], but many require external expert knowledge in the form of SLAs, QoS metrics, user-defined use cases, and weighing the importance of various resources. Our approach is automated, and infers the importance of system resources during different time frames by monitoring usage directly. Thereska et al [8] address the need to consider impact analysis in a proactive manner. They propose a "what-if" approach that supports interactive exploration of the results of system changes. Their analysis is focused on determining the technical impact of configuration changes on the system's performance, where our approach focuses more directly on assessing the operational impact for enterprise users.

**Dependency Discovery.** There has also been significant research on the importance of dependency analysis in determining the impact of a resource failure. The most similar approach to ours is a forensic analysis tool [9] to help system administrators identify entry points when investigating security intrusions. They load modules into the Linux kernel, and use the information gathered to detect dependency relationships between objects by tracking events in which one object affects the state of another object. They focus on three types of dependencies based on the objects being monitored: process/process, process/file and process/filename. Similarly, our approach uses the structure of the collected data records, including relationships between key fields, to determine dependencies. This differs from more sophisticated statistical approaches as used in [10][11]. In addition, the forensic analysis [9] focuses on files and programs, our approach includes a wider array of objects such as users, devices, network ports, remotes sites and routers.

Also, our approach collects data from the end-user workstations only, and doesn't require any modification of the system hardware or software resources. This is similar to the philosophies and techniques in [12][13]. Some approaches capture data using methods such as offline perturbation, and modification of system components [14][15][16]. Though these approaches might yield richer and more comprehensive topology results, the intrusiveness of these techniques could make implementation and management more difficult in production environments.

**Data Mining.** Data mining has been used for system management [17] and application management [18]. Our approach goes beyond previous work by abstracting and integrating system level events and application level events. As an example, in the mining of usage data to detect business workflow patterns, Aalst et al [18] mention the exploitation of timing data as an open problem in workflow mining. We use timing as the underlying fabric on which we integrate events from all system and application components.

## 4   Overview of Our Approach

Our approach is divided into four basic phases: Collection, Discovery, Mining and Assessment (Fig. 2). During the *Collection Phase*, we collect the operating system command output on various end-user workstations. The data is also time stamped to ensure consistency when linking records from different commands during the Discovery Phase, and pattern mining during the Mining Phase. In the *Discovery Phase*, we construct a single, enterprise system-wide dependency topology using the collected data. The topology is then used to compute transitive dependencies between resources and users during the Assessment Phase. The *Mining Phase* detects usage patterns based on when dependencies occur (schedule-based), and how different dependencies are related in terms of their activity status (demand-based). Finally, the *Assessment Phase* integrates the system topology and usage patterns to produce an impact assessment for a given technical event.

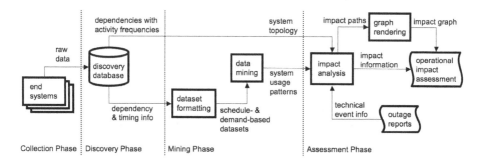

**Fig. 2.** Impact Assessment Dataflow

**Collection Phase.** We use cron-activated batch files to capture data about the current state of the workstation being monitored. The batch files execute common Linux operating systems (OS) commands like w(), ps(), lsof(), and traceroute(), to collect data about users, programs and processes, open files, and remote sites. The batch files also format the output for further processing during the Discovery Phase.

**Discovery Phase.** We use PostgreSQL views and scripts to load the OS output into a database, and extract dependencies in accordance with our dependency topology model in Fig. 3. The nodes correspond to fields in the command output, and each edge is labeled with the commands used to generate that specific type of dependency. As an example, the *w*() command gives the identifier of users logged onto the system, and is primarily used to distinguish real user accounts from accounts used to manage system services. Consider this sample *w*() output from the workstation *athena*:

```
USER    TTY     FROM                        IDLE    WHAT
adams   pts/0   achilles.cc.gt.atl.edu      4days   -bash
```

We derive the following three dependencies from this output:

- user | global | *adams* → site | global | *achilles.cc.gt.atl.edu*
- user | global | *adams* → program | *athena* | *–bash*
- program | *athena* | *–bash* → site | global | *achilles.cc.gt.atl.edu*

These dependencies correspond to the three edges in the topology model between the users, programs, and sites nodes.

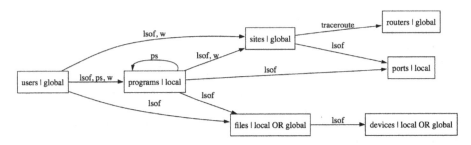

**Fig. 3.** Impact Topology Dependency Model

Each resource is represented by three values: *type | zone | identifier.* The resource types are defined in a relatively straightforward and intuitive manner. *Identifier* is the actual resource name, and *type* and *zone* are used to avoid machine-wide and system-wide name conflicts, respectively. Resources located exclusively on a particular end-system are assigned to that computer's *local zone.* Resources accessible by two or more resources located in different local zones are assigned to the system-wide *global zone.* As an example, a device can represent a (local) hard drive, or a (global) network attached storage system. A *system topology* view consists of the combined dependencies from one specific collection period. We use Graphviz to render the system topology and impact topology graphs.

**Mining Phase.** We mine the activity data for each dependency to find usage patterns. For each dependency, we extract the activity data from the database into the formats in Fig. 4. A schedule-based dataset captures the specific times a dependency is active, where the candidate attributes are the components of the timestamp $t_i$. The nominal attribute (i.e. class label) is 1 if dependency $d_j$ is active at time $t_i$, and 0 otherwise. In contrast, the demand-based dataset captures when a dependency is active relative to the activity status of other dependencies. The candidate attributes are the set of dependencies (not including $d_j$) that are active at time $t_i$, referred to as the *system status* at $t_i$. The nominal attribute is 1 if the dependency $d_j$ is active at any time during the $t_i$ to ($t_i$ + *duration*) time period, and 0 otherwise. The exact duration value is normally not known before the technical event occurs, but we can use common duration values for the advanced calculations. Schedule-based mining is similar to partial period pattern searches in time-series data, and demand-based mining is similar to autocorrelation analysis [19]. We use J48 and PART tools in WEKA [20] to generate the decision trees and rules, respectively, for the schedule-based and demand-based datasets. The trees and rules are stored as the *system usage patterns.*

Mining datasets for *dependency $d_j$* over all collection period *timestamps $t_i$*:

schedule-based: < { $day(t_i)$, $month(t_i)$, $date(t_i)$, $hour(t_i)$ }, $active(d_j, t_i)$ >

demand-based: < { $active(d_k, t_i)$ | $d_k \in$ Dependencies and $k \neq j$ }, $\bigvee_{\Delta t=0..(duration-1)} active(d_j, t_i + \Delta t)$ >

**Fig. 4.** Schedule- & Demand-Based Dataset Mining Formats

We also use the *activity frequency* and *correlation* values to reduce the number of dependencies to be considered during the Mining Phase. Dependencies with a very low activity frequency will be unlikely to cause an operational impact, and will also be likely to yield trivial patterns during the mining process. Dependencies with a very high activity frequency will, on the other hand, almost certainly cause an impact; however, they will also be likely to yield trivial patterns. Consequently, *dependencies with frequencies lower or higher than our established thresholds (e.g. 10% and 90%) are removed from mining consideration.* We calculate the correlation value for dependency pairs that have equivalent activity frequencies, or where the difference of their activity frequencies is smaller than an established tolerance (e.g. 2%). *If a pair of dependencies is strongly correlated (e.g. > 96.9%), then we can remove one of the dependencies from mining consideration.*

**Assessment Phase.** First, we use the *system topology* to calculate each path from a *failed resource* to a user who may be impacted by the given *technical event*. We then analyze the dependencies along each potentially impacted path. For each dependency, we use the *system usage patterns, time of failure, duration,* and *system status* information to determine the maximum likelihood that the dependency will be active during the outage period. For each path, we use the minimum likelihood of the dependencies on the path to determine the overall likelihood that the user will be operationally impacted by the failed resource. We remove any paths where the likelihood is less than a certain threshold, and return the remaining paths as the *operational impact assessment.*

## 5   Experimental Results

We tested our approach on a computer lab with six Linux–based end-user workstations, all of which are connected to a significantly larger campus infrastructure. The collector program was implemented as a Linux batch file on each workstation, and configured to collect data at roughly 5-minute intervals, which was then consolidated to one-hour groupings. We collected data from these systems over 35 days, and then aggregated the data on a central server to support the Discovery, Mining and Assessment Phases. We gathered more than 5000 distinct groups of data from the six end-systems, distributed over approximately 700 distinct collection times. The steps taken during the Discovery, Mining and Assessment Phases allowed us to significantly reduce this potentially overwhelming amount of data, making it much more manageable and operationally relevant. There are two significant motivations in reducing the size of the system and impact topologies: to reduce the amount of information processing needed to produce an impact assessment; and, to improve the clarity of the results for the system administrators and executive users, as shown in Table 1.

**Table 1.** Dependency Topology Sizes (Measured in Number of Dependencies/Edges)

|          | system-wide | | per technical event | | | |
|----------|------|------------|------|-----------|----------------------|------------|
|          | *all* | *real-users* | *all* | *freq < 0.1* | *0.1 ≤ freq ≤ 0.9* | *freq > 0.9* |
| **Mean**     | 3461 | 844 | 81  | 64  | 14  | 3  |
| **St. Dev.** | 1269 | 334 | 233 | 189 | 70  | 10 |
| **Skew**     | 1.3  | 0.7 | 4.2 | 5.3 | 7.2 | 3.9 |

The system topology data values were distributed fairly evenly around the mean. The impact topology values, however, were skewed significantly towards positive values. This was caused when certain technical events impacted an unusually large number of resources. As an example, most port or device failures only affected 4 to 12 resources. In contrast, technical events involving the *http* port on dionysos (*port | dionysos | http*), and a local device on hera (*device | hera | 8-1*), impacted 405 and 1,554 resources, respectively.

The initial topology, using all of the data gathered from one collection period, has an average of 3,461 dependencies. We reduce size of the system topology by 75% by identifying the subset of this topology that has a potential impact on one or more real users. Similarly, the initial impact topology for a given technical event has an average of 81 dependencies. We reduce the number of dependencies to be evaluated for the impact assessment by 79% by eliminating those dependencies with a frequency lower than our established threshold of 10%. Finally, an average of 14 dependencies needed to be evaluated with the system usage patterns for a given technical event. We determined that 1,893 of the dependencies collected during our testing had a frequency between 10% and 90%, inclusively. Further testing showed that 1,775 of these dependencies were strongly correlated (97% or more), such that we needed to perform usage pattern mining on only 118 distinct dependencies. Our practice results so far confirm these percentages: we've had to perform usage mining on an average of 2 of the 14 dependencies, and the usage patterns for the remaining 12 dependencies were strongly correlated to these results.

We will now demonstrate these principles with a practical example. Consider the technical event caused when the *mysql* port on the six end-systems used in our test environment are closed unintentionally by a faulty host firewall configuration. The comprehensive system topology for the entire testing period included over 92,000 distinct dependencies. Manually analyzing a topology of this size would be cumbersome and error-prone. We can use automated techniques to calculate more specifically which users are likely to be affected for this event, as shown in Fig. 5.

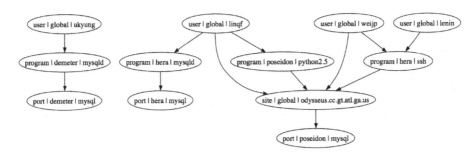

**Fig. 5.** Impact Topology Without Activity Frequencies

Using the impact topology results alone allows us to infer that the closed *mysql* port could potentially affect 4 of the 17 total users. We can leverage the system usage patterns to more specifically determine the impact. Fig. 6 gives an improved impact topology for this technical event, where each edge label represents the activity frequency for that dependency.

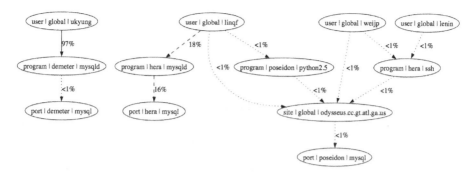

**Fig. 6.** Impact Topology with Activity Frequencies

We don't have enough information on the dependencies with a frequency < 10% to determine if they will be active during the outage period with any significant likelihood. Consequently, we remove the paths using these dependencies from consideration. The only path remaining for consideration is from *user | global | linqf* through *program | hera | mysqld* to *port | hera | mysql*. The next step is to use the timing and system status information from the technical event, along with the *system usage patterns*, to determine if there will be an impact on *user | global | linqf*.

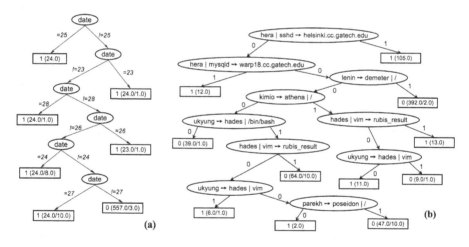

**Fig. 7.** Schedule-Based (a) and Demand-Based (b) Decision Trees

The two dependencies are strongly correlated, so we can use the same system usage pattern results for both dependencies. Fig. 7 shows the relevant decision tree results for these relationships. The scheduled-based decision tree has a correctly classified instances value of 96.57%, and we can use this as our measure of the likelihood of an impact. If the outage occurs between the 23rd and 28th of the month, then we would assess that user *linqf* has a 96.57% likelihood of being impacted during the outage period. Similarly, if the event occurs on the 22nd at 9pm, with an expected duration of 6 hours, then we would adjust our assessment such that user *linqf* has a 96.57% likelihood of being impacted between the hours of midnight and 3am on the 23$^{rd}$.

Now, suppose the event occurs on the 15$^{th}$ at 4pm, and lasts 6 hours. The schedule-based patterns do not indicate activity during this period, but the demand-based patterns might still indicate activity based on the status of other resources. Our approach will assess an impact if either set of patterns – schedule-based or demand-based – indicates that the dependency is likely to be active during the outage period. The demand-based decision tree has a correctly classified instances value of 95.57%, and was generated based on the designated outage period of 6 hours. As an example, if the *sshd* program on the computer named *hera* has an active connection to the *helsinki.cc.gatech.edu* site at the time of failure, then we can infer that the dependencies *user | global | linqf → program | hera | mysqld* and *program | hera | mysqld → port | hera | mysql* will also be active at some time during the 6-hour outage period. Consequently, we would assess that user *linqf* has a 95.57% likelihood of being impacted during the outage period.

This example demonstrates how the using the combination of system topology and system usage pattern information has allowed us to improve the clarity and operational relevance of our impact assessments. In the given scenario, the impact topology indicates that the closed *mysql* port might impact four different users. Incorporating the usage patterns allowed us to further determine which specific users had a significant likelihood of being affected during the outage period for the failed resource. This is precisely the kind of information that many system administrators need to make their impact assessments more operationally relevant for management executives.

## 6   Conclusion and Future Research

We described an operational impact assessment model and system (Section 4) that integrates events from all system and application components. By clustering events through simple data mining and statistical techniques, our system translates a low level event (e.g., failure of a device or router) into a probabilistic user level impact assessment meaningful to system administrators and managers. We demonstrate our approach by collecting and analyzing operational data at Georgia Tech for 35 days. Our experimental results (Section 5) show the promise of our approach in providing quantitative statistical support for operational impact analysis.

From the system management point of view, we consider the work described here as a concrete and significant first step. A natural next step is to apply our approach on systems of increasing scale and complexity. Through automated monitoring and analysis, we will collect a much larger event data set and build a more complete topology model of usage patterns. In addition to observed (real world) failures, we can also conduct controlled experiments by inducing faults in various resources to evaluate the accuracy and coverage of dependencies captured by our topology model. Trade-offs between the granularity/length of data collection and the accuracy/coverage of topology models (e.g., schedule-based and demand-based patterns) are another area of interesting research. Finally, a user-based assessment (e.g., feedback gathered from users via the help desk) matched to technical events (e.g., device failure) may provide a management-level validation of our approach and system.

From the technical point of view, we will investigate methods to deploy the collection systems more easily (e.g. Java applets). We will also examine ways to distribute the discovery and mining processes to the end systems, without sacrificing the accuracy of the results. This could improve the scalability of the overall system by reducing the bandwidth and processing costs when compared to our current, centralized approach. Future research will include incorporating our usage pattern mining techniques with more sophisticated dependency discovery systems. Our current approach allows us to integrate the dependency topology tightly with our usage mining techniques. Using more sophisticated dependency discovery systems might allow us to complement our current focus on the end-systems with improved visibility into the infrastructure.

# References

[1] Kar, G., Keller, S., Calo, S.: Managing Application Services over Service Provider Networks: Architecture and Dependency Analysis. NOMS (2000)

[2] Singh, A., Koropolu, M., Voruganti, K.: Zodiac: Efficient Impact Analysis for Storage Area Networks. USENIX FAST (2005)

[3] Assistant Secretary of Defense, National Information Infrastructure (ASD-NII): Department of Defense Instruction (DoDI) 8580.1, Information Assurance (IA) in the Defense Acquisition System (2004)

[4] Jobst, D., Preissler, G.: Mapping Clouds of SOA- and Business-related Events for an Enterprise Cockpit in a Java-based Environment. Intl. Symp. JAVA Prog. (2006)

[5] Hanemann, A., Schmitz, D., Sailer, M.: A Framework for Failure Impact Analysis and Recovery with Respect to Service Level Agreements. IEEE SCC (2005)

[6] EMC2|SMARTS Business Impact Manager:
http://www.emc.com/products/software/smarts/bim/

[7] IBM Tivoli Application Dependency Discovery Manager. http://www-306.ibm.com/software/tivoli/products/taddm/

[8] Thereska, E., Narayanan, D., Ganger, G.: Towards self-predicting systems: What if you could ask "what-if"? In: Workshop Database & Expert Systems Applications (2005)

[9] Sitaraman, S., Venkatesan, S.: Forensic Analysis of File System Intrusions using Improved Backtracking. In: IEEE Workshop on IWIA (2005)

[10] Brown, A., Kar, G., Keller, A.: An Active Approach to Characterizing Dynamic Dependencies for Problem Determination in a Distributed Environment. IM (2001)

[11] Ensel, C.: A Scalable Approach to Automated Service Dependency Modeling in Heterogeneous Environments. IEEE EDOC (2001)

[12] Aguilera, M., Mogul, J., Wiener, J., Reynolds, P., Muthitacharoen, A.: Performance Debugging for Distributed Systems of Black Boxes. SOSP (2003)

[13] Mortier, R., Isaacs, R., Barham, P.: Anemone: using end-systems as a rich network management platform. Microsoft Technical Report, MSR-TR-2005-62 (2005)

[14] Chen, M., Kiciman, E., Fratkin, E., Fox, A., Brewer, E.: Pinpoint: Problem Determination in Large, Dynamic Internet Services. DSN (2002)

[15] Kiciman, E., Fox, A.: Detecting Application-Level Failures in Component-Based Internet Services. IEEE Trans. Neural Networks 16(5), 1027–1041 (2005)

[16] Hariri, S., et al.: Impact Analysis of Faults and Attacks in Large-Scale Networks. IEEE Sec. & Priv. Mag., 49–54 (September-October 2003)

[17] Cohen, I., et al.: Capturing, indexing, clustering, and retrieving system history. SOSP (2005)
[18] van der Aalst, W.M.P., et al.: Workflow Mining: A Survey of Issues and Approaches. ACM TKDE 47(2), 237–267 (2003)
[19] Han, J., Kamber, M.: Data Mining: Concepts and Techniques, 2nd edn. Morgan-Kaufmann, San Francisco (2006)
[20] Witten, I., Frank, E.: Data Mining: Practical machine learning tools and techniques, 2nd edn. Morgan Kaufmann, San Francisco (2005)

# Virtualization-Based Techniques for Enabling Multi-tenant Management Tools

Chang-Hao Tsai[1], Yaoping Ruan[2], Sambit Sahu[2], Anees Shaikh[2], and Kang G. Shin[1]

[1] Real-Time Computing Laboratory, EECS Department
The University of Michigan, Ann Arbor, MI 48109-2121, USA
{chtsai,kgshin}@eecs.umich.edu
[2] IBM TJ Watson Research Center, Yorktown Heights, NY 10598, USA
{yaopruan,sambits}@us.ibm.com, aashaikh@watson.ibm.com

**Abstract.** As service providers strive to improve the quality and efficiency of their IT (information technology) management services, the need to adopt a standard set of tools and processes becomes increasingly important. Deploying *multi-tenant* capable tools is a key part of this standardization, since a single instance can be used to manage multiple customer environments, and multi-tenant tools have the potential to significantly reduce service-delivery costs. However, most tools are not designed for multi-tenancy, and providing this support requires extensive re-design and re-implementation.

In this paper, we explore the use of virtualization technology to enable multi-tenancy for systems and network management tools with minimal, if any, changes to the tool software. We demonstrate our design techniques by creating a multi-tenant version of a widely-used open source network management system. We perform a number of detailed profiling experiments to measure the resource requirements in the virtual environments, and also compare the scalability of two multi-tenant realizations using different virtualization approaches. We show that our design can support roughly 20 customers with a single tool instance, and leads to a scalability increase of 60–90% over a traditional design in which each customer is assigned to a single virtual machine.

## 1 Introduction

As service providers look for new ways to achieve high quality and cost efficiency in the way they manage IT infrastructure for customers, an important emerging theme is the need to adopt a standard set of management tools and processes. This goal is complicated by the complex variety of customer environments and requirements, as well as the increasingly distributed nature of infrastructure management in which technical teams provide support for systems and networks located across the globe.

One recent strategy being pursued by IT service providers to address this challenge is to deploy a relatively small set of "best-of-breed" management tools that support *multi-tenancy, i.e.,* a single instance can support multiple customers. Multi-tenant tools have a number of important advantages in terms of cost and simplicity. They require deployment of a much smaller infrastructure, in contrast to having a dedicated installation for

A. Clemm, L.Z. Granville, and R. Stadler (Eds.): DSOM 2007, LNCS 4785, pp. 171–182, 2007.

each customer, which can significantly reduce support costs for the infrastructure hosting the tool itself. Moreover, in some cases, multi-tenant tools have more advantageous software licensing models, for example, with a single license used to manage multiple customers. Finally, multi-tenant tools are a crucial element of the higher-level goal of consolidating tools to reduce training, management, and support costs.

A major barrier to adopting multi-tenant tools is that the desired management tool may not have been designed for multiple customer environments, and would thus require a significant rewrite to provide the needed support. Full multi-tenant support requires adequate, auditable, protection against the risk of data leakage between customers, performance that approaches the single-tenant case for each customer, and a relatively high density to realize the benefits of multi-tenancy.

In this paper, we explore the use of virtualization technology to enable multi-tenancy for systems and network management tools with minimal, if any, changes to the software itself. We consider virtualization at several layers, including full system virtualization, OS-level virtualization, and data virtualization. We describe and evaluate the trade-offs of these approaches through investigations of several design choices and experimental evaluations of their performance and scalability.

Our study focuses on OpenNMS, a popular open source, enterprise-grade network management tool that performs a number of functions including device discovery, service and performance monitoring, and event management [1]. We design multi-tenant-capable configurations of OpenNMS using the Xen virtual machine monitor (VMM) [2], and the OpenVZ virtual private server environment [3]. We then perform a number of detailed profiling experiments in which we measure the resource requirements and performance of OpenNMS in the virtual environments. These results also allow us to accurately configure Xen or OpenVZ in order to provide suitable performance. Finally, we compare the scalability of our virtualization-based designs with a baseline deployment in which each customer is assigned to a single Xen VM which houses the entire Open-NMS stack. We find that both Xen and OpenVZ can support multi-tenant deployments for nearly 20 customer networks (customer density with OpenVZ is slightly higher than with Xen), although each approach has its own relative advantages. Both, however, provide an overall scalability increase of 60–90% over the baseline configuration.

Many systems and network management tools adopt an architecture similar to Open-NMS, consisting of a web-based user interface application, a management server application which performs most of the monitoring or management functions, and a database that stores configuration information, collected data, and analysis reports. While our implementation considers multi-tenancy support in OpenNMS, we expect that the techniques and findings described in the paper will be applicable to a number of management tools that use this canonical architecture. Hence, our work represents an initial set of guidelines for leveraging virtualization technology to realize the increasingly important requirement to support multi-tenancy in systems management platforms.

The next section describes some background on network management systems. Section 3 illustrates our design choices in making the OpenNMS architecture multi-tenant-capable. We describe our testbed and experimental evaluation in Sect. 4. A brief discussion of related work appears in Sect. 5, and the paper concludes in Sect. 6.

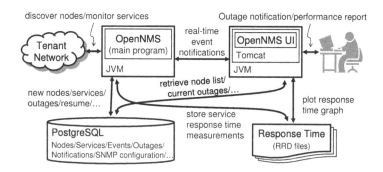

**Fig. 1.** OpenNMS architecture

## 2   Background

Network management is a standard service in current enterprise environments. These systems are a combination of hardware and software that monitors the topology, availability, and traffic of various network devices like routers and switches, as well as servers that provide services on the network.

While network management tools can be provided as a service, they differ from other services because they must connect to customer networks through firewalls at their network edge and customers may use network address translation (NAT) to employ private Internet addressing in the local network. For multi-tenant management tools, this presents two challenges. First, the tool cannot be deployed within one customer network because it needs to monitor multiple customer network domains and these private addresses are not publicly accessible. Second, private addresses may cause confusion to the tool because of overlapping addresses between customers.

We use a popular open-source NMS, OpenNMS, as our target application. OpenNMS is billed as an enterprise-grade network management platform, and is used in a variety of commercial and non-commercial environments [1]. OpenNMS monitors network-service availability, generates performance reports, and provides asset-management capability. Figure 1 shows major components of OpenNMS and their interactions.

The management server software is implemented in Java as a multi-threaded application. We call this part the *back-end*. The *front-end* user interface (UI) consists of a number of servlets and Java server pages (JSPs) deployed in an Apache Tomcat application server. Both the front-end and back-end connect to a PostgreSQL database for various management information. Response time of network services and SNMP counters are stored in Round Robin Database (RRD) files and later plotted in the user interface. Besides notifying users via the UI, OpenNMS can also be integrated with email or instant messaging systems to send timely notifications of critical events.

## 3   Design

In this section, we describe the design of our multi-tenant-capable OpenNMS using virtualization with minimum changes to the original system. With virtualization technology,

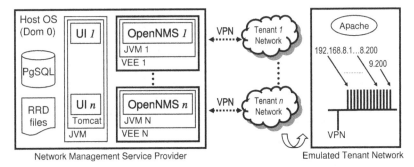

**Fig. 2.** Design overview of the multi-tenant-capable OpenNMS

the brute-force solution is to select a virtualization platform and run one OpenNMS tenant in each virtual execution environment (VEE), including all components described in Fig. 1. However, this solution is not efficient — as shown in our evaluation, memory becomes the bottleneck of the system. We propose an approach to virtualize only the back-end, and share a common database among all tenants.

An overview of this design is given in Fig. 2, where the OpenNMS back-end of each tenant sits in an VEE, and communicates with its managed network domain via VPN connections. The database and Tomcat are co-located in one VEE. Database queries from the back-ends are configured to use the tenant ID in the database name. All of these components can be organized together by configuration changes, to meet our goal of no modification to the source code.

### 3.1   Virtualization for the Back-End

The back-end of OpenNMS is the core of the system. It loads configuration files when it starts and instantiates internal service modules accordingly. The configuration files usually include customer-specific parameters such as the network address range for automatic service discovery, service-polling frequency, *etc.* Once the configurations are loaded, it starts probing of the customer network domain for each service accordingly.

We choose a virtualization implementation that provides low overhead but necessary isolation required by OpenNMS to work properly. First, it should provide file system virtualization so persistent states of each tenant such as configuration files are protected. Second, it should provide process and memory isolation so tenants on the same platform do not interfere with each other. Finally, since each tenant needs to communicate with its own network domain, the network layer should be virtualized as well. Especially when two tenants have identical private network addresses, packets from each tenant should be routed correctly. This requirement implies that each host should maintain its own protocol stack. For these reasons, virtualization technologies such as Java virtual machine (JVM) and FreeBSD Jail are not sufficient.

We use Xen and OpenVZ as our virtualization platforms in our implementation. Both of them provide virtualized network protocol stacks. We create multiple VEEs within a host and run an instance of OpenNMS in each VEE. Since each VEE also provides a resource boundary, performance isolation can also be implemented. We measure the performance of each tenant and identify the location where user-perceived performance is degraded.

### 3.2 VPN Connections

Traditionally, a management system is deployed inside each customer's network domain. With multi-tenancy, the system has to be located at a place where all customers can reach. However, most enterprise networks are not reachable from outside. Changing firewall configuration at each customer's network edge to accommodate this communication may introduce potential security risks. One approach to solve this problem is to use probing devices within each tenant's premise. While this approach might be feasible in real deployment, we choose to create Virtual Private Network (VPN) connections to each tenant's network. Creating VPNs is better for portability than probing devices, and is easier for setting up an experimental testbed. In this paper, we use OpenVPN [4], an open source SSL VPN solution. We configure OpenVPN to establish layer 2 (L2) VPN connections to tenant networks to support services such as BOOTP and DHCP servers, although most of the services can be monitored via a layer 3 (L3) VPN. When there are multiple L2 networks to be monitored, several VPN connections can be established simultaneously.

Using VPN connections to connect NMSs to tenant networks does incur some overhead in packet transmission due mainly to round-trip time, which depends on network congestion and the geographical distance between VPN endpoints. However, for management systems, this delay makes little impact on the results. For example, when monitoring service-availability, the added overhead does not pose any problem as long as the probing returns without timeout, which is 3 seconds.

### 3.3 Database Sharing

Since each OpenNMS instance only needs a database user account to store data in a PostgreSQL database server, we opt to use mechanisms built in database to provide the isolation for each tenant.

We configure each tenant to use a different database user name and database instance to store the data. This approach provides adequate security isolation, since data belongs to one tenant is not accessible by the others. As far as performance is concerned, database access usually is not the bottleneck in a multi-tenancy environment. High-availability database design can be used to prevent any database crash. We do not use these designs so as to compare results with the brute-force solution.

### 3.4 The Front-End

Similar to consolidating databases, we deploy multiple instances of the Java servlets and JSPs in Apache Tomcat. This allows customizing the front-end user interface to fit each customer's management policy and preferences. Each tenant has a different base URL to its web console. In addition to log-in credentials, access control can be applied to restrict access further.

## 4   Evaluation

In this section we describe our experimental evaluation which comprises two sets of experiments. The first set of experiments profiles and determines the working set and resource bottlenecks of our setup. The key results are: (i) memory is the bottlenecked resource, and (ii) the minimum memory required for each OpenNMS setup is about 144MB. The second set of experiments compares the benefit of our multi-tenancy approach with that of the baseline approach that is void of any multi-tenancy capabilities. We find that even with our "limited multi-tenancy" approach, as many as 60–90% more tenants can be supported with similar or better perceived quality.

### 4.1   Testbed Setup

We use two similarly-equipped machines to emulate the management server and the tenant networks. Each of them has an Intel Core 2 Duo E6600 CPU (without using Intel Virtualization Technology), 4GB of main memory, and two 7200rpm hard drives. The management station and the emulated tenant network are connected with a Gigabit Ethernet network. Debian GNU/Linux 4.0 is used as the host OS environment with PostgreSQL database server and Apache Tomcat 5.0. The OpenNMS we used in this study is version 1.2.9. Sun Java 5.0 is used to compile and run OpenNMS.

Our Xen-based implementation uses an experimental version of Xen, including a modified Linux kernel 2.6.18 as the kernel in both privileged and unprivileged domains. We optimize the setup by having the tenants share a common NFS-mounted /usr since all of them use the same program and do not need to contain identical files in their virtual disk images. Sharing file systems also improves the cache-hit ratio in the host OS. Another approach to reducing the file system size is to use copy-on-write disks. Unfortunately, this feature is not stable in our testing. The result is a 150MB root file system for each tenant and a 350MB /usr file system shared by all tenants. We also give each guest OS a 256MB swap space.

For the testbed using OpenVZ, we use a patch set (version 028stab027.1) for Linux kernel 2.6.18 in this work. A VEE created by OpenVZ shares the same patched Linux kernel but has its own root file system, network device, *etc.* We configure the software installation identically as in Xen.

In order to test our design, we emulate a tenant network as shown in Fig. 2. All tenants share the same emulated tenant network, which is created on a dummy network interface configured with 1,000 IP addresses. An Apache HTTP server listens on all IP addresses to create an illusion of 1,000 web servers. System parameters, such as increasing buffer size, are tuned to make sure that network and the client machine are not the bottlenecks.

### 4.2   Resource Profiling

The intent of this evaluation is to profile the resource usage of our proposed multi-tenancy-capable network management tooling using OpenNMS and provides parameters to use in multi-tenant evaluations. We determine resource bottlenecks, the working set for the proposed setup, and any trends as the number of clients being monitored are scaled. The first three parts of resource profiling are ran without any VMM.

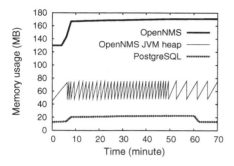 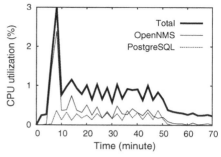

**Fig. 3.** Memory-usage profile of OpenNMS, PostgreSQL and JVM heap

**Fig. 4.** CPU-utilization profile of the entire system, OpenNMS, and PostgreSQL

**Memory is the Bottlenecked Resource.** We first ran OpenNMS with the database server within one OS, just as the typical setup for single tenant system. The OpenNMS is set up to use at most 256MB memory as JVM heap and monitor 200 hosts via a VPN connection.

Figure 3 presents the system memory used by OpenNMS, PostgreSQL and Open-NMS JVM heap usage as a function of time progression. When OpenNMS starts up, it first loads its configuration and previously-monitored hosts and services (none in this evaluation) from the database. It starts by discovering the clients to be monitored 5 minutes after the boot-up. During this stage, although the heap utilization is increased, memory used by the OpenNMS remains flat. Once auto-discovery starts, OpenNMS uses considerably more memory and the garbage collection of JVM kicks in periodically, generating a zig-zag shape of heap utilization between 49MB and 78MB. The increase in memory usage by the OpenNMS can be attributed to dynamic class loading and objects in the permanent generation, which is not included in heap utilization.

The auto-discovery procedure is paced by OpenNMS to avoid generating too much traffic in the network. Therefore, the duration of this stage is proportional to the number of probes and the number of hosts being monitored. Using the default configuration, it takes about 45 minutes to run all probes over 200 hosts. Since the emulated client network has only one Apache HTTP server running, most of the time is spent on waiting timeouts. Both OpenNMS and PostgreSQL use more memory as the auto-discovery procedure goes on.

After the auto-discovery completes, OpenNMS only periodically probes previously-discovered and manually-configured hosts and services, and thus, creates new Java objects at a slower rate, which leads to less-frequent garbage collection. PostgreSQL server also frees some memory as most data, such as event logs of each host, are not actively being used. The VPN connection, OpenVPN, uses 2.5MB memory constantly which is not plotted in the figure.

In terms of CPU utilization, which is plotted in Fig. 4 shows the CPU utilization as a function of progression of time. Note that the peak utilization occurs when the auto-discovery phase starts. The CPU utilization then stays around 1% during the auto-discovery stage and drops to almost 0 afterward, where the OS overhead is around 0.3%. From these two figures, we conclude that system memory is the potential bottleneck when multiple instances of OpenNMS are hosted on the same machine.

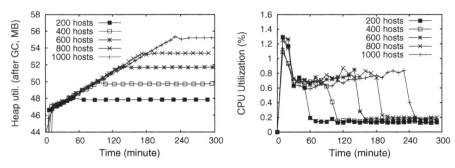

**Fig. 5.** Heap utilization vs. client network size    **Fig. 6.** CPU utilization vs. client network size

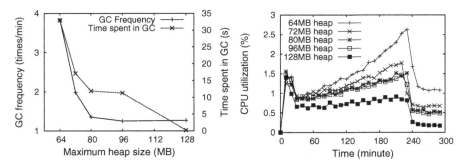

**Fig. 7.** GC frequency and time vs. heap size    **Fig. 8.** CPU utilization vs. heap size

**Effect of Client Network Size.** We then study the impact of the client network size on the resource utilization by varying the client size from 200 hosts to 1,000 hosts, *i.e.,* the typical network size in small to medium size businesses. The maximum JVM heap size is also 256MB as in the previous experiment.

While the memory used by OpenNMS does not differ much with different client network sizes, we observed that the heap utilization, after each garbage collection, is proportional to the number of hosts being monitored. From Fig. 5 we observe that for every 200 monitored hosts, OpenNMS uses 2MB of additional memory in heap. Comparing to the size of the OpenNMS process, this incremental cost is low.

Figure 6 shows that CPU utilization is only slightly affected by the client network size. This result reinforces our previous observation that system memory size is the bottleneck for OpenNMS when multi-tenancy is enabled.

**Effect of JVM Heap Size.** Next, we evaluate the effect of JVM heap size on our proposed multi-tenant-capable network management tool. We configure OpenNMS to monitor a client network consisting 1,000 hosts, and reduce the maximum heap size from the default 256MB to 64MB to investigate their relationship.

As we can see in Fig. 7, the garbage collection frequency is inversely related to the maximum heap size. The frequency is measured after auto-discovery is completed. When the maximum heap size is reduced to 64MB, garbage collection happens as frequent as 4 times a minute. In spite of this frequent garbage collection, the total time

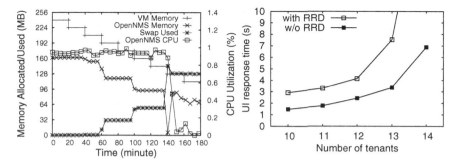

**Fig. 9.** Swap activity vs. VM memory size

**Fig. 10.** Scalability of the baseline multi-tenancy

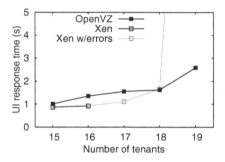

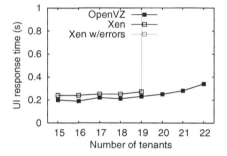

**Fig. 11.** Front-end UI response time with different number of tenants

**Fig. 12.** Front-end UI response time when response time logging is disabled

spent in the garbage collection in an hour is as little as 33 seconds, which is less than 1% CPU utilization. In addition, we observe that the JVM spent much less time in garbage collection if there are 128MB or more heap space, where a different garbage collection algorithm might be used. We also tried a 56MB heap configuration but the JVM could not survive.

The increase in CPU utilization is more pronounced in auto-discovery stage as can be seen in Fig. 8. With as little as 64MB heap size, OpenNMS uses as much as 2.5% CPU time at the end of auto-discovery stage. The increase in the CPU utilization with the number of host discovered suggests the garbage collector needs more time to sweep out dead objects among an increasing number of alive ones, and this phenomenon is more obvious when the heap size is smaller.

**Working Set Estimation.** Next, we determine the memory working set size for OpenNMS. While OpenNMS takes up as much as 160MB of memory to run, like most applications, the working set size is usually much smaller than the size of the total virtual memory segments that reside in physical memory. In the following, we take advantage of Xen's dynamic memory resizing capability and reduce the memory allocation of a VM from 256MB down to 96MB (at a rate of 16MB/20min), and monitor the swap space usage. In this experiment, only OpenNMS and OpenVPN are running in a VM,

PostgreSQL has been moved to domain 0 as the database server will be shared between multiple instances of OpenNMS.

In Fig. 9, we observe that the dirty memory pages begin to be swapped out to the swap partition when physical memory is reduced to 192MB. Swap space usage increases again when VM is reduced further by 32MB. When only 128MB is allocated, Linux suddenly swaps out all the memory used by OpenNMS. Although the working set was reloaded immediately, the dramatic drop in CPU utilization implies that most of the time were spent in dealing with page faults. Therefore, we conclude that OpenNMS with OpenVPN requires at least 144MB to perform smoothly.

### 4.3   Evaluation of Multi-tenancy Benefits

We evaluate the number of tenants that can be supported for both baseline multi-tenancy and our proposed multi-tenancy capability. The metric used for this evaluation is the increase in the number of tenants that can be supported by the same amount of resources while providing similar or better quality of service compared to the baseline multi-tenancy capability. The quality of service metric is the UI response time in the measurement process, and correctness of discovery and availability results.

For this evaluation, we configure the testbed so that each tenant has 400 emulated clients to be monitored. All the instances are started simultaneously, thus it can be considered as the worst-case scenario. We wait 2 hours for the auto-discovery process to complete and start polling results from the UI. For each tenant, we first log-in to the web console, list the number of hosts being monitored, and randomly pick 10 hosts to list their details. We report the average response time for the UI operations where the average is computed across all the tenants over all the clients.

**Scalability of Baseline Multi-tenancy.**   We first evaluate the scalability of a baseline multi-tenant OpenNMS installation, where each instance not only includes the back-end and OpenVPN but also the database and the Apache Tomcat server on top of a dedicated OS. Each tenant is hosted in a Xen VM with 256MB memory. Figure 10 shows that the UI response time increases with the number of tenants hosted. Although 14 tenants can be hosted on one server and discover all hosts and services, the UI response is an awfully 22s, which is completely unusable. If we set a response time threshold of 3s, only 10 tenants can be hosted.

While the bottleneck is the main memory size, the performance of the system can be improved by eliminating the disk activities resulting from keeping response time log files (RRD files). The UI becomes much more responsive and, as a result, the scalability improves to 12 tenants. However, we were not able to start 15 tenants due to out-of-memory errors.

**Proposed Multi-tenancy Scalability.**   We then evaluate the scalability of our proposed multi-tenancy solution, where the database and the Apache Tomcat server are shared among all the tenants. Figure 11 shows that the average response time is significantly reduced. Also note that 16 and 19 tenants can be hosted when Xen and OpenVZ based virtualization is used, respectively. Comparing to baseline multi-tenancy approach, our proposed multi-tenancy solution can support as much as 60–90% more number of tenants with similar or better UI response time.

When 17 tenants are hosted using Xen virtualization, we have observed some transient outages while the emulated network did not undergo any failure. When the number of tenants increased to 18 or more, there are many hosts that were not discovered and lots of false alarms. We considered these cases failed to meet the standard and plotted with dashed lines.

On the other hand, OpenVZ is able to host 19 tenants without any failure but failed to run with 20 tenants. The average response time is higher than that in Xen because Apache Tomcat and the database server also need to compete for main memory with OpenNMS JVMs — in Xen OpenNMS JVMs are confined in their own domains.

When more than 19 tenants are hosted, we observe heavy disk activities from reading and writing RRD files. In stead of optimizing disk performance, we evaluate the scalability again without the response time logging. The results are plotted in Fig. 12. The response time is reduced significantly again for both Xen and OpenVZ. Xen and OpenVZ can host 19 and 22 tenants respectively without any false alarms. When hosting more tenants, memory becomes bottleneck again and causes errors. Compared to the baseline multi-tenancy model, we observe 58–83% scalability improvements, while providing much better response time.

# 5   Related Work

The concept of multi-tenancy is usually applied to enterprise software such as ERP and CRM. It reduces the cost of operating a software application by sharing the associated hardware and software licensing cost with other customers. Successful multi-tenant-capable applications are usually designed from the ground-up [5]. In this work, we apply multi-tenancy to a specific kind of application, systems and network management, using virtualization as the enabler. Comparing to other applications, network management cannot live in application layer alone. It interacts with customers' network infrastructure and must deal with facts like IP address conflicts between customers.

One approach to handle IP address conflicts is to use network address translation (NAT) to map conflicting addresses into non-overlapped addresses in network management service provider's network. This approach is proposed with management payload address translation (MPAT) to deal with IP addresses in SNMP payload by Raz and Sugla in [6]. While it enables servicing multiple tenants with one network management software installation, this scheme cannot deal with unstructured use of IP addresses in protocols such as command line interface (CLI) of various network devices.

The overhead of virtualization has been evaluated by several researchers[7,8]. In particular, using Xen incurs some overhead in disk and network I/O and Linux-VServer, which is another OS-level virtualization mechanism and performs closely to native OS performance. As our evaluation result shows, the bottleneck of our testbed is either the amount of main memory or in the disk sub-system. Neither of them results from the use of virtualization. Implementing anticipatory scheduling in a VMM with guest context awareness as in [9] may improve disk throughput.

The memory footprint of each Xen VM is fixed in our implementation. Workload characterization helps us determine the optimal setting. Another approach to control memory allocation is to monitor its actual usage on-line [10,11]. Unfortunately, JVM heap size cannot be changed accordingly at run-time. Without increasing JVM heap size with VM memory size, JVM cannot benefit much from additional memory. On the othere hand, reducing VM memory allocation alone can lead to unnecessary swapping of dead objects.

## 6  Conclusion

In this paper we have described an approach to enabling multi-tenant capability in one of the popular network management tools, OpenNMS. We study the architecture of the management tool, and divide the system into different components including front-end, back-end engine, and storage database. We use virtualization as the base platform to ensure the isolation between different tenants. One single database is shared between multiple tenants to reduce the cost of hosting database servers and improve scalability. Our implementation using Xen and OpenVZ virtualization technology shows that both systems meet the requirements of multi-tenancy, and are able to provide about 20 tenants without reducing service quality.

## References

1. OpenNMS Group: OpenNMS. http://www.opennms.com
2. Barham, P., Dragovic, B., Fraser, K., Hand, S., Harris, T., Ho, A., Neugebauer, R., Pratt, I., Warfield, A.: Xen and the art of virtualization. In: SOSP 2003. Proceedings of the nineteenth ACM symposium on Operating systems principles, pp. 164–177. ACM Press, New York (2003)
3. OpenVZ Group: OpenVZ. http://www.openvz.org
4. OpenVPN Project: OpenVPN. http://www.openvpn.net
5. Fisher, S.: Service computing: The appexchange platform. In: SCC 2006. 2006 IEEE International Conference on Services Computing, IEEE Computer Society Press, Los Alamitos (September 2006) xxiv (Keynote)
6. Raz, D., Sugla, B.: Economically managing multiple private data networks. In: NOMS 2000. 2000 IEEE/IFIP Network Operations and Management Symposium, pp. 491–503 (2000)
7. Menon, A., Santos, J.R., Turner, Y., Janakiraman, G.J., Zwaenepoel, W.: Diagnosing performance overheads in the xen virtual machine environment. In: VEE 2005. 1st ACM/USENIX International Conference on Virtual Execution Environments, pp. 13–23 (2005)
8. Soltesz, S., Herbert-Pötzl, Fiuczynski, M.E., Bavier, A., Peterson, L.: Container-based operating system virtualization: A scalable, high-performance alternative to hypervisors. In: EuroSys 2006. 2006 EuroSys Conference (2006)
9. Jones, S.T., Arpaci-Dusseau, A.C., Arpaci-Dusseau, R.H.: Antfarm: Tracking processes in a virtual machine environment. In: USENIX 2006. 2006 USENIX Annual Technical Conference, pp. 1–14 (June 2006)
10. Waldspurger, C.A.: Memory resource management in vmware esx server. SIGOPS Operating Systems Review 36, 181–194 (2002)
11. Jones, S.T., Arpaci-Dusseau, A.C., Arpaci-Dusseau, R.H.: Geiger: Monitoring the buffer cache in a virtual machine environment. In: The 12th International Conference on Architectural Support for Programming Languages and Operating Systems (ASPLOS-XII), pp. 14–24 (2006)

# Offloading IP Flows onto Lambda-Connections

Tiago Fioreze, Mattijs Oude Wolbers, Remco van de Meent, and Aiko Pras

University of Twente, Enschede, The Netherlands
{t.fioreze,r.vandemeent,a.pras}@utwente.nl

**Abstract.** Optical networks are capable of switching IP traffic via lambda connections. In this way, big IP flows that overload the regular IP routing level may be moved to the optical level, where they get better Quality of Service (QoS). At the same time, the IP routing level is off-loaded and can serve smaller flows better. Within this context, this paper analyses the eligibility of IP flows to be moved to the optical level. In this analysis, we observe the percentage of IP traffic as well as the amount of IP flows moved to the optical level while using various definitions for an IP flow. The main contribution of this paper is to show how the amount of IP traffic transferred over lambda-connections considerably depends on the definition used for a flow.

## 1 Introduction

The use of lambda-switching in optical networks allows huge amounts of data to be transmitted over lambda-connections via multi-service optical switches. These optical switches are capable of making data forwarding decisions at different levels in the protocol stack [1]. Such capability enables therefore data packets to be fully switched at optical-level (lambda switching) instead of being forwarded (routed) at packet-level (packet forwarding).

Today, IP traffic from several specialized applications already profit from lambda-switched networks capabilities. Examples are grid applications [2] and High-Definition TeleVision (HDTV) broadcasting [3]. The question that may arise is whether there is also ordinary IP traffic, currently running over the existing IP network, that would be able to take advantage of these new lambda-switching capabilities. This paper investigates this question by focusing on the following research questions:

1. In current networks, how many IP flows would already be large enough to profit from being moved to the optical-level?
2. What fraction of the total IP data traffic do these flows represent? In other words, by what percentage would it be possible to offload the current IP network?

In order to answer these questions the following approach will be used: 1) Collect measurements from SURFnet6 [4], the Dutch research network; 2) Define a criterion that existing flows must satisfy to make them eligible to be moved to the optical-level; and 3) Analyze the collected traces in order to answer the research questions.

### 1.1 Related Work

The analysis of big IP flows in optical networks has already been addressed in other works [5] [6], but no substantial variation in the definition for a flow is found, as

A. Clemm, L.Z. Granville, and R. Stadler (Eds.): DSOM 2007, LNCS 4785, pp. 183–186, 2007.

concluded in a previous work of ours [7]. In [7], we showed that, in practice, IP flows are generally characterized by using the 5-tuple flow definition (source/destination address/port and protocol). Within this context, we performed our analysis by considering various definitions for a flow while observing the volume of IP traffic moved to the optical level. In contrast to this paper, in our previous work we collected 1 day of network traces divided in 30 minutes intervals and we only analyzed the flows with respect to their volume. In this paper, we collected 2 weeks of traces divided in different time intervals (5 and 30 minutes) as well as we observe the percentage of IP traffic and the amount of IP flows moved to the optical level.

## 2    Measurement and Analysis Setup

For our analysis SURFnet routed a NetFlow stream from the NetFlow-enabled core routers to a NetFlow collector located at our domain, where the incoming NetFlow stream was dumped into *pcap* files, using the *tcpdump* tool. This allowed us to adjust our analysis without the need for SURFnet to retransmit the data. The total amount of collected data was about 81 GB. The total amount of NetFlow reported bytes was 4.0 TB. However, since SURFnet uses 1:100 sampling, this accounts for some 0.40 PB of actual network traffic.

Our analysis consisted of varying the definition of a flow by using different levels of granularity. The higher the level of granularity is, the more restrictive the flow definition will be when grouping IP packets. Our flow definitions take into account different endpoints and have the following descending order of granularity: *App2App*: the 5-tuple flow definition; *HstHst*: set of packets with the same source and destination IP addresses; *Sub2Sub /24*: set of packets matching the 24 most significant bits of the source and destination addresses; *Sub2Sub /16*: set of packets matching the 16 most significant bits of the source and destination addresses; *Sub2Sub (NetFlow)*: set of packets matching the most significant bits of the source and destination addresses reported by NetFlow; *AS2AS*: set of packets with the same source and destination autonomous systems; and *Sub2Sub /8*: set of packets matching the 8 most significant bits of the source and destination addresses.

In order to check whether a certain IP flow is eligible to be moved to the optical level, we used the following criterion : *an IP flow is eligible if its total consumed bandwidth is equal or bigger than the minimal unit of transmission in SONET networks in a certain time interval: average throughput $\geq$ 50.112 Mbit/s*. Different time intervals (5 and 30 minutes) were used to check if they have an influence on the percentage of IP traffic as well as the amount of IP flows moved to the optical level. With such time intervals the threshold values for a flow to be considered eligible are 1.8 and 11 GBytes for 5 and 30 minutes intervals, respectively.

## 3    Results

This section shows the amount of flows that satisfied our criterion and the percentage of IP traffic eligible to be moved to the optical level. Figure 1 shows the amount of flows eligible for a lambda-connection while using various definitions for a flow as well as different time intervals (5 and 30 minutes interval). By using a small time interval (i.e.,

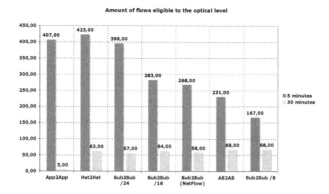

**Fig. 1.** The total amount of flows with 5 and 30 minutes time interval

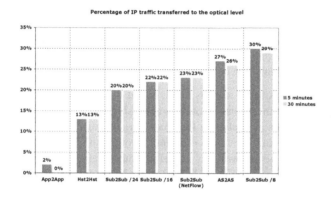

**Fig. 2.** Percentage of IP traffic with 5 and 30 minutes time interval

5 minutes) the number of flows eligible to move to the optical level is much higher than using a large time interval (i.e., 30 minutes). The reason is that in case a small time interval is used, the threshold value for a lambda-connection is also small (1.8 GBytes). As a consequence more flows satisfied our criterion. On the other hand, by using a big time interval, only a few very big flows of over 11GB in size, which last for a long period, are selected. It can also be seen in the graph — as could be expected — that lower granular flow definitions group more packets into fewer number of flows than higher granular flows.

A high number of flows does not directly imply that a large fraction of the IP traffic is eligble to be moved to the optical level. This can be seen in Figure 2, in which the percentage of IP traffic transferred to the optical level is shown, based on the total amount of collected data during 2 weeks (0.4 PB). It can also be seen that using different time intervals do not considerably change the percentage, but on the other hand the flow definition impacts the fraction considerably: the lower granular a flow definition is, the more packets will be grouped into flows, and, thus, the more traffic is selected to be moved over lambda-connections.

## 4    Conclusion

This paper presented various definitions for an IP flow and used them in conjunction with different time intervals to analyze their influence on moving flows to the optical level. The influence was observed in terms of percentage of IP traffic and amount of IP flows. Based on the analysis performed and in the obtained results, we can now answer our research questions.

1. *In current networks, how many IP flows would already be large enough to profit from being moved to the optical-level?*
   Based on our criterion, the number of flows that could be moved depends on the flow definition used as well as the time interval. During our 2 weeks of data analysis, between 390 and 450 flows would already profit from being moved to the optical-level if 5 minutes interval would be used in conjunction with high granular flow definitions. In case of the 30 minutes interval, between 55 and 70 flows.
2. *What fraction of the total IP data traffic do these flows represent? In other words, by what percentage would it be possible to offload the current IP network?*
   The fraction of IP traffic moved to the optical level strongly depends on the flow definition used. Higher granular flow definitions such as *App2App* and *Hst2Hst* allow between 0% and 13% of the total traffic. On the other hand, lower granular flow definitions allow between 20% and 30%.

The main contribution of this work is to show that the probability of finding IP flows eligible for lambda-connections increases when using less restrictive flow definitions. As future work, we aim at analyzing the characteristics of the eligible IP flows to the optical level by observing their size, duration, throughput, and recurrence. We would like to thank SURFnet for allowing us to perform measurements on their network. This paper was supported in part by the EC IST-EMANICS Network of Excellence (#26854).

## References

1. Leon-Garcia, A., Widjaja, I.: Communication Networks: fundamental concepts and key architectures, 2nd edn. McGraw-Hill, New York (2003)
2. Boutaba, R., Golab, W., Iraqi, Y., Li, T., Arnaud St., B.: Grid-Controlled Lightpaths for High Performance Grid Applications. Journal of Grid Computing 1(4), 387–394 (2003)
3. Rouskas, G.N.: Optical layer multicast: rationale, building blocks, and challenges. IEEE Network Magazine 17(1), 60–65 (2003)
4. SURFnet: SURFnet6 lighpaths mark start of the new Internet area (press release). Available in: http://www.surfnet.nl/info/en/artikel_content.jsp?objectnumber=107197
5. Mori, T., Kawahara, R., Naito, S., Goto, S.: On the characteristics of Internet traffic variability: spikes and elephants. In: International Symposium on Applications and the Internet. pp. 99–106 (2004)
6. Wallerich, J., Dreger, H., Feldmann, A., Krishnamurthy, B., Willinger, W.: A methodology for studying persistency aspects of internet flows. ACM SIGCOMM Computer Communication Review 35(2), 23–36 (2005)
7. Fioreze, T., Wolbers, M.O., Meent, R., Pras, A.: Finding elephant flows for optical networks. In: IM 2007. Application session proceedings of the 10th IFIP/IEEE International Symposium on Integrated Network Management, pp. 627–640. IEEE Computer Society Press, Los Alamitos (2007)

# Virtualized Interoperability Testing: Application to IPv6 Network Mobility

Ariel Sabiguero, Anthony Baire, Antoine Boutet, and César Viho

Institut de Recherche en Informatique et Systèmes Aléatoires
Campus Universitaire de Beaulieu
35042 Rennes CEDEX, France
asabigue@fing.edu.uy, {asabigue,abaire,aboutet,viho}@irisa.fr,

**Abstract.** Interoperability testing is an inherently distributed task. It connects different implementations together and determines if they interact according to their specifications, providing the expected services.

Deployment, configuration management and operation of an interoperability solution can be drastically improved with the use of virtualization techniques. Virtualized solution allows simpler and more reliable testing, as less equipment is required and full automation is achieved, providing means for better testing.

**Keywords:** Interoperability Testing, virtualization, management, reliability, cost.

## 1 Introduction

Interoperability testing is a discipline that requires deployment of several pieces of equipment. The way it addresses the verification of required properties in implementations is based on populating configurations with existing implementations and making them interwork.

In this work we present a solution based on the combined use of network virtualization and machine virtualization. The solution solves management problems that allows us to deploy several configuration scenarios with fixed hardware configurations. The operation of the virtualized test platform not only solves technical issues that previously were only addressed with inaccurate physical manipulations, but saves resources and time. Complete testbeds involving up to seven devices and five networks can be virtualized into a single physical host. The field of application is IPv6 Network Mobility testing following test specifications from IPv6 Ready Logo, an international certification program.

The IPv6 Network Mobility (NEMO) Basic Support protocol specification can be found in the Request For Comments (RFC) 3963 [1]. It is an extension to the Mobile IPv6 protocol and enables the support for the network mobility. This extension allows session continuity and reachability for every node in the Mobile Network as the network moves. The protocol is designed so that network mobility is transparent to the nodes inside the Mobile Network.

A. Clemm, L.Z. Granville, and R. Stadler (Eds.): DSOM 2007, LNCS 4785, pp. 187–190, 2007.
© IFIP International Federation for Information Processing 2007

## 2    Virtualized solution description

This section introduces the building blocks used in the construction of the virtualized environment. Technical details of configuration are beyond the scope of this work. Despite of that, we believe that a test engineer can deploy an equivalent platform with provided information.

### 2.1    Network Virtualization

Network Virtualization is the first step for deploying a virtualized test environment. This is a critical step since the network is the central component for making implementations interact with each other. Virtualized network shall not introduce any bias in the interactions while still allowing observability.

Our approach uses Virtual LANs defined by the IEEE 802.1Q standard [2] and software bridges. An intermediate solution, proposed in [3], introduced a partially virtualized network made of a Linux box and an Ethernet switch. In the present work the complete network is deployed in the GNU/Linux box.

Each node taking part in the test is configured to use one or more network interfaces. Each interface is connected to the virtual network and mapped to a separate VLAN in the Linux host OS.

To interconnect interfaces, their corresponding VLANs are associated to software bridges. The software bridge is responsible for implementing the collision domain semantic and connecting these interfaces spanned through different VLANs.

We achieve required connection between components, and each element can communicate with others in the same way as they would using physical hardware components. Moreover all the traffic between the elements transit through the software bridges, this allows full observability. Traffic recording requirements are achieved by recording all the traffic directly on the Linux bridge devices.

### 2.2    Machine Virtualization

The main goal behind machine virtualization is to collapse a set of virtual nodes into a single physical one. Benefits range from optimized resource allocation to separation of concerns of servers and services. We use virtualization to cut the explosion of nodes required for interoperability testing.

The goal is to collapse $m$ virtual hosts into $n$ physical ones without introducing any bias in the verdict. We expect $m >> n$, and preferably, $n = 1$. State of the art Network Mobility requirements are addressed from a single commodity PC.

For each node deployed on a virtual machine a set of network interfaces is configured. These devices are emulated by the VMware server. The guest system detect and accesses them like real physical interfaces and on the host system they are connected to their dedicated VLAN. The number of network interfaces depends on the role of the node in the test suite. A host node will require one interface for the test and a second interface for accessing the management network. If the node act as a router, then a third interface is needed.

## 2.3    Automated Virtualized Test Management

Test management and networking are centralized on the host system. Executing a single test case consists of executing various actions sequentially. Actions can be executed directly on the host system and remotely on guest systems through the management network. Mobility events can be performed by the host system.

Test case operation sequences follow the usual three-stage arrangement: preamble, test body and postamble. The preamble contains actions for setting up the initial topology by configuring the network and nodes. The postamble contains the opposite actions for resetting the testbed to its original state. The test body contains the actions that addresses directly the property or properties being verified by the test purpose.

Mobility testing implies topology changes during the execution of the test body. These mobility events are a very specific requirements that disallows full automation when using non-virtualized network. With the virtualized solution the mobility events can be implemented as two successive actions: mobile router VLAN is removed from the first bridge and added to the second bridge.

Any topology change can be automaticaly integrated in the test sequence and interleaved with other actions without requiring manual intervention. This reduces drastically the risk of network configuration errors (connecting a cable to the wrong network) as well as synchronization errors (not connecting a cable at the right time in the test sequence). Reliability and accuracy of test execution is enhanced, as field observations described in the next section.

# 3    Field Results

This section present results from field experience together with laboratory results. Not all the technologies used in our proposal are already accepted for certification purposes, thus, we can only present laboratory results.

## 3.1    Field Error Analysis

Manual operations are still required, and might always be required when there is no possibility to automate the IUT (Implementation Under Test). The conventional platform used for testing consists of several hubs, in which the different nodes are plugged test after test. Using IPv6 Ready Logo accepted technologies and practices, we studied the source of errors encountered during test execution.

Presented methodology completely remove network configuration errors, which account for almost one quarter of the field errors. A solution that automates the IUT fully solves synchronization, disappearing the source of errors too, removing up to 50% of total errors in that case.

## 3.2    Execution Time, Cost and Reliability

Figures presented here were gathered during real interoperability events and in laboratory. The addition of the management network, which solved the synchronization overhead and errors amongst the nodes of the test platform. The first solution was manually synchronized, even though automated and average times for test suite execution exceeded four hours -no time execution data was gathered with that tool-. With the addition of the parallel network, average execution times shrank to 2:50hs. Despite of that, some test executions might take up to 4:55hs. This is due to complexity of operation of the IUT or presence of unforseen problems. Due to this fact, when interoperability events are scheduled only two devices per day are scheduled, per test platform and test engineer. In laboratory executions, where conditions are better controlled, execution time averages 2:05hs.

The solution and methodology required by the IPv6 Ready Logo involves up to 7 test nodes, the test manager node and 5 network hubs are required. Presented solution can be completely collapsed inside a single physical computer, avoiding all network complexity and using standard Ethernet interfaces to connect to the IUT. State of the art hardware can handle the whole workload, thus the cost saving ratios can be estimated between 5:1 to 10:1.

Reliability of the collapsed testbed is drastically enhanced. Initial solution requires various equipments, the probability of failure is not negligible and increases accordingly the number of components. Reliability becomes more relevant in international interoperability events, where the complete platform has to be commuted. Transporting seven notebooks might sometimes lead to a broken node, leading to a non operational platform.

## 4    Conclusions

Presented methodology solves several problems found executing abstract test specifications for interoperability testing. The solution was successfully implemented. Experimental results show that execution errors due to unreliability of wireless technologies were removed without loosing automation. Complete virtualized environment for interoperability mobility testing in a single box provides cost savings and deployment facilities that simplifies execution and testing operations. Virtualization proved to be applicable to IPv6 in general and mobility testing in particular. Virtualization optimizes existing practices considering cost, reliability and fault tolerance of the testbed without introducing bias in the verdicts.

## References

1. Devarapalli, V., Wakikawa, R., Petrescu, A., Thubert, P.: RFC 3963: Network Mobility (NEMO) Basic Support Protocol (January 2005)
2. IEEE Standards for Local and Metropolitan Area Networks: Virtual Bridged Local Area Networks, IEEE Std.802.1q (1998)
3. Sabiguero, A., Viho, C.: Plug once, test everything. Configuration Management in IPv6 Interop Testing. In: Proceedings of the Fifteenth Asian Test Symposium. IEEE Computer Society Conference Publishing Services, pp. 443–448. IEEE Computer Society, Los Alamitos (2006)

# NADA – Network Anomaly Detection Algorithm

Sílvia Farraposo[1], Philippe Owezarski[2], and Edmundo Monteiro[3]

[1] School of Technology and Management of Leiria
Alto-Vieiro, Morro do Lena, 2411-901 Leiria, Apartado 4163, Portugal
[2] LAAS – CNRS, 7 Avenue du Colonel Roche
31077 Toulouse, CEDEX 4, France
[3] Laboratory of Communications and Telematics, Computer Science Department
Pólo II – Pinhal de Marrocos, 3030-290 Coimbra, Portugal
silvia@estg.ipleiria.pt, owe@laas.fr, edmundo@dei.uc.pt

**Abstract.** This paper deals with a new iterative Network Anomaly Detection Algorithm – NADA, which accomplishes the detection, classification and identification of traffic anomalies. NADA fully provides all information required limiting the extent of anomalies by locating them in time, by classifying them, and identifying their features as, for instance, the source and destination addresses and ports involved. To reach its goal, NADA uses a generic multi-featured algorithm executed at different time scales and at different levels of IP aggregation. Besides that, the NADA approach contributes to the definition of a set of traffic anomaly behavior-based signatures. The use of these signatures makes NADA suitable and efficient to use in a monitoring environment.

**Keywords:** Traffic Anomaly Identification, Anomaly Signature.

## 1 Introduction

The lack of security in networks is an issue that network administrators would like to solve on the fly, independently of the network size. Being anomalies a structural part of traffic, it is important to completely detect, classify (i.e., determining the type of anomaly) and identify (i.e., determining all the packets and flows involved in the anomaly) them in order to act adequately.

NADA aims being completely generic and work on any kind of time series issued from incoming traffic (online) or packet traces (offline). To illustrate NADA, in this paper we will consider three different data time series: Number of packets per unit of time; Number of bytes per unit of time; and Number of new flows per unit of time.

Other approaches for detecting traffic anomalies exist. However, as far as we know, none permits simultaneously the detection, classification and identification of traffic anomalies. At most, some recent works introduced some level of classification in the algorithms being proposed, using information provided by IP features [1] [2]. Nevertheless, anomaly classification and identification remains an important, unmet challenge, since none of the proposals exploited exhaustively the richness of IP

A. Clemm, L.Z. Granville, and R. Stadler (Eds.): DSOM 2007, LNCS 4785, pp. 191–194, 2007.
© IFIP International Federation for Information Processing 2007

feature information to provide accurate information by the involved parties. NADA's classification and identification stages are developed in an easy way for both configuring the tool and analyzing its outputs. This aspect is particularly important when one of the main goals is to limit the negative effects of an anomaly occurrence in real networks.

The rest of this paper is organized as follows: Section 2 gives an overview of the NADA algorithm presenting its main features. Section 3 presents anomaly signatures, and how these signatures can be used for anomaly classification, and section 4 concludes the paper, summarizing our ongoing research.

## 2   Network Anomaly Detection Algorithm – NADA

NADA has been defined as a multi-scale, multi-criteria, and multi-level of IP aggregation approach [3]. NADA's algorithm has two phases. The first one is devoted to the detection and classification of traffic anomalies, while the second phase targets the anomalous flows by fully identifying them.

The core idea used in NADA's detection stage is that any anomaly will be responsible for some level of variation at least on one of the criterions considered, at some time-scale and at some level of IP aggregation. Variations are pointed by using the formula below (1), in which $X$ is a data time series directly obtained from traffic traces, and $P$ is a data series that is obtained from $X$, and in which each value is the difference between two consecutive values of $X$. Each value $p_i$ of $P$ corresponds then to a variation. Significant variations might be associated to an anomaly. Significant variations were named deltoids by Cormode et al. [4] who used them to detect significant traffic changes.

$$X = \{x_1, x_2, ..., x_n\}, x_i = \{\# \, packets \,|\, \# \, bytes \,|\, \# \, flows\} / \Delta$$
$$P = \{p_1, p_2, ..., p_{n-1}\}, p_i = x_{i+1} - x_i$$
$$\begin{cases} pi \geq E(p) + k\sigma, select \\ pi < E(p) + k\sigma, reject \end{cases} \tag{1}$$

The mean and the standard deviation, $E(p)$ and $\sigma$ respectively, of each time series are calculated and used to define a threshold. Each value of the time series that exceeds the threshold might point a traffic anomaly. This sort of filtering can be more or less coarse grained depending on the value of the adjustment parameter $k$ of the formula, where smaller values of $k$ fine-grain the search. Currently, the value of $k$ is assigned manually, ranging from 0.5 to 2.5, being the value 2.0 the most used. These values were obtained empirically, after successive executions of NADA from where it was seen that for values of $k$ greater than 3.0 no significant variations are detected, while for values of $k$ smaller than 0.5 the formula is not effective because $E(p) + k\sigma \approx E(p)$.

The formula above is applied recursively. Each level of iteration uses a different level of traffic aggregation. At the first iteration the all IP space is considered, and time slots of duration $\Delta$, with possible anomalies, are spotted. At each new iteration, flows in the time slots previously spotted are analyzed, from more generic ones (mask /1) to more specific ones (mask /32).

The classification stage is based on behavior-based signatures. These signatures were obtained through the execution of NADA over several traces. The anomalies signaled by our algorithm presented always a set of characteristics that could be used to identify them in a univocal way. Finally, the purpose of anomaly identification is to allow its complete mitigation. This third stage then includes an exhaustive description of the anomaly, using all the information previously collected.

## 3  Classification Based on Anomaly Signatures

To assess the accuracy and performance of NADA, a set of traces created in the framework of the MetroSec Project, between 2004 and 2006 was used. This repository spans different types of anomalies, legitimate and illegitimate ones, with different levels of intensity. Also, different types of anomaly generators (as Hping, Iperf, Trinoo, TFN2k) were used in order to improve the quality of the database.

The successive utilization of NADA showed that anomalies of a specific type have a consistent signature. Such signatures are obtained by looking how the distribution of source and destination IP addresses and ports relate to each other in candidate-anomalous flows. Running NADA on the traces collected permitted the isolation of several types of anomalies. In this paper we will focus on DDoS attacks.

When analyzing the traces we have obtained two different types of DDoS signatures, depending on the number of destination ports that are flooded. It was also observed that these signatures are independent of the tool being used to perpetrate the attacks, and because of that may be considered as behavior-based signatures, instead of regular signatures, which are dependent of specific parameters of a specific anomaly.

Each behavior-based signature obtained can be represented as a sequence of four plots that constitute what we have called the graphical signature. Figure 1 is a representation of the DDoS signature behavior-based of type $n$IP sources using $n$Ports attacking $I$IP destination using $n$Ports. The four plots show how the different source and destination addresses/port relate to each other in flows associated to a DDoS. This sequence of shapes is detected at all levels of IP aggregation at the destination, ranging from /8 to /32. This signature is unique for a given type of attack when analyzing the correct time series, packets and bytes.

All plots in Figure 1 relate the distribution of source with destination information. So, the leftmost plot shows the IP sources that are flooding the destination IP address. The next plot, inserts information about the ports that were used by the sources. It can be seen that each packet sent was using a different port number. In the plot this is denoted by a full straight line. The third plot of the signature adds the port number information to each destination. In our DDoS case it is possible to see that different ports of the target are being flooded (diagonal line). Finally, the rightmost plot shows how destination ports are affected by the anomaly. This plot is important to differentiate network scan from port scan attacks.

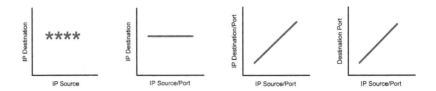

**Fig. 1.** DDoS behavior-based signature without noise. Type of DDoS: $n$ IP Sources, $n$ Source Ports : $1$ IP Destination, $n$ Destination Ports.

The Receiver Operating Characteristic (ROC) curves were used to obtain some information about the sensitivity of NADA (they are not showed due to the lack of space). The analysis of the curves permitted us to verify that NADA is efficient and that whatever the value of $k$ is, the detection probability is always higher than the rate of false alarms.

## 4 Conclusion

In this paper, we have presented NADA an algorithm for detecting, classifying and identifying anomalies of any type in network traffic, and that provides information about the parties responsible of the anomaly, in a way easily understandable by technicians who are operating and managing networks.

Moreover, the information provided by NADA is delivered in graphical and textual format. If the first format could be interesting for administrator to discover, at a glance, what is happening in the network, the latter one could be easily used to trigger other types of signals or actions, suited to the anomaly that is occurring.

To conclude this work, we intend to run NADA over traces for which we do not know about the presence of anomalies, to test the efficiency and robustness of NADA. Future work also includes the design of a election method for the $k$ factor, as it is for the moment hand made.

## References

1. Kim, S., Reddy, A., Vannucci, M.: Detecting Traffic Anomalies through Aggregate Analysis of Packet Header Data. In: Networking 2004, Athens (2004)
2. Lakhina, A., Crovella, M., Diot, C.: Mining Anomalies Using Traffic Feature Distributions. In: ACM SIGCOMM, Philadelphia (2005)
3. Farraposo, S., Owezarski, P., Monteiro, E.: A Multi-Scale Tomographic Algorithm for Detecting and Classifying Traffic Anomalies. In: IEEE ICC 2007, Glasgow (2007)
4. Cormode, G., Muthukrishnan, S.: What's New: Finding Significant Differences in Network Data Streams. In: IEEE/ACM Transactions on Networking, vol. 13 (2005)

# IT Service Management Automation – An Automation Centric Approach Leveraging Configuration Control, Audit Verification and Process Analytics

Naga Ayachitula[1], Melissa Buco[1], Yixin Diao[1], Bradford Fisher[2],
David Loewenstern[1], and Chris Ward[1]

[1] IBM Thomas J Watson Research Center
Hawthorne, NY 10532
[2] IBM
RTP, NC 27709
{nagaaka,mjbuco,diao,bradfish,davidloe,cw1}@us.ibm.com

**Abstract.** People, processes, technology and information are the service provider's resources for delivering IT services. Process automation is one way in which service providers can reduce cost and improve quality by automating routine tasks thereby reducing human error and reserving people resources for those tasks which require human skill and complex decision making. In this paper we propose a conceptual methodology for IT service management process automation in the area of configuration control, audit verification, and process analytics. We employ a complexity model to assist in identifying the opportunities for process automation. We recommend and outline an automated approach to the complex task of variance detection of the hierarchically defined Configuration Items in a Configuration Management Database (CMDB) against the Configuration Items in the IT environment. We also recommend the integration of this automated detection with human centric remediation for resolving the variances detected and outline an automated approach to the variance detection.

## 1 Introduction

Today's IT environments are generally large, complex, distributed, and constantly being changed. Although most changes are intended to fix or improve the environment, they can often have unexpected, undesirable, and costly effects on the environment. Therefore, it is recommended by best practices such as ITIL [1], the recognized standard for IT service management, that configuration of the environment be maintained in a CMDB and be carefully controlled. The CMDB includes attributes of and relationships between the configuration items (CIs) in the IT environment and serves as a source of authorized configuration information that can be used by all of the other ITIL processes. It also maintains relationships between configuration items and other Service Support artifacts (e.g. Change Records and Incident Records). Because the CMDB serves as the source of information for

A. Clemm, L.Z. Granville, and R. Stadler (Eds.): DSOM 2007, LNCS 4785, pp. 195–198, 2007.

decision making by many other process, the accuracy of the CMDB is important. Therefore, regular audits zare needed to verify that the CMDB correctly reflects the environment. This is an opportunity to detect and correct any errors in the CMDB as well as unauthorized changes that have been made to the IT environment. For an environment of even moderate size, these activities are time consuming and prone to human error which makes them prime candidates for automation.

## 2 Configuration Control, Audit Verification and Remediation

The Configuration Management process ensures accuracy by imposing configuration control, that is, by requiring controlling documentation for changes to information in the CMDB. [2] Thus the CMDB can then be regarded as repository of authorized information about CIs. The intent of configuration control is to prevent unauthorized changes to the IT environment and the CMDB. It is up to the discretion of the Configuration Manager to establish the policies regarding the extent and content of the controlling documentation required for a change. Correctness the contents of the CMDB can be ensured by regularly comparing against the actual IT environment. This requires discovering, either manually, via automated scans, or import from an authorized source information on what is actually in the IT environment. This gathered data may come from a variety of sources. The actual data may then be compared with that which was authorized in accordance with Configuration Management process to detect variances. Before comparison against the authorized data in the CMDB, the gathered data must be normalized and multiple sources reconciled. Based on the type of variance (e.g. unauthorized changed in the environment) an appropriate remediation is enacted.

## 3 Automation Centric Remediation Leveraging Configuration Control, Audit and Remediation and Process Analytics

The proposed methodology calls for using the IT complexity modeling tool to determine in a given business process which of the activities demand extensive coordination, communication, collaboration and require human interaction versus identifying repeatable patterns of activities that can be effectively automated, as illustrated in Figure 1. Below is an overview of the proposed automation in Figure 1.

1. Define which configuration item types should be part of the audit. Relationships between configuration items can be extensive. In order to make the comparison process feasible some scope for comparison has to be established around which set of CI relationships to compare. The scope in the proposed automation limits the CI relationship comparison to CI relationships which transverse "down" the CI relationship tree as defined in the authorized CI definition template.
2. Define the link rules for Authorized CI types to Actual CI types. A link rule provides a mechanism to uniquely identify CI instances. A link rule is typically one or more sets of attributes and criteria.
3. Search and retrieve all authorized CI instances for identified audit CI types.

4.  Search and retrieve all actual CI instances for identified audit CI types.
5.  Use the CI definition as a template to compare authorized CI instances with actual CI instances. The authorized CI template defines what CIs and relationship types to compare and how deep the compare should be.
6.  Write audit comparison and variance results.

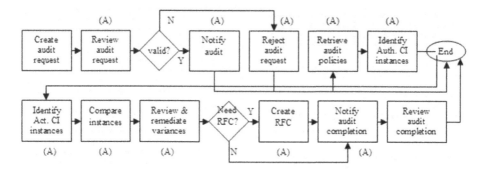

**Fig. 1.** Automation centric remediation process - activities labeled as (A) are automated activities

For the authorized CI to actual CI comparison, once the auditable CI data set is returned and the links are established between instances, comparison of the relationship and attributes for the CIs returned in the link and for all subsequent lower level CIs down the tree are also compared. For each comparison a result is written to the audit results.

## 4   Evaluation Using IT Process Complexity Model

We conducted a complexity evaluation for the process represented in Fig.1. Our discussion is based on the IT management complexity framework described in [3]. The per-task complexity was computed based on the complexity metrics introduced above along the three complexity dimensions. For example, task 7 compares and identifies variances between authorized and actual CI instances and involves high business item complexity. Once the per-task metrics have been computed, they can be aggregated to produce process-wide views to identify the complexity bottlenecks within this process and process-wide metrics to facilitate cross-process comparison. Per-task views are graphs showing all per-task metrics in bar charts. Fig. 2 provides a per-task view for all 11 tasks. The x axis indicates the tasks and the y axis indicates the metric values. All per-task metrics can be plotted separately or aggregated for three high-level views of execution complexity, coordination complexity, and business item complexity. The overall process complexity metrics are summarized in Table 1. We also conducted complexity evaluation for the automated process. As shown in Figure 2 and Table 1, tasks 2 to 7 and 9 to 10 have been automated and so have zero complexity associated with them. This reduces the number of tasks of this process from 11 to 3. In addition, automation also reduces the number of business

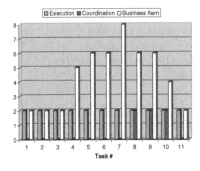
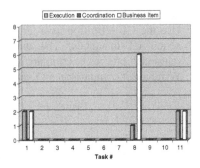

**Fig. 2** Per Task View of Processes without/with Automation

**Table 1** Complexity metrics for audit and remediation process in Figure 1

| Complexity Measure | Metric | Value Before | Value After |
|---|---|---|---|
| Execution | Number of Tasks | 11 | 3 |
| Coordination | Number of Shared Tasks | 0 | 0 |
| | Number of Cross-Role Links | 2 | 0 |
| Business Item | Number of Business Items | 8 | 2 |

items in this process from 8 to 2, since most of the required business items can be acquired and applied automatically in the new process.

## 5  Conclusions

Configuration control and audit verification exemplify areas which can benefit significantly from integration of as much automation as maturity and technology permit with human centric interactions for tasks such as remediation which are most efficiently handled by a human assisted by appropriate tooling. In this paper, we described a conceptual methodology for IT service management process automation in the area of configuration control, audit verification, and process analytics. We employed a complexity model to assist in identifying the opportunities for process automation. We outlined an automated approach to variance detection between authorized and actual and recommended integration of this automated detection with human centric remediation for resolving the variances detected.

## References

1. ITIL The Key to Managing IT Services: Service Support Version 2.3 (TSO for OGC) (2000)
2. Information technology — Service management (ISO/IEC 20000)
3. Diao, Y., Keller, A.: Quantifying the complexity of IT service management processes. In: Proceedings of the 17th IFIP/IEEE International Workshop on Distributed Systems: Operations and Management, Dublin, Ireland, pp. 61–73 (2006)

# Proposal on Network-Wide Rollback Scheme for Fast Recovery from Operator Errors

Kiyohito Yoshihara, Daisuke Arai, Akira Idoue, and Hiroki Horiuchi

KDDI R&D Laboratories Inc., 2-1-15 Ohara Fujimino-shi
Saitama 356-8502, Japan
{yosshy,di-arai,idoue,hr-horiuchi}@kddilabs.jp

**Abstract.** This paper proposes a new network-wide rollback scheme for fast recovery from operator errors, toward the high availability of networks and services. A technical issue arises from the fact that operators, who manipulate one or more diverse devices and services due to their network-wide dependency in a typical management task, are the major cause of failure. The lack of systems or tools fully addressing the issue motivated us to develop a new scheme. The underlying idea is that, for any operational device or service, the observable behavior is identical whenever the same setting is configured. High availability will thus be achieved by rolling the settings that may cause an abnormal state by an operator error, back to past ones with which devices and services were stable. Certain policies for the network-wide rollback are identified and a prototype implementation and preliminary results will be presented.

## 1 Introduction

As seen from its global acceptance, the Internet is becoming as another form of promising infrastructure like electricity, water and gas. At the same time, the ever-increasing scale of the networks constituted by diverse devices and services entails additional opportunities for network operations. We operate one or more devices and services in a typical management task, due to their network-wide dependency. For instance, when we install a new Web server, we configure a router, the DNS server and a firewall in order, as well as the Web server.

In contrast, it is reported in [1] that operators are the leading cause of failure, accounting for 51%, which was roughly estimated based on the number of identified outages in three Internet sites of 500 to 5000 computers. In order to make the networks and services dependable enough to be used with availability equivalent to existing infrastructures, the new technical issue arising is to enable fast recovery from operator errors while considering the diversity of devices and services as well as their network-wide dependency.

Certain systems [2,3] have been developed to address the issue, which presuppose errors on the part of the operator, provide undo utilities that allow the operator to roll a service back to a previous state, and minimize the Mean Time To Repair (MTTR) for higher availability; however, the systems take into account neither the diversity of services nor their dependency. The development

A. Clemm, L.Z. Granville, and R. Stadler (Eds.): DSOM 2007, LNCS 4785, pp. 199–202, 2007.

of additional software components for each service is required for the adoption. Moreover, their operational scope is restricted to a single service, and the resulting state is not necessarily consistent with that after past management tasks. We might exploit tools [4,5] for multi-vendor routers and switches; however, they are the same as the systems [2,3] in terms of the limited operational scope.

This paper proposes a new network-wide rollback scheme for fast recovery from operator errors, as work in progress. The proposed scheme will be differentiated by (1) the practicality by which we can deploy the proposed scheme with no modification to existing diverse devices and services and (2) the network-wide configuration management, via which we can roll an entire managed network back to a safe state, consistently with past management tasks. In the subsequent sections, we will initially present the proposed scheme, together with some policies specific to network-wide rollback, and then show the current state of the prototype implementation and preliminary results.

## 2   Proposal on Network-Wide Rollback Scheme for Fast Recovery from Operator Errors

### 2.1   Design Principle

The idea of the proposed scheme comes from a straightforward fact: for any operational device or service, its observable behavior is identical whenever the same setting is configured. Thus, we can expect fast recovery from operator errors when in an abnormal state after a management task, by rolling the current settings back to past ones, with which managed devices and services were in a stable state. We extend this idea to a network with the design principles below.

1. We develop a new server to achieve network-wide rollback. The server hooks all command requests to and responses from managed devices and services during a management task, and backups all settings of the devices and services, including those that were not operated whenever a task is completed. An ID is given, along with backup time and an associable comment, in order to identify a state in the network-wide rollback.
2. For a device and service, we describe two scripts for the backup and rollback of setting, and register them as well as the human-readable name, IP address and login credential with the server. Running one or more scripts can see a network of diverse devices and services rolled back to a stable state, with no modification to the devices and services.
3. To cope with addition/deletion of a device and service, we define compensation policies as retaining a state stably after the network-wide rollback over such changes. A simple example of the policy is to skip the rollback for a device not existed before. The resulting state should be consistent but may not always be the one occurred in the past management tasks.
4. We cannot always roll all necessary settings back at will, due to a transient state during the rollback: e.g. inability to reach a managed device a few hops away from the server, via the change of a routing table of a router on the path. With this in mind, we define ordering policies to avoid such side-effects.

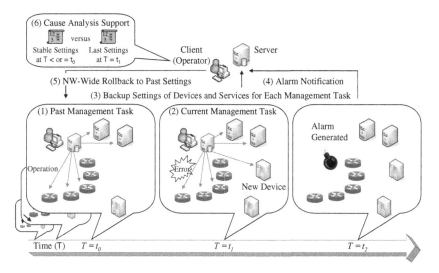

**Fig. 1.** Overview of System Operation Based on Proposed Scheme

## 2.2   Overview of System Operation Based on Proposed Scheme

We assume below that the enrollment of names, IP addresses, login credentials, and scripts of managed devices and services in the server has been completed.

When an operator performs a management task, he/she firstly logs into the server, and subsequently further logs into a target device and service from the server, via a usual terminal client (Fig.1 (1) and (2)). Every time the operator logs out from the device and service, the server backups all the settings of the managed devices and services, using the scripts (Fig.1 (3)). The backup can be on a regular basis and on demand from an operator.

In case of an alarm notification (Fig.1 (4)) from an external system, suspecting operator errors in the last management task (Fig.1 (2)), an operator logs into the server for fast recovery. Based on compensation and ordering policies, he/she then rolls all settings of the managed devices and services back (network-wide rollback) to the past ones in a stable state at $T \leq t_0$ (Fig.1 (5)), from the server.

Subsequently, an operator will conduct a cause analysis of the alarm. The proposed scheme supports the comparison of the last settings at $T = t_1$ with the others at $T \leq t_0$, and the verification of the commands hooked in the past management task (Fig.1 (6)). When the alarm is still alive after the network-wide rollback, there might be other causes, such as hardware failure, or software crash unable to reboot. Coping with the causes of the latter kind is future work.

## 3   Implementation and Preliminary Results

Figure 2 shows the prototype implementation for the evaluation of the proposed scheme. The development of the policy DB is underway.

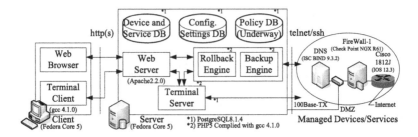

**Fig. 2.** Prototype Implementation Based on Proposed Scheme

The primary performance metric is the time of the network-wide rollback, for the faster it is completed, the shorter MTTR for high availability is accomplished. We applied the proposed scheme to the network of a router, a DNS server and a firewall assuming a barebones DMZ, as shown on the right side of Fig.2. The time was 142 sec., when they were sequentially rolled back accompanied with reboots, providing an upper bound of the rollback time for the network. We could reduce the time to 40 sec. by starting the rollback of the DNS server earlier than that of the router, followed by the router rollback soon after that. In the case of inverse order, the rollback of the DNS server failed until completion of the router rollback, due to the inability to reach its higher level DNS servers.

The above preliminary results reveal that the rollback time depends on an ordering policy. We are investigating compensation and ordering policies, and faster rollback operations that do not rely on time-consuming reboots. We will evaluate them in a carrier-scale network, using the above bound as a reference.

## 4    Conclusions

This paper proposed a new network-wide rollback scheme for fast recovery from operator errors, as a work in progress. The design principles and an overview of the system operation were presented. We will show the evaluation results shortly, using the completed version of the prototype implementation.

## References

1. Patterson, D.A.: A Simple Way to Estimate the Cost of Downtime. In: Proc. of the 16th Systems Administration Conference, pp. 185–188 (November 2002)
2. Brown, A.B., Patterson, D.A.: Undo for Operators: Building an Undoable E-mail Store. In: Proc. of USENIX 2003, pp. 1–14 (June 2003)
3. O'Brien, J., Shapiro, M.: Undo for anyone, anywhere, anytime. In: Proc. of the 11th workshop on ACM SIGOPS European workshop, ACM Press, New York (2004)
4. Shrubbery Networks, Inc.: Really Awesome New Cisco conflg Differ (RANCID) (URL available for May 2007) http://www.shrubbery.net/rancid/
5. AdventNet, Inc.: DeviceExpert (URL available for May 2007),
   http://manageengine.adventnet.com/products/device-expert/index.html

# AURIC: A Scalable and Highly Reusable SLA Compliance Auditing Framework

Hasan and Burkhard Stiller

Computer Science Department IFI, University of Zürich, Switzerland
{hasan,stiller}@ifi.uzh.ch

**Abstract.** Service Level Agreements (SLA) are needed to allow business inter-actions to rely on Internet services. Service Level Objectives (SLO) specify the committed performance level of a service. Thus, SLA compliance auditing aims at verifying these commitments. Since SLOs for various application services and end-to-end performance definitions vary largely, *automated* auditing of SLA compliances poses the challenge to an auditing framework. Moreover, end-to-end performance data are potentially large for a provider with many customers. Therefore, this paper presents a *scalable* and *highly reusable* auditing framework and a prototype, termed *AURIC* (*Au*diting *F*ramework for *I*nternet Servi*c*es), whose components can be distributed across different domains.

## 1 Introduction

Today, the Internet has become a platform for business. Various services are offered to enable business transactions to be accomplished. A *Service Level Agreement* (SLA) is negotiated between a provider and a customer in order to define a legally binding contract regarding the service delivery. While the TeleManagement Forum defines an SLA as "a formal negotiated agreement between two parties, sometimes called a Service Level Guarantee, it is a contract (or part of one) that exists between the service provider and the customer, designed to create a common understanding about services, priorities, responsibilities, etc." [17], in general, an SLA comprises in particular a service descrip-tion, the *expected performance level* of the service, the procedure for reporting prob-lems, the *time-frame for response and problem resolution*, the process for monitoring and reporting the service level, the consequences for the provider not meeting its obli-gations, and escape clauses and constraints [18]. The performance level of a service committed is specified in a set of *Service Level Objectives* (SLO). Thus, SLA compli-ance auditing aims at verifying that these SLOs are met. This task must be *automated* in order to be *efficient* and to enable *real-time reactions* in case of an SLA violation.

In fact, specifying SLAs on IP-based networks becomes viable through network de-vice instrumentations for Quality-of-Service (QoS) measurements, not only of transport but also of application services. However, application service SLAs still pose challeng-es to their compliance auditing, due to the *variety* and the potential *complexity* of SLOs. An example for a complex SLO is the following detail specification of service availability: "In most cases, service requests from authorised users will be accepted.

A. Clemm, L.Z. Granville, and R. Stadler (Eds.): DSOM 2007, LNCS 4785, pp. 203–215, 2007.

If a request from an authorised user is rejected or not responded within 15 seconds, then the next request for this service from the same user will be accepted. However, this next request must be made within the next 5 minutes and 1 minute must have been elapsed since the rejected or unresponded request." Thus, an *expressive* specification language is beneficial to formally specify such complex relations among various events.

A useful auditing framework must allow for the *distribution of auditing load* to separate auditor instances. The time and memory required for auditing may increase only *linearly* with an increasing number of audit data. Moreover, the framework must be *reusable* and *easily* adaptable to audit any *complex* SLO. Hence, this paper presents a *scalable* and *highly reusable generic* framework, termed *AURIC (Au*diting Framework for *I*nternet Services), which supports *secure inter-domain* interactions and provides all necessary core functionality to conduct *automatically* potentially *complex* audit tasks.

The remainder of this paper is organized as follows. Section 2 discusses related work. While Section 3 presents the AURIC architecture for SLA compliance auditing, Section 4 describes its prototypical implementation. An extensive evaluation of AURIC with respect to its scalability and reusability is presented in Section 5, which is followed by Section 6, where conclusions are drawn.

## 2     Related Work

Current approaches in SLA management address the *formal specification* of a complete SLA in a *specific area, e.g.*, network or web services, or concentrate on measurements of a pre-defined set of SLA parameters [1], [6], [8], [10], [12], [13]. Hence, to modify or to extend an existing solution, particularly a commercial product, for its application to an SLO with a different logic, a larger effort is needed than if the solution has been based on a generic framework like AURIC. Moreover, most approaches support only *simple SLO terms* and do not consider possible *inter-domain* auditing interactions and their *security* requirements. While [7] discusses all relevant details of related work, the following paragraphs summarize major issues only.

The Web Service Level Agreement (WSLA) Framework proposes a concept for SLA management including online monitoring of SLA violation and defines a language to specify SLAs [13]. However, it *focuses on web services and supports only simple SLO terms.* A condition in a WSLA's SLO is simply a logic expression with SLA parameters as variables. WSLA does not support conditional expressions for SLO specifications and the framework does not expect to process metered data consisting of more than one field, *e.g.*, <IPAddress, PacketLossRatio>. Since the timepoint at which the value of a measured metric is transferred is considered as the measurement timepoint, batch processing of measured data is not supported.

In the area of Grid services, Cremona [14] is an architecture and library for the creation and monitoring of WS-Agreements, whose specification is worked out by the Grid Resource Allocation and Agreement Protocol Working Group (GRAAP-WG) of the Global Grid Forum. Cremona supports the implementation of agreement management, however, SLO monitoring is considered application specific, thus, no support to its implementation is available, except an interface to retrieve monitoring results.

The Project TAPAS (Trusted and Quality-of-Service Aware Provision of Application Services) proposes SLAng, a language for expressing SLAs precisely [16]. SLAng is defined using an instance of the Meta-Object Facility model, and its violation semantics is defined using Object Constraint Language constraints. To reduce the possibility of disagreement over the amount of errors introduced by the mechanism for SLA violation detection, a contract checker is to be automatically generated by using the metamodel of the language and associated constraints as inputs for a generative programming tool [15]. However, this approach leads to performance problems. Thus, in order to eliminate various drawbacks mentioned above, this paper presents an architecture for SLA compliance auditing as described in the next section.

## 3   AURIC SLA Compliance Auditing Architecture

Based on the generic model and architecture for automated auditing [9], the AURIC architecture for SLA compliance auditing has been implemented, which covers three main functions: metering, accounting, and auditing, as depicted in Fig. 1.

**Metering and Accounting:** The quality level of a service being delivered must be metered to allow for the auditing of its SLA compliance. Metered data are collected and aggregated by accounting components to generate accounting data (termed Facts). Accounting data are passed to the non-repudiation (NR) module to generate evidence of service consumption. Generation and transfer of evidences require interactions between

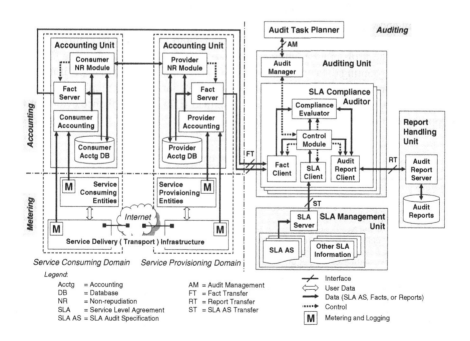

**Fig. 1.** AURIC SLA Compliance Auditing Architecture

NR modules from both sides. Accounting data and evidences are stored in the accounting database and the respective Fact server is notified, so that they are transferred to the
SLA compliance auditor. If non-repudiation is not required, an NR module simply acts
as a proxy between the accounting component and the database or the Fact server. The
architecture and protocols for non-repudiation of service consumption supporting fair-
ness and identity privacy in a mobile environment are available [7], [11].

**Auditing:** The main interactions between AURIC's components are for auditing. The
auditing unit provides an auditing service through the Audit Management (AM) interface. The audit manager waits for audit requests and forwards each audit task received
to an auditor. It also accepts requests relating to an audit task being conducted, *e.g.*, requests on its status and requests to stop an audit task. An audit task planner represents
an entity which requests an auditing service from an auditing unit. An auditor retrieves
data to be processed from various sources: accounting units, SLA management units,
and Report handling units. Each of these components provides for a service to access
its data through a data server component, namely a Fact server, an SLA server, and an
Audit Report server respectively. Note that an Audit Report server also receives requests to store Audit Reports. All SLOs committed are assumed to be specified in a language, which allows for an automated auditing. The resulted specifications are called
SLA Audit Specifications (SLA AS). Other SLA information, *e.g.*, user profile, service
profile, are not relevant at this stage, and thus, are not explicitly listed in the figure.

To communicate with various data servers, an auditor must contain the corresponding clients. The communication happens via the respective interface: SLA AS Transfer
(ST), Fact Transfer (FT), or Report Transfer (RT) interface. The auditor must also contain a compliance evaluator to examine accounting data and Audit Reports based on the
SLA AS obtained from the SLA client through the control module. The control module
configures and controls other components in carrying out their functions. The Fact client retrieves accounting data and delivers them to the compliance evaluator. If needed,
the Audit Report client retrieves and delivers Audit Reports to the compliance evaluator. Finally, this client sends Audit Reports obtained from the compliance evaluator to
a Report handling unit. Table 1 briefly discusses suitable protocols for those interfaces.

**Table 1.**   Auditing Interfaces

| Interface | Description |
|---|---|
| AM | A new protocol for this interface is needed, however, following two communication patterns are sufficient to enable management interactions in normal and erroneous situations: Request-Answer and Notification pattern. A request message is used to initiate or terminate an audit task or to obtain its status information. An answer is sent as a response to a request message and it may contain error description, if any. A notification can be sent at any time to inform the re-spective audit task planner of completion of an audit task or any error occured during an audit. |
| ST | A URL is used to locate a particular SLA AS. Existing protocols such as HTTPS and SSH File Transfer Protocol are very well suited to be used to transfer SLA AS securely from an SLA manager to the auditing unit. |
| FT | For the purpose of transferring Facts, Diameter [2] protocol is very well suitable. The Base Ac-counting message pair is sufficient. However, to allow for selection of Facts a new Diameter command must be defined. |
| RT | Diameter is also suitable here, since the types of interactions are the same as for FT interface. |

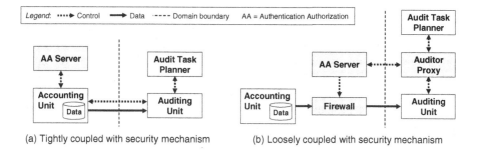

**Fig. 2.** Examples of Secured Access to Accounting Data

**Security Considerations:** Multi-domain support requires secure interactions and access control. Since in an SLA all parties involved are known in advance, security associations among those components can be established before interactions take place. Having these security associations in place, authentication and authorization (AA) can be accomplished. As an example, suppose that accounting unit and auditing unit are located in different administrative domains. There are several ways of doing access control, *e.g.*, based on Authentication, Authorization, and Accounting (AAA) architecture [3]. In Fig. 2 (a), an AA server is contacted by the accounting unit to authenticate and authorize the auditing unit before it is allowed to send data to the auditing unit.

Access control can also be provided without intervening auditing functionality as shown in Fig. 2 (b). An auditor proxy is inserted between audit task planner and auditing unit. The proxy analyses audit tasks and requests access to the relevant accounting unit from the AA server of the respective domain. If there is a security association between the two domains, the access request is accepted and the firewall is configured to allow data flows between the auditing unit and the accounting unit. On receipt of a positive response from the AA server, the proxy forwards the audit task to the auditing unit. Finally, if necessary, a secure communication channel can be established to transfer data confidentially, based on security associations between those domains.

## 4   Implementation

Based on the proposed architecture, a prototypical implementation of an SLA compliance auditing framework in C++ is provided. The implementation aims at showing that developing an auditor can be done basically through specialization of a set of base classes to implement the SLO specific application logic. Fig. 3 depicts the implementation architecture of a *specific* SLA compliance auditor. The auditor is specific, since the application logic to audit a *specific SLO* is implemented as an integral part of the auditor. Thus, the auditor does not require an SLA client component to retrieve the SLA AS (cf. Fig. 1). However, various application logic corresponding to different SLOs can be implemented at compile time before one is chosen to be applied through a configuration file at run time. Thus, the need of a parser.

Each Fact and Audit Report is represented as a list of attribute-value-pairs (AVPs). Diameter [2] is chosen as the protocol for transferring Facts and Audit Reports due to its extensibility and the capability of its accounting message to carry a list of AVPs. Thus, the functionality of a Fact client and a Report client (cf. Fig. 1) is merged into a single entity called a Fact and Report client, which consists of a Fact and Report transfer module implemented on top of the Open Diameter framework. The description of the Open Diameter implementation is given in [5]. Furthermore, to obtain a modular design, the author proposes to decompose an audit task into a sequence of subtasks:

1. ***Facts filtering***: Only Facts which are relevant for the SLO being audited are to be further processed. The filtered Facts are named *related Facts*.

2. ***Facts grouping***: Related Facts must be grouped, since they result from different service settings or observation periods. A group of Facts from a particular setting or period is named a *Fact-List*. A Fact-List being built is called an *open* Fact-List, whereas a Fact-List ready for auditing is called a *complete* Fact-List.

3. ***Property values calculation***: Each performance parameter of a service is characterized by a set of *properties*, whose values are calculated from the complete Fact-List examined in order to determine the compliance with the SLO.

4. ***Compliance calculation***: The *degree of compliance* with the SLO is calculated by applying the SLO specific compliance formula to the property values.

5. ***Report AVPs calculation***: The values for the report AVPs are calculated from various sources: the Fact-List, property values, and the compliance value.

6. ***Report generation***: As a result, a report is composed from the report AVPs.

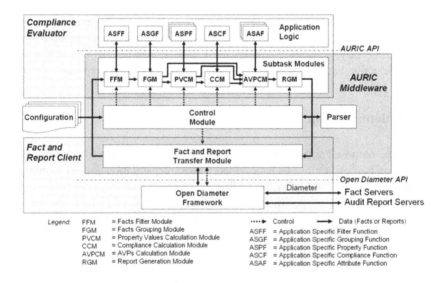

**Fig. 3.** Implementation Architecture of an SLA Compliance Auditor

Based on this decomposition, the compliance evaluator is developed, which consists of two parts: a sequence of subtask modules and a set of application logic. While the application logic implements SLO specific subtask functions, the subtask modules implement functionality which is common to all auditing applications, namely, management of Facts, Fact-Lists, and property values, as well as transfer of data between two subtask modules. The interface between a subtask module and its application logic is defined by the AURIC Application Programming Interface (API).

## 4.1    AURIC API

The auditing framework API provides five base classes to implement application logic (cf. Fig. 4). The parent class `SubtaskFunc` provides methods to parametrize the application specific subtask function derived, which are invoked by the auditing framework after the creation of the function based on the configuration file. Each base class offers a method `Process()`, whose purpose is described in Table 2 and which should be implemented by the developer of the auditing application.

**Table 2.** The Purpose of the API's `Process()` Methods

| Class | The Purpose of `Process()` Method |
|---|---|
| Filter-Function | To examine the accounting record encapsulated in the `Fact` object and return true or false to denote whether the record is related to the SLO being audited. A `Fact` object provides for methods to get information about the accounting record encapsulated in the object, *e.g.*, the value of a particular attribute. |
| Grouping-Function | To examine the accounting record encapsulated in the `Fact` object and assign the record to one or more Fact-Lists with the help of `OpenFactLists` object. An `OpenFactLists` object provides for methods to manipulate open Fact-Lists managed by the auditing framework, *e.g.*, to add a Fact into an open Fact-List and to close an open Fact-List. |
| Property-Function | To calculate a property value from the list of related accounting records encapsulated in the `FactList` object. A `FactList` object provides for methods to manipulate and to access information about accounting records encapsulated in the object, *e.g.*, the number of records, the sum of the value of a particular field of the records. |
| Compliance-Function | To calculate a compliance value from the list of property values encapsulated in the `PropertyValues` object. A `PropertyValues` object provides for methods to access property values. |
| Attribute-Function | To calculate a report attribute value from the list of related accounting records (encapsulated in `FactList` object), the list of property values (encapsulated in the `PropertyValues` object), and the compliance value. |

## 4.2    Development of a General SLA Compliance Auditor

A *general* SLA compliance auditor is an auditor which can be used to audit *any* SLO without the need to modify and recompile the application logic. To implement a general SLA compliance auditor, following items must be available: an audit specification *language* to define in detail *how* an SLO is to be audited and an implementation of those

```
class SubtaskFunc {
 public:
  virtual ~SubtaskFunc() {}
  virtual bool SetStringParam(
   unsigned int paramNo,
   const string& paramVal) {return false;}
  virtual bool SetNumberParam(
   unsigned int paramNo,
   float paramVal) {return false;}
  virtual bool SetBooleanParam(
   unsigned int paramNo,
   bool paramVal) {return false;}
};
class FilterFunction : public SubtaskFunc {
 public:
  virtual ~FilterFunction() {}
  virtual bool Process(
   const Fact& currentFact) = 0;
};
class GroupingFunction : public SubtaskFunc {
 public:
  virtual ~GroupingFunction() {}
  virtual void Process(const Fact& currFact,
   OpenFactLists& ofl) = 0;
};
```

```
class PropertyFunction : public SubtaskFunc {
 public:
  virtual ~PropertyFunction() {}
  virtual prop_value_t* Process(
   FactList& currentFactList) = 0;
};

class ComplianceFunction: public SubtaskFunc {
 public:
  virtual ~ComplianceFunction() {}
  virtual float Process(
   const PropertyValues& propertyValues) = 0;
};

class AttributeFunction : public SubtaskFunc {
 public:
  virtual ~AttributeFunction() {}
  virtual void Process(string& attrValue,
   FactList& currentFactList,
   const PropertyValues& propertyValues,
   float complianceValue) = 0;
};
```

**Fig. 4.** AURIC API

five application specific classes as an *interpreter* of the audit specification language used. An audit specification language, named *Sapta*, has been developed [7].

A Sapta specification for auditing an SLO consists of a set of *function definition subspecifications* and a set of *function invocation subspecifications*. Each set of function definition subspecifications defines the application logic corresponding to those five functions defined in Section 4.1 to audit a specific SLO, whereas each set of function invocation subspecifications defines which function definition subspecifications are to be invoked and with which values for their parameters. The function invocation subspecifications in Sapta is usable as a configuration file for auditing, which consists of a ComplianceCalculation subspecification and a ReportComposition subspecification. Furthermore, the following principle is followed in the design of Sapta: The management (storage and transport) of Facts and Fact-Lists should be transparent to a programmer of an audit specification. Accesses to and manipulations of Facts and FactLists are to be supported through specific language constructs. Thus, in addition to conventional language constructs such as iteration and conditional branches, Sapta defines constructs which allow for a convenient specification of audit subtasks, *e.g.*, time schedule to evaluate completeness of a Fact-List (cf. Chapter 4 in [7] for further details).

## 5   Evaluation

The AURIC framework is evaluated with respect to its key requirements defined in Section 1. The scalability of the architecture is analyzed with respect to the number of SLOs, while the load scalability of its implementation, in terms of processing delay and memory requirements, is evaluated with respect to the number of Facts to be processed.

## 5.1   Scalability of Auditing Framework

Suppose that there are $p$ parties in a multi-domain environment and two SLAs are negotiated between any two parties (in one SLA a party takes the role of a service provider, in the other SLA the role of a customer). This full mesh relationship results in $p*(p-1)$ SLAs. However, from the point of view of each party only $2*(p-1)$ SLAs are relevant. Unlike other approaches which use an auditor instance per SLA, AURIC defines an auditor instance per SLO. The number of SLOs ($n_{SLO}$) does not depend on the number of SLAs ($n_{SLA}$), but on the number of services ($n_{svc}$). Assuming that each service has a maximum of $c$ SLOs, then $n_{SLO}$ is bound by $c*n_{svc}$. Table 3 compares the scalability of AURIC architecture with the other approaches, where $n_A$ is the number of auditor instances required and $n_{A,max}$ is its upper bound. Although all approaches show a *linear scalability*, AURIC does have an *advantage* over the other: the number of services and SLOs grows much slower than the number of customers (SLAs).

With respect to the load scalability of an auditor, the number of Facts to be audited is crucial. There is a limit to the processing speed of an auditor, which determines the amount of Facts allowed per time unit. The amount of Facts can increase due to, *e.g.*, more sessions, which are generated. By *scaling up* the auditor, more Facts can be audited. However, this problem can also be solved by *scaling out* the auditor, since accounting data for the same SLO can be partitioned (*e.g.*, based on CustomerID) and delivered to several instances of auditors, all responsible for the same SLO.

**Table 3.** Scalability Comparison

| Approach | $n_A$ | $n_{A,max}$ | Order of $n_A$ |
|---|---|---|---|
| WSLA Framework, Cremona, TAPAS SLAng | $n_{SLA}$ | $2 * (p-1)$ | O(n) |
| AURIC | $n_{SLO}$ | $c * n_{svc}$ | O(n) |

**Auditor Processing Time:** To evaluate the processing time, three SLO specific auditors are implemented based on the AURIC framework. Each auditor is responsible for auditing one of the three SLOs: Service Breakdown SLO, Service Request SLO, and Downlink Throughput SLO. The measurement of the processing time is done on a host with a Pentium 4 CPU 1.80 GHz, 512 MB main memory. Facts to be processed are delivered at once in a single batch to the auditor, and experiments are carried out with different numbers of Facts. In each experiment the time needed by those Facts to pass processes from the first to a certain subtask module is measured. Each experiment is run 10 times with the same configuration to obtain an average value of the processing time. For example, results show that it takes *in average* 7.94 s (with a *standard deviation* of 0.16 s) to process 100,000 Facts delivered at once through the sequence of *all* subtask modules in auditing the service breakdown SLO.

Fig. 5 (a) depicts as an example the average processing time *per Fact* in *each* subtask module for auditing service breakdown SLO. Other use cases see similar results. The time required by an auditor to accomplish its task is determined by the total number of Facts to be processed, the number of *related* Facts after being *filtered*, the number of

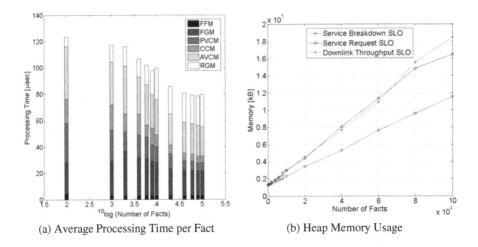

(a) Average Processing Time per Fact          (b) Heap Memory Usage

**Fig. 5.** Load Scalability

*Fact-Lists* after being *grouped*, and the *complexity* of the SLO defined. In all use cases, for a large number of Facts the processing time per Fact in each subtask module exhibits a relative constant value as expected. Thus, AURIC shows a scalable implementation.

**Auditor Heap Memory Usage:** Memory requirements of the auditor are important, especially in relation to the number of Facts. Hence, for those three use cases the memory usage is obtained from /proc files [4]. The virtual memory usage of the heap determines the dominating aspect, thus, all other memory usage is omitted. If all Facts are delivered *at once* to the auditor, a *linear* increase of heap memory usage with an increasing number of Facts is expected, since more memory will be needed to store more Facts. This behavior is shown in Fig. 5 (b), showing that the AURIC implementation scales.

### 5.2   Reusability of Auditing Framework

High reusability is a very important property to be fulfilled by an auditing framework. AURIC's reusability is shown by demonstrating that most of the auditing components do not need to be adapted or replaced, when developing a new auditing application based on the framework. Assuming the example of the following application logic to determine compliances of Facts with a certain SLO:

- If a `Fact` belongs to the SLO to be audited then `ff1(Fact)` is true.
- The value of `gf1(Fact, OpenFactLists)` identifies the `FactList` to which the `Fact` belongs (*e.g.*, all accounting records about (un)availability of service S within a month are to be grouped in order to decide on SLO compliance). If a `FactList` is complete, then `gf2(FactList)` is true.

- A `FactList` complies with the SLO if the value of `cf1(pf1(FactList), pf2(FactList))` is 1 (*e.g.*, if service S may down at most 3 times which are longer than 5 minutes, and the total downtime may not exceed 30 minutes, then `pf1()` would count the number of breakdowns longer than 5 minutes and `pf2()` would calculate the total downtime).

- If a `FactList` does not comply with the SLO a report consisting of `pf1(FactList)`, `pf2(FactList)`, `af1(FactList)`, and `cf1(pf1(FactList), pf2(FactList))` is to be generated.

This logic is easily implemented into AURIC by writing those five application-specific functions. Fig. 6 depicts the *simplified* code snippets. Having defined these subclasses, the programming job is done and an executable auditor for this specific SLO can be compiled. All other functionality is provided automatically by the framework, *e.g.*, interactions with Fact/Report servers to obtain Facts and to deliver Audit Reports, management of Facts, Fact-Lists, property values, and execution of methods invoked by audit subtasks, as well as transfer of data between audit subtasks.

```
class FF_SLO1 : public FilterFunction {
 public:
  bool Process(const Fact& currentFact)
    {return ff1(currentFact);}
};
class GF_SLO1 : public GroupingFunction {
 public:
  void Process(const Fact& currentFact,
               OpenFactLists& ofl) {
    thisFactListId = gf1(currentFact, ofl);
    ofl.Assign(thisFactListId, currentFact);
    if (gf2(ofl.GetFactList(thisFactListId)))
      {ofl.CloseFactList(thisFactListId);}
  }
};
class PV_SLO1 : public prop_value_t {
// define variables to store a property value
};
class PF_1_SLO1 : public PropertyFunction {
 public:
  prop_value_t* Process(FactList& currFL) {
    PV_SLO1* pv = new PV_SLO1;
    // assign pf1(currFL) to variables in pv
    return ((prop_value_t*)pv);
  }
};
```

```
class PF_2_SLO1 : public PropertyFunction {
 public:
  prop_value_t* Process(FactList& currFL) {
    PV_SLO1* pv = new PV_SLO1;
    // assign pf2(currFL) to variables in pv
    return ((prop_value_t*)pv);
  }
};
class CF_SLO1 : public ComplianceFunction {
 public:
  float Process(const PropertyValues& pVal) {
    PV_SLO1& pv1 = (PV_SLO1&)
      pVal.GetPropertyValue(1);
    PV_SLO1& pv2 = (PV_SLO1&)
      pVal.GetPropertyValue(2);
    return (cf1(pv1, pv2));
  }
};
class AF_SLO1 : public AttributeFunction {
 public:
  void Process(string& attrValue,
       FactList& currentFactList,
       const PropertyValues& propertyValues,
       float complianceValue) {
    attrValue = af1(currentFactList);
  }
};
```

**Fig. 6.** Deriving Application Specific Functions

```
ComplianceCalculation CC_SLO1 {
       FF_SLO1
    >> GF_SLO1
    >> PF_1_SLO1, PF_2_SLO1
    >> CF_SLO1
}
```

```
ReportComposition RC_SLO1 {
       [Field1 eq GF_SLO1 >> AF_SLO1],
       [Field2 eq PF_1_SLO1],
       [Field3 eq PF_2_SLO1],
       [Field4 eq CF_SLO1]
}
```

**Fig. 7.** Example Configuration in Sapta

Before invoking the newly developed auditor, a configuration file written in Sapta needs to be created. The framework consults this file to determine, which subclasses are to be used by each audit subtasks and to determine the composition of an Audit Report. For the example above, the content of the configuration file is shown in Fig. 7. Furthermore, it is likely that several SLOs share the same application logic for specific functions, *e.g.*, a `PropertyFunction` to determine the average value of a certain field in the accounting records. This subclass needs to be coded once and can be used for various SLOs through auditor configurations. Thus, the framework also supports reuse of application logic without code duplication in addition to the reuse of its own components.

## 6    Summary and Conclusions

Existing approaches in SLA compliance auditing lack a *general applicability* and concentrate on formal specifications of SLAs rather than on the auditing of SLOs. These pure specification approaches lead to the potential unawareness of system designers on how manifold and complex an SLO for application services can be beyond a guarantee of traditional QoS parameters. Thus, AURIC has been designed based on a *generic model and architecture*. Since the architecture neither assumes specific services nor specific SLOs, it is *general* and applicable to the full range of Internet service types. Furthermore, AURIC architecture is shown to be *linearly scalable* with respect to the number of SLOs due to the possibility to employ an auditor per SLO and to divide the load. The framework implementation also shows a linear scalability of the processing time and memory usage with respect to the number of Facts to be audited.

AURIC framework's functionality is *highly reusable*, which is achieved through the functional decomposition of an audit task into a sequence of subtasks to allow for a modular specification, and through the separation of common audit functionality from SLO-specific auditing logic, as well as a formal language *Sapta* to specify complex audit tasks in full detail. The framework implements the required common audit functionality and offers an API to implement the application logic for auditing a specific SLO. Using AURIC framework, a developer does not need to be concerned about the control of data flow, management of audit data, and data transport. Therefore, the efforts to develop an auditing application based on AURIC framework are largely reduced.

### Acknowledgments

The work has been performed partially in the framework of the EU IST Project Akogrimo (IST-2004-004293), the EU IST Project Daidalos II (IST-2005-026943), and the EU IST Network of Excellence EMANICS (IST-NoE-026854).

## References

1. Agilent Technologies: Measuring Web Quality of Service with the New HTTP Test in FireHunter 4.0; White Paper, Agilent Technologies Inc. (November 2002)
2. Calhoun, P., Loughney, J., Guttman, E., Zorn, G., Arkko, J.: Diameter Base Protocol; IETF, RFC 3588 (September 2003)

3. de Laat, C., Gross, G., Gommans, L., Vollbrecht, J., Spence, D.: Generic AAA Architecture; IETF, RFC 2903 (August 2000)
4. Duddi, S.: Demystifying Footprint; mozilla. org. (March 2002)
5. Fajardo, V.I.: Open Diameter Software Architecture (2004)
6. G-NE GmbH: Konzeptionsansatz: Qualitätssicherung in IT-Outsourcing-Projekten mittels einer unabhängigen Prüfinstanz; Confidential Document (2002)
7. Hasan: A Generic Auditing Framework for Compliance Verification of Internet Service Level Agreements; ETH Zürich, Switzerland, PhD Thesis, Shaker Verlag GmbH, Aachen (2007)
8. Hasan (ed.): A4C Framework Design Specification; Deliverable D341, Sixth European Union Framework Programme, IST Project "Daidalos" (September 2004)
9. Hasan, Stiller, B.: A Generic Model and Architecture for Automated Auditing. In: Schönwälder, J., Serrat, J. (eds.) DSOM 2005. LNCS, vol. 3775, Springer, Heidelberg (2005)
10. Hasan, Stiller, B.: Auditing Architecture for SLA Violation Detection in QoS-Supporting Mobile Internet; IST Mobile and Wireless Comm. Summit 2003, Aveiro, Portugal (June 2003)
11. Hasan, Stiller, B.: Non-repudiation of Consumption of Mobile Internet Services with Privacy Support. In: WiMob 2005. IEEE International Conference on Wireless and Mobile Computing, Networking and Communications, Montreal, Canada (2005)
12. Itellix Software: Wisiba; Datasheet (2003)
13. Keller, A., Ludwig, H.: The WSLA Framework: Specifying and Monitoring Service Level Agreements for Web Services. Journal of Network and Systems Management 11(1), 57–81 (2003)
14. Ludwig, H., Dan, A., Kearney, R.: Cremona: An Architecture and Library for Creation and Monitoring of WS-Agreements. In: International Conference on Service Oriented Computing, New York, USA (November 2004)
15. Skene, J., Emmerich, W.: Generating a Contract Checker for an SLA Language. In: EDOC 2004. Workshop on Contract Architectures and Languages, Monterey, California (2004)
16. Skene, J., Lamanna, D.D., Emmerich, W.: Precise Service Level Agreements. In: 26th International Conference on Software Engineering, Edinburgh, UK (May 2004)
17. Telemanagement Forum: SLA Management Handbook; V1.5. GB917 (2001)
18. Verma, D.C.: Service Level Agreements on IP Networks. Proceedings of the IEEE 92(9) (September 2004)

# Customer Service Management for Grid Monitoring and Accounting Data

Timo Baur[1] and Samah Bel Haj Saad[2]

[1] Munich Network Management Team
Leibniz Rechenzentrum Garching
Boltzmannstr. 1
D-85748 Garching
[2] Munich Network Management Team
Universität der Bundeswehr München
Werner-Heisenberg-Weg 39
D-85579 Neubiberg

**Abstract.** Experiences with the management of Grid specific monitoring and accounting data have shown that current approaches do not sufficiently support a distinction between providers, users and customers of a Grid. This gap can be filled by the use of Customer Service Management techniques which enable customers to individually monitor and control their subscribed services. We adapt a Customer Service Management scenario to Grid environments and outline an architecture dedicated to the management and visualization of monitoring and accounting data. To proof the concept, a prototype based on standard Grid components which manages user's needs and interactions with the resource provider is presented.

## 1 Introduction

Customer oriented services have become a strategic success factor of the IT industry. In the past, methods for Customer Service Management (CSM) helped to establish customer-oriented interfaces between internet service providers and customers, which enable a logical view and management of a customer's subscribed services. With the increasing interest of science and business in Grids, the integration of these methods within Grid infrastructures now become an important challenge.

A CSM interface offers the possibility to get current and appropriate information about the condition of services [1], e.g. a monitoring or an accounting service. This enables a customer to ask for internal processes and service states at the providers sites that are related to the provisioning of his subscribed resources and services (e.g. maintenance times).

In this paper, we discuss how methods of CSM can be adapted to a Grid environment in order to support customer needs and to inform and notify them about service states and relevant data. As a concrete example, we develop a concept based on CSM to visualize monitoring and accounting relevant data as a customer specific service for VOs in a Grid environment.

A. Clemm, L.Z. Granville, and R. Stadler (Eds.): DSOM 2007, LNCS 4785, pp. 216–228, 2007.

This paper is organized as follows: In section 2, we discuss related work and the state of the art of CSM in Grid environments. Moreover, in section 3, we introduce monitoring and accounting services as a use case. In section 4, a generic CSM scenario is applied to a Grid. We provide a description of CSM functionalities and indicate, where an adaptation or usage of Grid concepts and components can be applied. Finally in section 5, we address the implementation of a prototype that gathers monitoring and accounting information for specific Grid customers.

## 2   State of the Art

Currently, many companies and research institutions are developing and running CSM tools to manage their networks, among others the CSM system of the German Research Network (DFN) and the pan-european research and education backbone Geant2. In the area of Grid systems, where service and customer [2] orientation as well as QoS and SLA integration [3], [4], [5] are still challenging issues, CSM tools have not been applied yet. Many tools, e.g., MapCenter [6], Ganglia [7] or MonALISA [8] have been designed to cope with new Grid monitoring challenges, but most work is provider centric and does not take into account the requirements of customer-orientation.

CSM extends the provider's service management towards the customers and enables them to monitor and control up-to-date and meaningful information about service specific QoS parameters [9]. Additionally, it respects the management issues in the full life-cycle of the subscribed Grid services, e.g, inquiry, order, configuration, problem, quality, accounting and change management [10]. By using CSM it is easier for a customer to identify failures and to receive more accurate information about his subscribed services. If needed, this also enables a Grid customer to provide a better quality of service to his own customers and users.

After the shift from computational to service Grids and many approaches to the management of distributed Grid resources as well as accompanying managability services (like for instance the Open Grid Service Infrastructure OGSI [11] and the Common Resource Model CRM [12]), the adaptation of stateful web services as a platform within the Open Grid Service Architecture OGSA [13] has brought new methods for the operation and management of integrated, distributed and manageable Grid environments. Furthermore, specifications like the WS-Resource Framework (to handle resource states), WS-Notification (to handle events), WSLA [14] respectively WS-Agreement (to handle service level agreements) or WS-Security (to handle authorization issues) have been invented and many of them are already used in current Grid middleware.

This situation introduces new opportunities as well as difficulties to adapt CSM mechanisms in Web and Grid service environments. Grid and Web service architectures equally drive a new paradigm of horizontal, inter-organizational and distributed deployments and provide various, distributed service access points at the sites of multiple providers. While on the other side, multiple customer organizations choose their endpoints from multiple providers and access them from different locations.

Grids are heterogenous, highly dynamic and loosely coupled environments that make use of virtualization concepts and introduced the concept of virtual organizations (VOs), whose management was e.g. discussed in [15], [16].

VOs as understood in this work, are dynamic collections of individuals, institutions and resources [17], established to achieve common business objectives. Providing customer oriented data and services to VOs is a new aspect to CSM and results in the challenge for CSM to support multiple virtual organizations.

## 3   CSM in a Grid Monitoring and Accounting Scenario

In our scenario, different scientific communities, organized as VOs, wish to use the german Grid infrastructure D-Grid to solve their computational problems on shared resources for computation. For the usage and management of these resources, the VO's members need to access monitoring and accounting data.

Our research focuses on the problem how this data can be provided from a Grid infrastructure to different Grid users that belong to VOs.

This involves the following questions:

- Which data is to be shared for the monitoring and accounting of Grid resources and their usage ?
- How can the data be made available and accessible ?
- Which data from a shared resource belongs to a given user or VO ?
- How can provider-centric data be mapped to the customers ?
- How can data about the usage, quality of services and the states of accompanying resources be retrieved by a user ?
- How can the data for Grid users be visualized in a dedicated way ?

CSM as a concept is a useful approach to solve these questions, enabling the customer to retrieve and manage specific monitoring and accounting data.

Monitoring collects and provisions information about the usage, claim and affiliation of resources. Based on this information, accounting measures the accurate degrees of utilization (time, duration, host, user, provider, etc.) of the Grid resources and provides them to a billing component.

For Grid computing, monitoring and accounting of data is required with respect to different Grid users and their needs. A definition of a users roles, rights, subscribed services and accompanying resources is necessary. For example, [2] proposed different types of Grid users and a categorization as service end users, service providers and infrastructure system administrators. Methods to specify VOs as well as roles of their members and a specification of VO membership services can be found in [16]. For the scope of this paper, a VO membership service is assumed, which is able to provide data about the delegation of services and users to VOs. We use the CSM approach to customize the provisioned Grid services based on the information about the customers and their delegations.

As illustrated in figure 1 for the example of Grid monitoring, accounting and billing, Grid service customers need monitoring and accounting information to determine whether they are getting the service levels they are paying for. CSM should allow the monitoring and controlling of service level agreements (SLAs) negotiated between providers and customers, in order to increase the perceived value of the services to the users as well as to lower the operational costs of service management for the service provider. This offers benefits for a services provider and also for its customer while respecting Service Level Agreements (which contain all agreements about the delivery of the service) and Service Level Specification (SLSs) (which is its technical description) [18]. CSM should provide the necessary mechanisms to map the SLA and SLS settings onto the actual configuration of the service providers equipment.

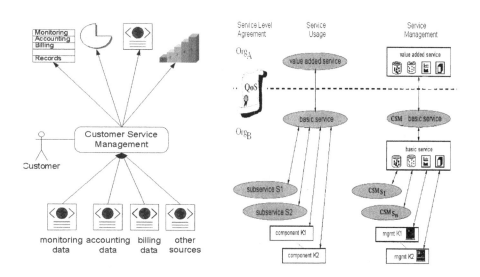

**Fig. 1.** CSM-based refinement of data

**Fig. 2.** A generic CSM scenario [1]

The provider does not have to provide all monitoring and accounting data to the end user who is not interested in the details of what is happening in underlying services (e.g. in the organization of the resource provider or the middleware). The user only needs information about the condition and the quality of the specific services he has subscribed to or which have been delegated to him.

Nevertheless, the customer and his users require information (and its visualization) in all phases of the lifecycle of the service provisioning:

- before service provisioning (e.g. procurement, signing a contract or a SLA)
- during service provisioning (e.g. control of the quality and states, failures, changes, maintenance times, statistics)
- after service provisioning (e.g. accounting, billing, optimization)

# 4   Architecture

In the following, we first report about a generic concept for CSM as specified in [1]. This concept points out different service types: At the provider side, there are basic services for the service management and their subservices as well as resources. The provider should also have a CSM basic service which provides logical views to the customer's side. At the customer side, there are value added services, representing the logical view produced by the CSM. While we discuss these service types in detail, we adapt every type to the specific situation in the Grid scenario. We further discuss aggregate levels in the distribution of metadata archives which provide - as subservices - the necessary data to the customer service management interface.

## 4.1   The CSM Approach

From a contractual point of view, as described in [1], customer and provider negotiate about QoS parameters which reflect the characteristics of the service. Based on these negotiations, a SLA is signed.

As shown in figure 2, CSM differentiates between the provider's and the customer's organization. This distinction enables the customer to find the best provider and service for the solution of a given problem.

For the provisioning of the service, the provider offers the service to his customer which can use the service itself or, in turn, can set up a value-added-service on top of it. For management purposes, the provider uses some kind of network and system management facilities (such as management platforms, trouble ticket systems and various other tools) that are necessary for the operation, administration, management and provisioning of the service. The customer will use similar facilities in his environment for the same aspects.

A Customer Service Management application is considered as a value added service in a customer's domain. It uses a basic CSM service at a CSM provider's domain. This service in turn uses services, sub-services and resources in its managed (service) network as shown in figure 2.

In a Grid environment, usually a Grid service provider ($Org_B$ in figure 2) puts Grid services on the disposal of different communities as customer organizations (shown as $Org_A$ in figure 2), which use them to run their applications. They are organized as VOs. Thus, in a Grid, $Org_A$ is a $VO_{1...n}$ (see figure 3). On the provider side, there may be a basic organization $Org_B$ ($RO_{Gridserviceprovider}$ in figure 3) or, in the recursive case, a $VO_{1...m}$.

Furthermore, the provider needs to gather data from subservices in his own organization as well as from external organizations. Thus, a provider's subservices can be provisioned by the provider itself, another provider in the role of an organization or a provider in the role of another VO.

## 4.2   Value Added Management Services

On the side of the customer's organization, a CSM application can act as a value added service, offering an interface to the users to manipulate and manage their basic services.

In our Grid scenario, this means that the customer needs to receive available data from existing basic Grid monitoring and accounting services. This data should be already tailored to the context of the VO he is associated with. It is desired within a user-friendly interface that the data will be processed and visualized in a form wished by the user and /or the customer.

As the advancements in sciences and engineering put higher demands on tools for a high-performance large-scale visual data exploration and analysis, the interface should be designed to assist the customer in the use of appropriate visualization methods for his data sets.

The customer can also provide the functionality and information to his own customers as a value added service if there is no conflict of agreements.

### 4.3   CSM Basic Service

To be able to realize the value added service in the customer's domain, a CSM Basic Service must be provided at the CSM provider's network endpoint. The purpose of this service is to provide logical views for specific customers on the content of the provisioned services.

In [1] the CSM Basic Service is divided into two coupled services: An 'operative CSM provider' and an 'administrative CSM provider'. On the one hand, the 'operative CSM provider' is responsible for the technical and operational aspects, particularly the retrieval of customized and service-specific information as well as the provisioning of usage and management functionalities of the subscribed services. In addition, this information can comprehensively reflect SLA and QoS parameters fixed in contracts.

On the other hand, the 'administrative provider' is responsible for the administration of access rights (authorization) and the identification of customers (authentication). It also provides the definition, which service functionalities have been leased and how CSM information must be presented [1]. It should also include information about the provider's policies and the SLAs with the customers.

In a Grid environment, the information about which resources and services have been leased should be available as a part of a VO membership service [16]. Using a coupling to such a service, a customized complex of services and subservices can be provisioned dynamically [19]. Such complex services are able to provide a dedicated functionality which is needed by a given VO. In a CSM basic service which is coupled to a VO management, authorization, policies and SLAs as well as the required views to present data are dependent on the VO they are executed in. The usage as well as the management side of the service, authorization and authentication (AA), policies and SLAs as well as the usage and management of the presentations need to be VO dependent (see also figure 3).

Authorization and authentication may be realized by the use of a VO membership service or identity provider. Also, VO-specific Attribute Release Policies (ARP) may be defined to restrict the retrieval of data and functionality. The proposed architecture embeds and extends access control.

But furthermore, it is necessary to realize functionalities like the handling of presentations and transformations, as well as policies and SLA issues dedicated to particular VOs. To describe how the data should be presented, VO-based transformation rules are available from a VO dependent presentation management, e.g. provided as dedicated XSLT transformations. They can be processed by the presentation mapper of the CSM Basic Service or delivered to a customer's application, being processed there (as in the case of AJAX - Asynchronous Java script And XML).

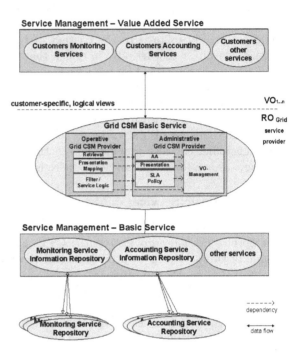

**Fig. 3.** The Grid CSM approach to data provisioning

The usage of the CSM Basic Service at the 'operative provider' is determined by the VO based management information from the 'administrative provider': the possibility to retrieve data by the AA module; the presentation mapping by the presentation module and the set of data filtered and chosen by a service logic by the SLA, policy and VO management modules.

### 4.4   Basic Services for Service Management

'The basic services for Service Management represent arbitrary services in the IT environment [...] on the providers side' [1]. In fact, these services realize the functionalities which are provisioned to the customer. They can also offer management functionality for other services on the provider side. In a CSM scenario, these services are subservices of the CSM basic service, which acts as the interface to the customer.

In Grids, these services are often implemented on the basis of a service oriented architecture (SOA). It must be pointed out, that in a SOA based on web services also mechanisms such as WS-Security, WSLA [14] respectively WS-Agreement (for SLAs) and WS-Notification (for Events) are available, which can be used to implement the functionalities of a CSM basic service. Nevertheless, to collect information from the provider side, a customer should not be enforced to develop own applications to access accounting and monitoring information and a user interface is needed.

In section 3, a basic service (or several distributed) for monitoring and accounting was considered. This service incorporates at least one database as a management information repository in which the information is collected. These services may be arbitrarily complex and consist of several subservices, e.g. local monitoring and accounting services and the accompanying sensors on the resources. They provide domain-specific metadata, e.g. in the form of XML files. For every organizational domain in a Grid environment (a traditional resource provider or a VO), an information repository contains raw data for monitoring and accounting. This data is collected from multiple subservices and resources.

### 4.5 Subservices and Resources

The measured information is published through middleware using specific interfaces which depend on the used Grid service.

Basically, the monitoring and accounting subservices act as information repositories (or directories for mediation), recursively gathering their information from other repositories or - at the end of the chain - sensor services which implement the metering functionality.

For resources to be shared, sensors and repositories must be able to exchange basic monitoring, accounting as well as usage data in a common [20] and machine-readable format [21]. For accounting, so called 'Usage Records' have been defined by the Open Grid Forum as a format for the exchange, as well as for the structured storage and utilization of accounting data in the Grid. They contain information about the use of resources and are based on a XML format. For monitoring, standardized information models like the OGF GLUE schema, CIM dialects or the Resource Description Framework RDF may be used.

### 4.6 Aggregate Elements

It is not only necessary that subservices and resources of the monitoring and accounting infrastructure are structured in an intelligent way so that they are able to hierarchically aggregate the correct information sources. The structure of the aggregated information retrieved from the subservices is also of importance. Thus, aggregate elements can be defined in the data, as done e.g. for accounting records in [22], where extended elements are introduced for the use across Grids and with heterogeneous extensibility. Such aggregate elements encapsulate a single aggregate accounting record. Elements of this kind also exist for monitoring services, bundling the information of multiple services in service groups (e.g., by using WS-ServiceGroups) or as database entries which contain aggregate data.

### 4.7 Summary of the Grid CSM Approach

Figure 3 summarizes the adapted CSM architecture as applied to the Grid monitoring and accounting scenario. Most importantly, in a Grid, the customer organization $Org_A$ may be a $VO_{1...n}$. A provider organization $RO$ inhabits the role of $Org_B$ from the CSM scenario model. As pointed out in section 4.1), depending on the case, this provider organization $RO$ may also be a $VO_{1...m}$, e.g. when a Customer Service Management between VOs is to be realized.

Between the layers of customer and provider, there is a mapping that is understood in terms of usage and management of the CSM basic service. It may be realized e.g. by providing protocols for the management of the presentation and transformation rules, the service level specifications, the policy rules, the identity providers and the VO management service.

Furthermore, a mapping between the Monitoring Service Information Repository as a Basic Service at the provider's site and the Monitoring Service Repositories as subservices can be perceived. It must be emphasized, that these repositories are provisioned by subservice providers, which are located in the local organization of the provider but also by subservice providers from remote ROs and VOs. The model may also be applied in a recursive way, gathering the data from another CSM Basic Service in a subproviders domain. This kind of stackability enables the sharing of data or functionality across different provider organizations which build different tools with CSM functionality.

## 5    Implementation

In the following, we report, how the introduced Grid components have been implemented to realize a CSM prototype with a monitoring and accounting functionality for the German D-Grid initiative, which is building a shared Grid infrastructure for many different scientific communities.

To satisfy a maximum of requirements in the D-Grid (see [23] and [24]) while assuring a homogeneous management of basic services and underlying heterogenous resources from different resource providers, a SOA based on Globus Toolkit 4 was selected.

As the prototype was built from bottom up with a top down architecture in mind, the following sections begin with the description of the components used on resources, continue with the description of subservices, the basic services at the provider's side, the basic CSM service, and conclude with a CSM application providing the value added services.

### 5.1    Basic Services, Subservices and Resources

As a central underlying information system, the Monitoring and Discovery System MDS4 which is part of the Globus Toolkit 4, has been selected and installed in a testbed. In MDS4, sites and VOs may maintain one or more repositories to record available containers, resources, and services [25]. A distributed repository (implemented as a network of MDS4 DefaultIndexServices) was built, which gathers monitoring data from the resource providers in the Grid. For this purpose, a structure of repositories has been suggested, that introduces a central repository at every resource provider's site as well as a repository for every VO in the Grid, hosted on a machine that belongs to the VO. The data from the repositories at the different resource providers are brought together in the VO repositories by means of pushing with regular intervals.

To measure status information about computing resources, standard MDS4 information providers have been used, placed on the local scheduling systems (e.g. Torque or SGE) at the Grid sites. To give the resource providers the opportunity to describe their sites, provide contact information, send maintenance messages and to advertise their geographical location into topological maps, an additional sensor has been created.

For accounting, a prototype was created based on components of SGAS (Swegrid Accounting System) [26]. The prototype collects information about scheduled jobs and stores it in Resource Usage Records in the central database of a SGAS server [27].

## 5.2 CSM Basic Service

A tailored WebMDS system was installed to provide the presentation mapping functionality of a CSM basic service. WebMDS is an application for the Tomcat application server and provides logical views on the sites and computing resources on the raw data from the Grid by applying XSL-transformations, defined in the presentation management part of the architecture.

The setup is able to produce views on static VOs as they are specified by the trees connecting the metadata archives of the resource providers and their VO specific roots. At present time, all customers can select views on all existing VO specific information repositories.

The system is able to view the states of the computing resources and services of the VOs DGI, AstroGrid, MediGrid, C3-Grid, HEP, InGrid, TextGrid and Test at a website. The customer can select the VO he wishes to monitor on top of the webpage. To the left of the page, a presentation view on the selected VO's data can be chosen. Different XSLT transformations that generate HTML have been provided for this purpose, e.g. views on computing elements, clusters and workernodes, a drill-down view, a detailed service list, a XML-View, and a dynamic map of the geographic location of Grid sites as well as their maintenance status. For accounting, a view has been implemented, which is able to exhibit the most important data from accounting Usage Records such as CPU time, user host, provider host, start job time and end job time. For accounting, a view has been implemented, which is able to exhibit the most important data from accounting Usage Records such as CPU time, user host, provider host, start job time and end job time.

## 5.3 CSM Application

A usual web browser located in the domain of the customer can be used as a CSM application. HTML-GET Parameters are exchanged with the CSM basic service, defining the name of the repository and the kind of logical view the customer wants to see. This enables the customers to use web links given to them by the provider or to implement their own personal web sites or applications which retrieve the dynamic information from the CSM by using standard HTML queries. It is possible to receive XML documents in the style of a Representational State Transfer (REST), containing full or refined sets of resource metadata of a specific VO. The setup, including the XSLT-Transformations, can act as a basis for further integration of user interfaces in Grid Portals or as a basis for other applications, services or monitoring and accounting systems.

A quantitative experimental evaluation on the dynamic system performance characteristics of the MDS4 components central to the prototype has been presented by its developers in [25].

## 6 Conclusions

An architecture for the realization of Customer Service Management in a monitoring and accounting scenario was outlined. It is based on a CSM Basic service, a VO management service as well as additional modules for SLA, AA, presentation and policy management.

We presented an application of methods from CSM to the management and monitoring of Grid services to enable the refinement of granular customer and VO oriented views. A VO specific monitoring and accounting system for the productive Grid infrastructure relating to the D-Grid Integration Project was implemented. It was shown that the traditional models for CSM in principle still hold in Grid environments, but should be extended by a coupling of Grid services to VO management to support faster organizational dynamics as well as shorter lifecycles of customer organizations.

The concept can be applied to a broad scope of Grid services such as distributed metadata repositories or other areas which need a customer specific provisioning as e.g. parallel and distributed simulation services.

Further work is going to implement a CSM basic service that uses a dynamic VO membership service. It is also intended to integrate the repositories of additional VOs as well as necessary transformations to handle the corresponding VO specific data.

**Acknowledgements.** Parts of this work have been funded by the German Federal Ministry of Education and Research under contract 01 AK 800 B and by the EC IST-EMANICS Network of Excellence #26854.

The authors wish to thank the members of the Munich Network Management (MNM) Team for helpful discussions and valuable comments on previous versions of this paper. The MNM Team founded by Prof. Dr. Heinz-Gerd Hegering is a group of researchers of the University of Munich, the Munich University of Technology, the University of Federal Armed Forces Munich and the Leibniz Supercomputing Centre of the Bavarian Academy of Sciences. Its web-server is located at http://www.mnm-team.org.

## References

1. Langer, M.: Konzeption und Anwendung einer Customer Service Management Architektur (engl. Conception and Application of a Customer Service Management). PhD thesis, Technische Universität München (2001)
2. Norman, M.: Types of grid users and the Customer-Service Provider relationship: a future picture of grid use. In: Proceedings of the 2006 UK e-Science All Hands Meeting (2006)

3. Sahai, A., Graupner, S., Machiraju, V., van Moorsel, A.: Specifying and Monitoring Guarantees in Commercial Grids through SLA. In: Proceedings of the 3rd IEEE International Symposium on Cluster Computing and the Grid, IEEE Computer Society Press, Los Alamitos (2003)

4. Chen, H., Jin, H., Mao, F., Wu, H.: Q-GSM: A QoS Oriented Grid Service Management Framework. In: Zhang, Y., Tanaka, K., Yu, J.X., Wang, S., Li, M. (eds.) APWeb 2005. LNCS, vol. 3399, Springer, Heidelberg (2005)

5. Magana, E., Serrat, J.: QoS Aware Policy-Based Management Architecture for Service Grids. In: Proceedings of the 14th IEEE International Workshops on Enabling Technologies, IEEE Computer Society Press, Los Alamitos (2005)

6. Bonnassieux, F., Harakaly, R., Primet, P.: The MapCenter Approach. In: Fernández Rivera, F., Bubak, M., Gómez Tato, A., Doallo, R. (eds.) Grid Computing. LNCS, vol. 2970, Springer, Heidelberg (2004)

7. Brent, N.C., Matthew, L.M., David, E.C.: The Ganglia Distributed Monitoring System: Design, Implementation,and Experience. In: Parallel Computing, vol. 30(7) (2004)

8. Legrand, I.C., Newman, H.B., Voicu, R., Cirstoiu, C., Grigoras, C., Toarta, M., Dobre, C.: MonALISA: An Agent Based, Dynamic Service System to Monitor, Control and Optimize Distributed Systems. In: CHEP 2004 (2004)

9. Langer, M., Loidl, S., Nerb, M.: Customer Service Management: Towards a Management Information Base for an IP Connectivity Service. In: Proceedings of the 4th IEEE Symposium on Computers and Communications, IEEE Computer Society Press, Los Alamitos (1999)

10. Nerb, M.: Customer Service Management als Basis für interorganisationales Dienstmanagement (engl. Customer Service Management as Basis for Interorganizational Service Management). PhD thesis, Technische Universität München (2001)

11. Tuecke, S., Czajkowski, K., Foster, I., Frey, J., Graham, S., Kesselman, C., Maquire, T., Sandholm, T., Snelling, D., Vanderbilt, P.: Open Grid Services Infrastructure (OGSI) Version 1.0. Technical report, Global Grid Forum (2003)

12. Stokes, E., Butler, N.: Common Resource Model (CRM). Technical report, Global Grid Forum (2003)

13. Foster, I., Kishimoto, H., Savva, A., Berry, D., Grimshaw, A., Horn, B., Maciel, F., Siebenlist, F., Subramaniam, R., Treadwell, J., Von Reich, J.: The Open Grid Services Architecture, Version 1.5. Technical report, Global Grid Forum (2006)

14. Keller, A., Ludwig, H.: Defining and Monitoring Service Level Agreements for dynamic e-Business. In: LISA 2002. Proceedings of the 16th USENIX System Administration Conference (2002)

15. Dreo Rodosek, G., Hegering, H.G., Stiller, B.: Dynamic Virtual Organizations as Enablers for Managed Invisible Grids. In: Proceedings of the 2006 IEEE/IFIP Network Operations and Management Symposium (NOMS), Vancouver, Canada (2006)

16. Schiffers, M.: Management dynamischer Virtueller Organisationen in Grids (engl.: Management of Dynamic Virtual Organizations in Grids). PhD thesis, Ludwig-Maximilians-Universität München (2007)

17. Foster, I., Kesselman, C., Tuecke, S.: The anatomy of the grid: Enabling scalable virtual organizations, vol. 15 (2001)

18. Betgé-Brezetz, S., Martinot, O., Delégue, G., Marilly, E.: Pro-Active SLA Assurance for Next Generation Network. In: WTC 2002. World Telecommunication Congress, Paris, France (2002)

19. Baur, T., Bel Haj Saad, S.: Virtualizing Resources: Customer Oriented Cross-Domain Monitoring for Service Grids. In: Proceedings of the 10th IFIP/IEEE Symposium on Integrated Management, IEEE Computer Society Press, Los Alamitos (2007)

20. Koo, M.y.: Accounting Interchange Natural Language Description (Requirements). Technical report, Global Grid Forum (2002)

21. Rodosek, G., Göhner, M., Golling, M., Kretzschmar, M.: Towards an Accounting System for Multi-Provider Grid Environments. In: IM 2007. Proceedings of the 10th IFIP/IEEE International Symposium on Integrated Management, IEEE Computer Society Press, Los Alamitos (2007)

22. Chen, X., Khan, A., Kant, D.: Aggregate Accounting Record Recommendation. Technical report, Global Grid Forum (2006)

23. gentschen Felde, N., Baur, T., Garschhammer, M., Reiser, H.: Anforderungen an das Monitoring, Ergebnisse aus den Erhebung bei den Communities und Ressourcenanbietern im D-Grid (engl.: Requirements for monitoring, results of a study of communities and resource providers). In: Rückemann, C.-P. (ed.): Ergebnisse der Studie und Anforderungsanalyse in den Fachgebieten Monitoring, Accounting, Billing bei den Communities und Ressourcenanbietern im D-Grid, Fachgebiete Monitoring, Accounting und Billing im D-Grid-Integrationsprojekt, pp. 45–63 (2006)

24. Rückemann, C.P., Göhner, M.: Anforderungen an das Accounting (engl.: Requirements for accounting). Technical report, D-Grid (2006)

25. Schopf, J., Raicu, I., Perlman, L., Miller, N., Kesselman, C., Foster, I., D'Arcy, M.: Monitoring and Discovery in a Web Services Framework: Functionality and Performance of Globus Toolkit MDS4. In: Proceedings of the 15th IEEE International Symposium on High Performance Distributed Computing, IEEE Computer Society Press, Los Alamitos (2006)

26. Elmroth, E., Gardfjell, P., Mulmo, O., Sandholm, T.: An OGSA-Based Bank Service for Grid Accounting Systems. In: Applied Parallel Computing. State-of-the-art in Scientific Computing, Springer, Heidelberg (2004)

27. Baur, T., Bel Haj Saad, S., Göhner, M.: Customer Service Management für Grid Monitoring und Accounting (engl.: Customer Service Management for Grid monitoring and accounting). Technical report, D-Grid (2007)

# LINUBIA: A Linux-Supported User-Based IP Accounting

Cristian Morariu, Manuel Feier, and Burkhard Stiller

Department of Informatics IFI, University of Zurich, Switzerland
{morariu,stiller}@ifi.uzh.ch, manuel@feier.ch

**Abstract.** Obtaining information about the usage of network ressources by individual users forms the basis for establishing network billing systems or network management operations. While there are already widely used accounting techniques available for measuring IP network traffic on a per-host basis, there is no adequate solution for accounting per-user network activities on a multiuser operating system. This work provides a survey on existing approaches to this problem and identifies requirements for a user-based IP accounting module. It develops a suitable software architecture LINUBIA and proposes a prototypical implementation for the Linux 2.6 operating system, which is capable of providing per-user accounting for both the IPv4 and the IPv6 protocol.

## 1 Introduction and Problem Statement

The Internet is rapidly growing and fundamentally influencing economic, cultural, and social developments worldwide. While more and more people take advantage of this global network and new services are being deployed every day, more network resources are consumed. This creates the need for effective accounting mechanisms that are closely coupled to authentication mechanisms, *e.g.,* in support of network management tasks, charging requirements, or intrusion detection systems for systems and users. Often it becomes necessary to know what amount and which type of network traffic a specific network user is generating.

Today, as networking is moving towards an all-IP network [9] an accounting system integrated into the IP layer seems the most straight forward solution. This approach allows for the same accounting mechanisms to be used regardless of the application and the transport protocol carried over IP, or the data link layer and physical connection the IP runs on top of.

Although the accounting of IP network traffic has received wide attention since the beginning of the Internet [18], existing systems have a major drawback by looking strictly to the IP packet captured on the wire. Such an approach allows for the mapping of each IP packet to an end-system, which sends or receives the packet, but it is unable to specify, which user was responsible for generating the traffic. Multiuser operating systems often use a single IP address, which is shared among different individual users. Since multiple users may be connected remotely at the same time to the same machine and may have different applications that generate IP traffic being transported over the

A. Clemm, L.Z. Granville, and R. Stadler (Eds.): DSOM 2007, LNCS 4785, pp. 229–241, 2007.

network, it is impossible to identify how much traffic each of theses users generated by just looking into the IP traffic at the router level.

Therefore, this paper proposes the user-based IP accounting architecture named LIN-UBIA, which uses a Linux kernel extension and a library for accessing this extension, for mapping each IP packet sent or received to the responsible user. This solution allows for splitting network costs in case of usage-based charging or may allow detection of the user or process that was responsible for illegal IP traffic.

Fig. 1 depicts a typical scenario for using the new user-based IP accounting infrastructure. In an enterprise network users are typically authenticated by using a centralized authentication server such as LDAP (Light-weight Directory Access Protocol) [15] or Kerberos [12] and they may access the network from any terminal or working station that is configured to use the central authentication server. Upon authentication the device to which the user logged on to starts to meter the network usage and sends periodic accounting records to the accounting server. Since the network usage is mapped to user identifiers (ID) and a user uses the same ID with any device he is allowed to connect to, the accounting server may aggregate the network usage from different devices within the network and present users with detailed and aggregated information about network traffic they created.

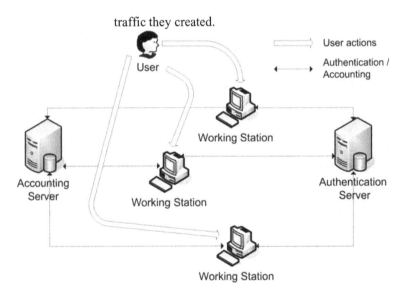

**Fig. 1.** Enterprise Scenario

The remainder of the paper is structured as follows. Section 2 presents a brief overview on related work in the field of IP accounting followed by Section 3, which outlines the design of the new approach. Section 4 gives major implementation details. While Section 5 discusses evaluation results, finally, Section 6 draws conclusions and provides ideas about future work.

## 2   Related Work

Some of the first guidelines for measuring internet traffic have been proposed in [18]. The IETF defined a generic AAA architecture (Authentication, Authorization, and Accounting) [10] that formed the basis for RADIUS [14] and Diameter [2] protocols. The AAA architecture and its related protocols do not define how measurements need to be done, but specify how to transport and collect the data measured. SNMP (Simple Network Management Protocol) [3] allows network administrators to monitor and manage network traffic performance. Each network device in a SNMP managed network has a management agent that resides on that device. The management agent collects information from different counters and configuration parameters of the managed device and makes them available to a Network Monitoring Station (NMS) via the SNMP protocol. The information collected via SNMP is typically highly aggregated (e.g., summary of data transferred on an interface or average data rate during the last n seconds). RTFM (Real-time Flow Monitoring) [1] and RMON (Remote Monitoring) [19] also use SNMP for transporting measured data. None of these solution offers any support for user-based IP accounting.

Commercial accounting systems, such as NetFlow [6], NARUS [11], or Juniper's J-Flow Accounting [8], lack the support for accounting on a per-user basis. The authors of [4] propose a method for accounting TCP connections on a per-user basis. Their solution is based on introducing an additional step in the TCP connection set-up phase for checking the authenticity of the user. If a TCP session is started all the traffic is reported to the user, who started the session. [20] proposes to use multiple IP addresses on a multi-user devices and use a distinct IP address for every user. This would allow traditional IP traffic accounting systems to be used for user-based IP accounting. NIPON [13] and [21] introduce an agent-based solution, where an agent is set up on a host with multiple users; this agent is designed to collect required traffic information directly on that host, but without having to change the operating system (kernel), so that it can also be used with closed source systems, like Solaris or Windows. The solution is based on capturing all traffic on the network interface to identify local traffic and to correlate it to local users. The drawback of this solution is the need to monitor all traffic on the link in case of shared links such as Fast Ethernet.

The UTAdragon project (Useful Traffic Accounting Dragon) [17] retrieves network data by collecting network and process information using the /proc/net interface. Data about open network connections and processes that use them are collected and recombined to create a table showing, which system user has consumed how much network traffic. The accounting data is stored in a MySQL Database, allowing further processing or aggregation. UserIPAcct (User IP Accounting) [16] is an extension to the Linux kernel originally developed in 1994. The development has stopped in 2000 and the latest beta version available addresses kernel 2.2. This system extends the Linux kernel in a way that it becomes able to attribute IP traffic to local system users. This code is not compatible with modern Linux kernels (*e.g.*, 2.6) and also does not support IPv6.

Comparing to existing work, LINUBIA proposes a user-based IP accounting system embedded into the latest generation of the Linux kernel (v2.6) and capable of performing accounting for IPv4 as well as IPv6 traffic. Moreover, LINUBIA reports measured traffic separated on different transport protocols. An important difference to previous approaches is having not only a Linux kernel extension for user-based IP accounting, but a solution that can easily integrate into existing authentication and accounting systems by using standard protocols such as LDAP and Diameter. Havingthe accounting module embedded into the Linux kernel enables, besides traffic accounting, later extensions to perform IP traffic access control based on users or applications which generated the traffic. The solution proposed here follows an architecture close to the one proposed in [16].

## 3   Design

Based on the following use cases a summary of the main requirements for the new user-based IP accounting architecture, termed LINUBIA is derived. Based on these requirements that have been identified the design of the proposed solution is detailed.

### 3.1   Motivating Use Cases

*Network Traffic Billing System*
The first scenario deals with the case of a grid infrastructure spanning across a larger area on top of which customers may run their own grid applications. A grid user will typically install its applications on multiple nodes and these run typically with the user's privileges. The grid operator may use the user-based accounting module in order to split network costs (traffic created by grid applications is typically high) among all customers based on the amount of traffic they created.

*Individual Load Monitoring and Abuse Detection*
The second scenario addresses the case of an institution, for example a university, which offers its students the possibility to use the Web for research and communication purposes, but does not want them to excessively waste precious network bandwidth for sharing videos, filesharing, and the like. The system setup is done in a way that a student can log into one of many computers at the university with his personal credentials. The user account information is stored in a centralized LDAP directory, so a specific student has uses the same user ID (UID) in every system he logs into. A script can regularly copy usage information to a database server, where it is stored and accumulated with the traffic footprint of other users in order to detect possible anomalies in the traffic under investigation. The system administrator has the possibility to monitor network usage of students, independent of applications or the computer they use. With the help of this information he can detect and quantify abuses, suspend accounts of the respective users, or initiate further investigations.

*Service Load Measuring*
The third scenario handles the identification of applications, which generate abnormal traffic. For example, on a Linux server different services may be operational, some of them may not be using well-known ports (*e.g.,* a bit-torrent client, which constantly changes ports it is running on). On that router connecting this server to the Internet, the administrator can monitor how much traffic this server created, but he can only

identify applications based on port numbers. In case of applications that change these ports the use a user-based IP accounting module eases traffic monitoring for these type of applications.

## 3.2 Requirements

Based on these use cases above as well as a general observation of achieving a practical and implementable solution the following four key requirements for IP accounting LINUBIA have been identified:

- The IP accounting module shall account for IPv4 and IPv6 traffic information on a per-user bases operating the Linux operating system.
- The IP accounting module shall allow for application-based traffic accounting.
- An API interface shall be available for configuring the IP accounting module and retrieving accounted for data.
- The performance impact of the IP accounting module on the networking subsystem should be kept minimal.

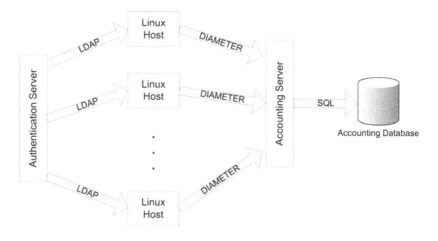

**Fig. 2.** Network Architecture

## 3.3 LINUBIA Architecture

The architecture of an enterprise network having LINUBIA running on the Linux end-hosts, consists of both a network architecture (cf. Fig. 2) that defines the network components required for LINUBIA and a end-host architecture (cf. Fig. 3) that defines the software components required within an end-system to support LINUBIA.

Two types of devices may be identified: regular Linux hosts, which may be used by users and the accounting domain infrastructure (consisting of an authentication server, a data aggregation server, and a storage server). Linux nodes use an authentication server for verifying user credentials. Whenever a user logs in to a Linux host all the processes started by the user will run with the global UID of the user. Each Linux host has LINUBIA enabled. Accounted for data is encapsulated in accounting records and it is transported from each Linux host to an accounting server using the Diameter protocol. The accounting server further stores the accounting records in a central database. For supporting this an accounting client runs on each host, collects the data accounted by LINUBIA and sends it to an accounting server using the Diameter protocol.

### 3.3.1    End-Host Accounting Architecture

This section shall describe in detail the different components and their interactions required within an end-host in order to support user-based IP accounting. Regular operating systems do not offer a function to autonomously measure user-specific IP traffic. Therefore, a host needs to be modified in order to be able to perform such a task. Fig. 3 shows how this can be achieved by modifying the Linux operating system kernel, which resides between the networking hardware and applications in the user space. The kernel allows network applications to access the TCP/IP stack via the network socket interface; it contains routines to send outgoing IP packets to the network and deliver incoming packets to the destination applications. These routines and the kernel have to be extended in order to measure, store and export the desired accounting information associated with each accounting-relevant IP network operation. This is done by a kernel accounting extension that consists of a number of components which are added to the kernel.

The *information storage* component is responsible for the temporary storage of accounting information collected. Each incoming or outgoing packet triggers a lookup

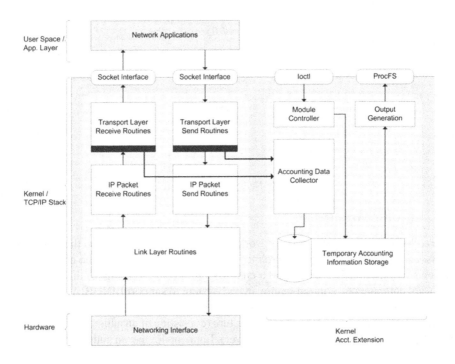

**Fig. 3.** End-Host Architecture

in this component for finding the record entry for the username responsible with the transfer thus the efficiency of the *information storage* component highly impacts the overall performance of the accounting module. The *data collector* component retrieves the necessary information from the IP networking subsystem and puts it in the storage component. The *output generation* component reformats the internal data before exporting it to user space via the proc filesystem (`procfs`). The *module controller* provides facilities to manage records stored, for example to reset all records of a specific user. It uses the `ioctl` interface.

This architecture is designed to extract and export user-specific IP accounting information from the kernel to user space for further processing. The data is stored temporarily in the main memory by the kernel module. Data aggregation and persistent storage are done outside the kernel. in order to keep low the load on the kernel.

### 3.3.2  Integrated View

Fig. 4 shows the integration of the host specific architecture into the network architecture. In addition to the kernel-based accounting architecture sketched in 3.3.1 two additional components are required for building accounting applications on top of LIN-BUIA. The first component is an accounting library that provides the API for querying and configuring the accounting module. It enables applications to access the kernel interfaces of the accounting extension.

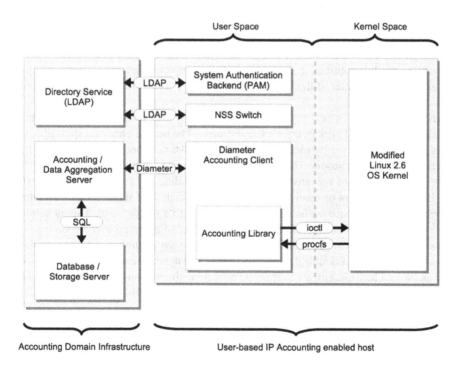

**Fig. 4.** Integrated View

The second component is a Diameter accounting client that uses this library to fetch the user-based IP accounting records from the kernel and sends them to a remote data aggregation server using the Diameter protocol. The aggregation server can evaluate and store the accounting data persistently, for example by using a separate database server.

A flexible system authentication back-end and Name Service Switch (NSS) configuration allows that a unique user account of a centralized user database (on a remote directory) can be used on any user host; the suggested interface being used for this is LDAP. The intention is that multiple hosts use the same user database and therefore the same UIDs for individual users, making users and associated accounting records uniquely identifiable across distinct hosts.

# 4   Implementation

The implementation of the host-based extension is based on the code layout of the useripacct project [16] and is entirely written in the C programming language [5]. Compared to the other investigated approaches, LINUBIA supports 64 bit counters, provides realtime traffic statistics and allows parallel accounting of IPv4 as well as IPv6. The accounting system was implemented for modern 2.6 series Linux kernels and supports both IPv4 and IPv6.

The information triplet to be extracted from each IP network operation consists of the IP packet size, the packet owner (user), and the network and transport protocols involved with the operation. Unfortunately, the required routines and protocol headers are distinct for IPv4 and IPv6, and for incoming traffic, the information cannot be retrieved at the IP layer, like it is the case for outgoing traffic. This required the embedding of the accounting module routines in the transport layer implementation. A shortcoming of this approach is a scatter of the LINUBIA code across several files in the Linux kernel network subsystem.

The *data collector* can extract the size of a packet from IP packet headers; the sum of the transferred IP packet sizes equals the IP traffic. The network and transport protocol types can be determined by identifying the kind of the network routine or by also inspecting the IP packet header. The user information can be determined by looking up the ownership properties of the network socket corresponding to a packet. As it is possible that IP packets are sent or received that have no associated local network socket, there are rare situations where traffic cannot be attributed to a regular user. This is handled by directing such accounting information to the record of a special user "nobody".

The *information* storage component is implemented as a number of records that are connected in groups of doubly-linked lists within a hash table. Each record contains the UID as the primary identification attribute as well as the measured IP traffic values for different network and transport protocols. Users are dynamically added when they start using IP-based networking.

Upon request, the *output generation* component loops through these lists to create a table with all users and their traffic records which is exported to the `proc` file system. The user space library reads a special item in the `proc` filesystem that is exported by the kernel extension and contains the temporary accounting information. The library recreates the record structures so that they can be easily accessed by other applications,

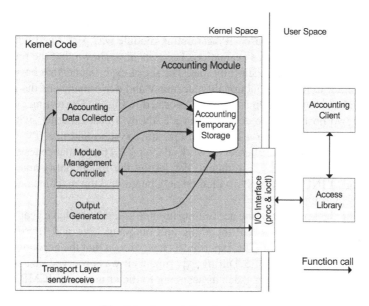

**Fig. 5.** Implementation Architecture

such as the accounting client. It also provides functions to send commands to the *module controller*, using the `ioctl` interface. The accounting client sends locally detected accounting records to the accounting server using the Diameter protocol. Within Diameter, records are structured as sets of (predefined) Attribute- Value Pairs (AVP). The sample accounting client and sample server communicate in regular intervals by using accounting sessions, where an accounting session contains current records for one user, as delivered by the accounting library. Besides the accounting Attribute-Value-Pairs (AVPs) proposed in [2], a set of parameters have been defined as shown in Tab. 1.

A patch containing the user-based IP accounting module for the 2.6.17 version of the Linux kernel may be found at *http://www.csg.uzh.ch/staff/morariu/linubia*.

**Table 1.** New AVPs for Linux User-Based IP Accounting

| AVP Name | AVP Code | AVP Name | AVP Code |
|---|---|---|---|
| Linux-Input-IPV4-Octets | 5001 | Linux-Input-IPV4-TCP-Octets | 5101 |
| Linux-Output-IPV4-Octets | 5002 | Linux-Output-IPV4-TCP-Octets | 5102 |
| Linux-Input-IPV6-Octets | 5003 | Linux-Input-IPV4-UDP-Octets | 5103 |
| Linux-Output-IPV6-Octets | 5004 | Linux-Output-IPV4-UDP-Octets | 5104 |
| Linux-Input-TCP-Octets | 5005 | Linux-Input-IPV6-TCP-Octets | 5105 |
| Linux-Output-TCP-Octets | 5006 | Linux-Output-IPV6-TCP-Octets | 5106 |
| Linux-Input-UDP-Octets | 5007 | Linux-Input-IPV6-UDP-Octets | 5107 |
| Linux-Output-UDP-Octets | 5008 | Linux-Output-IPV6-UDP-Octets | 5108 |

## 5   Evaluation

The evaluation of the user-based IP accounting module was performed both in terms of functional and performance evaluation. The tests have shown that the requirements described in Sect. 3.2 have been fully met. The set of experiments that have been per-formed in order to test the functionality, accuracy and performance of the accounting module used a network set-up as the one described in Fig. 6. The testing environment consists of two hosts that are connected in a LAN by a Fast Ethernet switch as seen in the figure. Both hosts run a Linux 2.6 operating system and use IPv4 as well as IPv6. Both hosts have Fast Ethernet network adapters. All performance tests have been per-formed in a laboratory environment. For testing the functionality and robustness of the module LINUBAIA was installed on an Ubuntu desktop machine and used in a production environment.

For testing the accuracy of the accounting module several tests have been performed in which TCP, UDP, and ICMP incoming and outgoing IPv4 and IPv6 traffic was generated and accounted for. The experiments have shown that the accounting module correctly accounts for IP traffic. During experiments it was observed that some traffic cannot be mapped to any user (such as scanning traffic or incoming ICMP messages). Such traffic is accounted for the system user by the accounting module. Another obser-vation concerns ICMP traffic that appears to be exclusively mapped to the system user and not to the user who actually sent the message. The reason for this is that raw socket operations are considered critical and only possible for user root, also for security rea-sons (a regular user can only execute the ping program because it has the SUID-bit set, thus being executed under root context).

Tab. 2 shows the results of a first test consisting of a 256 MB file transfer over a Fast Ethernet link with and without LINUBIA using IPv4 and IPv6. The purpose of this test was to identify the impact of accounting on the performance of the Linux network subsystem. As the table shows there is only a small impact (0.83 for IPv4 and 0.41 for IPv6) on performance observed when running with LINUBIA enabled.

In Tab. 3 observed and estimated maximum throughput on a Linux box with and without LINUBIA are shown. For estimating the maximum throughput the Iperf [7] tool was used. The test with Iperf affirms that the measuring results are correct. Although

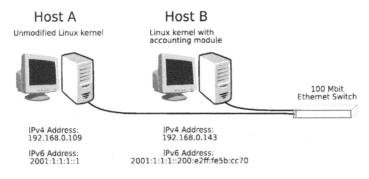

**Fig. 6.** Testing environment

**Table 2.** Average time for a 256 MB file transfer over a Fast Ethernet connection with and without the user-based IP accounting enabled (average numbers of 20 runs)

|  | Unmodified IPv4 | Accounting IPv4 | Unmodified IPv6 | Accounting IPv6 |
|---|---|---|---|---|
| Average time | 21.815 s | 21.998 s | 22.102 s | 22.193 s |
| Std. deviation | 0.062 s | 0.208 s | 0.010 s | 0.204 s |

**Table 3.** Average maximum throughput observed and calculated by Iperf over an Fast Ethernec connection, with and without the user-based IP accounting module enabled.

|  | Unmod. IPv4 | Acct. IPv4 | Rel. diff. (%) | Unmod. IPv6 | Acct IPv6 | Rel. diff. (%) |
|---|---|---|---|---|---|---|
| Manual (Mbps) | 93.880 | 93.099 | 0.839 | 92.661 | 92.281 | 0.412 |
| Iperf (Mbps) | 94.080 | 91.700 | 2.595 | 92.880 | 92.870 | 0.012 |

the values are not totally equal, the dimensions are the same and the performance loss is marginal.

During the evaluation phase of LINUBIA the architecture and its implementation have been tested to check the functionality they provide and the performance impact on the Linux kernel network subsystem. These tests have shown that LINUBIA delivers the required accounting results, especially a per-user network activities result on a multi-user operating system, while having a small impact on the performance of the endsystem under investigation.

# 6   Conclusions and Future Work

This paper demonstrates by a design and prototypical implementation that a userbased IP accounting approach is technically possible on modern Linux (2.6 series) operating systems. Additionally, it can be used also in the same version with the upcoming IPv6 network protocol and it can be integrated into an existing accounting infrastructure, such as Diameter. On one hand, users are not supposed to have only one computer device of their own (not to mention sharing one device with other users), but rather to have several devices for different purposes. On the other hand, the more computers become commodities for daily life and will be used by different people (producing networking-related and other costs), the more important it becomes to establish accounting systems, which offer a clear and secure user identification on the end-device and will probably have an integrated character. The current implementation shows a clear proof of concept. Compared to traditional device-based accounting mechanisms, a user-based approach allows the mapping of network services usage not only to a device, but more specific, to the user which consumed those services.

Improvements are possible, *e.g.*, with the storage component, which can be done with a smaller memory footprint and also more efficiently by utilizing advanced data structures that will help to optimize access times. Another interesting issue determines the linkage of the networking subsystem to the socket interface, which also implies a link to the process management of the operating system. An advanced accounting module can offer IP accounting not only per user, but also per process. This allows for the identification, the management, or schedulability of processes not only by their CPU usage or memory consumption, but also by their network resource consumption. Finally, this leads to the creation of network filters or firewalls that allow for or deny network access to specific applications or users running on a host, instead of only allowing or denying specific services. The current LINUBIA implementation treats all traffic the same, thus producing an overall network consumption report for each user. An interesting improvement would be separated accounting for different services (differentiated based on DSCP number or destination Autonomous System).

## Acknowledgment

This work has been performed partially in the framework of the EU IST Project EC-GIN (FP6-2006-IST-045256) as well as of the EU IST NoE EMANICS (FP6-2004-IST-026854).

## References

1. Brownlee, N., Mills, C., Ruth, G.: Traffic Flow Measurement: Architecture; RFC 2722 (October 1999)
2. Calhoun, P., Loughney, J., Guttman, E., Zorn, G., Arkko, J.: Diameter Base Protocol; RFC 3588 (September 2003)
3. Harrington, D., Presuhn, R., Wijnen, B.: An Architecture for Describing SNMP Management Frameworks; RFC 2271 (January 1998)
4. Edell, R.J., McKeown, N., Varaiya, P.P.: Billing Users and Pricing for TCP. IEEE Journal on Selected Areas in Communications 13(7) (September 1995)
5. Feier, M.: Design and Prototypical Implementation of a User-based IP Accounting Module for Linux, Diploma Thesis, University of Zürich, Switzerland (February 2007)
6. Flexible NetFlow Homepage (May 2007), http://www.cisco.com/en/US/products/ps6601/products_data_sheet0900aecd804b590b.html
7. Iperf Homepage: (May 2007), http://dast.nlanr.net/Projects/Iperf/
8. Juniper Homepage (May 2007), http://www.juniper.net/
9. Koukal, M., Bestak, R.: Architecture of IP Multimedia Subsystem. In: 48th International Symposium ELMAR-2006 focused on Multimedia Signal Processing and Communications, Zadar, Croatia (June 2006)
10. de Laat, C., Gross, G., Gommans, L., Vollbrecht, J., Spence, D.: Generic AAA Architecture; RFC 2903 (August 2000)
11. Narus Homepage (May 2007), http://www.narus.com/
12. Neuman, B.C., Ts'o, T.: Kerberos: An Authentication Service for Computer Networks. IEEE Communications 32(9), 33–38 (1994)
13. NIPON: Nutzerbasiertes IP Accounting (May 2007), http://www.icsy.de/forschung/nipon/
14. Rigney, C., Willens, S., Rubens, A., Simpson, W.: Remote Authentication Dia. In: User Service (RADIUS); RFC2865 (June 2000)

15. Sermersheim, J. (ed.): Lightweight Directory Access Protocol (LDAP): The Protocol; RFC 4511 (June 2006)
16. UserIPacct Homepage (May 2007),
    `http://ramses.smeyers.be/homepage/useripacct/`
17. UTA Dragon Homepage (May 2007),
    `http://www.crash-override.net/utadragon.html`
18. Vinton, G. (ed.): Guidelines for Internet Measurement Activities; RFC 1262, (October 1991)
19. Waldbusser, S.: Remote Network Monitoring Management Information Base; RFC 2819 (May 2000)
20. Zhang, G., Reuther, B.: A Model for User Based Traffic Accounting. In: 31st EUROMICRO Conference on Software Engineering and Advanced Applications, Porto, Portugal (August 30–September 3, 2005)
21. Zhang, G., Reuther, B., Mueller, P.: Distributed Agent Method for User Based IP Accounting. In: 7th CaberNet Radicals Workshop, Bertinoro, Forlí, Italy (October 13-16, 2002)

# Efficient Web Services Event Reporting and Notifications by Task Delegation

Aimilios Chourmouziadis and George Pavlou

Centre for Communication Systems Research, School of Electronics
and Physical Sciences, University of Surrey,
GU27XH Guildford, United Kingdom,
{A.Chourmouziadis,G.Pavlou}@surrey.ac.uk
http://www.ee.surrey.ac.uk/CCSR/

**Abstract.** Web Services are an XML technology recently viewed as capable of being used for network management. A key aspect of WS in this domain is event reporting. WS-based research in this area has produced a collection of notification specifications, which consider even aspects such as filtering to reduce machine and network resource consumption. Still though, additional aspects need to be addressed if WS event reporting is to be used efficiently for network management. This paper borrows an idea in network management that of policy based task delegation and applies it in the context of WS-based management by using the WS-Notification standard messages, to increase event reporting efficiency. More specifically, we are adding functionality to the entity that produces events making it capable of performing a set of tasks apart from simple ones such as collecting and reporting notification data. This functionality allows an entity, such as a manager, capable of delegating tasks of various complexities to an event reporting entity where they can be performed dynamically. As a proof of concept that the approach is feasible and increases efficiency we analyze a complex event reporting scenario where task delegation is used. We compare this approach for performance to a plain WS-based event system and also to simple SNMP traps.

## 1 Introduction

The growing use of the eXtensible Markup Language (XML) for data representation, coupled with the development of many XML standards and technologies such as Web Services (WS), has spurred research in a variety of fields other than the ones these technologies were originally designed for. One such field is network management.

One significant aspect of network management is event reporting. To use WS for event reporting two problems have to be addressed (a) asynchronous communication (push) (b) efficiency. The former is required since the time of the production of an event is not known and thus synchronous (pull) style communication is not possible. Efficiency is also an important aspect since for example it does not make sense to produce events that nobody is interested in receiving, or to produce events that someone is not interested to receive as this will make unnecessary use of resources.

A. Clemm, L.Z. Granville, and R. Stadler (Eds.): DSOM 2007, LNCS 4785, pp. 242–255, 2007.

In order to provide asynchronous communication between WSs, a callback mechanism is required. A Uniform Resource Locator (URL) is such a mechanism but is inadequate since (a) it only allows a single protocol to be defined to reach a service, (b) it can not describe all transport mechanism types, and, (c) it doesn't necessarily convey interface information. The proprietary WS-Addressing [1] specification solved this problem by defining two mechanisms that can be used as an efficient callback mechanism: (a) endpoint references, (b) message-information headers [2]. Despite its drawbacks [3] this specification has opened the way for three specification documents to be defined: WS-Events [4], WS-Eventing [5], and WS-notification [6].

In the HP WS-Events specification [4], the consumer of an event can (a) discover event-types an event producer supports, (b) subscribe to an event, (d) perform data filtering, (e) define an expiration date for receiving events, and, (f) provide a callback URL for an event. Filtering mechanisms are not specified in [4] but the means for unwanted events not to be produced or consumed are provided. In WS-Eventing [5] things become clearer; this specification supports the XML Path (XPath) for event filtering and WS-Addressing to provide a better callback mechanism. In WS-Notification [6] more features are added. [6] allows (a) consumers to receive content in an application-specific or raw format (b) define several types of expressions for filtering (XPath etc), (c) define event-types a consumer needs to receive with expressions called topics, (d) provide support for notification brokering.

All the above standards are on the right track for providing efficient and reliable event reporting communication. Still WS notifications can be used more efficiently for network management. Consider the management scenario where a manager has to be notified when an interface of a Quality of Service (QoS) enabled network fails. Upon receiving this event, the manager needs to determine the traffic contracts affected and requests for more data. In cases such as the previous, event reporting triggers actions at the event receiver which in turn requests for more system data or performs other changes i.e. configuration. Finding a way to perform a set of actions, normally performed by the entity receiving an event, in order for the tasks to be performed by the entity producing them, would make the notification process more efficient. The process where an entity is given the task to perform a set of actions for another entity is called task delegation. Task delegation can be used for WS-event reporting as long as the entity with the responsibility to perform a set of tasks is not a very resource-constrained system. This is more a reality today [7] (dumb agent myth).

Using WS-based event reporting with task delegation can be important for two reasons. The first one applies to data retrieval. In many event-reporting scenarios event data represents a small amount of the data carried over the network in comparison to the HTTP and the Simple Object Access Protocol (SOAP) header data. The use of WS notifications is not justified in these cases since WS perform badly when retrieving small amounts of data [8], [9]. As such, adding additional data, normally retrieved after the receipt of an event, in the initial report in order to reduce latency and traffic overhead can be beneficial. Secondly by task delegation a higher degree of autonomy can be achieved as the manager's supervision is limited.

A prominent way to perform task delegation for WS-based event reporting is through policies and the WS-Notification messages support their use. Delegating tasks though policies to improve the communication between entities in the event reporting process is not a new idea. Applying it to WSs to check if it is feasible and if potential benefits can be gained from it, is something that needs to be explored. As such a WS-based event service has been built supporting task delegation with the use of WS-Notification messages and policies. To prove the viability and the gains of the approach, an event reporting scenario is analyzed based on a QoS enabled network. We analyze the performance of event reporting for three systems: (a) A WS-based notification system where only event data are reported and then a set of actions triggered by the event are performed to collect more data (b) A WS-based event system where event data and data collected from subsequent tasks are gathered and sent by the entity that produces events in the initial report (c) An SNMP trap system.

The remainder of this paper is structured as follows. In section 2, details of the event reporting scenario based on a QoS-enabled Traffic Engineered (TE) on which we will comparing the three systems are provided.   Section 3 analyzes the WS-notification standard  messages used for event reporting in our scenario and it is shown how to use these messages to configure our event service to perform a set of tasks of varying complexity. Section 4 presents the WS-notification compliant messages that need to be sent for configuring an event service for handling event tasks, and the interactions between the different entities of the event reporting process. Section 5  presents a perfornance evalution between the two WS-based systems and a system based on SNMP  traps. Section 6 presents our conclusions.

## 2   QoS Event Reporting Scenario

### 2.1  QoS Management System

Providing QoS in a single or across different domains is a widely researched topic. QoS is currently provided on the basis of Service Level Agreements (SLAs). An SLA is a set of terms that clients and providers of services have to abide by when they are accessing or providing a service respectively.   The technical part of an SLA is a Service Level Specification (SLS) and it represents the means to define QoS-based IP services [10]. IP Differentiated Services [11] (DiffServ) is considered the most prominent framework for providing QoS-based services. All QoS-based services are quantified by means of performance parameters such as throughput, delay, loss and delay variation. One of the means to support the DiffServ architecture is over Multi-Protocol Label Switching (MPLS) traffic engineered networks.

Monitoring and event reporting of the network status and its resources is an essential process in order to ensure a QoS network's operation. To ensure the latter the use of Traffic Engineering (TE) is required. TE requires the collection of various data in order to ensure the network's smooth operation. This is achieved by a suitable monitoring and event reporting system which is scalable in terms of network size, customers' size etc. This constitutes a significant challenge in QoS-networks.

Previous examples of research in monitoring and event reporting has been performed in the TEQUILA [12], and the ENTHRONE frameworks [13].   These systems used in these frameworks are mostly based on the Manager-Agent paradigm. This is the paradigm we also adopted to collect data either with WS or SNMP for event reporting (Fig. 1). This system performs three kinds of operations: active, passive measurements and event reporting. Active measurements are performed by injecting synthetic network traffic. Passive measurements are conducted using Management Information Bases (MIBs) from SNMP and involve measuring throughput, load and packet loss at the traffic class (Per Hop Behavior-PHB), traffic contract (Service Level Specification-SLS) and the path (Label Switched Path - LSP) level. In Fig. 1, the manager is responsible for configuring software on the agents attached to the routers it needs to retrieve data from so as to perform active or passive measurements or event reporting. The agent operates either on a dedicated PC attached to a router or, if future routers support such functionality, on the router itself.

To perform measurements for our scenario at the PHB, LSP or SLS level we selected two of the SNMP MPLS MIBs to represent management data. These are the Label Switching Router (LSR) MIB [14] and the Forwarding Equivalence Class to Next Hop Label Forwarding Entry (FEC-To-NHLFE) MIB [15]. The former is used to perform PHB and LSP measurements and the latter is used for SLS measurements. For WS, equivalent MIBs had to be built and be deployed as WS interfaces.

## 2.2 Management Information Retrieval for QoS WS-Based Event Reporting

Retrieving management data from a managed system in our scenario requires facilities to be able to pick data in a bulk or selective way. This is achieved by the parser presented in [16]. Selective and bulk retrieval is achieved by dispatching appropriate queries. The reason behind building our own parser is to keep resource usage, latency and traffic overhead low. Thus selective retrieval at SOAP level is not

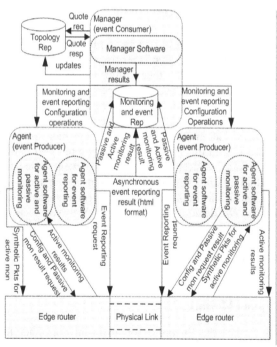

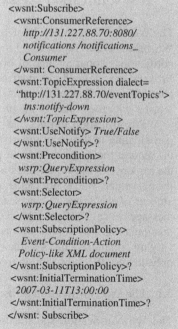

**Fig. 1.** Management system for monitoring and event reporting (manager-agent paradigm)

**Fig. 2.** WS Notification Subscription message [6]

an option since more data than required would have to be retrieved, encoded and selected. At the same time XPath can be a heavy-weight tool for management tasks especially if large documents need to be searched or loaded in memory. In addition processing raw data is less intesive than processing a verbose XML document.

We use our parser in our event reporting scenario to collect management data.

### 2.3  QoS Event Reporting Scenario

We consider an event reporting scenario in which the manager is notified that an MPLS interface failed in the ingress router. Upon receiving this event the manager needs to collect more data so as to determine the LSPs and SLSs that are affected by the failing interface so as to take appropriate measures. To apply this event reporting scenario, we have built and deployed a WS event service (Fig. 1) at the agent side. The event service is configured to perform a number of management tasks normally performed after the receipt of a notification, dynamically before dispatching the event report to the manager. By having the manager delegate tasks to other management entities its burden is minimized and the event process becomes more efficient. To demonstrate the benefits of such an approach, two WS-based event reporting approaches are considered which are analyzed in section 5. For both approaches WS-Notification compliant messages are used to configure the event source for notifications and for event reporting. A comparison to SNMP traps is also provided.

## 3  WS-Notification Messaging for Event Reporting

The WS-Notification family of specifications defines a  system architecture to support WS-based event reporting. In this architecture a *publisher* is an entity sending notifications about a range of events called *topics* to other entities called *consumers*. *Brokers* are defined as intermediate entities between producers and consumers controlling the flow of events with filtering. For a consumer to receive events it must register with the broker or the producer by selecting the appropriate topics.

WS-Notification defines the features and messages exchanged between entities participating in the event reporting process. In this paper we are only interested in (a) the request message a consumer sends to a producer to register for an event topic, (b) the response to the request message, and, (c) the event messages the producer sends to the consumer. We do not tackle aspects such as brokering, topic filtering, etc, as these are out of the scope of our scenario.  We demonstrate the use of WS-Notification messages to (a) configure the event service we have built for event reporting and task manipulation, (b) report events and, (c) investigate potential benefits of adding varying complexity tasks to the event producer. As such, in the next two sections we only address WS subscription (request and response) and notification messages.

### 3.1  The WS Notification Subscription Message

The WS-Notification specification defines that in order for an event consumer to receive a notification from a producer, it has to send a subscription message. The format of such message is given in Fig. 2. Here, the *consumer reference* tag is a URL providing a call-back mechanism for event delivery.  The *topic expression* tag defines the event topics a consumer can register to receive. Our event service implementation supports four general topics, (a-b) a threshold is exceeded going upwards-downwards (notify-high or notify-low), (c-d) the state of a unit has changed to active-inactive (notify-up or notify-down).The *UseNotify* tag is used by a consumer to select whether events will be formatted in an application specific way or in a WS-Notification *Notify* message. In addition, the selector and precondition expressions are used for data filtering. To define the period for which an event consumer registers for events, the termination time of the subscription has to be specified (*InitialTerminationTime*).

In the subscription message, the *subscription policy* element is a component used to specify application-specific policy requirements/assertions. The semantics on how an event producer will react to these assertions depends on the application-specific grammar used. A non -normative way to define policies is the WS-Policy standard. The greater vision of IBM for using the policy element is to be able to define concrete policies that allow a service to describe its approaches for subscription management or to specify directives that the event source must follow.

The response to a subscription may contain lots of data. Primarily though it contains the address of a WS defining messages that can be exchanged to manipulate subscription resources and fault information for subscription failure.

The *Notify* message contains the following: (a) a *topic* header that describes the event topic an event consumer subscribed initially to receive (b) a *producer reference* element that describes the endpoint of the service that produced the event, and (c) *message* elements where the actual payload of a notification is inserted. Our event service supports both *Notify* and application specific messages.

## 3.2 Policy-Like Configuration of Events for Network Management

Apart from the IBM specifics on policies, the vision of policies for network and service management is described in [17]. According to [17] policies are an aspect of information influencing the behavior of objects in a system. All policies can be expressed as a hierarchy where a high level policy goal can be refined into multiple levels of lower level policies. Effectively policies are rules used as the means to successfully achieve a goal. Furthermore, policies can be broadly classified into (a) *authorization* policies that define what is permitted, or not, to be performed in a system, and, (b) *obligation* policies that define what must be performed, or not, in order to guide the decision making process of a system. Both types of policies can be defined using an event-condition-action model of definition. Thus it is evident that policies can be reduced to set of rules, actions, utility functions that can be used to (a) ensure compliance, (b) define behavior, and, (c) achieve adaptability of a system.

In the network management world events are viewed as a state that usually demands an action to be taken. An event can be comprised of information about (a) the event itself, (b) the condition that produces it, and, (c) the type of actions to be performed after event generation. All this information is consistent with the network management view of policies (event-condition-action). As such, it is possible to use WS-Policy or any domain specific grammar to configure an event process as a policy. Thus the *subscription policy* element and any domain specific grammar can be used so as to pass to an event service (event producer), data in order to configure the event information, the event production condition and any event tasks-actions as policies.

In our event service implementation we use the *subscription policy* element to send to the event producer an XML document that consists of three sections: (a) general event data, (b) the conditions that trigger event-production, and, (c) subsequent actions. This document configures events as policies and its grammar is validated through an XML schema. Details on this are given in section 4. The grammar configuring events as policies constitutes by no means a formal policy. Still we can use it within the WS-Notification subscription policy element so as to be able to configure an event source to perform a set of varying complexity tasks. This allows us to delegate a set of tasks that the manager would otherwise perform to other entities (event service) so that WS event reporting is made more efficient.

## 4  Event Reporting Scenario Operations

### 4.1  Event Reporting Process Description

To configure the event service developed for the QoS event reporting scenario that we presented, the event consumer has to send a subscription message to the event producer. In reference to Fig. 1, the consumer is the manager and the producer is the agent. In Fig. 3 these roles are assumed by XML SOAP messaging services and WSs.

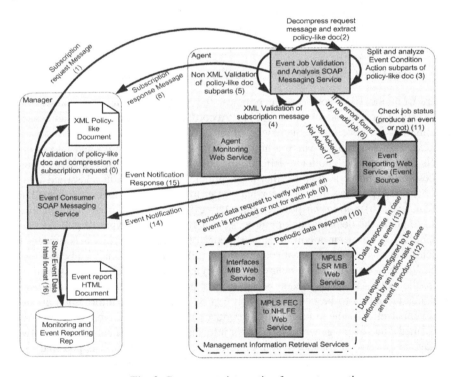

**Fig. 3.** Components interaction for event reporting

An overview of the operations that need to be performed for a receiver of events to actually start receiving notifications is given in Fig. 3. Here the subscription process starts by validating the event condition action policy-like document to avoid subscription request failure. Then the request is compressed and sent to the agent. At the agent the subscription request is decompressed, the policy-like document is extracted and split into its event-condition-action sub-parts. After SAX parser validation of each message part, the XML policy-like document is also searched for any discrepancies not captured by XML validation. This is necessary since inter-dependencies between different elements of the policy-like document exist and cannot be expressed by an XML schema. If errors are found the manager's SOAP messaging service is notified. On the opposite case, the agent's messaging service adds an event job to the event service. An event job can still be rejected for various reasons (job exists etc). Successful or unsuccessful addition of a job is reported to the manager. Apart from adding a job, the event service supports features such as (a) resume, (b) suspend, (c) remove, and, (d) update.

Upon successful addition of a job, the event sub-part is processed, and event data are collected using the Java reflection API to dynamically invoke the appropriate WSs exposing management data. Selective data retrieval is performed using the parser developed in [16]. Because we use our parser to filter data when collecting it, the *selector* and *precondition* expressions offered by the WS-Notification standard for filtering are not used. Following the data collection phase, the condition part of the policy-like document is processed to determine whether an event has been produced. If no event is produced the process is repeated according to the granularity of operations. If an event is produced, the action sub-parts of the policy-like document are executed.

The actions in our event reporting scenario involve tasks to gather extra data to determine the LSPs and SLSs affected by a failing interface. Calling the appropriate WSs to gather these data is performed dynamically and any queries to retrieve management data are formed on the fly using recursive methods since these queries can contain data not known in advance. When the event data and data from the configured tasks are collected, an event report is sent to the manager which confirms its receipt. The event report data is stored in HTML format.

## 4.2 Policy-like Event Configuration Document

The policy-like document consists of an event, a condition and an action part. The event part (Fig. 4) consists

```
<ns:EventSpec name="" jobid="" date="" time="">
  <ns:OIDsToMonitor>...</ns:OIDsToMonitor> {1}
  <ns:EventTask actionid="">
    <ns:ServiceEndpoint>...
    </ns:ServiceEndpoint> {1}
    <ns:Method namespace="">...</ns:Method> {1}
    <ns:Use>...</ns:Use> {1}
    <ns:Style>...</ns:Style>{1}
    <ns:MethodParams>
      <ns:Param name="" pmid="" namespace=""
        type="">
      <ns:Param> +
    </ns:MethodParams> ?
    <ns:Result resid="" type="" namespace=""
    qname="" name="">
      <ns:ResultParam pmid="" type="">...
      </ns:ResultParam>*
      <ns:ResultFormat forid="" dependsON="">
        <ns:FormatValue>...</ns:FormatValue>?
        <ns:FormatPattern>...</ns:FormatPattern> ?
      </ns:ResultFormat> ?
    </ns:Result> *
  </ns:EventTask> {1}
</ns:EventSpec> +
```

**Fig. 4.** Event part of the policy like document

```
<ns:EventCondition jobrefid="">
 <ns:MonitoringObjectType    monid="">
 <ns:granularity>...</ns:granularity> {1}
 <ns:window>...</ns:window>{1}
 </MonitoringObjectType> {1}
 <ns:Threshold>
  <ns:tType>...</ns:tType> {1}
  <ns:value>...</ns:value> {1}
  <ns:clearvalue> </ns:clearvalue> ?
 </ns:Threshold> {1}
</ns:EventCondition> +
```

**Fig.5.** Condition part of the policy like document

of sections which define (a) which parameter(s) need(s) to be monitored (*OIDstoMonitor*), (b) how to retrieve the data to be monitored (*EvenTask and its sub-elements*), and, (c) how to handle and process the retrieved data (*Result and its sub-elements*). The condition part of the document (Fig. 5) contains information to determine

```
<ns:ActionOnEvent jobrefid=""actionid="">
 <ns:ServiceEndpoint>...
 </ns:ServiceEndpoint> {1}
 <ns:Method namespace="">...
 </ns:Method> {1}
 <ns:Use>...</ns:Use> {1}
 <ns:Style>...</ns:Style>{1}
 <ns:MethodParams>
  <ns:Param name="" pmid=""namespace=""
  type="">
  <ns:Param> +
 </ns:MethodParams> ?
 <ns:Result resid="" type="" namespace=""
 qname=""  name="">
   <ns:ResultParam pmid=""type="">...
   </ns:ResultParam>*
   <ns:ResultFormat forid="" dependsON="">
    <ns:FormatValue>...</ns:FormatValue>?
    <ns:FormatPattern>...</ns:FormatPattern> ?
   </ns:ResultFormat> ?
  </ns:Result> *
</ns:ActionOnEvent>
```

**Fig. 6.** Action part of the policy like document

whether an event has been produced or not, such as (a) the type of monitor used (mean monitor, variance monitor, etc), (b) the measurement granularity, (c) the smoothing window size, and, (d) the clearing value that re-enables event reporting if it has been disabled. The action part(s) of the document contains data on how to call the appropriate WS to perform a task and also on how to process the result of any WS calls (Fig. 6).

## 5  Scenario Measurements

### 5.1  Evaluation Setup

For the evaluation aspects of our scenario, a big number of LSPs need to be setup for some measurements. As this is difficult in a small test-bed, we resorted to other means for evaluating the SNMP performance overhead. For traffic overhead, the average size of each message is calculated by looking into it and analyzing the size of its subparts. For latency a similar number and type of objects as in the MPLS MIBs are instantiated and the Advent-Net SNMP v3.3 is used to access a Net-SNMP agent. For WS, the software used is Apache Axis 1.3, JAXP 1.3, SAAJ 1.3 and JAXM 1.1. Java's zip facilities are used to compress/decompress messages and Java's reflection API was used to make WS dynamic calls. All MIBs are deployed with literal encoding so that the verboseness of XML tags is reduced and traffic overhead is minimized. The manager and agent were deployed on a 1000MHz/256MB RAM and 466MHz/192MB RAM machine respectively running Red-hat Linux 7.3, thus simulating a lower end system for the agent.

## 5.2  Measurements

The measurements presented in this section demonstrate the potential benefits of data filtering and task delegation for event reporting. Two WS-based approaches are examined. In the first, the manager is notified about a failing interface, and then queries the agent to determine the affected LSPs and SLSs. In the second approach the agent is configured by the manager to perform dynamically the set of tasks the latter would otherwise perform, and sends back all the collected data. The second approach is more complex since it requires the event service to call the appropriate WSs to determine the affected LSPs and SLSs at run time. This also requires forming parser queries to retrieve management data on the fly, since these queries may also contain data that are not known in advance.Through task delegation and filtering we show that the second approach is plausible and results in traffic and latency benefits. SNMP's, traffic and latency performance was also measured for comparison.

For SNMP traffic overhead measurements we rely on previous research performed in [8] and [18]. In these papers the traffic overhead for SNMP operations is given by:

$$L_{get, getNext} \approx n1 * (54 + 12 + 2L_1 + L_2) \tag{1}$$

$$L_{getBulk} \approx 54 + 1 * (6 + L_1) + n_1 (6 + L_1 + L_2) \tag{2}$$

$$L_{trapSNMPv\ 1} = 49 + n_1 * (3 + L_1 + L_2) \tag{3}$$

$$L_{trapSNMPv\ 2} = 75 + L_3 + n_1 * (3 + L_1 + L_2) \tag{4}$$

In equations (1), (2), (3) and (4) $L_1$ is the size of the Object Identifier (OID) of a variable, $L_2$ is the variable value size, $n_1$ is the number of OIDs to retrieve and $L_3$ is the trap OID. Taking into account the size (Table 1) of the data that needs to be reported the traffic overhead for SNMP can be computed.

**Table 1.** Information size in ASN.1 format inside an SNMP message

| Monitoring | Measurement Type | mplsXCLspId. mplsXCIndex. mplsXCInSegmentIndex. mplsXCOutSegmentIndex | mplsInSegmentInterface. mplsInSegmentIndex / mplsOutSegmentInterface. mplsOutSegmentIndex | mplsFTNDscp. mplsFTNIndex | mplsFTNActionPointer. mplsFTNIndex |
|---|---|---|---|---|---|
| | L1/L2 | 16-19 (Max 16000 LSPs) / 6 (CR-LDP) | 14-16 (Max 16000 Ifs) / 1-4 | 14-16/ 1-3 (Max 16000 LSPs) | 14-16/ (16-20) (Max 16000 LSPs) |
| | Measurement Type | IfOperStatus. ifIndex | IfAdminStatus. ifIndex | Trap OID L3=10 | Event Reporting |
| | L1/L2 | 10+(1-3)/1 | 10+(1-3)/1 | | |

For the measurements, the ingress router is configured to have 900 and 30 LSPs to simulate big and small networks respectively, each of which is assigned to a different customer. The reason behind assigning a different customer to each LSP is to keep things simple with respect to validity checks to the resulting event data. A further assumption is the number of LSPs and SLSs affected by the failing interface, which is considered to be six. Although it is not easy to determine a plausible number of LSPs assigned to each interface, six is a reasonable number for small networks. This number may not be realistic for large networks, but the aim is to keep the volume of data to be retrieved relatively low. This way we can show that WS can benefit from sophisticated retrieval mechanisms and exhibit superior performance to SNMP even if a small volume of data is retrieved (not shown in [8] and [9]). Additionally, keeping the same number of affected SLSs and LSPs for both small and large networks we can keep the traffic latency comparison between them on the same terms.

For the manager or agent to determine, for each WS approach the affected LSPs and SLSs, three queries must be sent. These queries: (a) determine the interface indices of the LSPs associated with this interface, (b) use the previous step indices to determine the affected LSPs, and, (c) determine the affected SLSs using the LSP IDs from the previous step. Parts of the three queries are the following:

$$\{\text{mplsInSeg mentInterface}[\ ], \text{mplsOutSeg mentInterface}[\ ]\}$$
$$\{\text{value} = \text{ifIndex}, \text{value} = \text{ifIndex}\} \tag{5}$$

$$\{\text{mplsXCLsp Id}[\ ]\}$$
$$\{\text{mplsInSegmentXCIndex} = \text{mplsInSegmentIndex}_1 \text{ OR} \tag{6}$$
$$\text{mplsOutSegmentXCIndex} = \text{mplsOutSegmentIndex}_1 \text{ OR} ...\}$$

$$\{\text{mplsFTNDscp}[\ ]\}$$
$$\{\text{mplsFTNActionPointer} = \text{mplsXCLspId.mplsXCIndex.} \tag{7}$$
$$\text{mplsXCInSegmentIndex.mplsXCOutSegmentIndex OR} ...\}$$

The measurements for our scenario are presented in Figures 7, 8, 9 and 10. In Fig. 7 configuration latency for the WS-based event services is quite significant since (de)compression of the subscription request, and XML validation takes place for both the first (S) and the second WS-based approach (C)  (WS(C)/ WS(S) config). Configuring the event service though is not a time critical task and happens once for a specific event-job. Therefore, we do not consider configuration latency in the event reporting overall latency of the WS approaches since it is not a time critical task.

Comparing the two WS-based approaches in terms of latency for small networks, it can be seen that the difference is very small (Fig 8). This occurs because the latency benefit from performing local WS calls for the WS approach with task delegation is counter-balanced from the latency incurred from performing dynamic WS calls and building data queries on the fly. For big networks though, latency decreases by around 75 ms if task delegation is used (Fig. 7). Comparing the WS-based approaches with SNMP, latency is about the same in the case of small networks (Fig. 8). For big networks SNMP suffers from a substantial increase in latency (Fig. 7). This occurs for two reasons, the first one being that SNMP does not offer facilities for task delegation so that data retrieval operations can be performed locally. The second reason is that SNMP does not offer filtering capabilities. Therefore determining the LSPs and SLSs affected from the failing interface requires retrieving more data than required from the relevant tables in the MPLS MIBs so as to be processed by the manager.

As far as traffic overhead is concerned 2700 bytes are saved by task delegation for both small and large networks (Fig. 9). This reduction occurs since SOAP and HTTP header data for the second WS approach are less. For every time an event is produced, our approach will save more traffic and latency. Therefore in the initial configuration of the event service we can select to monitor with a small expression all

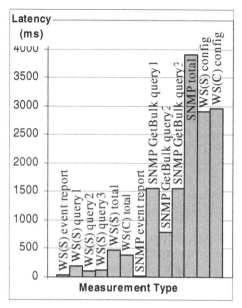

**Fig. 7.** Latency measurements for SNMP and for the two WS based approaches (900 LSPs)

**Fig. 8.** Latency measurements for SNMP and for the two WS based approaches (30 LSPs)

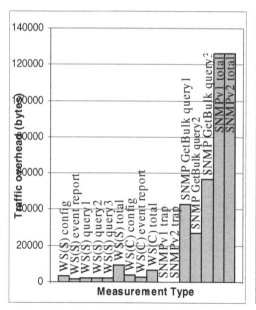

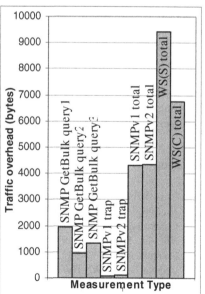

**Fig. 9.** Traffic measurements for SNMP and the two WS based approaches (900 LSPs)

**Fig. 10.** Traffic measurements for SNMP (30 LSPs) and total traffic for the WS schemes.

the interfaces of the ingress (relevant) router. The latter is not possible with SNMP without increasing traffic overhead since all MIB variables that need to be monitored must be defined. SNMP's traffic overhead for big networks is 120 kilobytes more due to lack of filtering and task delegation facilities (Fig. 10). For smaller networks SNMP's traffic overhead is less by 2300 bytes when compared to the WS approach based on task delegation (Fig 10). If more events are produced though, configuration traffic overhead included in the total traffic overhead of any WS based approach (3767 bytes for WS(C)) will not be included again since this happens only once for each event job. As such SNMP's traffic overhead becomes worse than the WS event reporting by task delegation approach by 1467 (3767-2300) bytes for each new event (Fig 9).

## 6  Conclusions

In this paper we have shown that facilities such as task delegation for WS event reporting can lead to significant gains in latency and traffic overhead since many of the tasks that must be performed upon receipt of an event report can be performed locally at the agent. We have also shown that such facilities have major performance gains for WS against SNMP. Offering such facilities is plausible today since the technical characteristics of devices used for management have increased.

Our work though on event reporting can also be improved by refining our policy-like grammar to meet closely the requirements of policy management. Currently our event reporting system is manually configured to perform a set of tasks dynamically at run-time. The essence of policy-based management for event reporting though would be to design an event reporting system that will autonomously deduce the actions to perform. This is in our future goals. Finally it is in our goals to apply our event reporting system to other fields and more resource constrained environments.

Nevertheless our event reporting system has great application potential. Through a realistic scenario we have demonstrated that sophisticated facilities for WS event reporting can lead to significant gains. Distributing task load for event reporting is extremely important, resulting in more distributed scalable, self adaptive systems.

## References

[1] Box, D., et al.: Web Services addressing, http://www.w3.org/Submission/ws-addressing/
[2] Vinoski, S.: IONA Technologies "Web Services Notifications". IEEE Internet Computing 8(2), 86–90 (2004)
[3] Vinoski, S.: IONA Technologies "More Web Services Notifications". IEEE Internet Computing 8(3), 90–93 (2004)
[4] Catania,N.,etal.:WS-EVENTS2.0.HP, http://devresource.hp.com/drc/specifications/wsmf
[5] Box, D., et al.: WS-Eventing, http://www.w3.org/Submission/WS-Eventing/
[6] Graham, S., et al.: Web Services Base Notification, http://www-128.ibm.com/
[7] Flattin, J.P: Web-Based Management of IP networks and Systems. ©Wiley series (2003)
[8] Pras, A., et al.: Comparing the Performance of SNMP and WS-Based Management. IEEE eTNSM 1(2) (2004)

 [9] Pavlou, G., Flegkas, P., Gouveris, S.: On Management Technologies and the Potential of Web Services. IEEE Communications Magazine 42(7), 58–66 (2004)
[10] Blake, S., et al.: An Architecture for Differentiated Services. RFC 2475, (December 1998)
[11] Goderis, D., et al.: SLS Semantics and Parameters. draft-tequila-sls-02.txt (August 2002)
[12] Asgari, H., Egan, R., Trimintzios, P., Pavlou, G.: Scalable monitoring support for resource management and service assurance. IEEE Network 18(6), 6–18 (2004)
[13] ENTHRONE, 2nd phase 1/9/2006, http://www.enthrone.org/
[14] Srinivasan, C., et al.: MPLS Label Switching Router MIB. RFC 3813 (June 2004)
[15] Nadeau, T., et al.: MPLS Forwarding Equivalence Class To Next Hop Label Forwarding Entry MIB. RFC 3814 (June 2004)
[16] Chourmouziadis, A., Pavlou, G.: Efficient Information Retrieval in Network Management Using Web Services. DSOM. In: Proceedings, October 23-25, 2006, Dublin, Ireland (2006)
[17] Sloman, M.: Policy Driven management for Distributed Systems. JNSM 2(4) (1994)
[18] Lima, W., et al.: Evaluating the performance of Web Services and SNMP notifications. NOMS. In: 10th IEEE/IFIP pp. 546–556 (2006)

# Transactions for Distributed Wikis
# on Structured Overlays[*]

Stefan Plantikow, Alexander Reinefeld, and Florian Schintke

Zuse Institute Berlin
{Plantikow,Reinefeld,Schintke}@zib.de
http://www.zib.de

**Abstract.** We present a transaction processing scheme for structured overlay networks and use it to develop a distributed Wiki application based on a relational data model. The Wiki supports rich metadata and additional indexes for navigation purposes.

Ensuring consistency and durability requires handling of node failures. We mask such failures by providing high availability of nodes by constructing the overlay from replicated state machines *(cell model)*. Atomicity is realized using two phase commit with additional support for failure detection and restoration of the transaction manager. The developed transaction processing scheme provides the application with a mixture of pessimistic, hybrid optimistic and multiversioning concurrency control techniques to minimize the impact of replication on latency and optimize for read operations. We present pseudocode of the relevant Wiki functions and evaluate the different concurrency control techniques in terms of message complexity.

**Keywords:** Distributed transactions, content management systems, structured overlay networks, consistency, concurrency control.

## 1 Introduction

*Structured overlay networks (SONs)* provide a scalable and efficient means for storing and retrieving data in distributed environments without central control. Unfortunately, in their most basic implementation, SONs do not offer any guarantees on the ordering of concurrently executed operations.

Transaction processing provides concurrently executing clients with a single, consistent view of a shared database. This is done by bundling client operations in a transaction and executing them as if there was a global, serial transaction execution order. Enabling structured overlays to provide transaction processing support is a sensible next step for building *consistent* decentralized, self-managing storage services.

We propose a transactional system for an Internet-distributed content management system built on a structured overlay. Our emphasis is on supporting

---

[*] This work was partially supported by the EU projects SELFMAN and CoreGRID.

A. Clemm, L.Z. Granville, and R. Stadler (Eds.): DSOM 2007, LNCS 4785, pp. 256–267, 2007.

transactions in dynamic decentralized systems where nodes may fail at a relatively high rate. The chosen approach provides clients with different concurrency control options to minimize latency.

The article is structured as follows: Section 2 describes a general model for distributed transaction processing in SONs. The main problem addressed is masking the unreliability of nodes. Section 3 presents our transaction processing scheme focusing on concurrency control. This scheme is extended to the relational model and exemplified using the distributed Wiki in Section 4. Finally, in Section 5, we evaluate the different proposed transaction processing techniques in terms of message complexity.

## 2   Transactions on Structured Overlays

Transaction processing guarantees the four ACID properties: *Atomicity* (either all or no data operations are executed), *consistency* (transaction processing never corrupts the database state), *isolation* (data operations of concurrently executing transactions do not interfere with each other), *durability* (results of successful transactions survive system crashes). Isolation and consistency together are called *concurrency control*, while *database recovery* refers to atomicity and durability.

*Page model.* We only consider transactions in the *page model* [1]: The database is a set of uniquely addressable, single objects. Valid elementary operations are reading and writing of objects, and transaction abort and commit. The model does not support predicate locking. Therefore, phantoms can occur and consistent aggregation queries are not supported. The page model can naturally be applied to SONs. Objects are stored under their identifier using the overlay's policy for data placement.

### 2.1   Distributed Transaction Processing

Distributed transaction processing guarantees the ACID properties in scenarios where clients access multiple databases or different parts of the same database located on different nodes. Access to local databases is controlled by *resource manager (RM)* processes at each participating node. Additionally, for each active transaction, one node takes the role of the *transaction manager (TM)*. The TM coordinates with the involved RMs to execute a transaction on behalf of the client. The TM also plays an important role during the execution of the distributed atomic commit protocol.

Distributed transaction processing in a SON requires distribution of resource and transaction management. The initiating peer can act as TM. For resource management, it is necessary to minimize the communication overhead between RM and storing node. Therefore, in the following, we assume that each peer of the overlay performs resource management for all objects in its keyspace partition.

## 2.2   The Cell Model for Masking Churn

Distributing the resource management over all peers puts tight restrictions on messages delivered under transaction control. Such messages may only be delivered to nodes that are currently responsible for the data. This property is known as *lookup consistency*. Without lookup consistency, a node might erroneously grant a lock on a data item or deliver outdated data. It is an open question how lookup consistency can be guaranteed efficienty in the presence of frequent and unexpected node failures *(churn)*. Some authors (e.g. [2]) have suggested protocols that ensure consistent lookup if properly executed by *all* joining and leaving nodes. Yet large-scale overlays are subject to considerable amounts of churn [3] and therefore correct transaction processing requires masking it.

*Cell model.* Instead of constructing the overlay network using single nodes, we propose to build the overlay out of *cells*. Each cell is a dynamically sized group of physical nodes [4] that constitute a *replicated state machine (RSM, [5])*. Cells utilize the chosen RSM algorithm to provide replicated, atomic operations and high availability. This can be exploited to

- mask churn and therefore guarantee lookup consistency,
- provide stable storage for transactional durability,
- ensure data consistency using atomic operations,
- minimize overhead for routing to replicas (cell nodes form a clique).

For the underlying nodes, we assume the *crash-stop* failure model. This model is common for SONs because it is usually unknown wether a disconnected node will rejoin again later. We do not cover the distribution of physical nodes on cells, nor do we consider Byzantine failures. We assume that cells never fail unexpectedly and always execute the overlay algorithm orderly. If too many cell nodes fail, the cell destroys itself by executing the overlay's leave protocol. The data items are re-distributed among neighboring cells. For simplification, we also assume that the keyspace partition associated to each cell does not change during transaction execution.

**Fig. 1.** Cell routing using dirty reads

*Cell routing.* The execution of replicated operations within the cells comes at a considerable cost: RSMs are implemented using some form of atomic broadcast which in turn depends on an implementation of a consensus protocol. Yet, modern consensus algorithms like *Fast Paxos* [6] require at least $N(\lfloor 2N/3 \rfloor + 1)$ messages for consensus between $N$ nodes. While this cost is hardly avoidable for consistent replication, it is as well unacceptable for regular message routing. Hence we propose to use dirty reads (i.e. to read the state of one arbitrary node). When the state of a node and its cell are temporarily out of sync, routing errors may occur. To handle this, the presumed target cell will pre-deliver the message using a replicated operation (Fig. 1). Pre-delivery first checks, wether the presumed target cell is currently responsible for the message. If that is the case, the message is delivered and processed regularly. Otherwise, message routing is restarted from the node that initiated pre-delivery.

Replicated operations will only be executed at a node after all of its predecessor operations have been finished. Therefore, at pre-delivery time, the presumed target cell either actually is responsible for the message or a previously executed replicated operation has changed the cell's routing table consistently such that the *correct* follow-up routing hop or target cell for the message is known. A messages reaches its destination under the assumption that cell routing table changes are sufficiently rare, and intermediate hops do not fail.

# 3  Concurrency Control and Atomic Commit in SONs

In this section, we present appropriate concurrency control and atomic commit techniques for overlays based on the cell model.

*Atomic Operations.* Using RSMs by definition [5] allows the execution of atomic and totally ordered operations. This already suffices to implement transaction processing, e.g. by using *pessimistic two phase locking (2PL)* and an additional distributed atomic commit protocol. However, each replicated operation is expensive, thus any efficient transaction processing scheme for cell-structured overlays should aim at minimizing the number of replicated operations.

*Optimistic concurrency control (OCC).* OCC executes transactions against a *local* working copy (working phase). This copy is validated just before the transaction is committed (validation phase). The transaction is aborted if conflicts are detected during validation. As every node has (a possibly temporarily deviating) local copy of its cell's shared state, OCC is a prime candidate for reducing the number of replicated operations by executing the transaction against single nodes of each involved cell.

## 3.1  Hybrid Optimistic Concurrency Control

Plain OCC has the drawback that long-running transactions using objects which are frequently accessed by short-running transactions may suffer starvation due to consecutive validation failures. This is addressed by *hybrid optimistic concurrency control (HOCC, [7])* under the assumption of *access invariance*, i.e. repeated executions of the same transaction have identical read and write sets.

HOCC works by executing *strong two phase locking (SS2PL)* for the transaction's read and write sets at the beginning of the validation phase. In case of a validation failure, locks are kept and the transaction logic is re-executed. Now, access invariance ensures that this second execution cannot fail because all necessary locks are already held by the transaction. However, it is required that optimistically read values do not influence the result of the re-execution phase. Otherwise, consistency may violated.

The use of SS2PL adds the benefit that no distributed deadlock detection is necessary if a global validation order between transactions is established. A possible technique for this has been described by Agrawal et. al [8]: Each cell $v$ maintains a strictly monotonic increasing timestamp $t_v$ for the largest, validated transaction. Before starting the validation, the transaction manager suggests a validation time stamp $t > t_v$ to all involved cells. After each such cell has acknowledged that $t > t_v$ and updated $t_v$ to $t$, the validation phase is started. Otherwise the algorithm is repeated. Gruber [9] optimized this approach by including the current $t_v$ in every control message.

## 3.2 Distributed Atomic Commit

*Distributed atomic commit (DBAC)* requires consensus between all transaction participants on the transaction's termination state (committed or aborted). If DBAC is not guaranteed, the ACID properties are violated.

We propose a blocking DBAC protocol that uses cells to treat TM failures by replicating transaction termination state. Every transaction is associated with a unique identifier (TXID). The overlay cell corresponding to that TXID is used to store a *commit record* holding the termination state and the address of the TM node (an arbitrary, single node of the TXID cell). If no failures occur, regular *two-phase atomic commit (2PC)* is executed. Additionally, after all prepared-messages have been received and before the final commit messages are sent, the TM first writes the commit record. If the record is already set to abort, the TM aborts the transaction. If RMs suspect a TM failure, they read the record to either determine the termination state or initiate transaction abort. Optionally, RMs can restore the TM by selecting a new node and updating the record appropriately. Other RMs will notice this when they reread the modified record.

## 3.3 Read-Only Transactions

In many application scenarios simple read-only transactions are much more common than update transactions. Therefore we optimize and extend our transaction processing scheme for read-only transactions by applying techniques similar to *read-only multiversioning (ROMV, [10])*.

All data items are versioned using unique timestamps generated from each node's loosely synchronized clock and globally unique identifier. Additionally, we maintain a *current version* for each data item. This version is accessed and locked exclusively by HOCC transactions as described above and implicitly associated with the cell's maximum validation timestamp $t_v$. The current version decouples ROMV and HOCC.

Our approach moves newly created versions to the future such that they never interfere with read operations from ongoing read-only transactions. This avoids the cost associated with distributed atomic commit for read-only transactions but necessitates it to execute reads as replicated operations. Read-only transactions are associated with their start time. Every read operation is executed as a replicated operation using the standard multiversioning rule [11]: The result is the oldest version which is younger than the transaction start time. If this version is the current version, the maximum validation timestamp $t_v$ will be updated. This may block the read operation until a currently running validation is finished. Update transactions create new versions of all written objects using $t > t_v$ during atomic commit.

# 4  Algorithms for a Distributed Wiki

In this section, we describe the basic algorithms of a distributed content management system built on a structured overlay with transaction support.

## 4.1  Mapping the Relational Model

So far we only considered uniquely addressable, uniform objects. In practice, many applications use more complex, relational data structures. This raises the question of how multiple relations with possibly multiple attributes can be stored in a single structured overlay. To address this, first, we assume that the overlay supports range queries [12,13] over a finite number of index dimensions.

Storing multiple attributes requires mapping them on index dimensions. As the number of available dimensions is limited, it is necessary to partition the attributes into disjoint groups and map these groups instead. The partition must be chosen in such a way that fast primary-key based access is still possible. Depending on their group membership, attributes are either primary, index, or non-indexed data attributes. Multiple relations can be modeled by prefixing primary keys with a unique relation identifier.

## 4.2  Notation

Table 1 contains an overview of the pseudocode syntax from [14]. Relations are represented as sets of tuples and written in CAPITALS. Relation tuples are addressed by using values for the primary attributes in the fixed order given by the relation. For reasons of readability, tuple components are addressed using unique labels (Such labels can easily be converted to positional indexes). Range queries are expressed using labels and marked with a "?".

## 4.3  Wiki

A *Wiki* is a content management system that embraces the principle of minimizing access barriers for non-expert users. Wikis like www.wikipedia.org comprise

**Table 1.** Pseudocode notation

| Syntax | Description |
|---|---|
| **Procedure** Proc $(arg_1, arg_2, ..., arg_n)$ | Procedure declaration |
| **Function** Fun $(arg_1, arg_2, ..., arg_n)$ | Function declaration |
| **begin ... commit (abort) transaction** | Transaction boundaries |
| ADDRESS$_{"ZIB"}$ | Read tuple from relation |
| ADDRESS$_{"ZIB"}$ $\leftarrow$ $("Takustr.\ 7", "Berlin")$ | Write tuple to relation |
| $\Pi_{attr_1, ..., attr_n}(M) = \{\pi_{attr_1, ..., attr_n}(t) \mid t \in M\}$ | Projection |
| $\forall t \in$ tuple set : RELATION $\overset{+}{\leftarrow} t$ bzw. $\overset{-}{\leftarrow} t$ | Bulk insert and delete |
| $\text{DHT}^?_{key_1 = "a",\ key_2}$ $or$ $\text{DHT}^?_{key_1 = "a",\ key_2 = *}$ | Range query with wildcard |

millions of pages written in a simplified, human-readable markup syntax. Each page has a unique name which is used for hyperlinking to other Wiki pages. All pages can be read and edited by any user, which may result in many concurrent modification requests for hotspot pages. This makes Wikis a perfect test-case for our distributed transaction algorithm.

Modern Wikis provide a host of additional features, particularly to simplify navigation. In this paper we exemplarily consider backlinks (a list of all the other pages linking to a page) and recent changes (a list of recent modifications of all Wiki pages). We model our Wiki using the following two relations:

| Relation | Primary attributes | Index attributes | Data attributes |
|---|---|---|---|
| CONTENT | *pageName* | *ctime* (change time) | *content* |
| BACKLINKS | *referencing* (page), *referenced* (page) | - | - |

Wiki operations use transactions to maintain global consistency invariants:

- CONTENT always contains the current content for all pages,
- BACKLINKS contains proper backlinks for all pages contained in CONTENT,
- users cannot modify pages whose content they have never seen (explained below).

The function WikiRead (Alg. 4.1) delivers the content of a page and all backlinks pointing to it. This requires a single read for the content and a range query to obtain the backlinks. Both operations can be executed in parallel.

The function WikiWrite (Alg. 4.2) is more complex because conflicting writes by multiple users must be resolved. This can be done by serializing the write requests using locks or request queues. If conflicts are detected during (atomic) writes by comparing last read and current content, the write operation is aborted. Users may then manually merge their changes and retry. This approach is similar to the compare-and-swap instructions used in modern microprocessors and to the concurrency control in version control systems.[1] We realize the compare-and-swap in WikiWrite by using transactions for our distributed Wiki. First, we precompute which backlinks should be inserted and deleted. Then, we compare the current and old page content and abort if they differ. Otherwise all updates are performed by writing the new page content and modifying BACKLINKS. The update operations again can be performed in parallel.

---

**Algorithm 4.1.** WikiRead: Read page content

1: **function** WikiRead ($pageName$)
2:     **begin transaction** $read\text{-}only$
3:         $content \leftarrow \pi_{content}(\text{CONTENT}_{pageName})$
4:         $backlinks \leftarrow \Pi_{referenced}(\text{BACKLINKS}^{?}_{referencing=pageName,\ referenced})$
5:     **commit transaction**
6:     **return** $content, backlinks$
7: **end function**

---

**Algorithm 4.2.** WikiWrite: Write new page content and update backlinks

1: **procedure** WikiWrite ($pageName, content_{old}, content_{new}$)
2:     $refs_{old} \leftarrow \text{Refs}(content_{old})$
3:     $refs_{new} \leftarrow \text{Refs}(content_{new})$
4:     $refs_{del} \leftarrow refs_{old} \setminus refs_{new}$          — precalculation
5:     $refs_{add} \leftarrow refs_{new} \setminus refs_{old}$
6:     $txStartTime \leftarrow \text{CurrentTimeUTC}()$
7:     **begin transaction**
8:         **if** $\pi_{content}(\text{CONTENT}_{pageName}) = content_{old}$ **then**
9:             $\text{CONTENT}_{pageName} = (txStartTime,\ content_{new})$
10:             $\forall t \in \{(ref,\ pageName) \mid ref \in refs_{add}\}:\ \text{BACKLINKS} \overset{+}{\leftarrow} t$
11:             $\forall t \in \{(ref,\ pageName) \mid ref \in refs_{del}\}:\ \text{BACKLINKS} \overset{-}{\leftarrow} t$
12:         **else**
13:             **abort transaction**
14:         **end if**
15:     **commit transaction**
16: **end procedure**

---

The list of recently changed pages can be generated by issuing a simple range query inside a transaction and sorting the results appropriately.[2]

## 4.4   Wiki with Metadata

Often it is necessary to store additional metadata with each page (e.g. page author, category). To support this, we add a third relation METADATA with primary

---

[1] Most version control systems provide heuristics (e.g. merging of different versions) for automatic conflict resolution that could be used for the Wiki as well.

[2] The complete range query is: $\{\text{CONTENT}^{?}_{pageName=*,\ ctime=*}\}^{\overleftarrow{ctime}}_{\#<resultLimit}$.

---

**Algorithm 4.3.** SetPageMetadata: Write page metadata attributes

---

**Require:** *changeEnv* environment describing changes to be made
1: **procedure** SetPageMetadata ($pageName$, $content_{old}$, $changeEnv$)
2:     **begin transaction**
3:         **if** $\pi_{content}(\text{CONTENT}_{pageName}) = content_{old}$ **then**
4:             $\forall(anAttrName \Leftarrow anAttrValue) \in changeEnv$ :
5:                 $\text{METADATA}_{pageName,\ anAttrName} \leftarrow anAttrValue$
6:         **else**
7:             **abort transaction**
8:         **end if**
9:     **commit transaction**
10: **end procedure**

---

key attributes *pageName* and *attrName* and data attribute *attrValue*. Alternatively we could also add metadata attributes to CONTENT. But this would not be scalable as current overlays only provide a limited number of index dimensions.

Modifying page metadata (Alg. 4.3) requires verifying that the page has not been changed by some other transaction. Otherwise new metadata could be associated wrongly to a page (This is similar to storing wrong backlinks). For reading page metadata, a simple range query suffices [14].

## 5   Evaluation

The presented algorithms for ensuring consistency mainly require the atomicity property while only few restrictions are placed on the serial execution order of operations. Thus in theory, a high degree of concurrency is possible. This is especially interesting for range queries like RecentChanges which can utilize the overlay's capabilities to multicast to many nodes in parallel.

Table 2 shows the communication overhead of various concurrency control schemes. We compare the different schemes using an example transaction that consists of $k$ serial steps. Each step executes data operations in parallel on $N$ cells (one operation per cell).

**Table 2.** Comparison of concurrency control methods

| Transaction type | One-time overhead for $N$ cells | Ops per step on $N$ cells in parallel | Total for $k$ serial steps |
|---|---|---|---|
| (1) Atomic Write | $1\,L$ | $1\,R$ | $1\,L + 1\,R$, because $k, N = 1$ |
| (2) Read-Only Trans. | $N\,L$ | $N\,R$ | $N\,L + kN\,R$ |
| (3) Pess. 2PL + 2PC | $N\,L + 2N\,R$ | $N\,R$ | $N\,L + (k+1)N\,R$ |
| (4) Hyb. Opt. + 2PC | $N\,L + 2N\,R$ | $N\,U$ | $N\,L + (k-1)N\,U + 2N\,R$ |
| (5) Hyb. Opt. + 2PC + Validation Error | $N\,L + 3N\,R$ | $2N\,U$ | $N\,L + (2k-2)N\,U + 3N\,R$ |

(2) to (4) use the 2PC variant described in 3.2. For our evaluation, we assume that no failures occur during the commit.

For every scheme, we distinguish the number and type of operations necessary to carry out the transaction: $U$ is a simple unreplicated operation, $R$ is a replicated operation, and $L$ is a lookup (routing) operation. The cost is split into one-time (initial and DBAC) overhead, the cost per step, and the total cost. Totals include DBAC costs and take the possible combined sending of messages into account (e.g. combining last write operation with validate and prepare). The evaluated concurrency control schemes are:

(1) a simple, replicated operation on a single cell,
(2) a read-only multiversioning transaction (Sec. 3.3),
(3) a pessimistic 2PL transaction,
(4) a HOCC (Sec. 3.1) transaction without validation failure, and
(5) a HOCC transaction with validation failure and re-execution of transaction logic.

HOCC reduces the number of necessary replicated operations for $k > 1$. For $k = 1$ and a transaction on a single cell, ACID is already provided by using a RSM and no DBAC is necessary. For $k = 1$ and a transaction over multiple cells, HOCC degenerates into 2PL: the data operations on the different cells are combined with validate-and-prepare messages and executed using single replicated operations.

Read-only transactions use more replicated operations but save the DBAC costs of HOCC. This makes them well-suited for quick, parallel reads. But long running read transactions might be better off using HOCC if the performance gained by optimism outweights DBAC overhead and validation failure chance.

Using cells yields an additional benefit. If replication was performed above the overlay layer, additional routing costs of $(r-1)N$ lookup messages would be necessary ($r$ is the number of replicas).

# 6    Related Work

Mesaros et. al describe a transaction processing scheme for overlays based on 2PL [15]. Lock conflicts are resolved by giving higher priority to older transactions and forcing the loosing transaction into the 2PL shrinking phase. Transactions are executed by forming a dynamic multicast group consisting of all participating nodes. The article does not address issues of lookup consistency and replication.

OceanStore [16] uses a two-tier approach for multiversioning-based replication. On the first layer, a small set of replicas forms a primary ring. On the second layer, additional replicas cache object versions. Replicas are located using the Tapestry overlay network. Primary ring replicas use a Byzantine agreement protocol to serially execute atomic operations.

Etna [17] is a system for executing atomic read and write operations in a Chord-like overlay network. Operations are serialized using a primary copy and replicated over $k$ sucessors using a consensus algorithm.

Both articles do not describe how full transaction processing can be built on top of atomic operations. For OceanStore, multiversioning [11] is proposed [16]. The inherent cost of replicated transaction execution is handled using the caching tier. However, this comes at the price of reduced consistency.

As an alternative to our solution for atomic commitment, Moser et al. [18] describe a non-blocking approach based on Paxos commit. Their solution treats the set of all replicas of all accessed items as a whole and fixes this set at commit time. They suggest the use of symmetric replication [19] to achieve availability. Instead of using RSMs inside cells, encoding schemes like Reed-Solomon codes could be used, as proposed by Litwin et al. [20] to ensure proper availability.

## 7  Summary

We presented a transaction processing scheme suitable for a distributed Wiki application on a structured overlay network. While previous work on overlay transactions has not addressed node unreliability, we identified this as a key requirement for consistency and proposed the cell model as a possible solution.

The developed transaction processing scheme provides applications with a mixture of concurrency control techniques to minimize the required communication effort. We showed core algorithms for the Wiki that utilize overlay transaction handling support and evaluated different concurrency control techniques in terms of message complexity.

## References

1. Gray, J.: The transaction concept: Virtues and limitations. In: Proceedings of the 7th Intl. Conf. on Very Large Databases, pp. 144–154 (1981)
2. Ghodsi, A.: Distributed k-Ary System: Algorithms for Distributed Hash Tables. PhD thesis, KTH Stockholm (2006)
3. Li, J., Stribling, J., Gil, T.M., Morris, R., Kaashoek, M.F.: Comparing the performance of distributed hash tables under churn. In: Voelker, G.M., Shenker, S. (eds.) IPTPS 2004. LNCS, vol. 3279, Springer, Heidelberg (2005)
4. Schiper, A.: Dynamic group communication. Distributed Computing 18(5), 359–374 (2006)
5. Schneider, F.B.: The state machine approach: A tutorial. Technical Report TR 86-800, Dept. of Comp. Sci., Cornell University (December 1986)
6. Lamport, L.: Fast paxos. Technical Report MSR-TR-2005-112, Microsoft Research (January 2006)
7. Thomasian, A.: Distributed optimistic concurrency control methods for high-performance transaction processing. IEEE Transactions on Knowledge and Data Engineering 10(1), 173–189 (1998)
8. Agrawal, D., Bernstein, A.J., Gupta, P., Sengupta, S.: Distributed optimistic concurrency control with reduced rollback. Distributed Computing 2, 45–59 (1987)
9. Gruber, R.E.: Optimistic Concurrency Control for Nested Distributed Transactions. PhD thesis, Massachusetts Institute of Technology (June 1989)

10. Mohan, C., Pirahesh, H., Lorie, R.: Efficient and flexible methods for transient versioning of records to avoid locking by read-only transactions. In: SIGMOD 1992. Proceedings of the 1992 ACM SIGMOD Intl. Conf. on Management of data, pp. 124–133. ACM Press, New York (1992)
11. Reed, D.P.: Naming and synchronization in a decentralized computer system, PhD thesis. Technical Report MIT-LCS-TR-205, MIT (September 1978)
12. Schütt, T., Schintke, F., Reinefeld, A.: Structured Overlay without Consistent Hashing: Empirical Results. In: GP2PC 2006. Proceedings of the Sixth Workshop on Global and Peer-to-Peer Computing (May 2006)
13. Andrzejak, A., Xu, Z.: Scalable, efficient range queries for grid information services. In: P2P 2002. 2nd IEEE Intl. Conf. on Peer-to-Peer Computing, IEEE Computer Society Press, Los Alamitos (2002)
14. Plantikow, S.: Transactions for distributed wikis on structured overlay networks (in German). Diploma thesis, Humboldt-Universität zu Berlin (April 2007)
15. Mesaros, V., Collet, R., Glynn, K., Roy, P.V.: A transactional system for structured overlay networks. Technical Report RR2005-01, Université catholique de Louvain (UCL) (March 2005)
16. Rhea, S., Eaton, P., Geels, D., Weatherspoon, H., Zhao, B., Kubiatowicz, J.: Pond: The OceanStore Prototype. In: Proceedings of the 2nd USENIX Conf. on File and Storage Technologies, pp. 1–14 (2003)
17. Muthitacharoen, A., Gilbert, S., Morris, R.: Etna: A fault-tolerant algorithm for atomic mutable DHT data. Technical Report MIT-CSAIL-TR-2005-044 and MIT-LCS-TR-993, CSAIL, MIT (2005)
18. Moser, M., Haridi, S.: Atomic commitment in transactional DHTs. In: First CoreGRID European Network of Excellence Symposium (2007)
19. Ghodsi, A., Alima, L.O., Haridi, S.: Symmetric replication for structured peer-to-peer systems. In: The 3rd Intl. Workshop on Databases, Information Systems and peer-to-Peer Computing (2005)
20. Litwin, W., Schwarz, T.: LH*RS: a high-availability scalable distributed data structure using Reed Solomon Codes. In: SIGMOD 2000. Proceedings of the 2000 ACM SIGMOD Intl. Conf. on Management of Data, pp. 237–248. ACM Press, New York (2000)

# Author Index

# Lecture Notes in Computer Science

Sublibrary 5: Computer Communication Networks and Telecommunications

For information about Vols. 1– 4427
please contact your bookseller or Springer

Vol. 4104: T. Kunz, S.S. Ravi (Eds.), Ad-Hoc, Mobile, and Wireless Networks. XII, 474 pages. 2006.

Vol. 4074: M. Burmester, A. Yasinsac (Eds.), Secure Mobile Ad-hoc Networks and Sensors. X, 193 pages. 2006.

Vol. 4033: B. Stiller, P. Reichl, B. Tuffin (Eds.), Performability Has its Price. X, 103 pages. 2006.

Vol. 4026: P.B. Gibbons, T. Abdelzaher, J. Aspnes, R. Rao (Eds.), Distributed Computing in Sensor Systems. XIV, 566 pages. 2006.

Vol. 4003: Y. Koucheryavy, J. Harju, V.B. Iversen (Eds.), Next Generation Teletraffic and Wired/Wireless Advanced Networking. XVI, 582 pages. 2006.

Vol. 3996: A. Keller, J.-P. Martin-Flatin (Eds.), Self-Managed Networks, Systems, and Services. X, 185 pages. 2006.

Vol. 3976: F. Boavida, T. Plagemann, B. Stiller, C. Westphal, E. Monteiro (Eds.), NETWORKING 2006. Networking Technologies, Services, and Protocols; Performance of Computer and Communication Networks; Mobile and Wireless Communications Systems. XXVI, 1276 pages. 2006.

Vol. 3970: T. Braun, G. Carle, S. Fahmy, Y. Koucheryavy (Eds.), Wired/Wireless Internet Communications. XIV, 350 pages. 2006.

Vol. 3964: M.Ü. Uyar, A.Y. Duale, M.A. Fecko (Eds.), Testing of Communicating Systems. XI, 373 pages. 2006.

Vol. 3961: I. Chong, K. Kawahara (Eds.), Information Networking. XV, 998 pages. 2006.

Vol. 3912: G.J. Minden, K.L. Calvert, M. Solarski, M. Yamamoto (Eds.), Active Networks. VIII, 217 pages. 2007.

Vol. 3883: M. Cesana, L. Fratta (Eds.), Wireless Systems and Network Architectures in Next Generation Internet. IX, 281 pages. 2006.

Vol. 3868: K. Römer, H. Karl, F. Mattern (Eds.), Wireless Sensor Networks. XI, 342 pages. 2006.

Vol. 3854: I. Stavrakakis, M. Smirnov (Eds.), Autonomic Communication. XIII, 303 pages. 2006.

Vol. 3813: R. Molva, G. Tsudik, D. Westhoff (Eds.), Security and Privacy in Ad-hoc and Sensor Networks. VIII, 219 pages. 2005.

Vol. 3462: R. Boutaba, K.C. Almeroth, R. Puigjaner, S. Shen, J.P. Black (Eds.), NETWORKING 2005. XXX, 1483 pages. 2005.